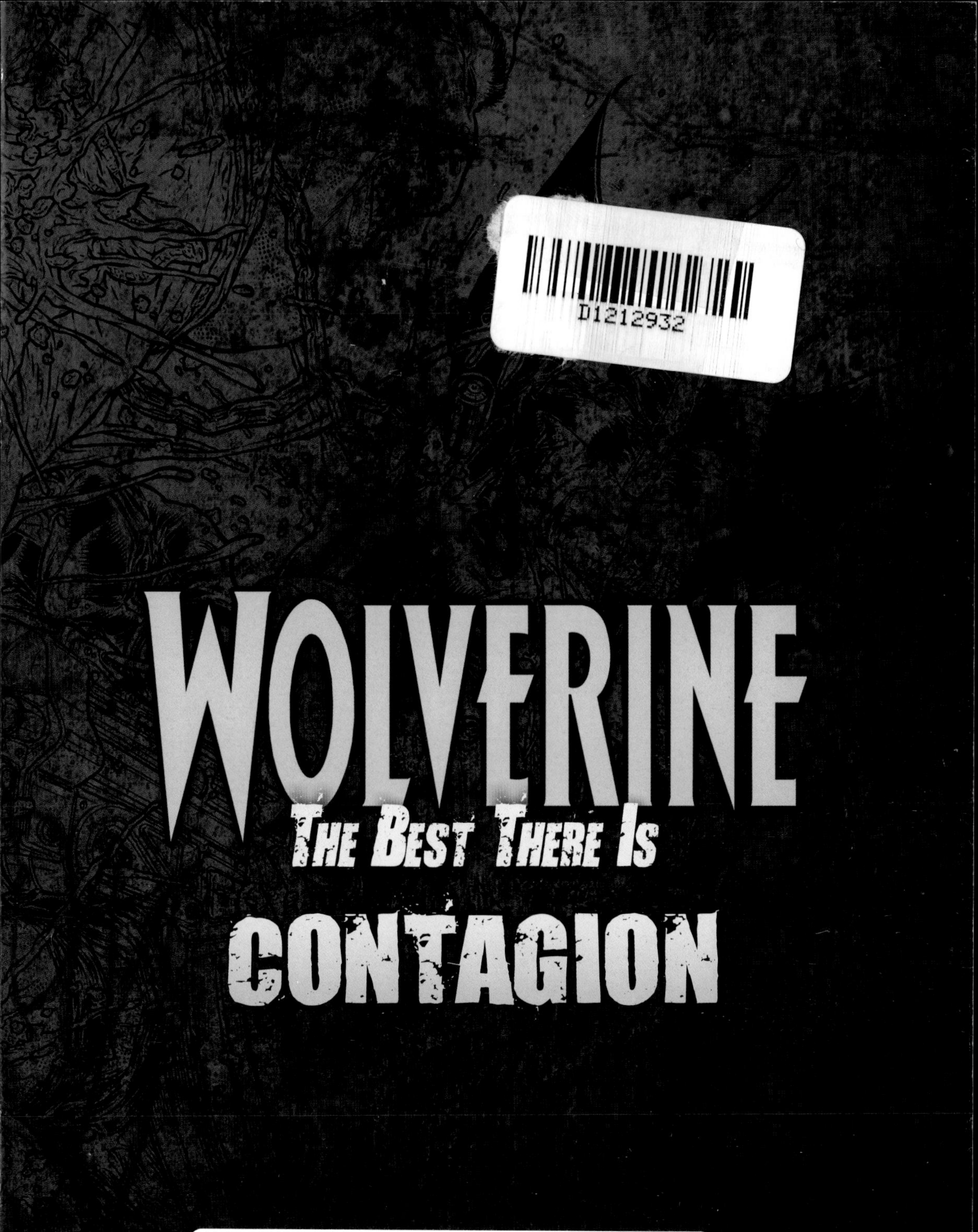

WOLVERINE

THE BEST THERE IS

CONTAGION

WOLVERINE: THE BEST THERE IS — CONTAGION. Contains material originally published in magazine form as WOLVERINE: THE BEST THERE IS #1-6. First printing 2011. Hardcover ISBN# 978-0-7851-4446-5. Softcover ISBN# 978-0-7851-4432-8. Published by **MARVEL WORLDWIDE, INC.**, a subsidiary of **MARVEL ENTERTAINMENT, LLC. OFFICE OF PUBLICATION:** 135 West 50th Street, New York, NY 10020. Copyright © 2010, 2011 and 2012 Marvel Characters, Inc. All rights reserved. Hardcover: $24.99 per copy in the U.S. and $27.99 in Canada (GST #R127032852). Softcover: $15.99 per copy in the U.S. and $17.50 in Canada (GST #R127032852). Canadian Agreement #40668537. All characters featured in this issue and the distinctive names and likenesses thereof, and all related indicia are trademarks of Marvel Characters, Inc. No similarity between any of the names, characters, persons, and/or institutions in this magazine with those of any living or dead person or institution is intended, and any such similarity which may exist is purely coincidental. **Printed in the U.S.A.** ALAN FINE, EVP -- Office of the President, Marvel Worldwide, Inc. and EVP & CMO Marvel Characters B.V.; DAN BUCKLEY, Publisher & President - Print, Animation & Digital Divisions; JOE QUESADA, Chief Creative Officer; JIM SOKOLOWSKI, Chief Operating Officer; DAVID BOGART, SVP of Business Affairs & Talent Management; TOM BREVOORT, SVP of Publishing; C.B. CEBULSKI, SVP of Creator & Content Development; DAVID GABRIEL, SVP of Publishing Sales & Circulation; MICHAEL PASCIULLO, SVP of Brand Planning & Communications; JIM O'KEEFE, VP of Operations & Logistics; DAN CARR, Executive Director of Publishing Technology; JUSTIN F. GABRIE, Director of Publishing & Editorial Operations; SUSAN CRESPI, Editorial Operations Manager; ALEX MORALES, Publishing Operations Manager; STAN LEE, Chairman Emeritus. For information regarding advertising in Marvel Comics or on Marvel.com, please contact John Dokes, SVP Integrated Sales and Marketing, at jdokes@marvel.com. For Marvel subscription inquiries, please call 800-217-9158. **Manufactured between 5/30/11 and 6/27/2011 (hardcover), and 5/30/11 and 12/19/11 (softcover), by R.R. DONNELLEY, INC., SALEM, VA, USA.**
10 9 8 7 6 5 4 3 2 1

WOLVERINE
THE BEST THERE IS
CONTAGION

WRITER
CHARLIE HUSTON

ARTIST
JUAN JOSE RYP

COLORIST
ANDRES MOSSA

LETTERER
VC'S CLAYTON COWLES

COVER ART
BRYAN HITCH, PAUL NEARY & PAUL MOUNTS

ASSISTANT EDITOR
JODY LEHEUP

EDITORS
SEBASTIAN GIRNER & JORDAN D. WHITE

SPECIAL THANKS TO MADISON CARTER, JEFF CHRISTIANSEN, MIKE FICHERA,
ROB LONDON, MIKE O'SULLIVAN, MARKUS RAYMOND & STUART VANDAL

COLLECTION EDITOR: JENNIFER GRÜNWALD • EDITORIAL ASSISTANTS: JAMES EMMETT & JOE HOCHSTEIN
ASSISTANT EDITORS: ALEX STARBUCK & NELSON RIBEIRO • EDITOR, SPECIAL PROJECTS: MARK D. BEAZLEY
SENIOR EDITOR, SPECIAL PROJECTS: JEFF YOUNGQUIST • SENIOR VICE PRESIDENT OF SALES: DAVID GABRIEL
SVP OF BRAND PLANNING & COMMUNICATIONS: MICHAEL PASCIULLO • BOOK DESIGN: JEFF POWELL

EDITOR IN CHIEF: AXEL ALONSO • CHIEF CREATIVE OFFICER: JOE QUESADA
PUBLISHER: DAN BUCKLEY • EXECUTIVE PRODUCER: ALAN FINE

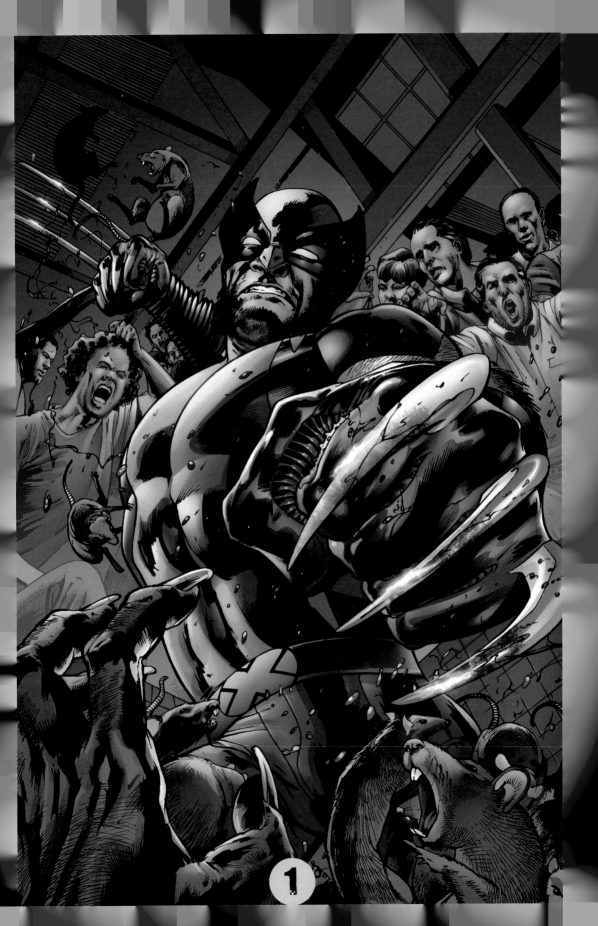

1

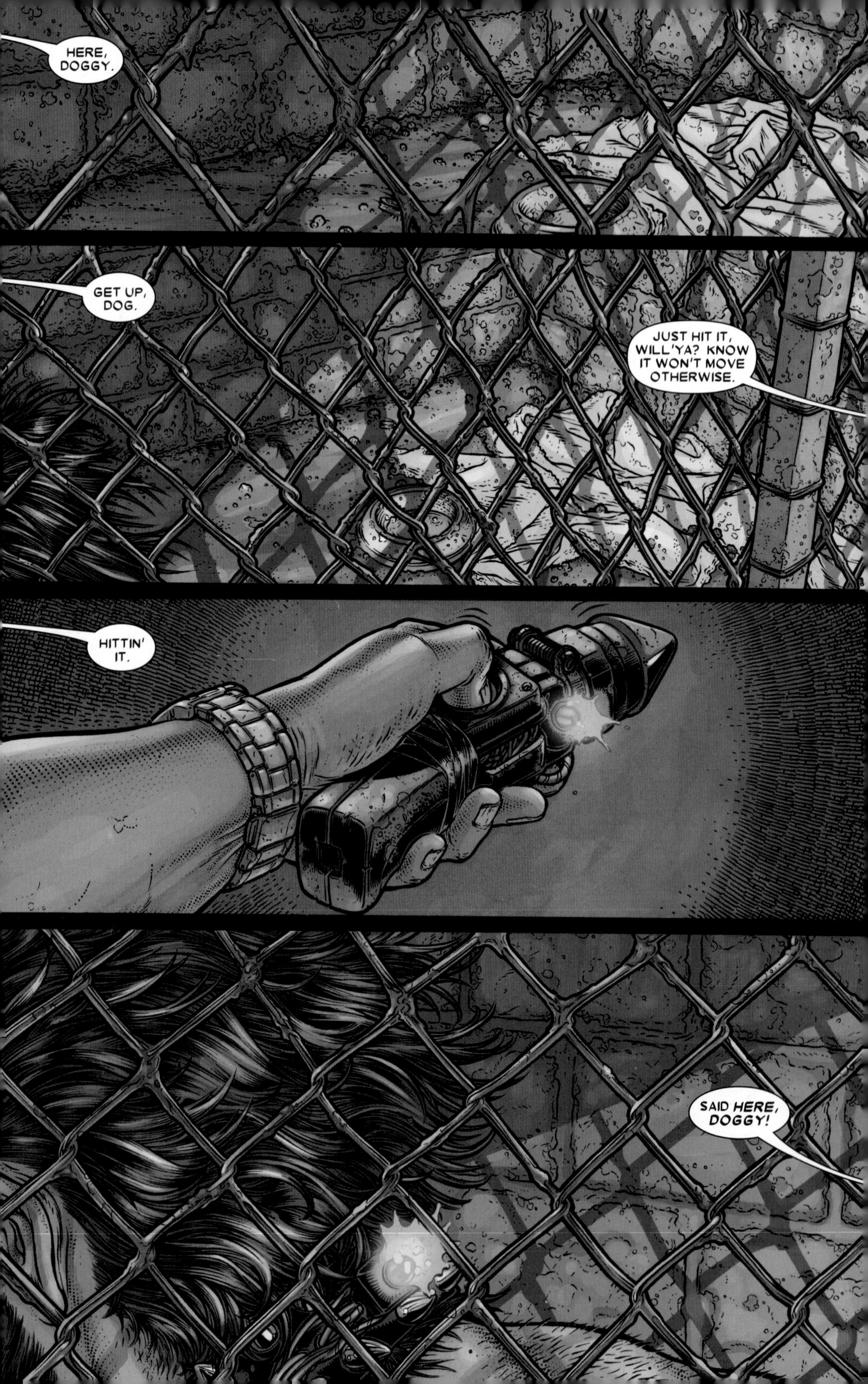
HERE, DOGGY.
GET UP, DOG.
JUST HIT IT, WILL'YA? KNOW IT WON'T MOVE OTHERWISE.
HITTIN' IT.
SAID HERE, DOGGY!

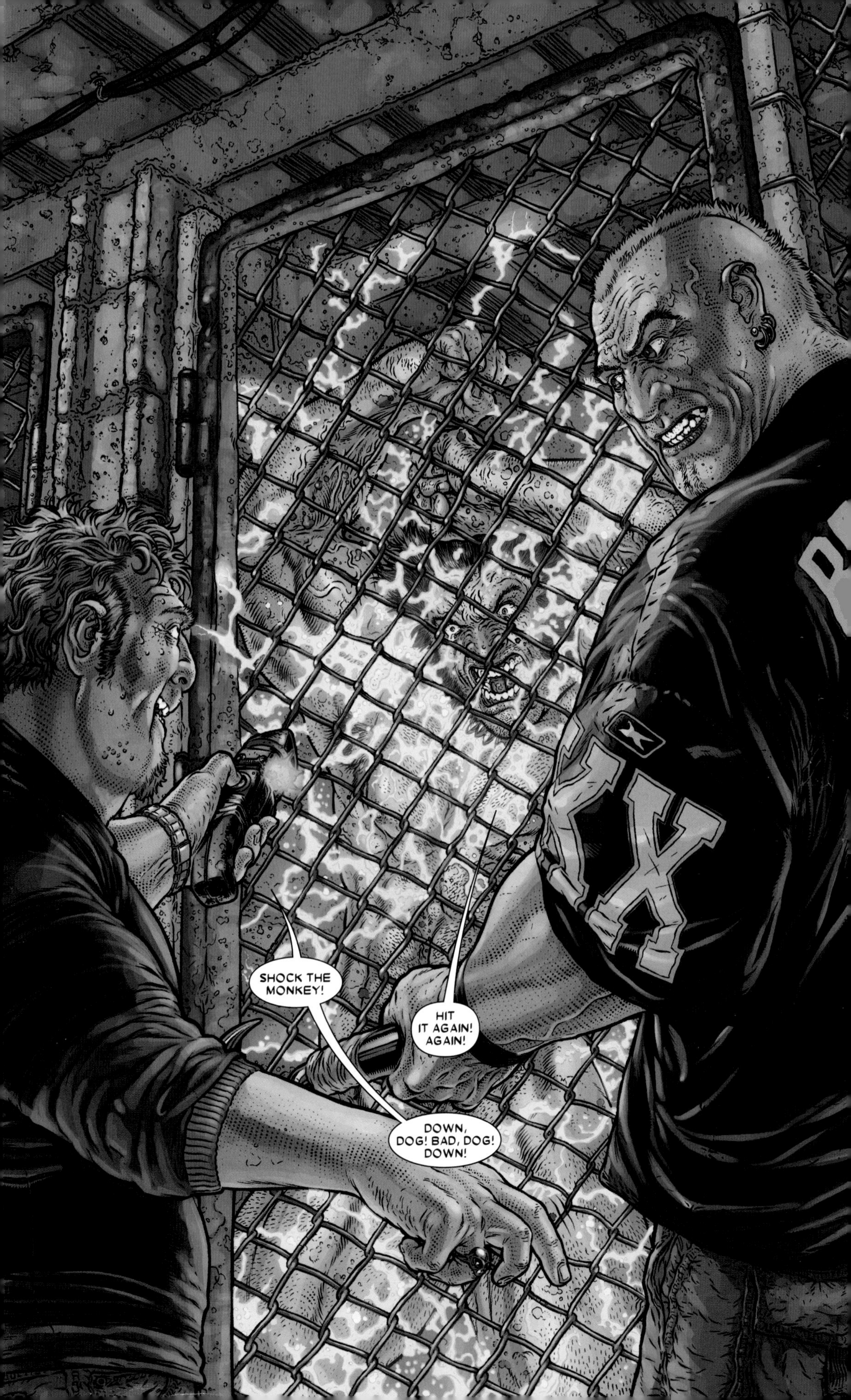
SHOCK THE MONKEY!
HIT IT AGAIN! AGAIN!
DOWN, DOG! BAD, DOG! DOWN!

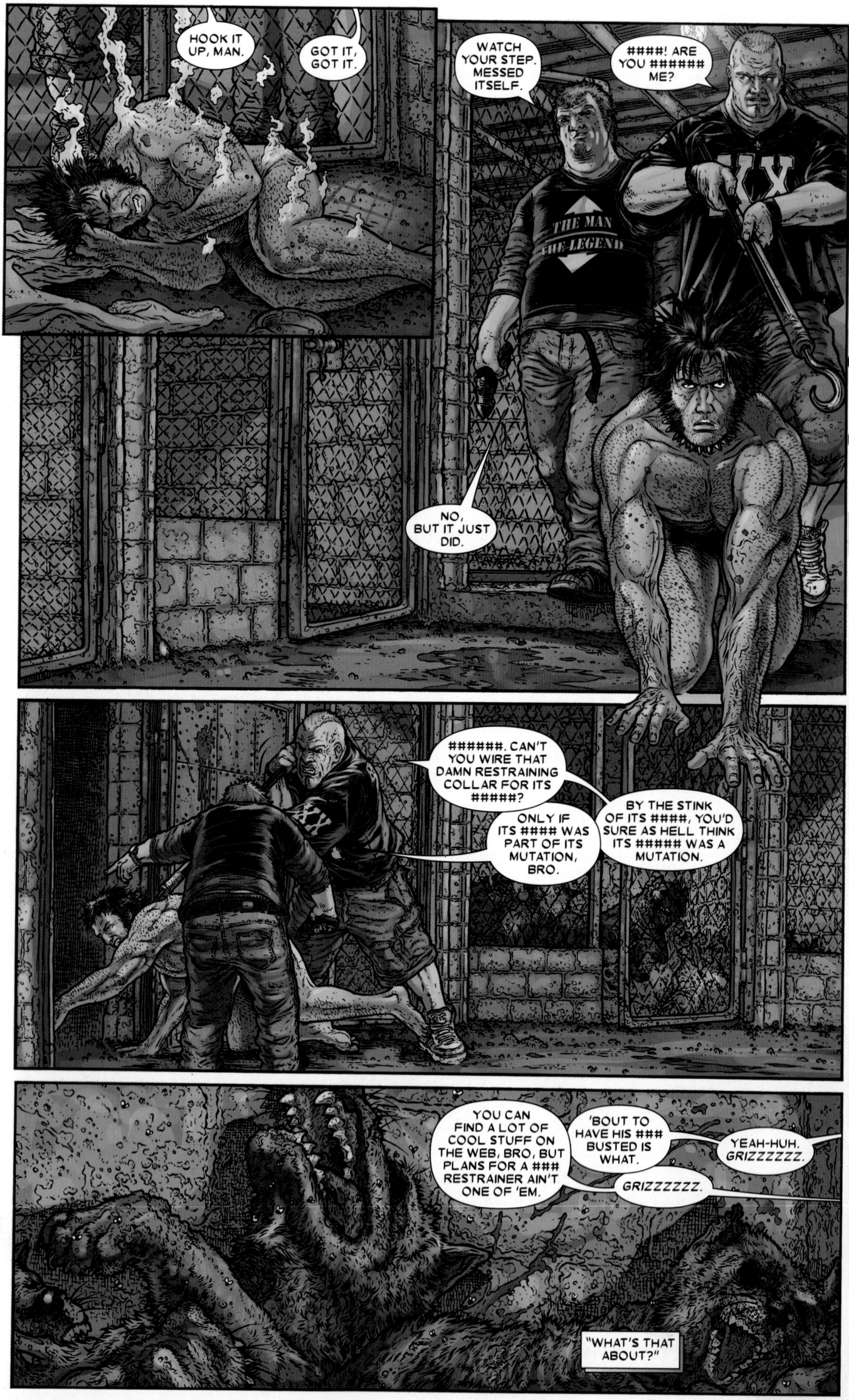
HOOK IT UP, MAN.
GOT IT, GOT IT.
WATCH YOUR STEP. MESSED ITSELF.
####! ARE YOU ###### ME?
NO, BUT IT JUST DID.
######. CAN'T YOU WIRE THAT DAMN RESTRAINING COLLAR FOR ITS #####?
ONLY IF ITS #### WAS PART OF ITS MUTATION, BRO.
BY THE STINK OF ITS ####, YOU'D SURE AS HELL THINK ITS ##### WAS A MUTATION.
YOU CAN FIND A LOT OF COOL STUFF ON THE WEB, BRO, BUT PLANS FOR A ### RESTRAINER AIN'T ONE OF 'EM.
'BOUT TO HAVE HIS ### BUSTED IS WHAT.
YEAH-HUH. GRIZZZZZZ.
GRIZZZZZZ.
"WHAT'S THAT ABOUT?"

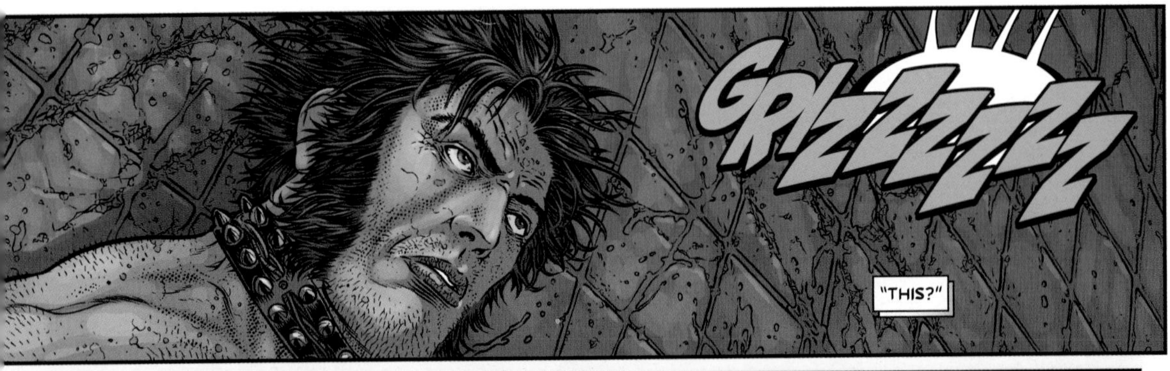
GRIZZZZZZZ
"THIS?"

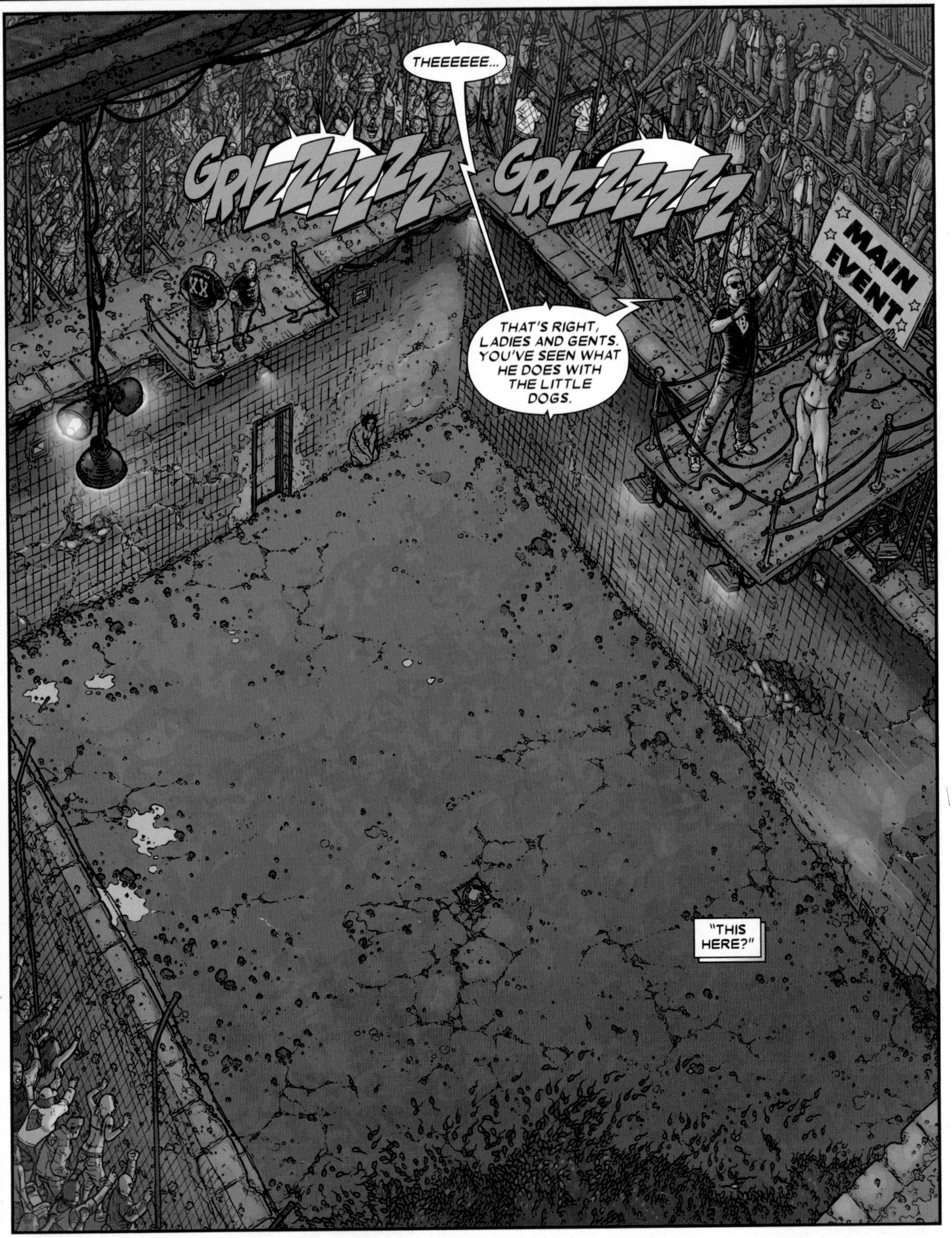
THEEEEEE...
GRIZZZZZZZ
GRIZZZZZZZ
MAIN EVENT
THAT'S RIGHT, LADIES AND GENTS. YOU'VE SEEN WHAT HE DOES WITH THE LITTLE DOGS.
"THIS HERE?"

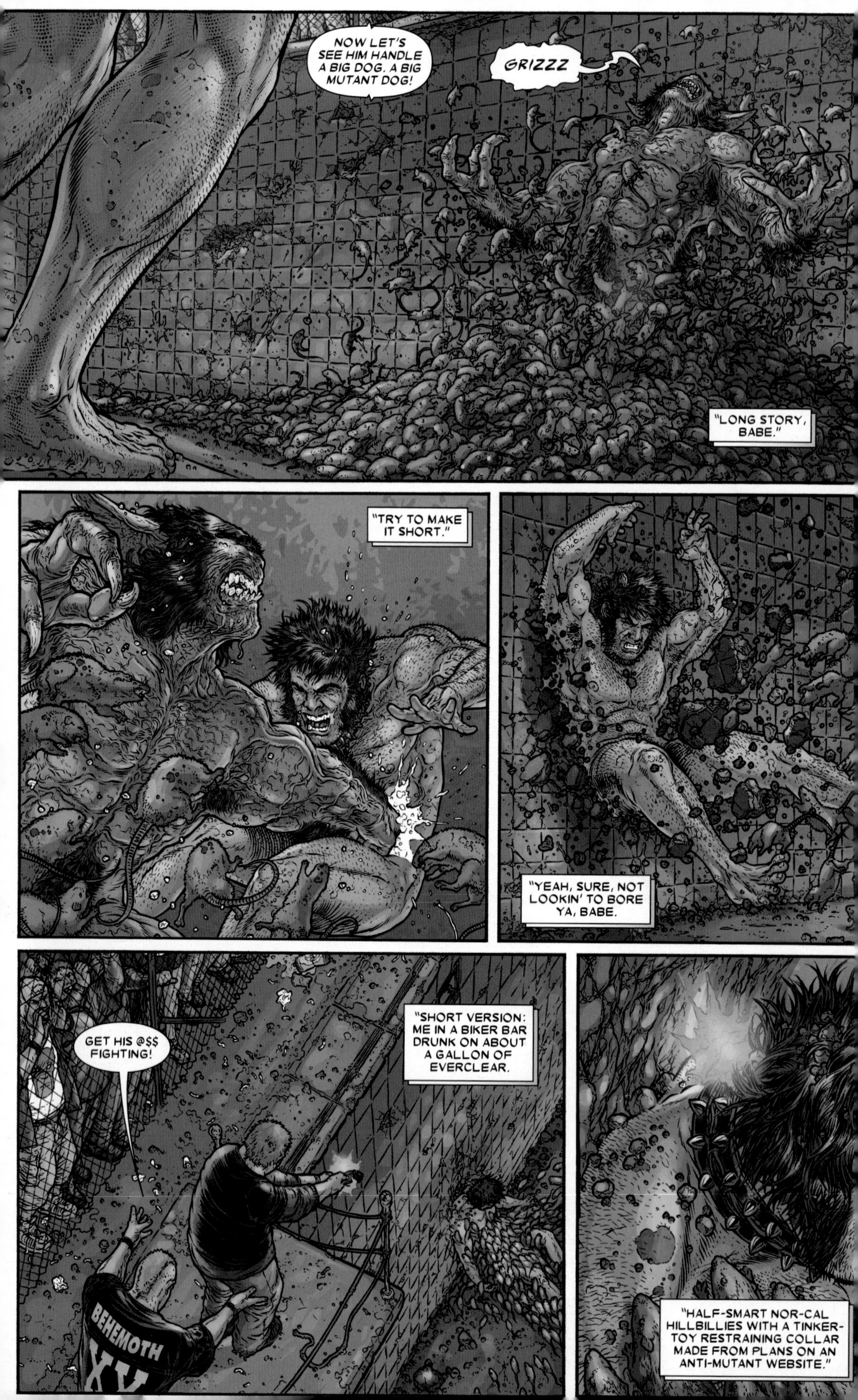
NOW LET'S SEE HIM HANDLE A BIG DOG. A BIG MUTANT DOG!
GRIZZZ
"LONG STORY, BABE."
"TRY TO MAKE IT SHORT."
"YEAH, SURE, NOT LOOKIN' TO BORE YA, BABE.
GET HIS @$$ FIGHTING!
"SHORT VERSION: ME IN A BIKER BAR DRUNK ON ABOUT A GALLON OF EVERCLEAR.
BEHEMOTH XV
"HALF-SMART NOR-CAL HILLBILLIES WITH A TINKER-TOY RESTRAINING COLLAR MADE FROM PLANS ON AN ANTI-MUTANT WEBSITE."

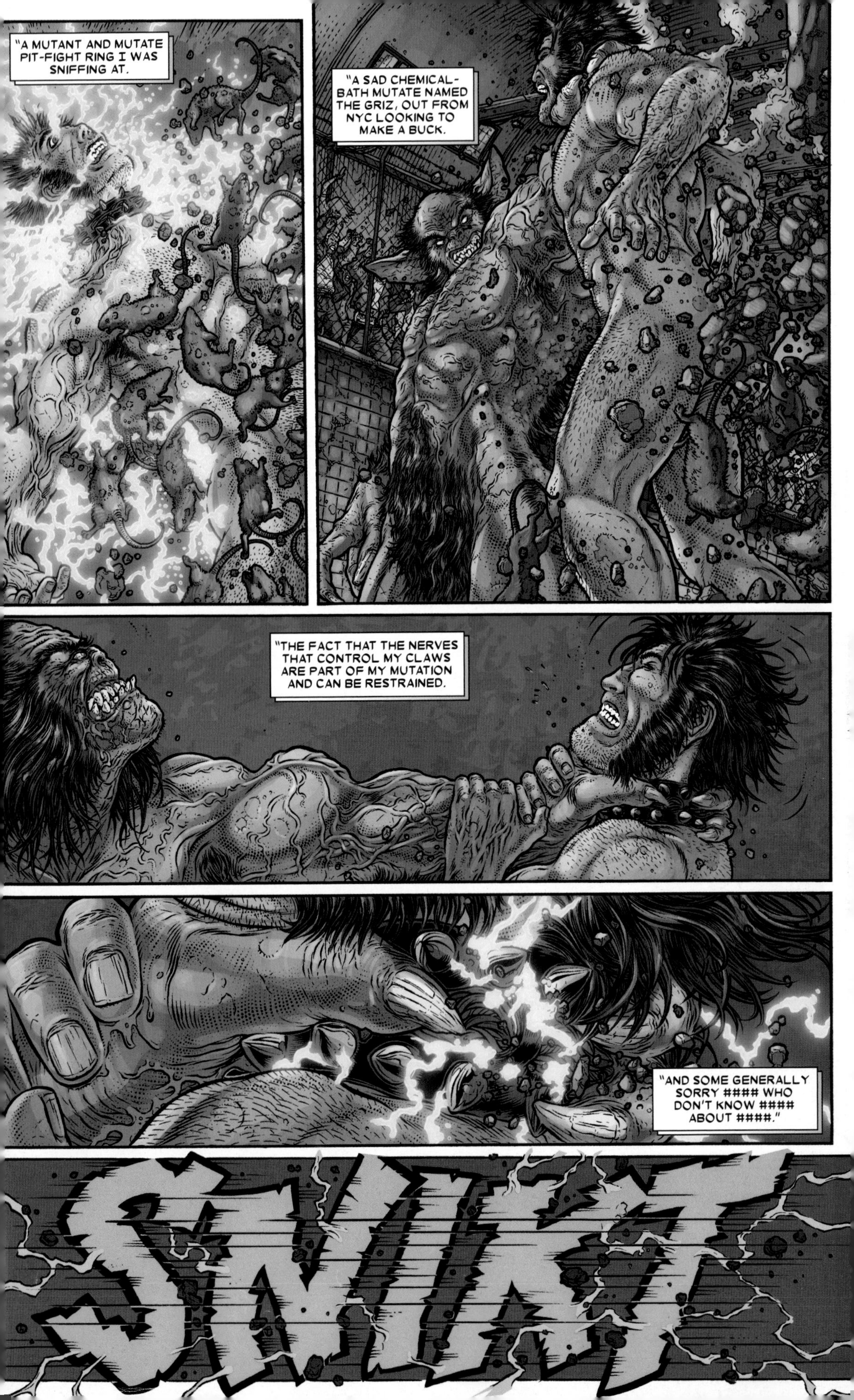
"A MUTANT AND MUTATE PIT-FIGHT RING I WAS SNIFFING AT.
"A SAD CHEMICAL-BATH MUTATE NAMED THE GRIZ, OUT FROM NYC LOOKING TO MAKE A BUCK.
"THE FACT THAT THE NERVES THAT CONTROL MY CLAWS ARE PART OF MY MUTATION AND CAN BE RESTRAINED.
"AND SOME GENERALLY SORRY #### WHO DON'T KNOW #### ABOUT ####."
SNIKT

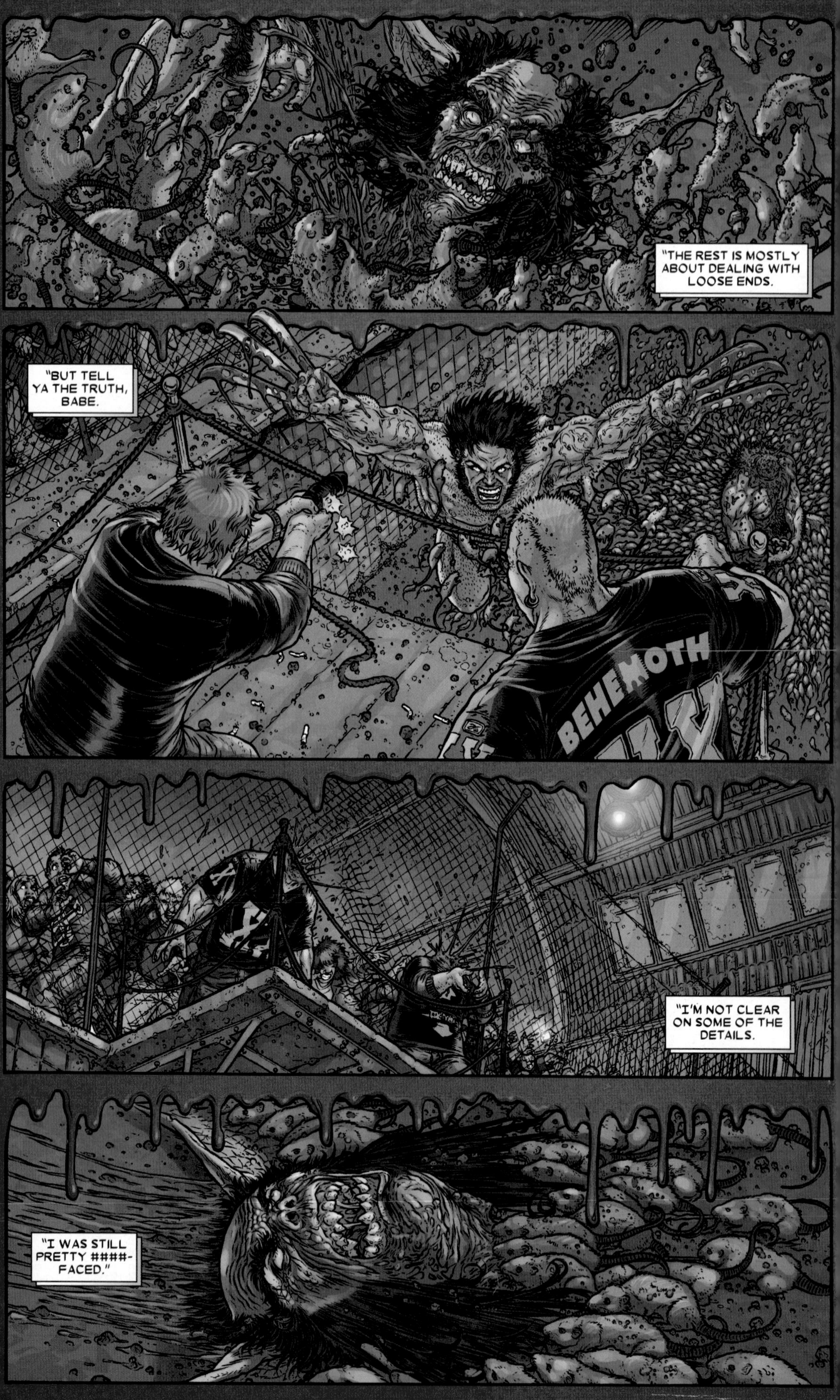
"THE REST IS MOSTLY ABOUT DEALING WITH LOOSE ENDS.
"BUT TELL YA THE TRUTH, BABE.
BEHEMOTH
"I'M NOT CLEAR ON SOME OF THE DETAILS.
"I WAS STILL PRETTY ####-FACED."

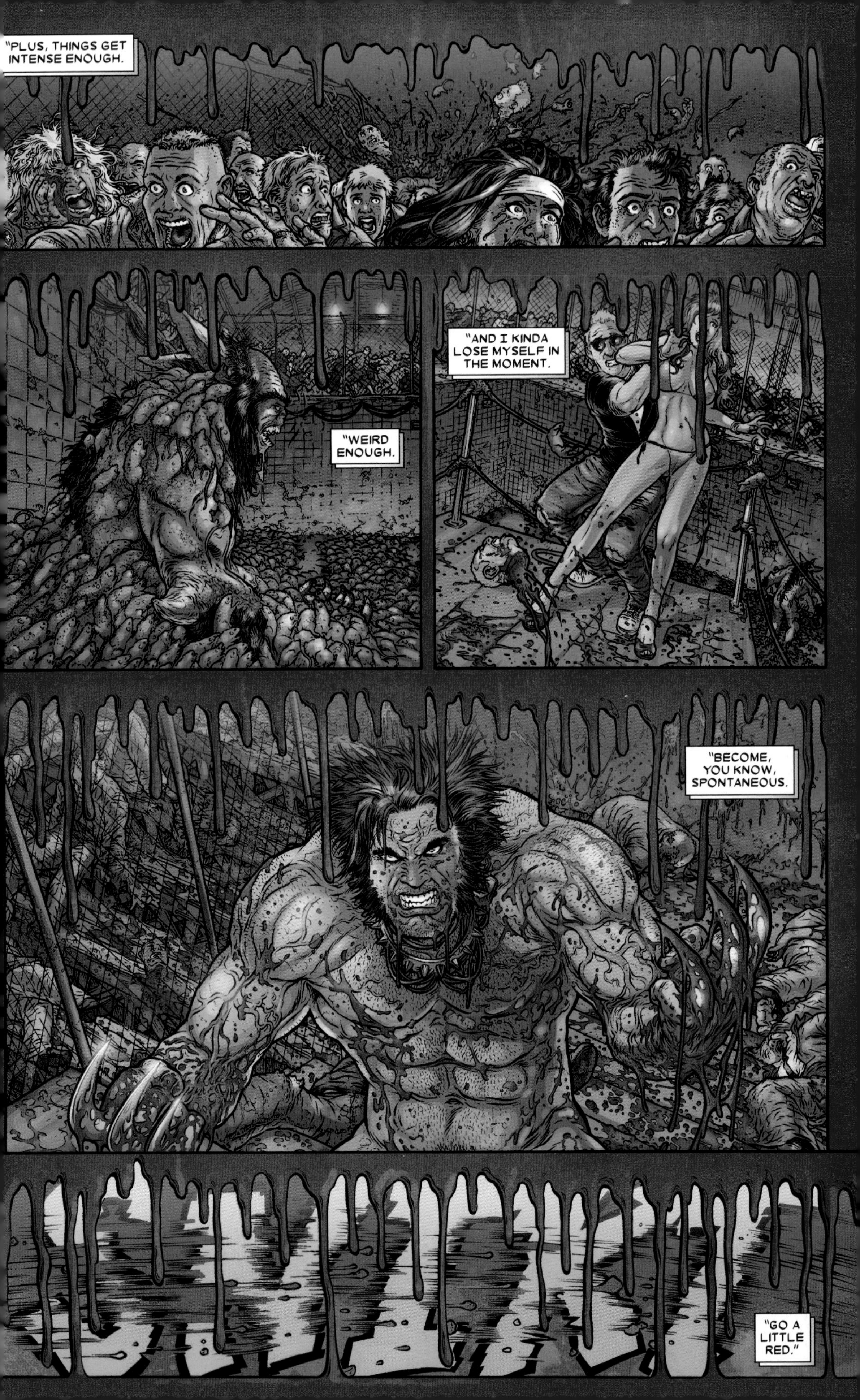
"PLUS, THINGS GET INTENSE ENOUGH.
"WEIRD ENOUGH.
"AND I KINDA LOSE MYSELF IN THE MOMENT.
"BECOME, YOU KNOW, SPONTANEOUS.
"GO A LITTLE RED."

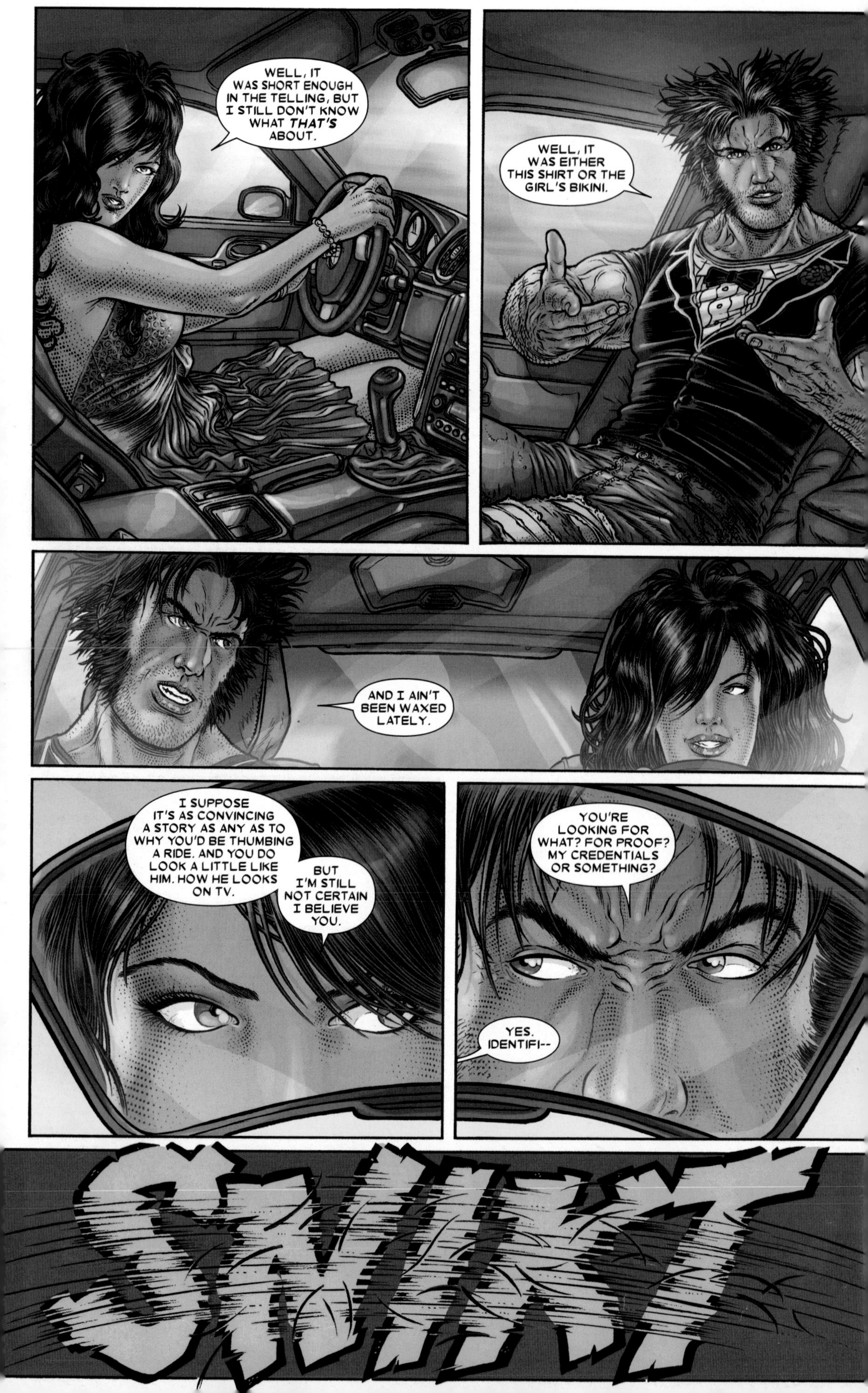
WELL, IT WAS SHORT ENOUGH IN THE TELLING, BUT I STILL DON'T KNOW WHAT *THAT'S* ABOUT.
WELL, IT WAS EITHER THIS SHIRT OR THE GIRL'S BIKINI.
AND I AIN'T BEEN WAXED LATELY.
I SUPPOSE IT'S AS CONVINCING A STORY AS ANY AS TO WHY YOU'D BE THUMBING A RIDE. AND YOU DO LOOK A LITTLE LIKE HIM. HOW HE LOOKS ON TV.
BUT I'M STILL NOT CERTAIN I BELIEVE YOU.
YOU'RE LOOKING FOR WHAT? FOR PROOF? MY CREDENTIALS OR SOMETHING?
YES. IDENTIFI--
SNIKT

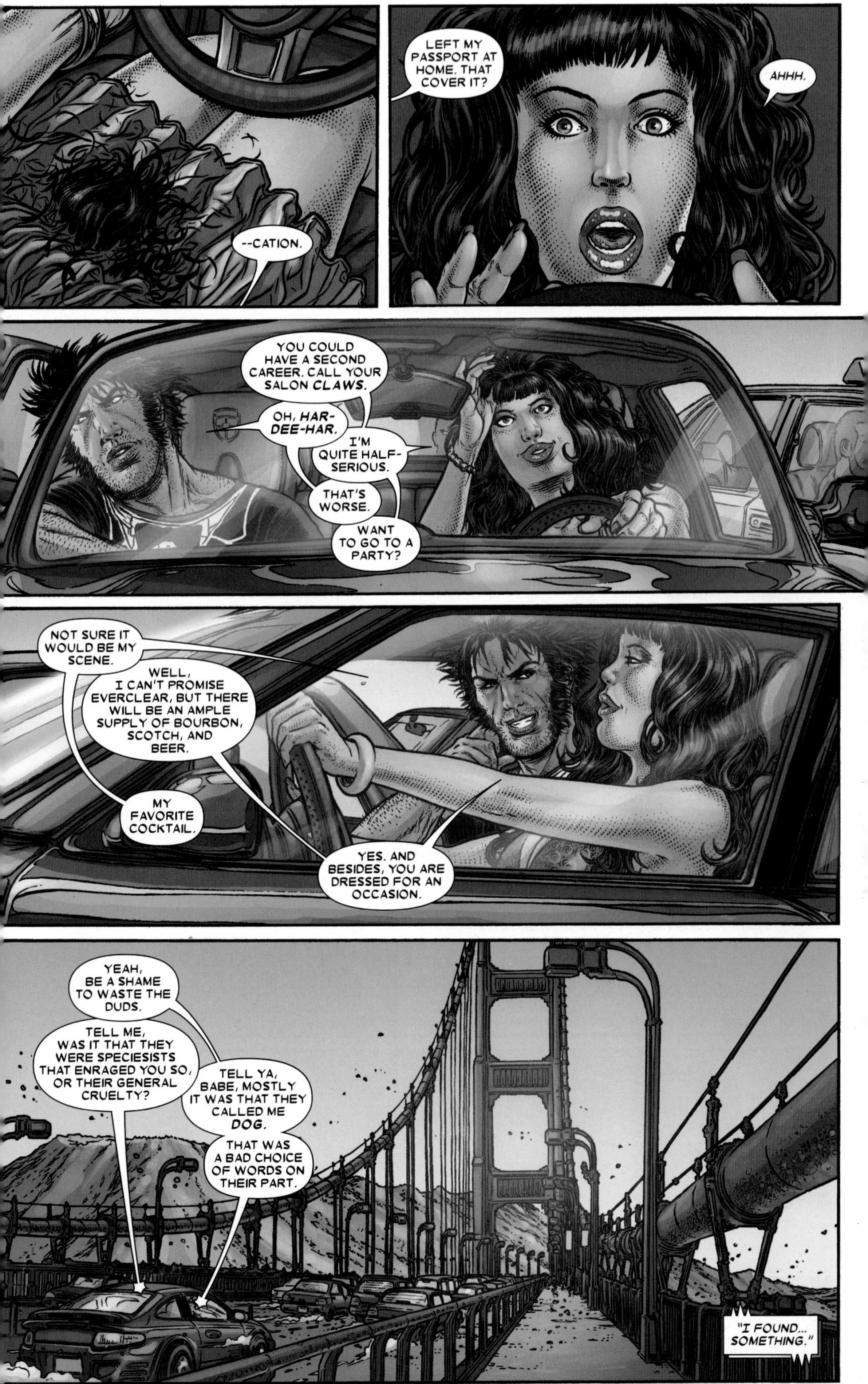
--CATION.
LEFT MY PASSPORT AT HOME. THAT COVER IT?
AHHH.
YOU COULD HAVE A SECOND CAREER. CALL YOUR SALON **CLAWS.**
OH, **HAR-DEE-HAR.**
I'M QUITE HALF-SERIOUS.
THAT'S WORSE.
WANT TO GO TO A PARTY?
NOT SURE IT WOULD BE MY SCENE.
WELL, I CAN'T PROMISE EVERCLEAR, BUT THERE WILL BE AN AMPLE SUPPLY OF BOURBON, SCOTCH, AND BEER.
MY FAVORITE COCKTAIL.
YES. AND BESIDES, YOU ARE DRESSED FOR AN OCCASION.
YEAH, BE A SHAME TO WASTE THE DUDS.
TELL ME, WAS IT THAT THEY WERE SPECIESISTS THAT ENRAGED YOU SO, OR THEIR GENERAL CRUELTY?
TELL YA, BABE, MOSTLY IT WAS THAT THEY CALLED ME **DOG.**
THAT WAS A BAD CHOICE OF WORDS ON THEIR PART.
"I FOUND... SOMETHING."

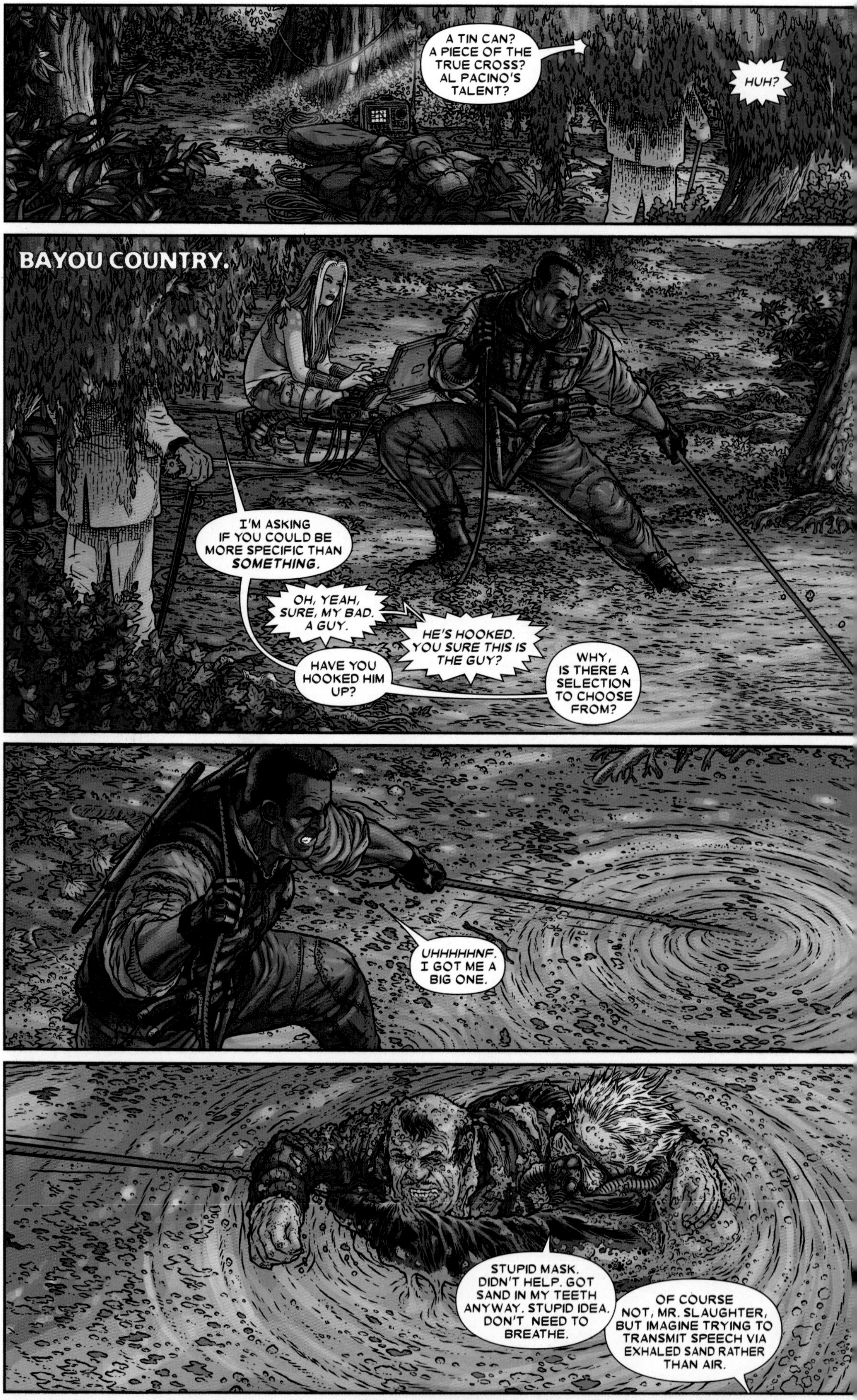

A TIN CAN? A PIECE OF THE TRUE CROSS? AL PACINO'S TALENT?
HUH?
BAYOU COUNTRY.
I'M ASKING IF YOU COULD BE MORE SPECIFIC THAN SOMETHING.
OH, YEAH, SURE, MY BAD. A GUY.
HAVE YOU HOOKED HIM UP?
HE'S HOOKED. YOU SURE THIS IS THE GUY?
WHY, IS THERE A SELECTION TO CHOOSE FROM?
UHHHHHNF. I GOT ME A BIG ONE.
STUPID MASK. DIDN'T HELP. GOT SAND IN MY TEETH ANYWAY. STUPID IDEA. DON'T NEED TO BREATHE.
OF COURSE NOT, MR. SLAUGHTER, BUT IMAGINE TRYING TO TRANSMIT SPEECH VIA EXHALED SAND RATHER THAN AIR.

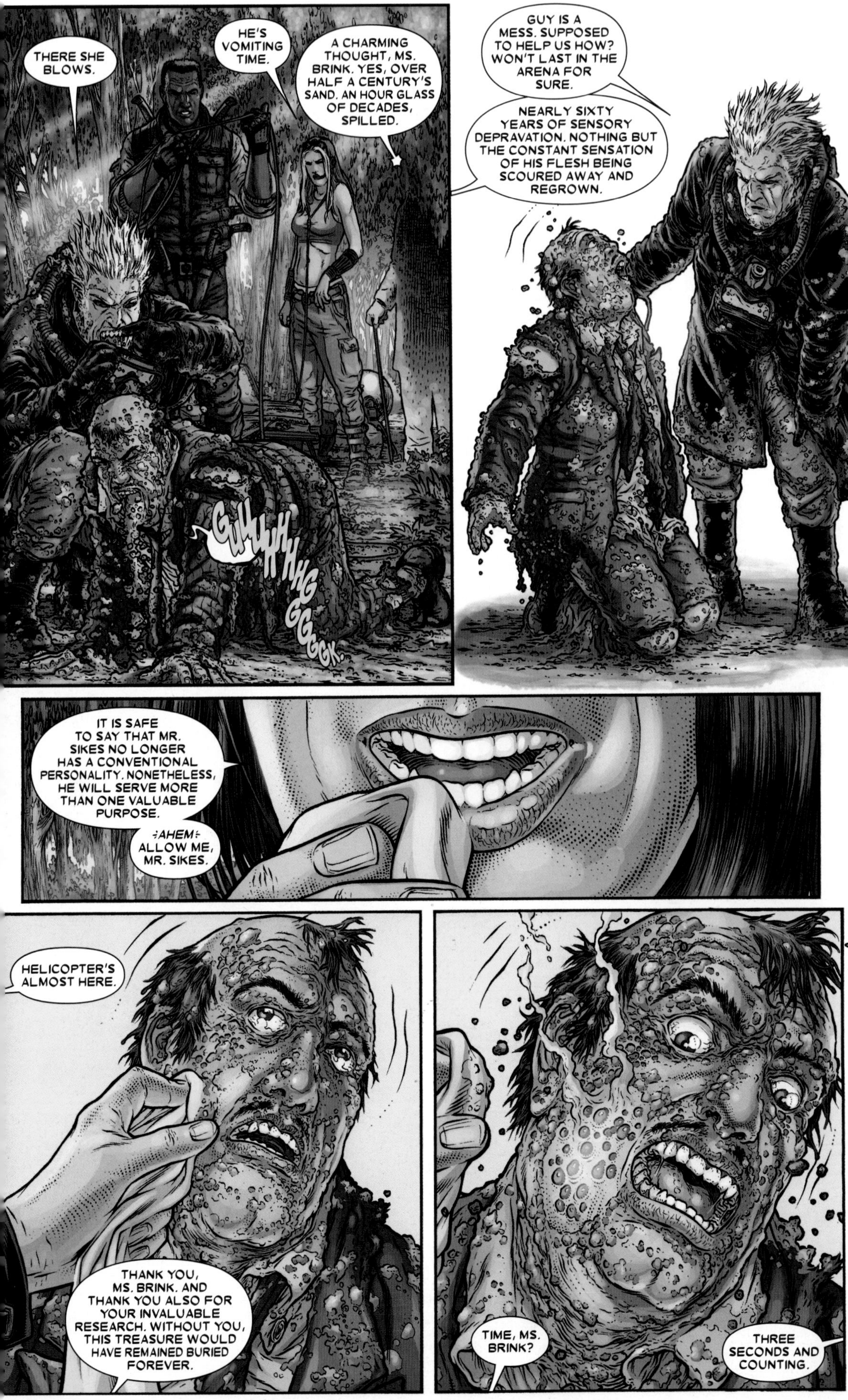
THERE SHE BLOWS.
HE'S VOMITING TIME.
A CHARMING THOUGHT, MS. BRINK. YES, OVER HALF A CENTURY'S SAND. AN HOUR GLASS OF DECADES, SPILLED.
GUUUHHHHGGGGGK.
GUY IS A MESS. SUPPOSED TO HELP US HOW? WON'T LAST IN THE ARENA FOR SURE.
NEARLY SIXTY YEARS OF SENSORY DEPRAVATION. NOTHING BUT THE CONSTANT SENSATION OF HIS FLESH BEING SCOURED AWAY AND REGROWN.
IT IS SAFE TO SAY THAT MR. SIKES NO LONGER HAS A CONVENTIONAL PERSONALITY. NONETHELESS, HE WILL SERVE MORE THAN ONE VALUABLE PURPOSE.
AHEM ALLOW ME, MR. SIKES.
HELICOPTER'S ALMOST HERE.
THANK YOU, MS. BRINK. AND THANK YOU ALSO FOR YOUR INVALUABLE RESEARCH. WITHOUT YOU, THIS TREASURE WOULD HAVE REMAINED BURIED FOREVER.
TIME, MS. BRINK?
THREE SECONDS AND COUNTING.

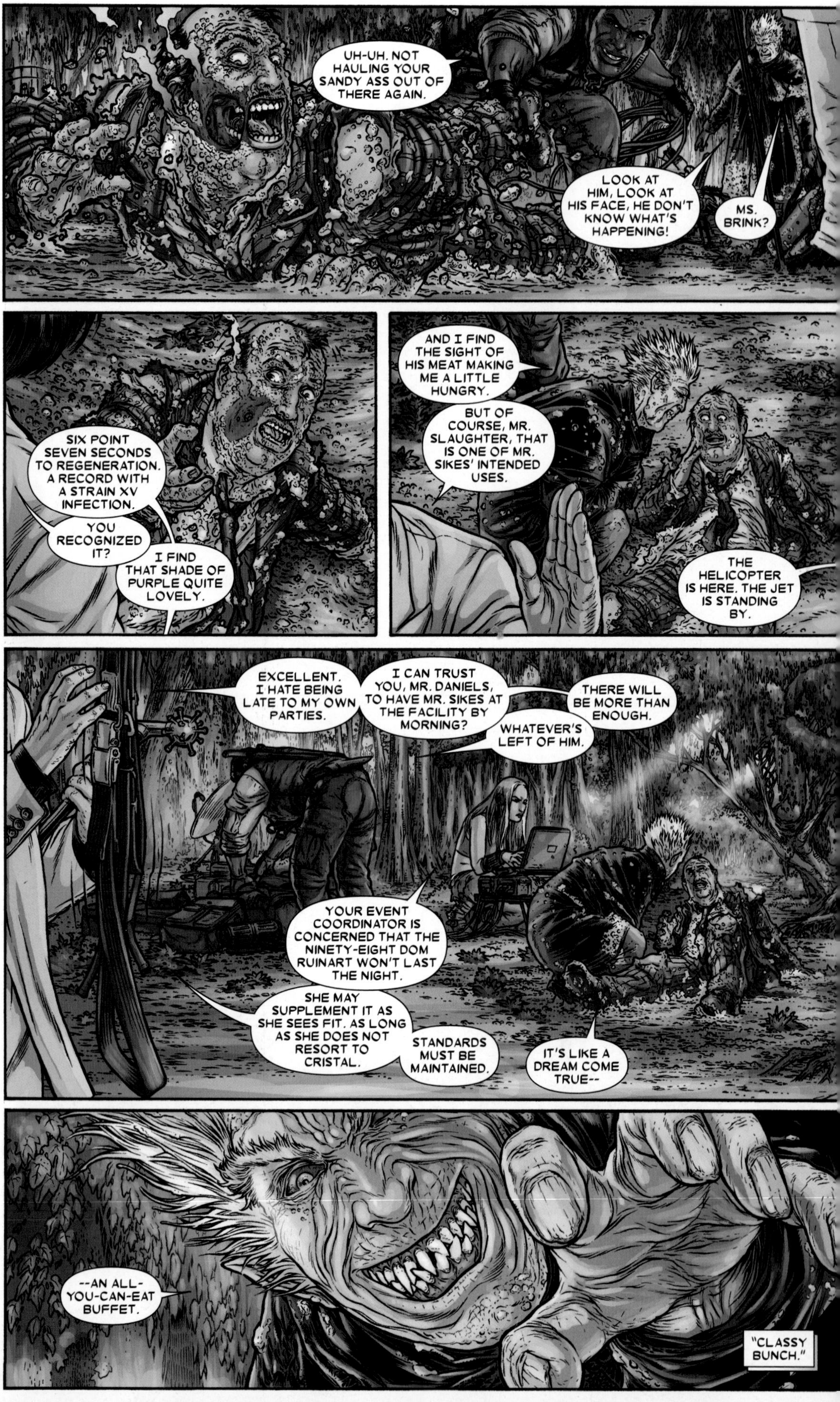
UH-UH. NOT HAULING YOUR SANDY ASS OUT OF THERE AGAIN.
LOOK AT HIM, LOOK AT HIS FACE, HE DON'T KNOW WHAT'S HAPPENING!
MS. BRINK?
SIX POINT SEVEN SECONDS TO REGENERATION. A RECORD WITH A STRAIN XV INFECTION.
YOU RECOGNIZED IT?
I FIND THAT SHADE OF PURPLE QUITE LOVELY.
AND I FIND THE SIGHT OF HIS MEAT MAKING ME A LITTLE HUNGRY.
BUT OF COURSE, MR. SLAUGHTER, THAT IS ONE OF MR. SIKES' INTENDED USES.
THE HELICOPTER IS HERE. THE JET IS STANDING BY.
EXCELLENT. I HATE BEING LATE TO MY OWN PARTIES.
I CAN TRUST YOU, MR. DANIELS, TO HAVE MR. SIKES AT THE FACILITY BY MORNING?
THERE WILL BE MORE THAN ENOUGH.
WHATEVER'S LEFT OF HIM.
YOUR EVENT COORDINATOR IS CONCERNED THAT THE NINETY-EIGHT DOM RUINART WON'T LAST THE NIGHT.
SHE MAY SUPPLEMENT IT AS SHE SEES FIT. AS LONG AS SHE DOES NOT RESORT TO CRISTAL.
STANDARDS MUST BE MAINTAINED.
IT'S LIKE A DREAM COME TRUE--
--AN ALL-YOU-CAN-EAT BUFFET.
"CLASSY BUNCH."

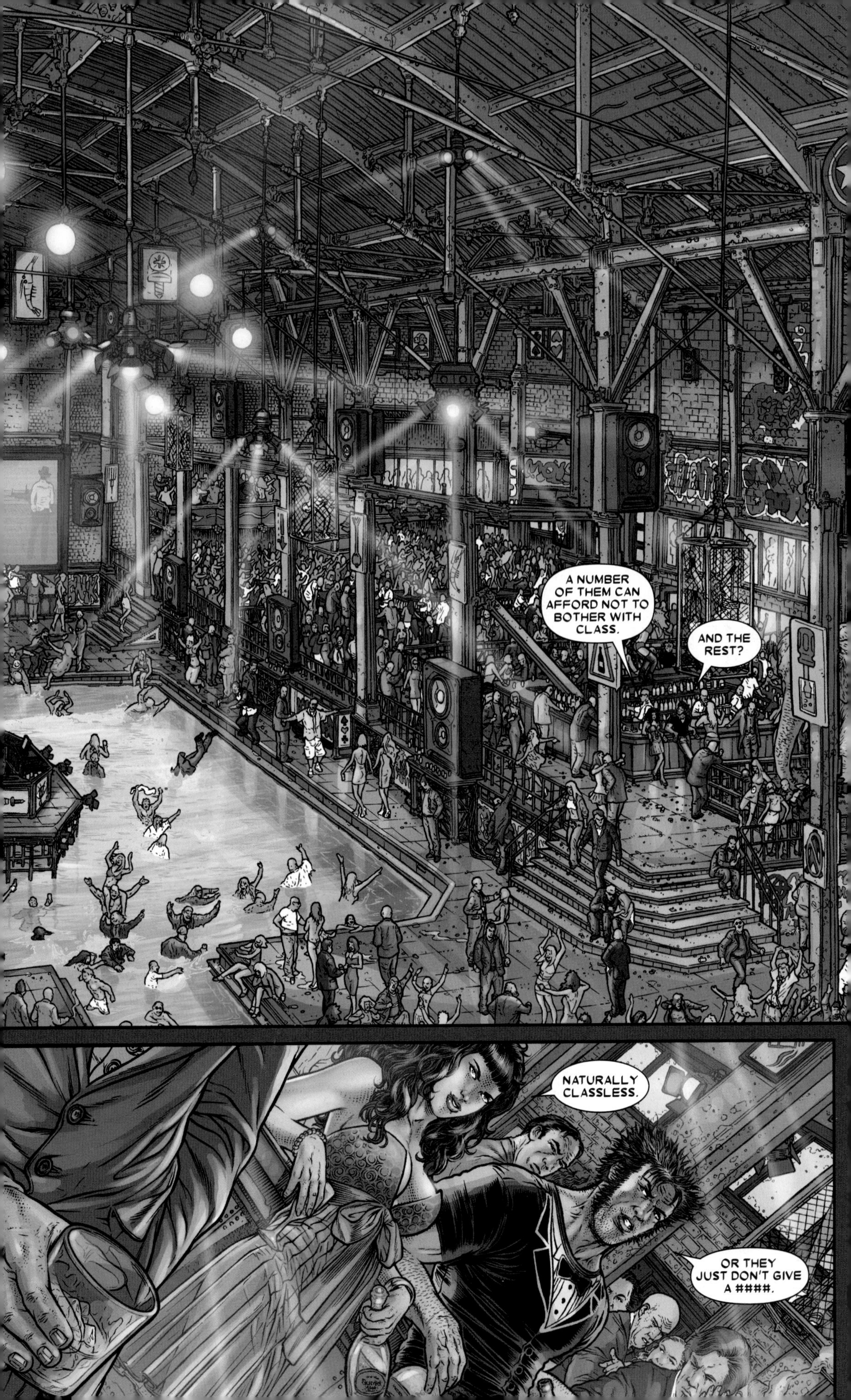
A NUMBER OF THEM CAN AFFORD NOT TO BOTHER WITH CLASS.
AND THE REST?
NATURALLY CLASSLESS.
OR THEY JUST DON'T GIVE A ####.

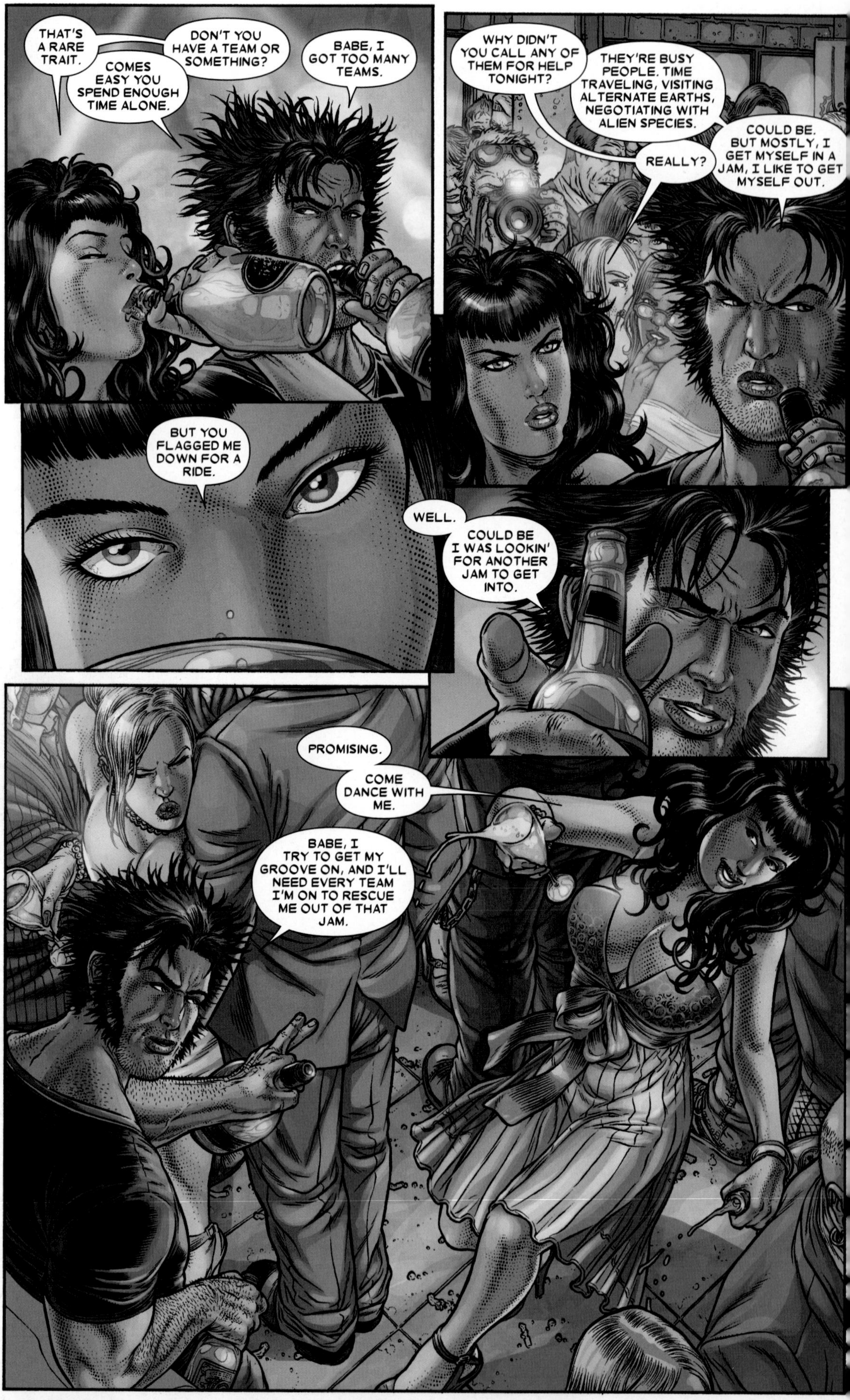
THAT'S A RARE TRAIT.
DON'T YOU HAVE A TEAM OR SOMETHING?
COMES EASY YOU SPEND ENOUGH TIME ALONE.
BABE, I GOT TOO MANY TEAMS.
WHY DIDN'T YOU CALL ANY OF THEM FOR HELP TONIGHT?
THEY'RE BUSY PEOPLE. TIME TRAVELING, VISITING ALTERNATE EARTHS, NEGOTIATING WITH ALIEN SPECIES.
REALLY?
COULD BE. BUT MOSTLY, I GET MYSELF IN A JAM, I LIKE TO GET MYSELF OUT.
BUT YOU FLAGGED ME DOWN FOR A RIDE.
WELL.
COULD BE I WAS LOOKIN' FOR ANOTHER JAM TO GET INTO.
PROMISING.
COME DANCE WITH ME.
BABE, I TRY TO GET MY GROOVE ON, AND I'LL NEED EVERY TEAM I'M ON TO RESCUE ME OUT OF THAT JAM.

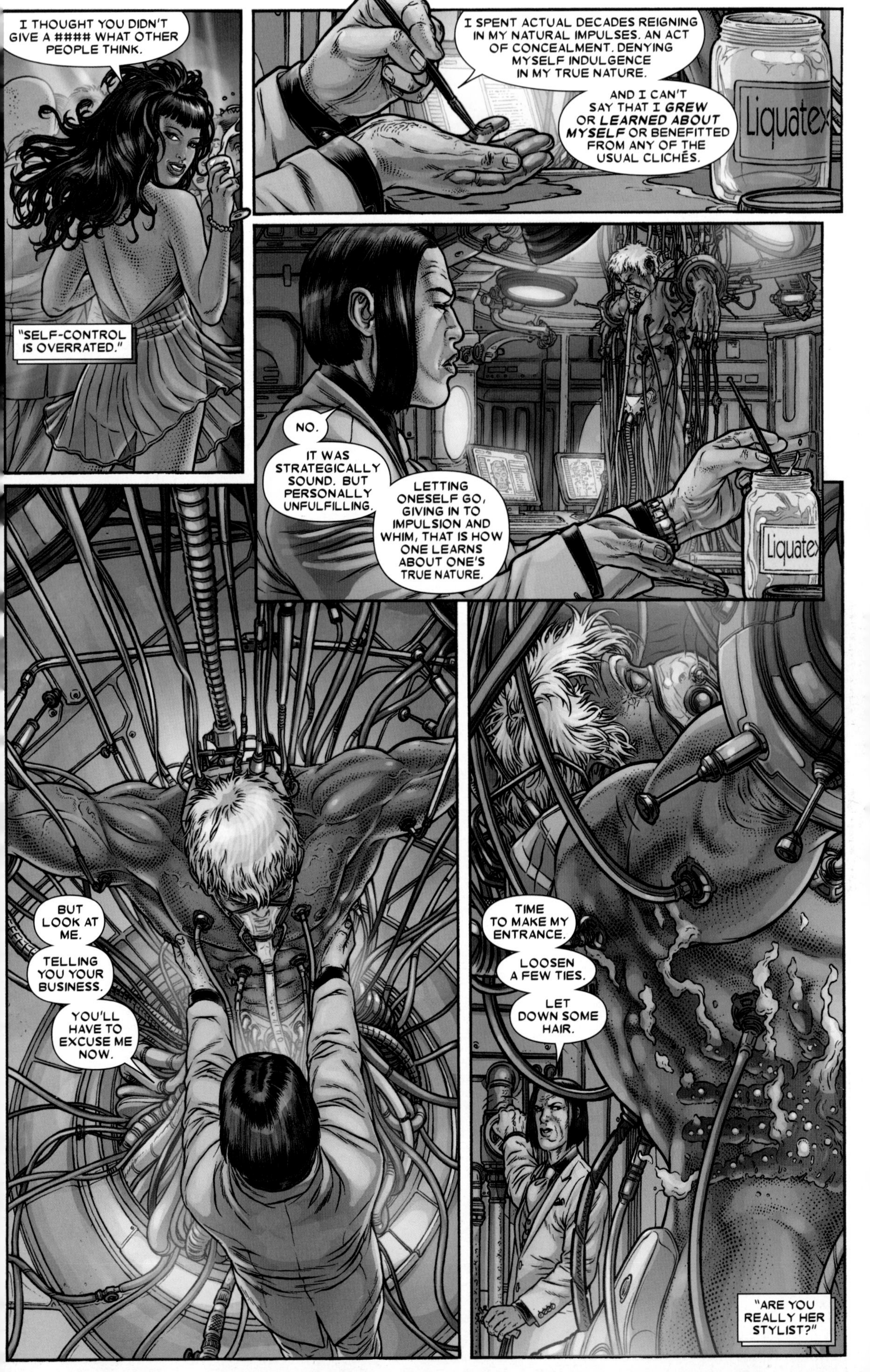
I THOUGHT YOU DIDN'T GIVE A #### WHAT OTHER PEOPLE THINK.
"SELF-CONTROL IS OVERRATED."
I SPENT ACTUAL DECADES REIGNING IN MY NATURAL IMPULSES. AN ACT OF CONCEALMENT. DENYING MYSELF INDULGENCE IN MY TRUE NATURE.
AND I CAN'T SAY THAT I GREW OR LEARNED ABOUT MYSELF OR BENEFITTED FROM ANY OF THE USUAL CLICHÉS.
Liquatex
NO.
IT WAS STRATEGICALLY SOUND. BUT PERSONALLY UNFULFILLING.
LETTING ONESELF GO, GIVING IN TO IMPULSION AND WHIM, THAT IS HOW ONE LEARNS ABOUT ONE'S TRUE NATURE.
Liquatex
BUT LOOK AT ME.
TELLING YOU YOUR BUSINESS.
YOU'LL HAVE TO EXCUSE ME NOW.
TIME TO MAKE MY ENTRANCE.
LOOSEN A FEW TIES.
LET DOWN SOME HAIR.
"ARE YOU REALLY HER STYLIST?"

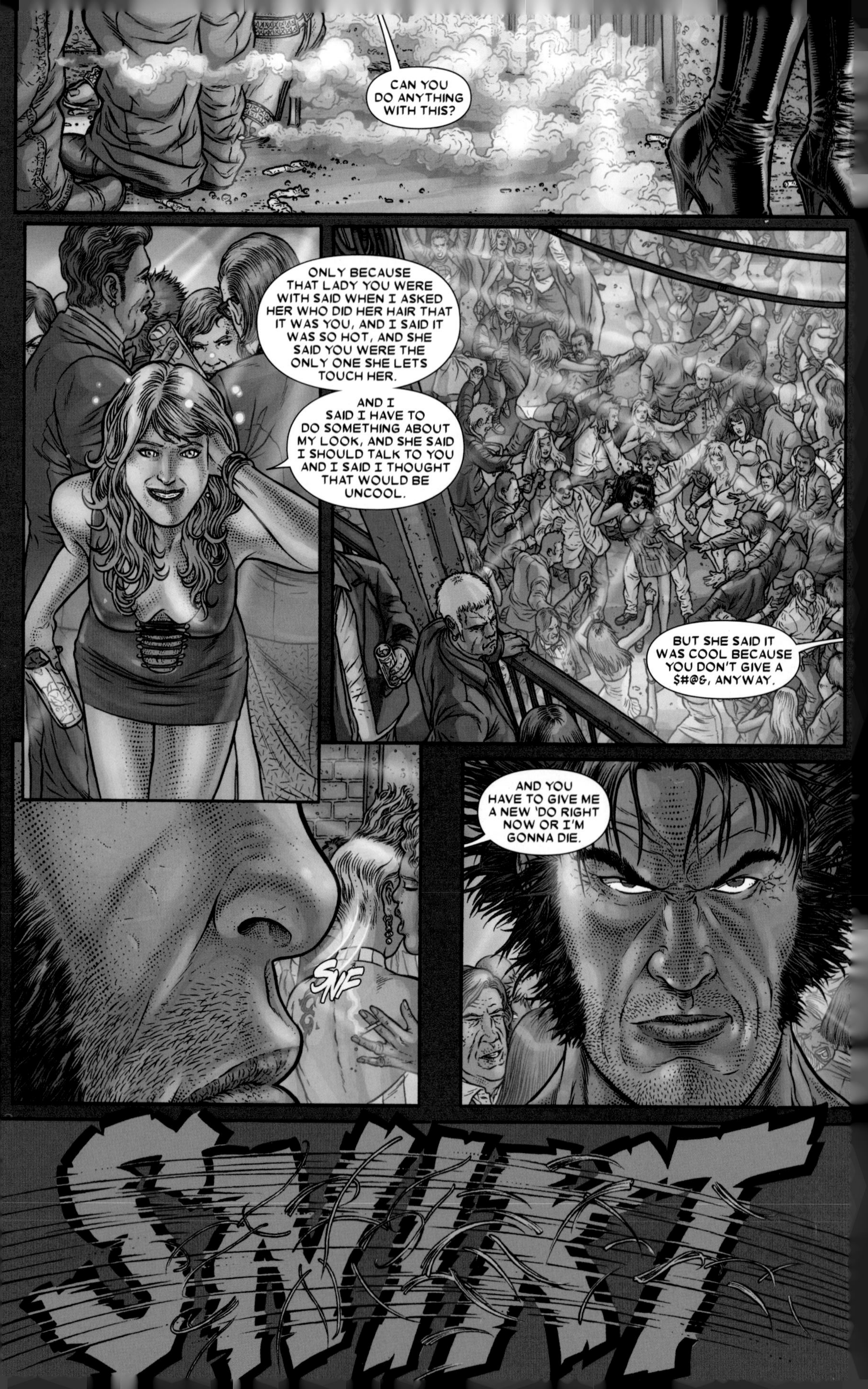
CAN YOU DO ANYTHING WITH THIS?
ONLY BECAUSE THAT LADY YOU WERE WITH SAID WHEN I ASKED HER WHO DID HER HAIR THAT IT WAS YOU, AND I SAID IT WAS SO HOT, AND SHE SAID YOU WERE THE ONLY ONE SHE LETS TOUCH HER.
AND I SAID I HAVE TO DO SOMETHING ABOUT MY LOOK, AND SHE SAID I SHOULD TALK TO YOU AND I SAID I THOUGHT THAT WOULD BE UNCOOL.
BUT SHE SAID IT WAS COOL BECAUSE YOU DON'T GIVE A $#@&, ANYWAY.
SNF
AND YOU HAVE TO GIVE ME A NEW 'DO RIGHT NOW OR I'M GONNA DIE.
SNIKT

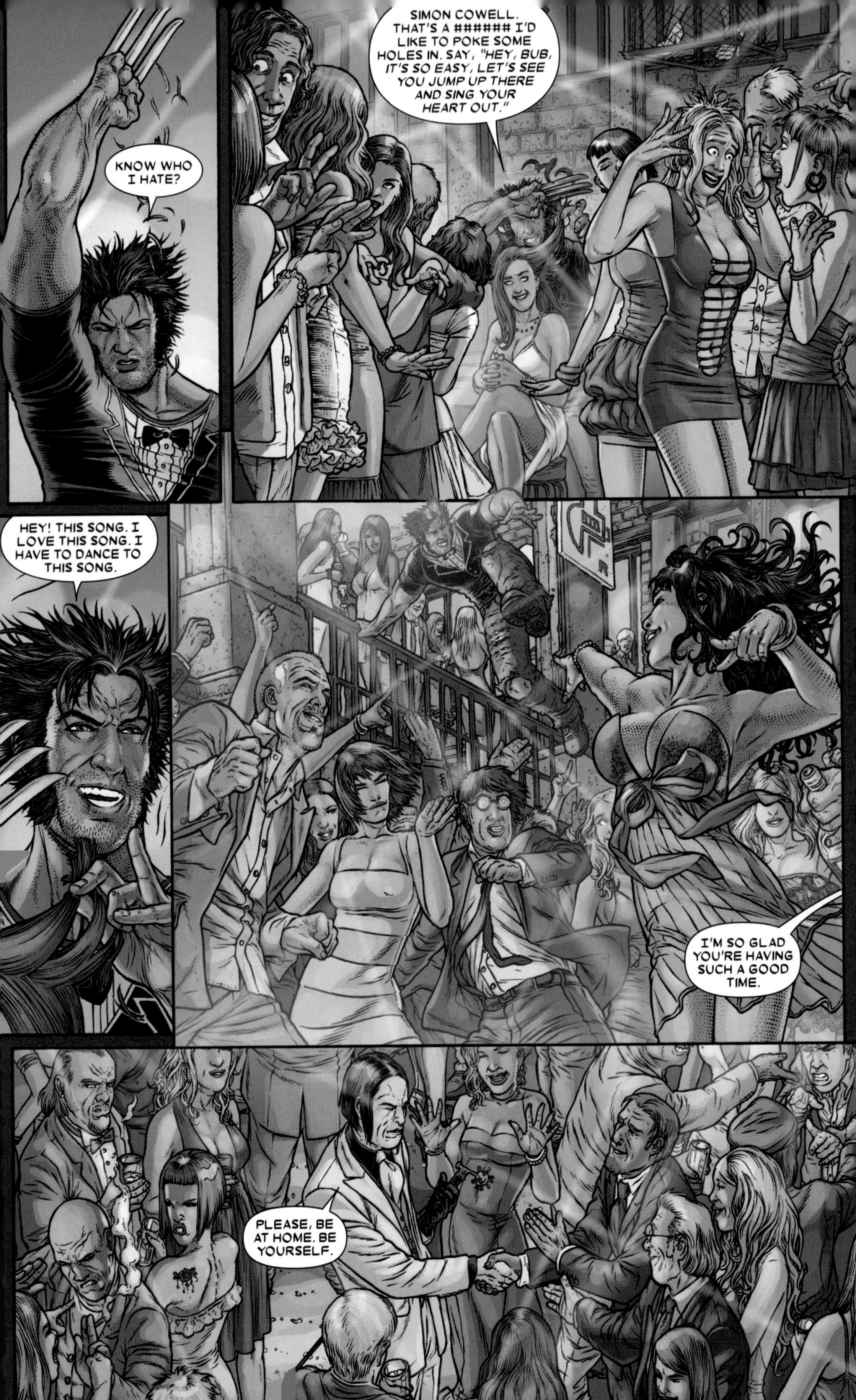
KNOW WHO I HATE?
SIMON COWELL. THAT'S A ###### I'D LIKE TO POKE SOME HOLES IN. SAY, "HEY, BUB, IT'S SO EASY, LET'S SEE YOU JUMP UP THERE AND SING YOUR HEART OUT."
HEY! THIS SONG. I LOVE THIS SONG. I HAVE TO DANCE TO THIS SONG.
I'M SO GLAD YOU'RE HAVING SUCH A GOOD TIME.
PLEASE, BE AT HOME. BE YOURSELF.

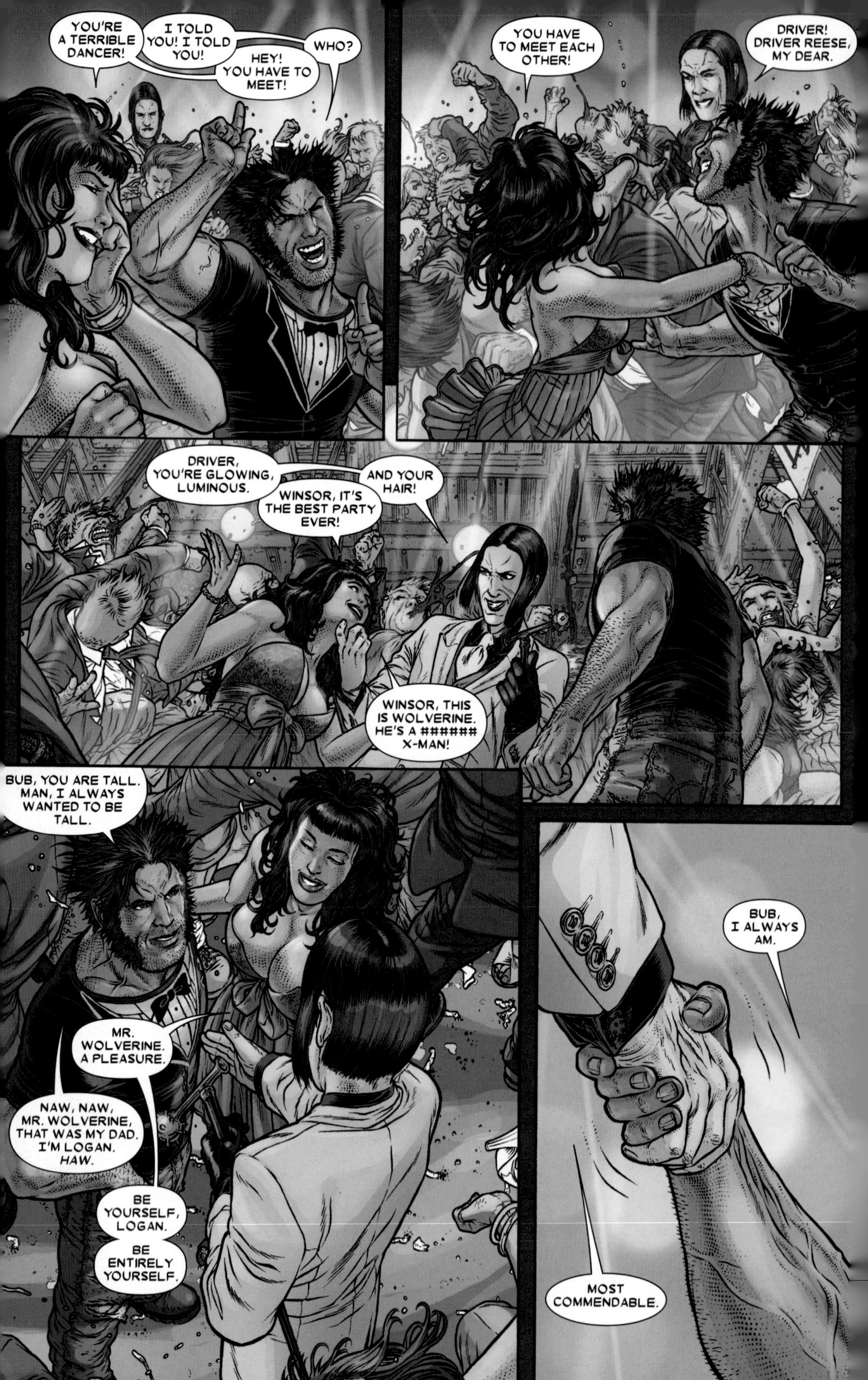

YOU'RE A TERRIBLE DANCER!
I TOLD YOU! I TOLD YOU!
HEY! YOU HAVE TO MEET!
WHO?
YOU HAVE TO MEET EACH OTHER!
DRIVER! DRIVER REESE, MY DEAR.
DRIVER, YOU'RE GLOWING, LUMINOUS.
AND YOUR HAIR!
WINSOR, IT'S THE BEST PARTY EVER!
WINSOR, THIS IS WOLVERINE. HE'S A ###### X-MAN!
BUB, YOU ARE TALL. MAN, I ALWAYS WANTED TO BE TALL.
MR. WOLVERINE. A PLEASURE.
NAW, NAW, MR. WOLVERINE, THAT WAS MY DAD. I'M LOGAN. HAW.
BE YOURSELF, LOGAN.
BE ENTIRELY YOURSELF.
BUB, I ALWAYS AM.
MOST COMMENDABLE.

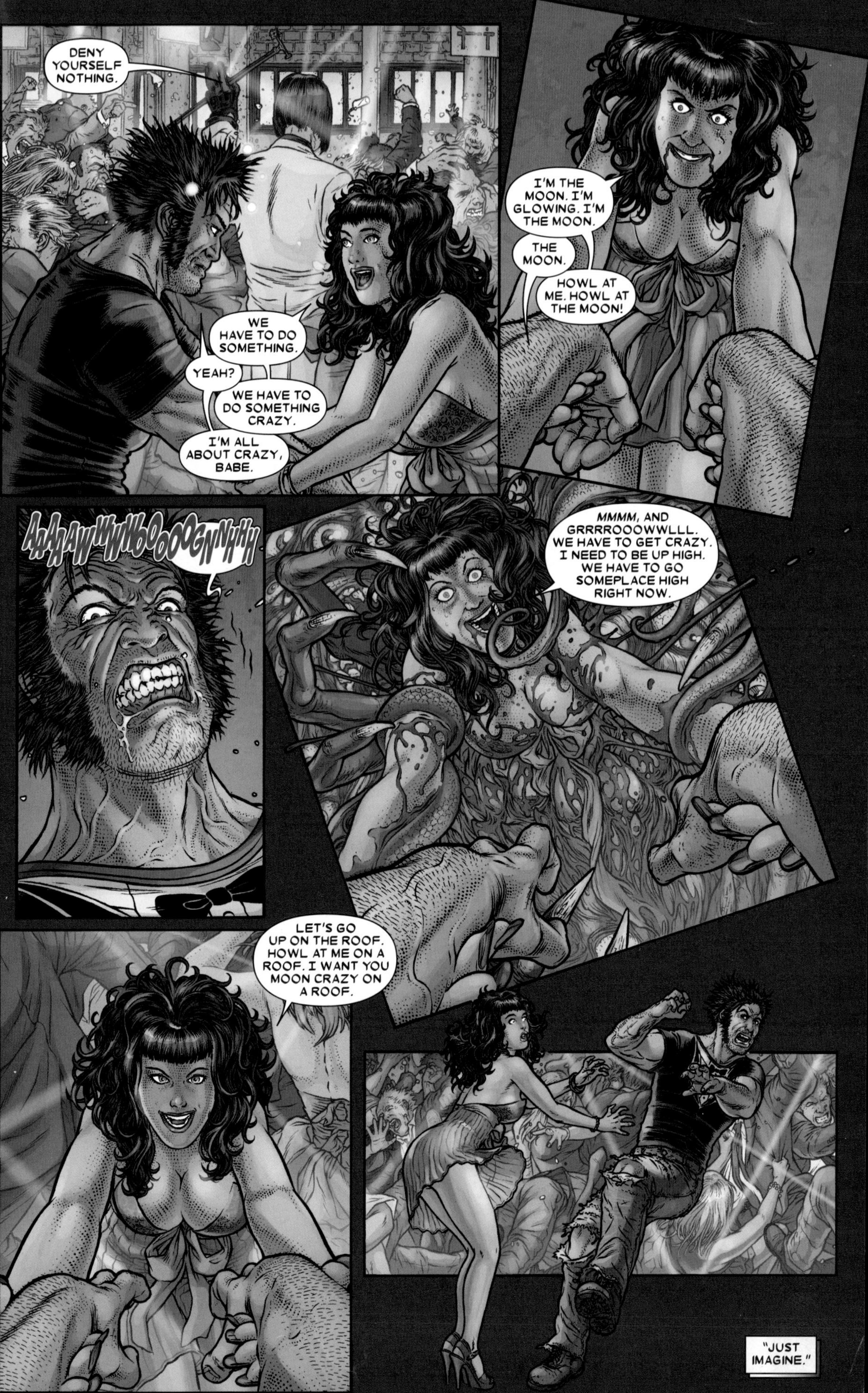
DENY YOURSELF NOTHING.
WE HAVE TO DO SOMETHING.
YEAH?
WE HAVE TO DO SOMETHING CRAZY.
I'M ALL ABOUT CRAZY, BABE.
I'M THE MOON. I'M GLOWING. I'M THE MOON.
THE MOON.
HOWL AT ME. HOWL AT THE MOON!
AAAAAWWWWOOOOOGNHHH
MMMM, AND GRRRROOOWWLLL. WE HAVE TO GET CRAZY. I NEED TO BE UP HIGH. WE HAVE TO GO SOMEPLACE HIGH RIGHT NOW.
LET'S GO UP ON THE ROOF. HOWL AT ME ON A ROOF. I WANT YOU MOON CRAZY ON A ROOF.
"JUST IMAGINE."

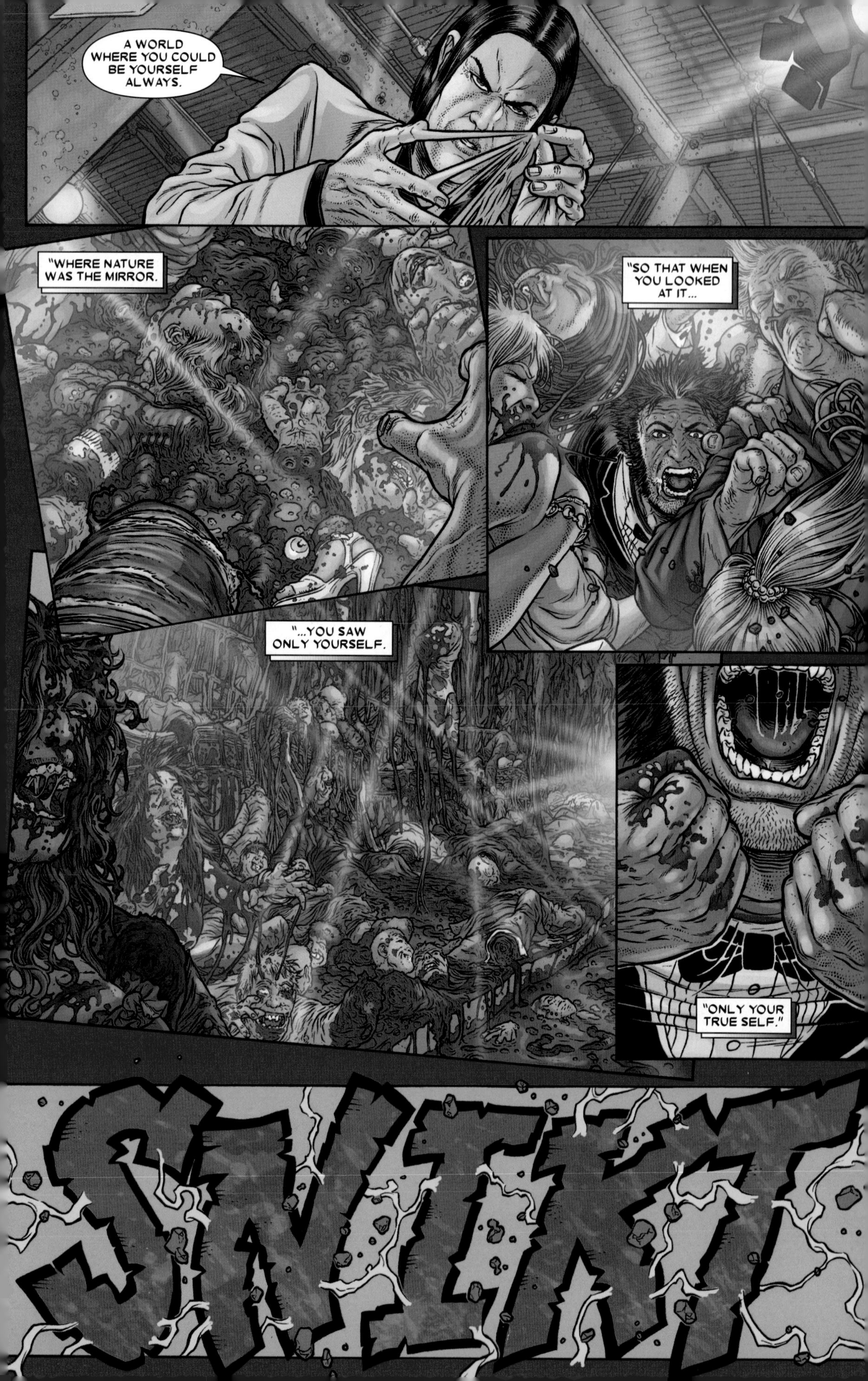
A WORLD WHERE YOU COULD BE YOURSELF ALWAYS.
"WHERE NATURE WAS THE MIRROR.
"SO THAT WHEN YOU LOOKED AT IT...
"...YOU SAW ONLY YOURSELF.
"ONLY YOUR TRUE SELF."

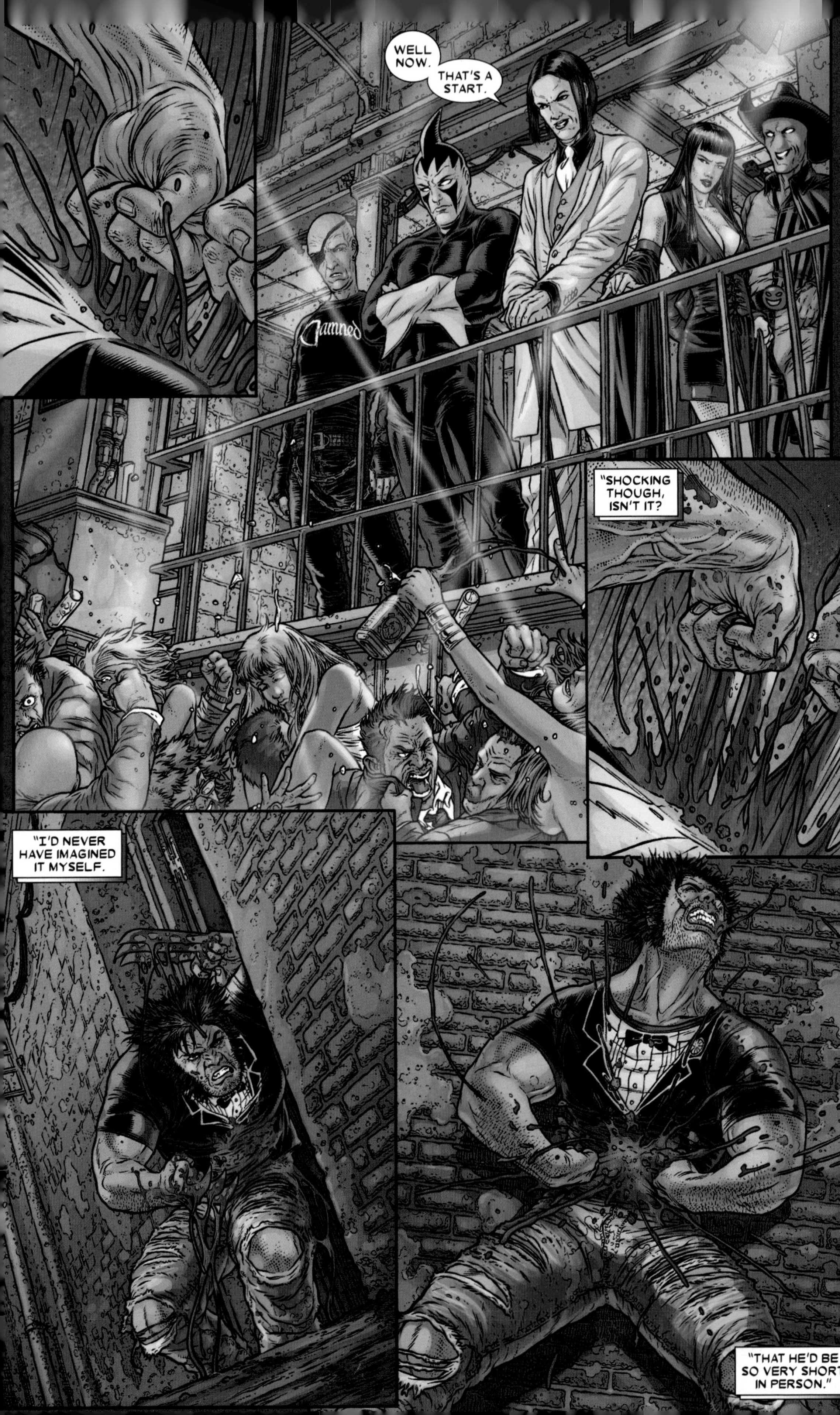
WELL NOW.
THAT'S A START.
"SHOCKING THOUGH, ISN'T IT?
"I'D NEVER HAVE IMAGINED IT MYSELF.
"THAT HE'D BE SO VERY SHORT IN PERSON."

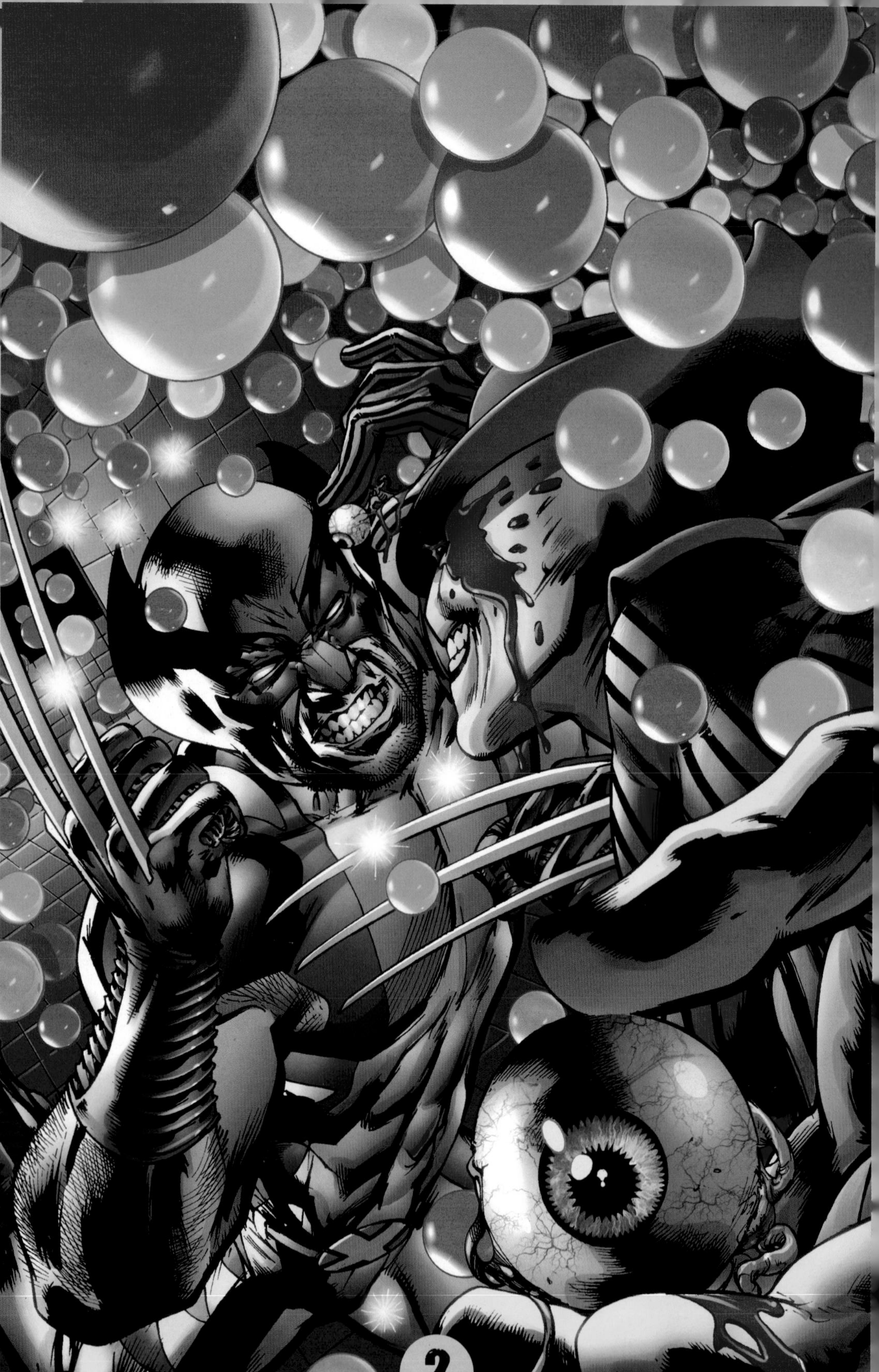
2

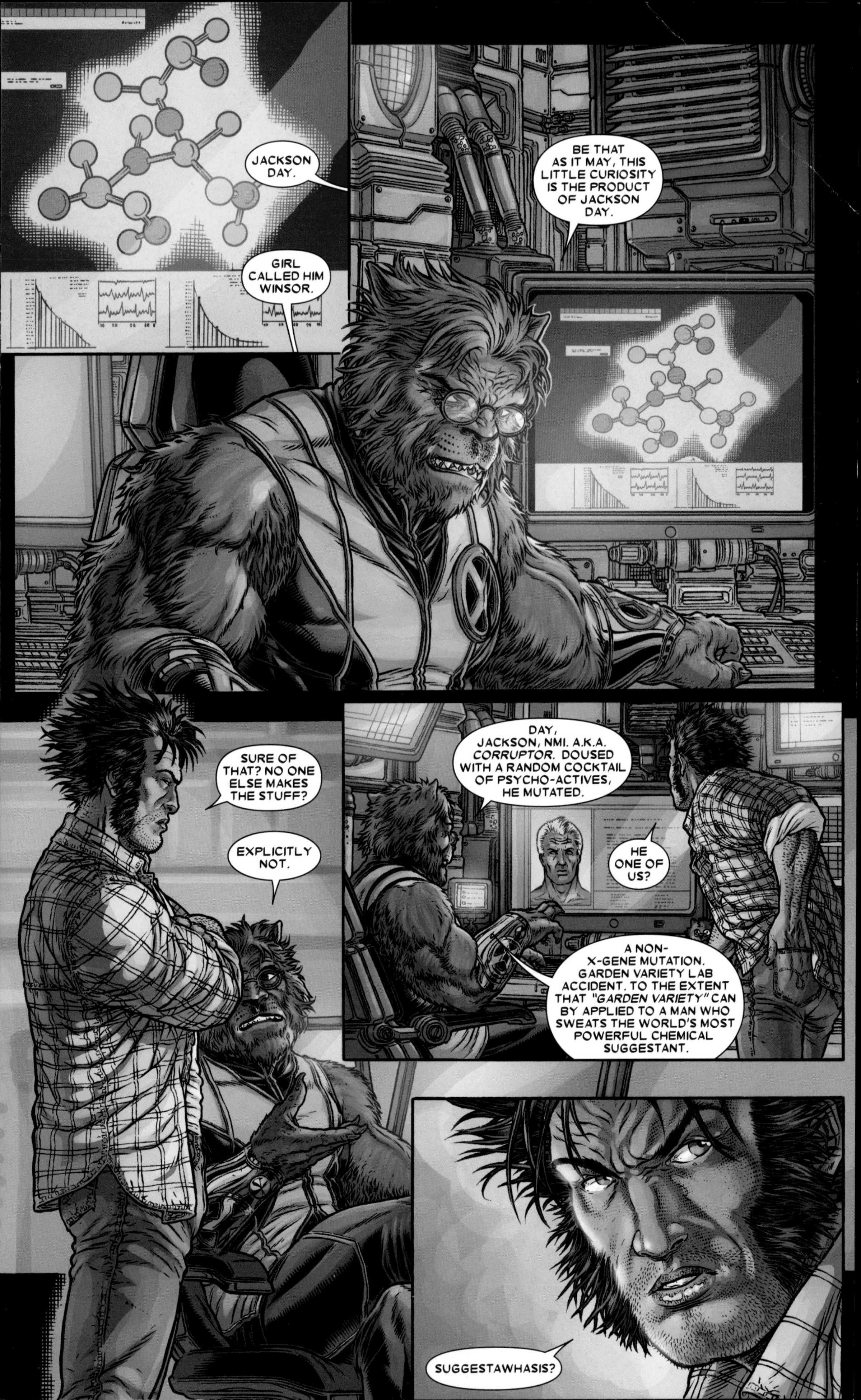
JACKSON DAY.
BE THAT AS IT MAY, THIS LITTLE CURIOSITY IS THE PRODUCT OF JACKSON DAY.
GIRL CALLED HIM WINSOR.
SURE OF THAT? NO ONE ELSE MAKES THE STUFF?
EXPLICITLY NOT.
DAY, JACKSON, NMI. A.K.A. CORRUPTOR. DOUSED WITH A RANDOM COCKTAIL OF PSYCHO-ACTIVES, HE MUTATED.
HE ONE OF US?
A NON-X-GENE MUTATION. GARDEN VARIETY LAB ACCIDENT. TO THE EXTENT THAT "GARDEN VARIETY" CAN BY APPLIED TO A MAN WHO SWEATS THE WORLD'S MOST POWERFUL CHEMICAL SUGGESTANT.
SUGGESTAWHASIS?

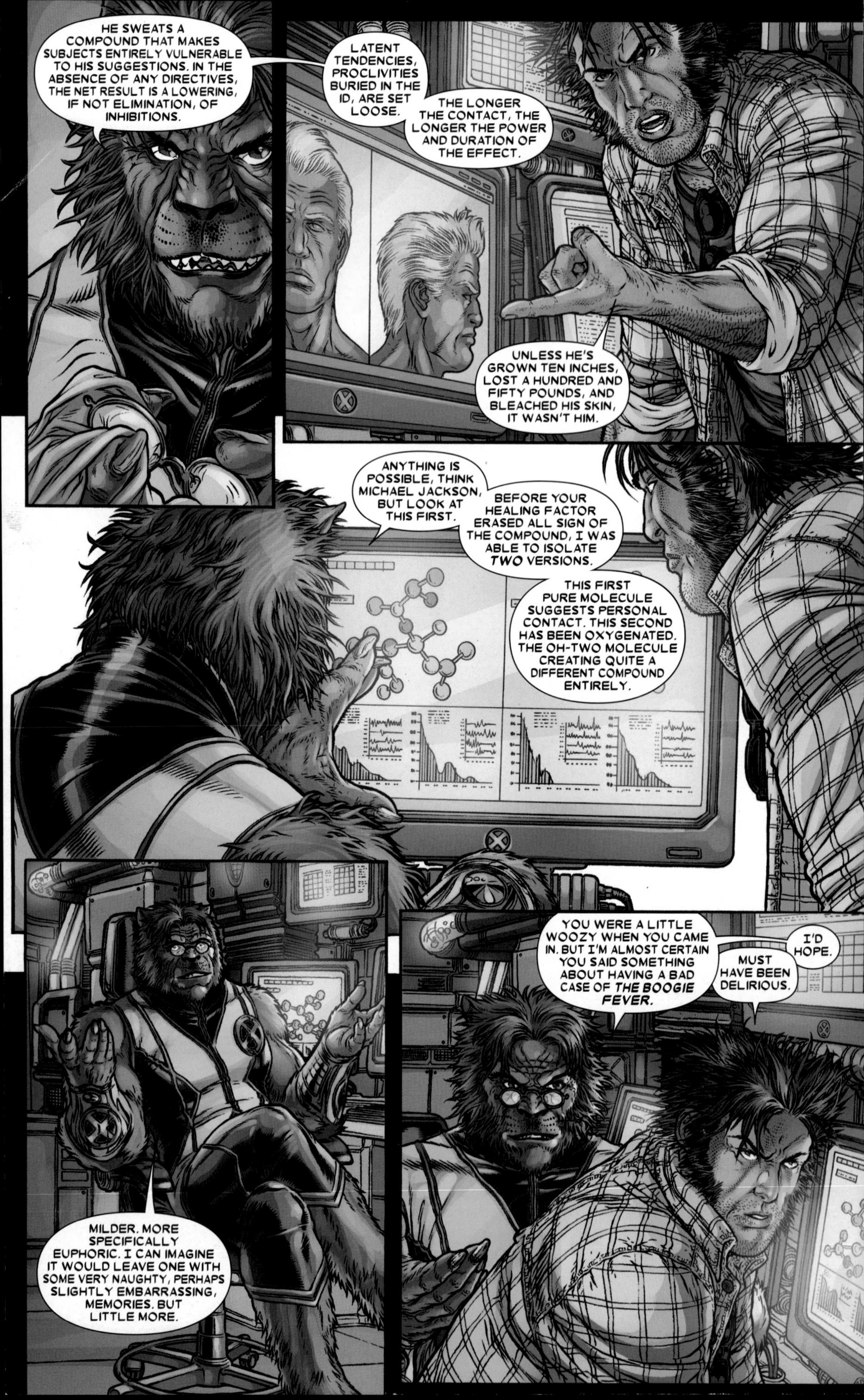

HE SWEATS A COMPOUND THAT MAKES SUBJECTS ENTIRELY VULNERABLE TO HIS SUGGESTIONS. IN THE ABSENCE OF ANY DIRECTIVES, THE NET RESULT IS A LOWERING, IF NOT ELIMINATION, OF INHIBITIONS.
LATENT TENDENCIES, PROCLIVITIES BURIED IN THE ID, ARE SET LOOSE.
THE LONGER THE CONTACT, THE LONGER THE POWER AND DURATION OF THE EFFECT.
UNLESS HE'S GROWN TEN INCHES, LOST A HUNDRED AND FIFTY POUNDS, AND BLEACHED HIS SKIN, IT WASN'T HIM.
ANYTHING IS POSSIBLE, THINK MICHAEL JACKSON, BUT LOOK AT THIS FIRST.
BEFORE YOUR HEALING FACTOR ERASED ALL SIGN OF THE COMPOUND, I WAS ABLE TO ISOLATE *TWO* VERSIONS.
THIS FIRST PURE MOLECULE SUGGESTS PERSONAL CONTACT. THIS SECOND HAS BEEN OXYGENATED. THE OH-TWO MOLECULE CREATING QUITE A DIFFERENT COMPOUND ENTIRELY.
MILDER. MORE SPECIFICALLY EUPHORIC. I CAN IMAGINE IT WOULD LEAVE ONE WITH SOME VERY NAUGHTY, PERHAPS SLIGHTLY EMBARRASSING, MEMORIES. BUT LITTLE MORE.
YOU WERE A LITTLE WOOZY WHEN YOU CAME IN. BUT I'M ALMOST CERTAIN YOU SAID SOMETHING ABOUT HAVING A BAD CASE OF *THE BOOGIE FEVER.*
I'D HOPE.
MUST HAVE BEEN DELIRIOUS.

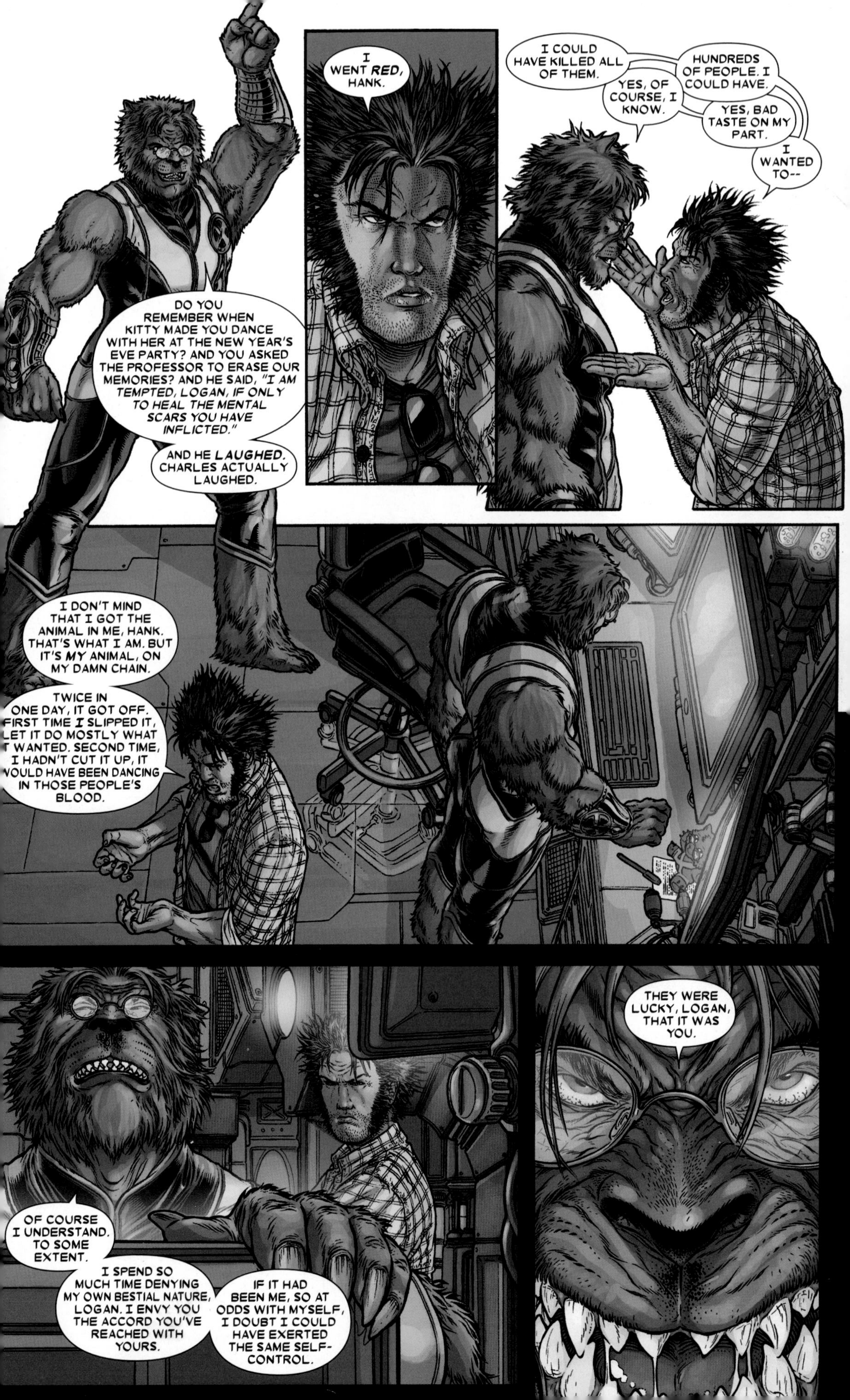

DO YOU REMEMBER WHEN KITTY MADE YOU DANCE WITH HER AT THE NEW YEAR'S EVE PARTY? AND YOU ASKED THE PROFESSOR TO ERASE OUR MEMORIES? AND HE SAID, "I AM TEMPTED, LOGAN, IF ONLY TO HEAL THE MENTAL SCARS YOU HAVE INFLICTED."
AND HE LAUGHED. CHARLES ACTUALLY LAUGHED.
I WENT RED, HANK.
I COULD HAVE KILLED ALL OF THEM.
HUNDREDS OF PEOPLE. I COULD HAVE.
YES, OF COURSE, I KNOW.
YES, BAD TASTE ON MY PART.
I WANTED TO--
I DON'T MIND THAT I GOT THE ANIMAL IN ME, HANK. THAT'S WHAT I AM. BUT IT'S MY ANIMAL, ON MY DAMN CHAIN.
TWICE IN ONE DAY, IT GOT OFF. FIRST TIME I SLIPPED IT, LET IT DO MOSTLY WHAT IT WANTED. SECOND TIME, I HADN'T CUT IT UP, IT WOULD HAVE BEEN DANCING IN THOSE PEOPLE'S BLOOD.
OF COURSE I UNDERSTAND. TO SOME EXTENT.
I SPEND SO MUCH TIME DENYING MY OWN BESTIAL NATURE, LOGAN. I ENVY YOU THE ACCORD YOU'VE REACHED WITH YOURS.
IF IT HAD BEEN ME, SO AT ODDS WITH MYSELF, I DOUBT I COULD HAVE EXERTED THE SAME SELF-CONTROL.
THEY WERE LUCKY, LOGAN, THAT IT WAS YOU.

"SOME OF 'EM MAYBE, HANK."

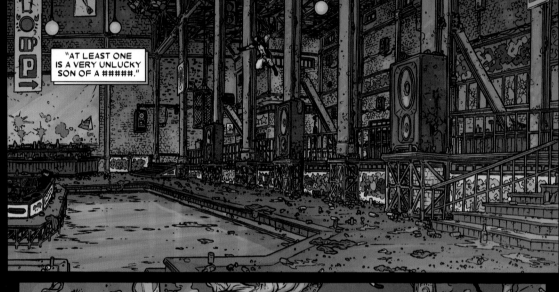

"AT LEAST ONE IS A VERY UNLUCKY SON OF A #####."

KKKK

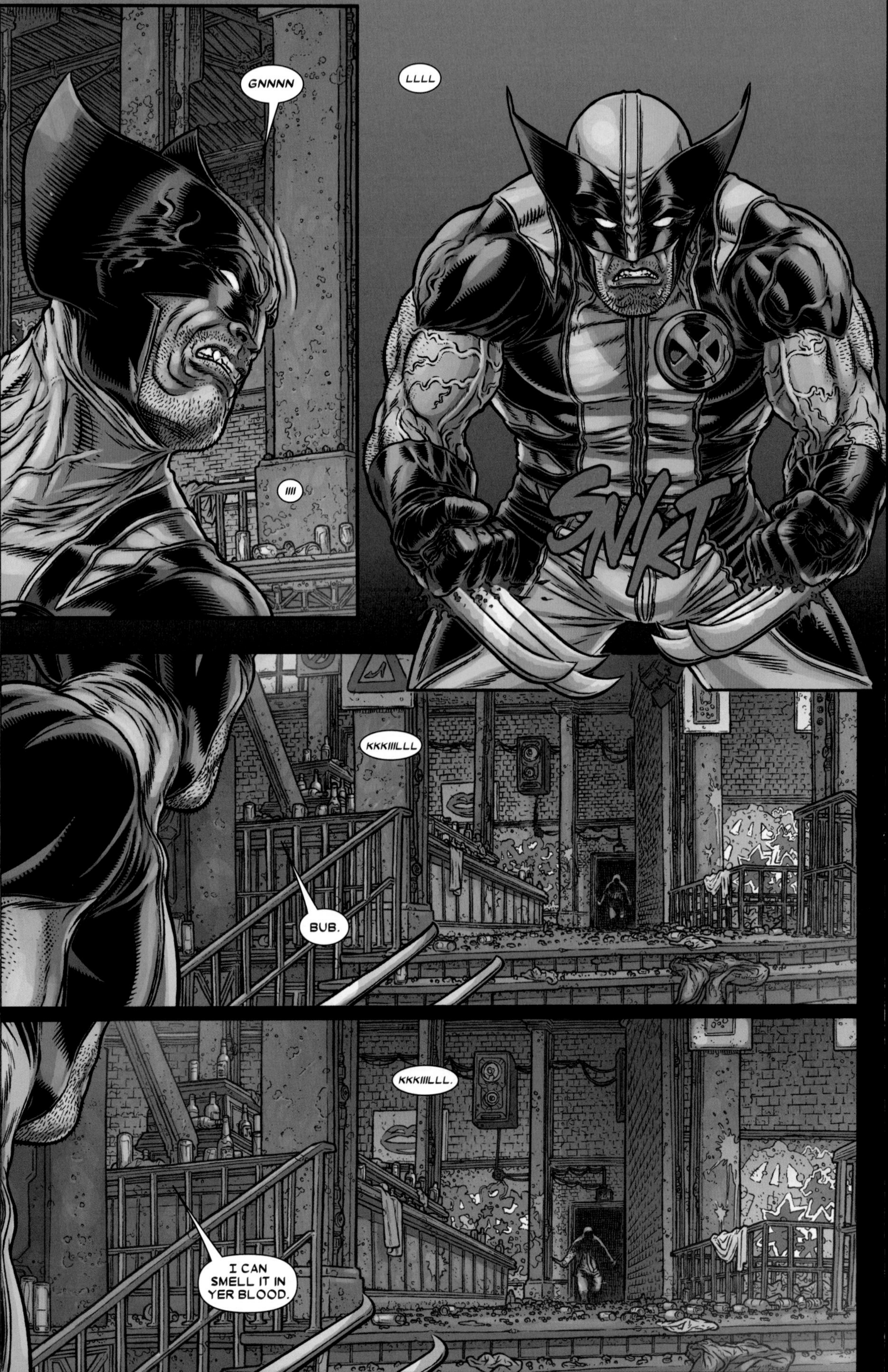
GNNNN
LLLL
IIII
SNIKT
KKKIIILLL
BUB.
KKKIIILLL.
I CAN SMELL IT IN YER BLOOD.

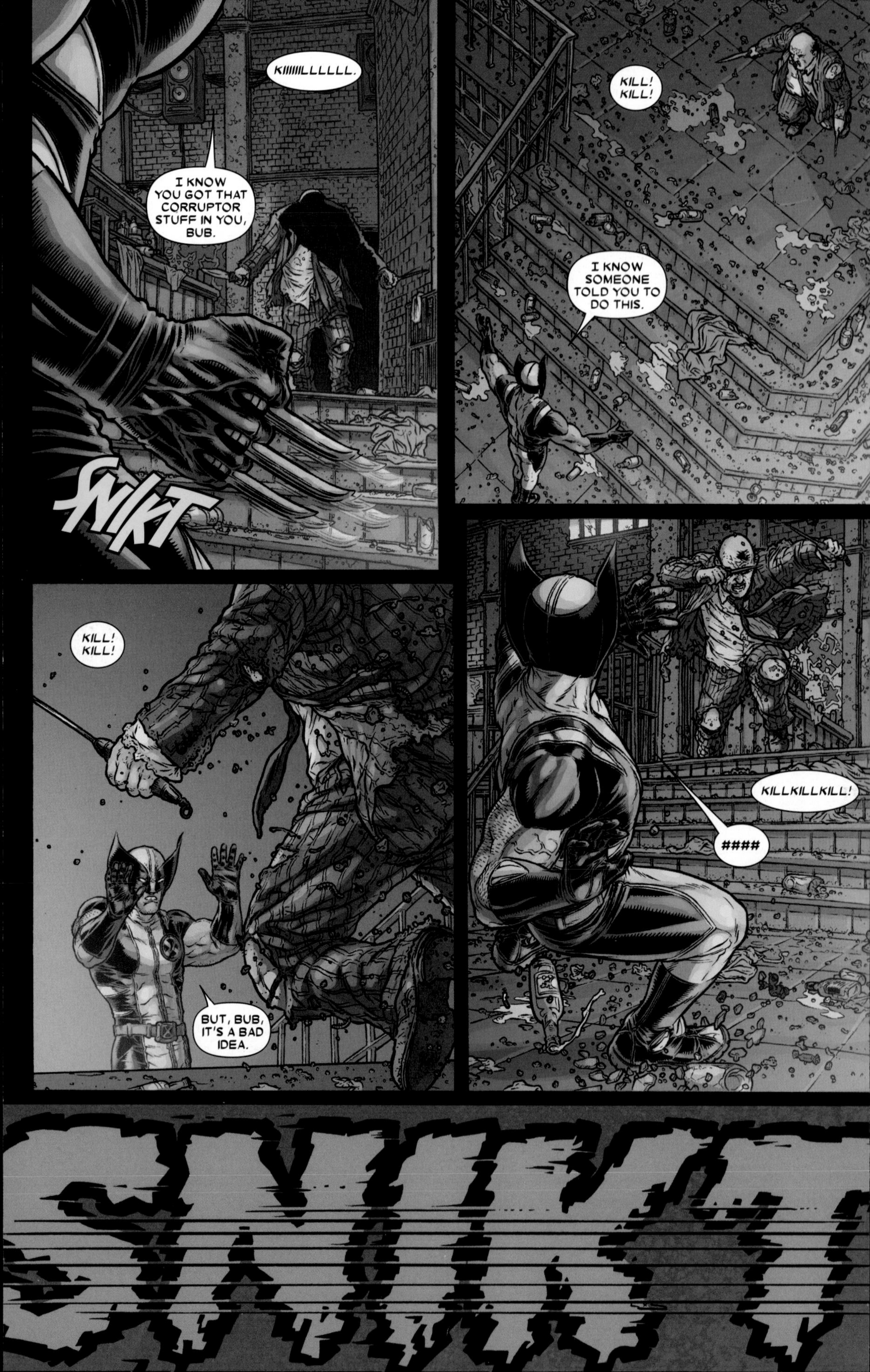
KIIIIIILLLLLL.
I KNOW YOU GOT THAT CORRUPTOR STUFF IN YOU, BUB.
SNIKT
KILL! KILL!
I KNOW SOMEONE TOLD YOU TO DO THIS.
KILL! KILL!
BUT, BUB, IT'S A BAD IDEA.
KILLKILLKILL!
####

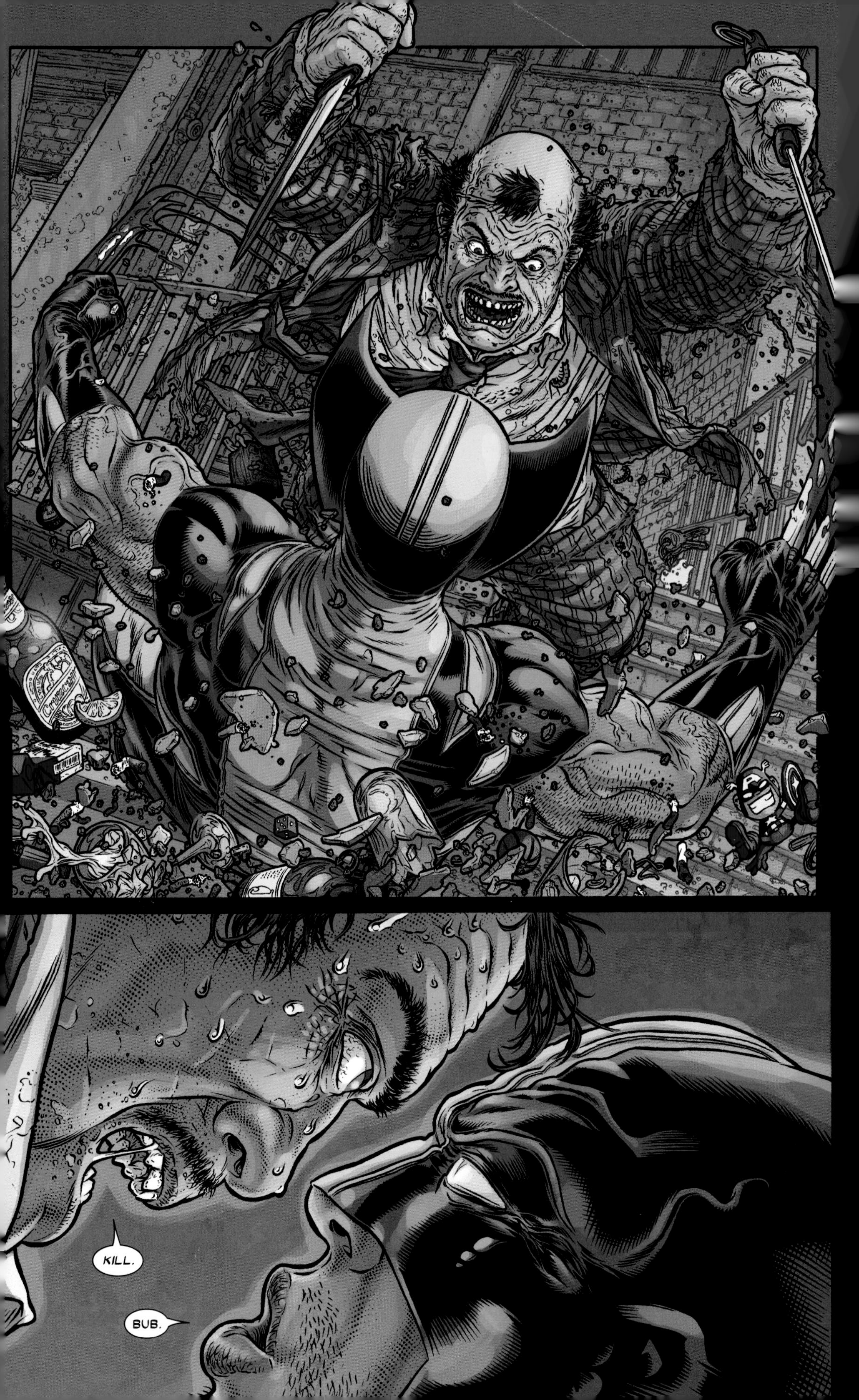
KILL.
BUB.

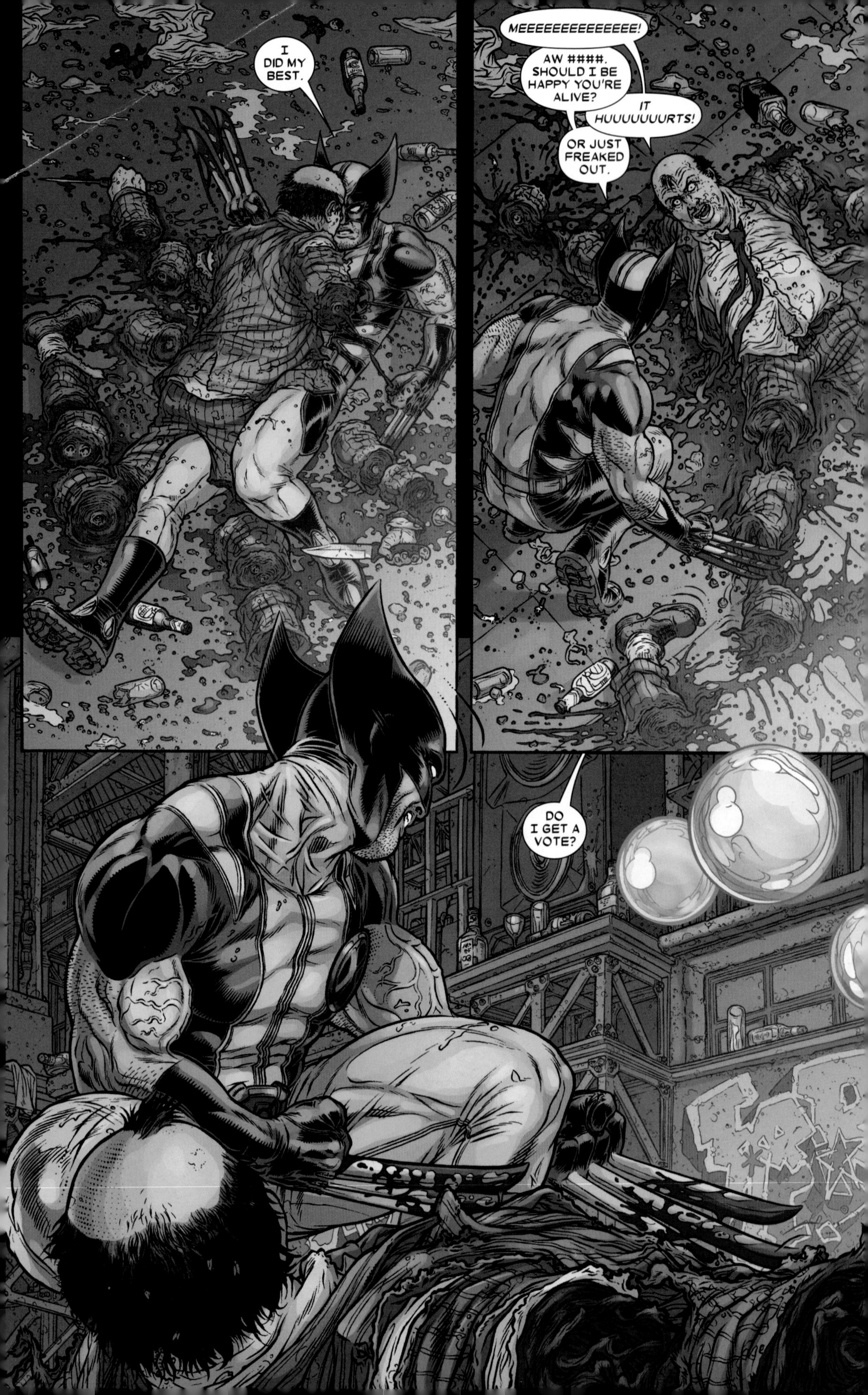
I DID MY BEST.
MEEEEEEEEEEEEEE!
AW ####. SHOULD I BE HAPPY YOU'RE ALIVE?
IT HUUUUUUURTS!
OR JUST FREAKED OUT.
DO I GET A VOTE?

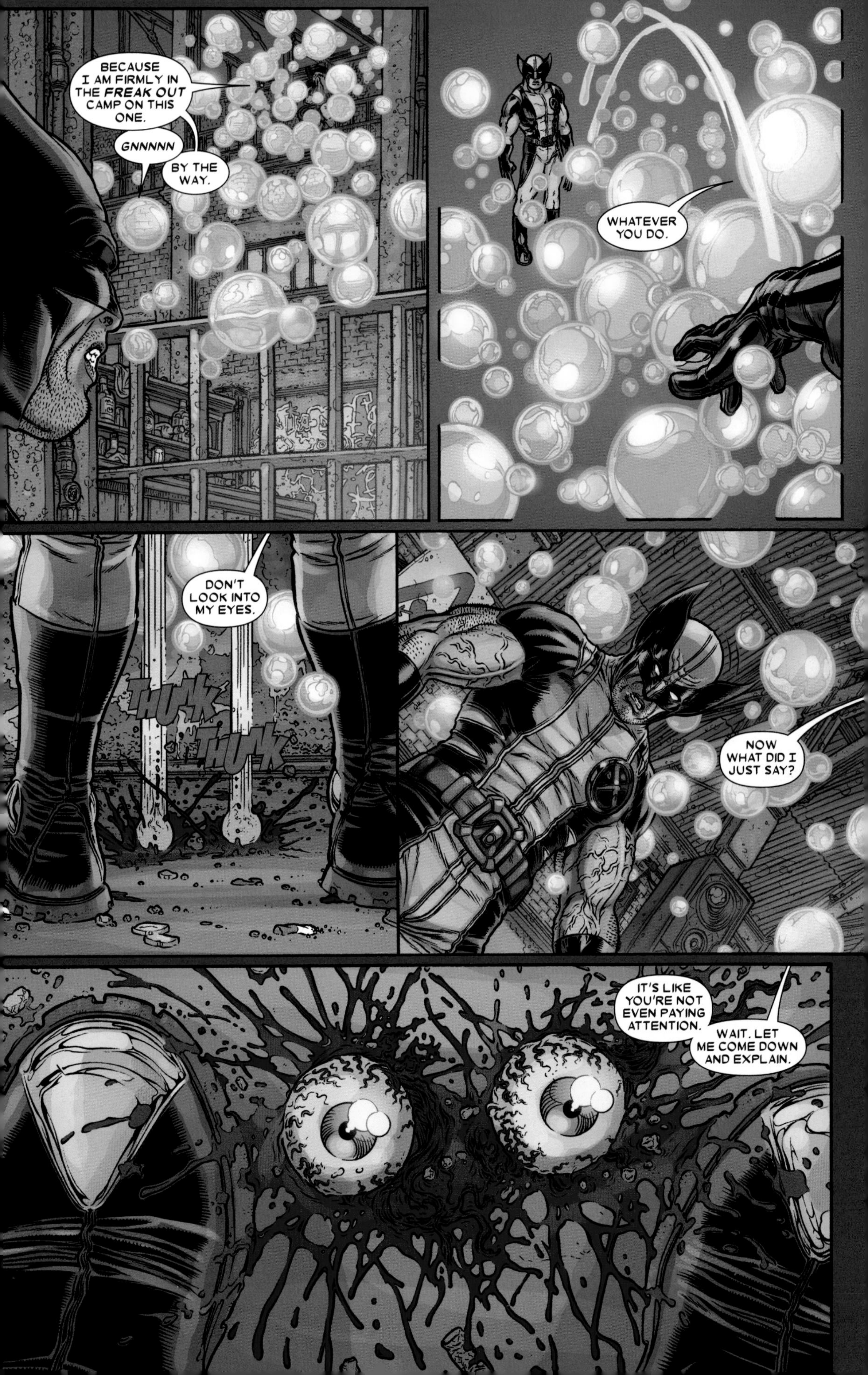
BECAUSE I AM FIRMLY IN THE FREAK OUT CAMP ON THIS ONE.
GNNNNN
BY THE WAY.
WHATEVER YOU DO.
DON'T LOOK INTO MY EYES.
THUK
THUK
NOW WHAT DID I JUST SAY?
IT'S LIKE YOU'RE NOT EVEN PAYING ATTENTION.
WAIT. LET ME COME DOWN AND EXPLAIN.

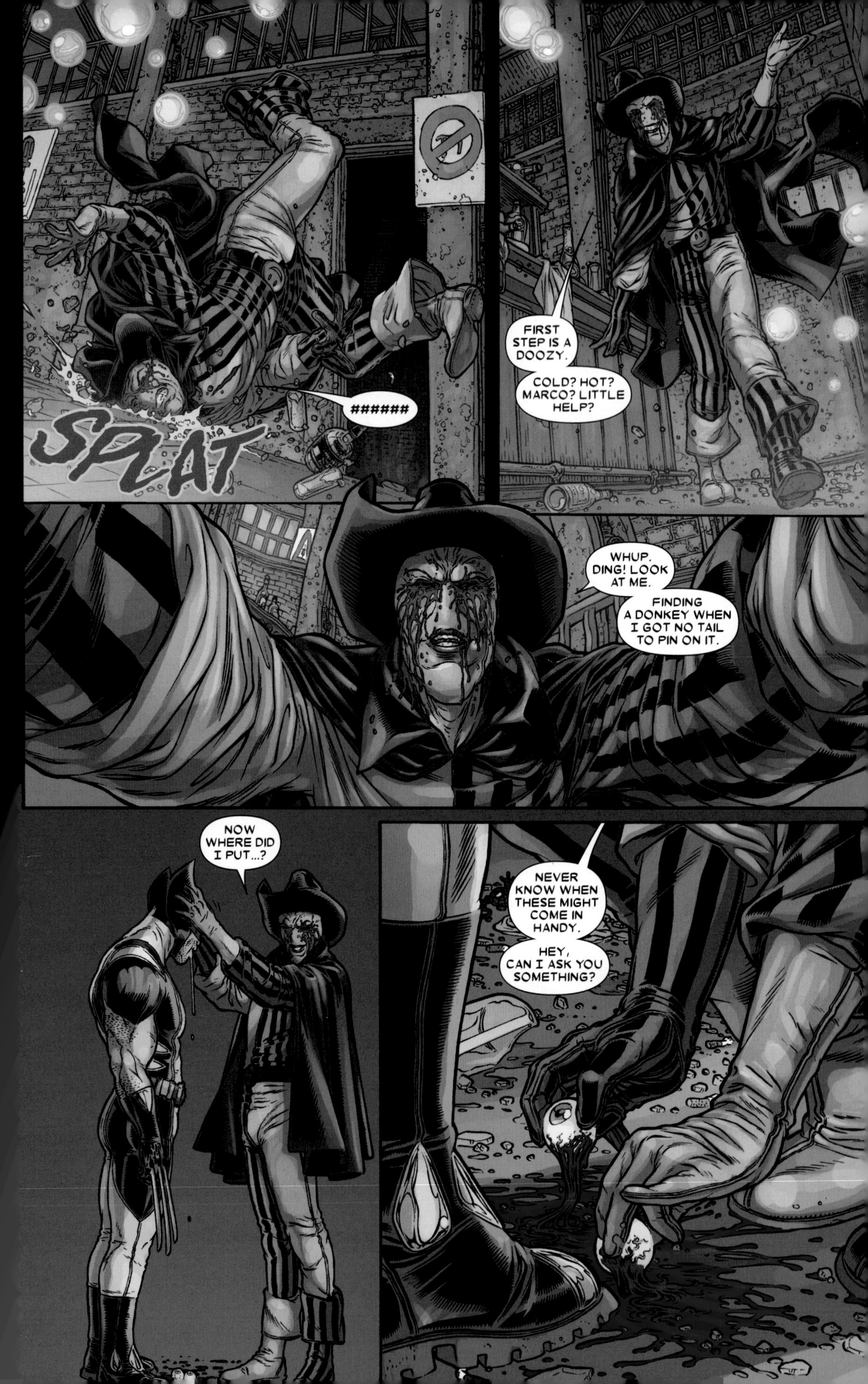
SPLAT
######
FIRST STEP IS A DOOZY.
COLD? HOT? MARCO? LITTLE HELP?
WHUP. DING! LOOK AT ME.
FINDING A DONKEY WHEN I GOT NO TAIL TO PIN ON IT.
NOW WHERE DID I PUT...?
NEVER KNOW WHEN THESE MIGHT COME IN HANDY.
HEY, CAN I ASK YOU SOMETHING?

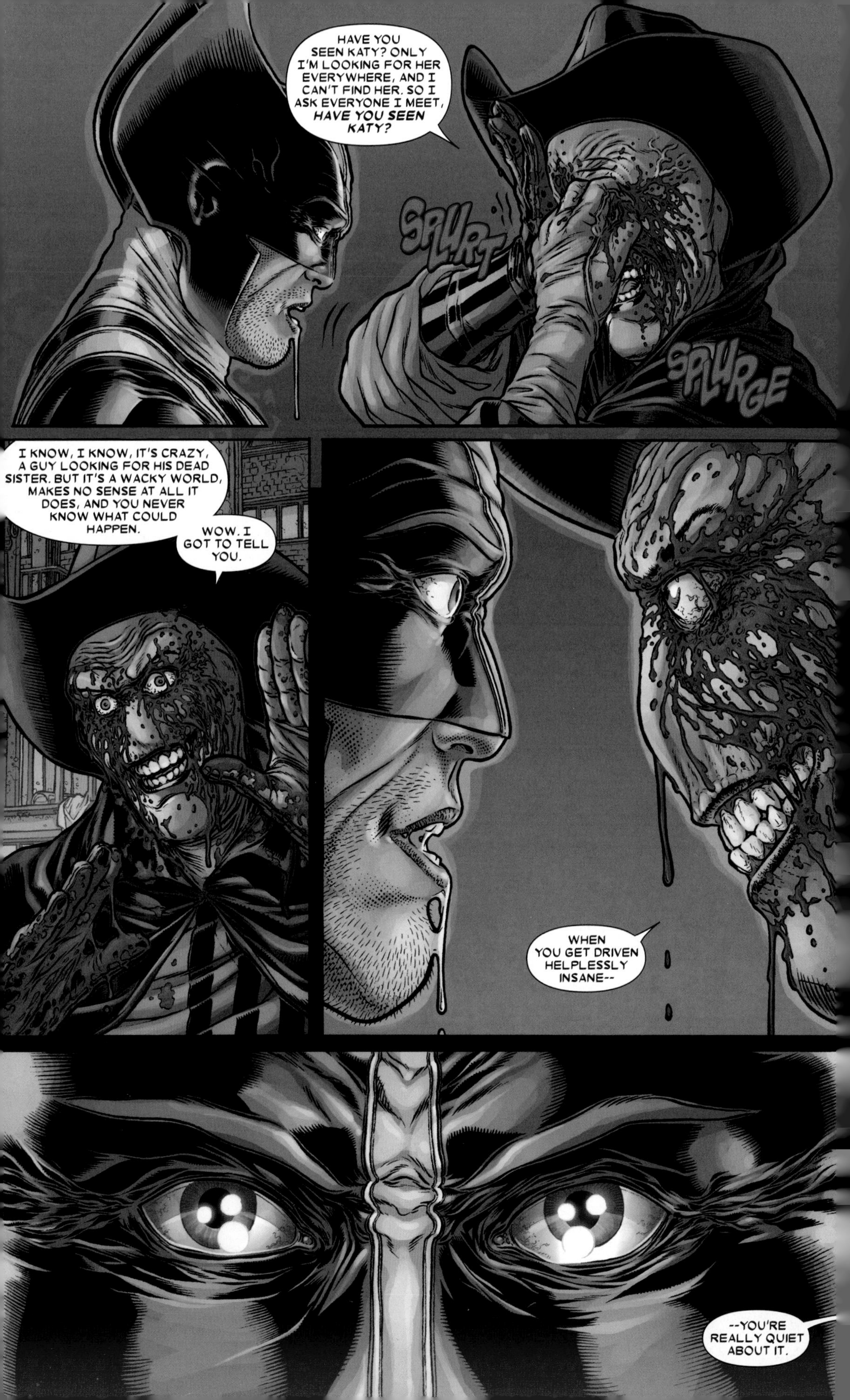
HAVE YOU SEEN KATY? ONLY I'M LOOKING FOR HER EVERYWHERE, AND I CAN'T FIND HER. SO I ASK EVERYONE I MEET, *HAVE YOU SEEN KATY?*
SPLURT
SPLURGE
I KNOW, I KNOW, IT'S CRAZY, A GUY LOOKING FOR HIS DEAD SISTER. BUT IT'S A WACKY WORLD, MAKES NO SENSE AT ALL IT DOES, AND YOU NEVER KNOW WHAT COULD HAPPEN.
WOW. I GOT TO TELL YOU.
WHEN YOU GET DRIVEN HELPLESSLY INSANE--
--YOU'RE REALLY QUIET ABOUT IT.

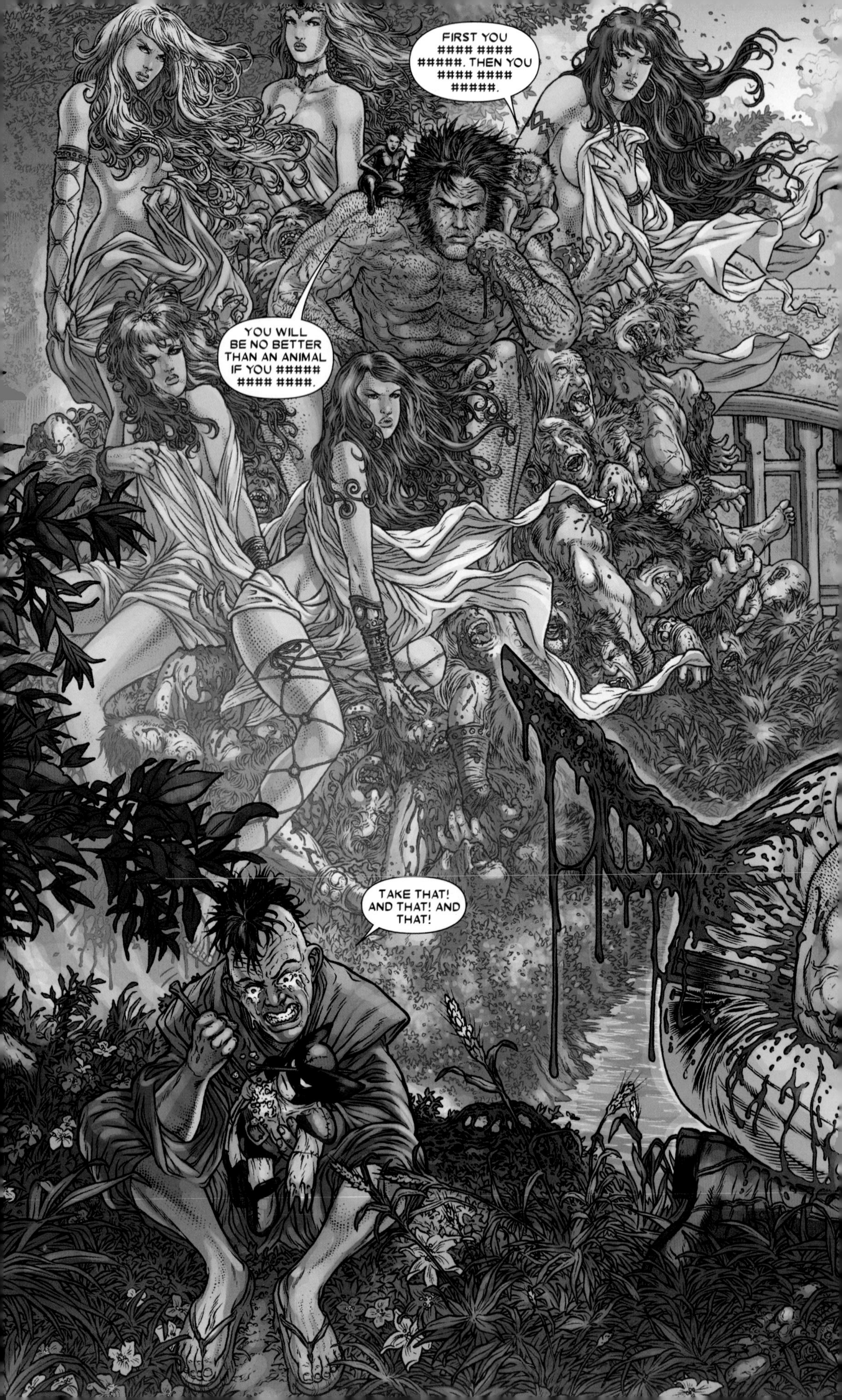

FIRST YOU #### #### #####. THEN YOU #### #### #####.
YOU WILL BE NO BETTER THAN AN ANIMAL IF YOU ##### #### ####.
TAKE THAT! AND THAT! AND THAT!

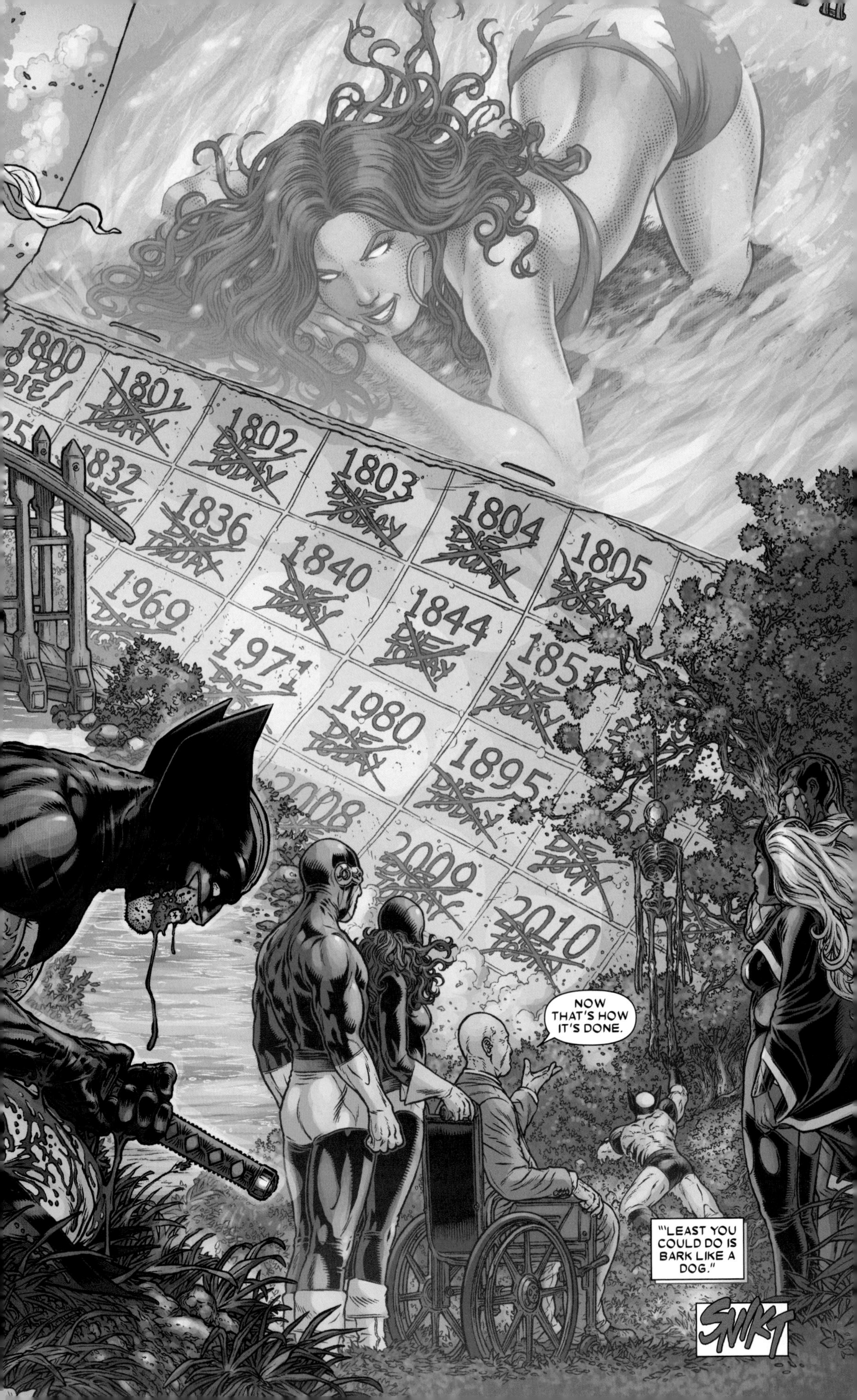
NOW THAT'S HOW IT'S DONE.
"'LEAST YOU COULD DO IS BARK LIKE A DOG."
SNIKT

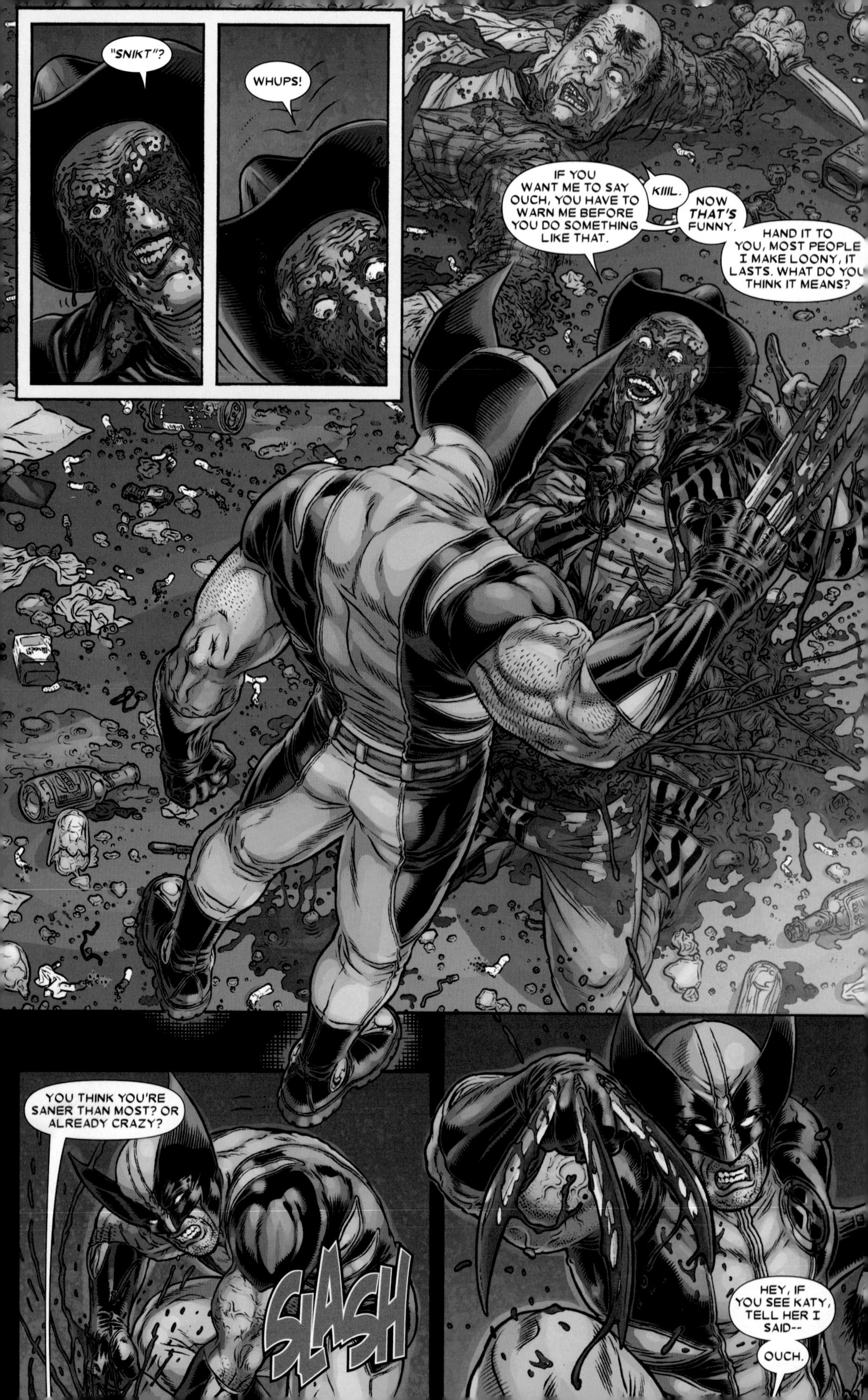
"SNIKT"?
WHUPS!
IF YOU WANT ME TO SAY OUCH, YOU HAVE TO WARN ME BEFORE YOU DO SOMETHING LIKE THAT.
KIIL.
NOW THAT'S FUNNY.
HAND IT TO YOU, MOST PEOPLE I MAKE LOONY, IT LASTS. WHAT DO YOU THINK IT MEANS?
YOU THINK YOU'RE SANER THAN MOST? OR ALREADY CRAZY?
SLASH
HEY, IF YOU SEE KATY, TELL HER I SAID--
OUCH.

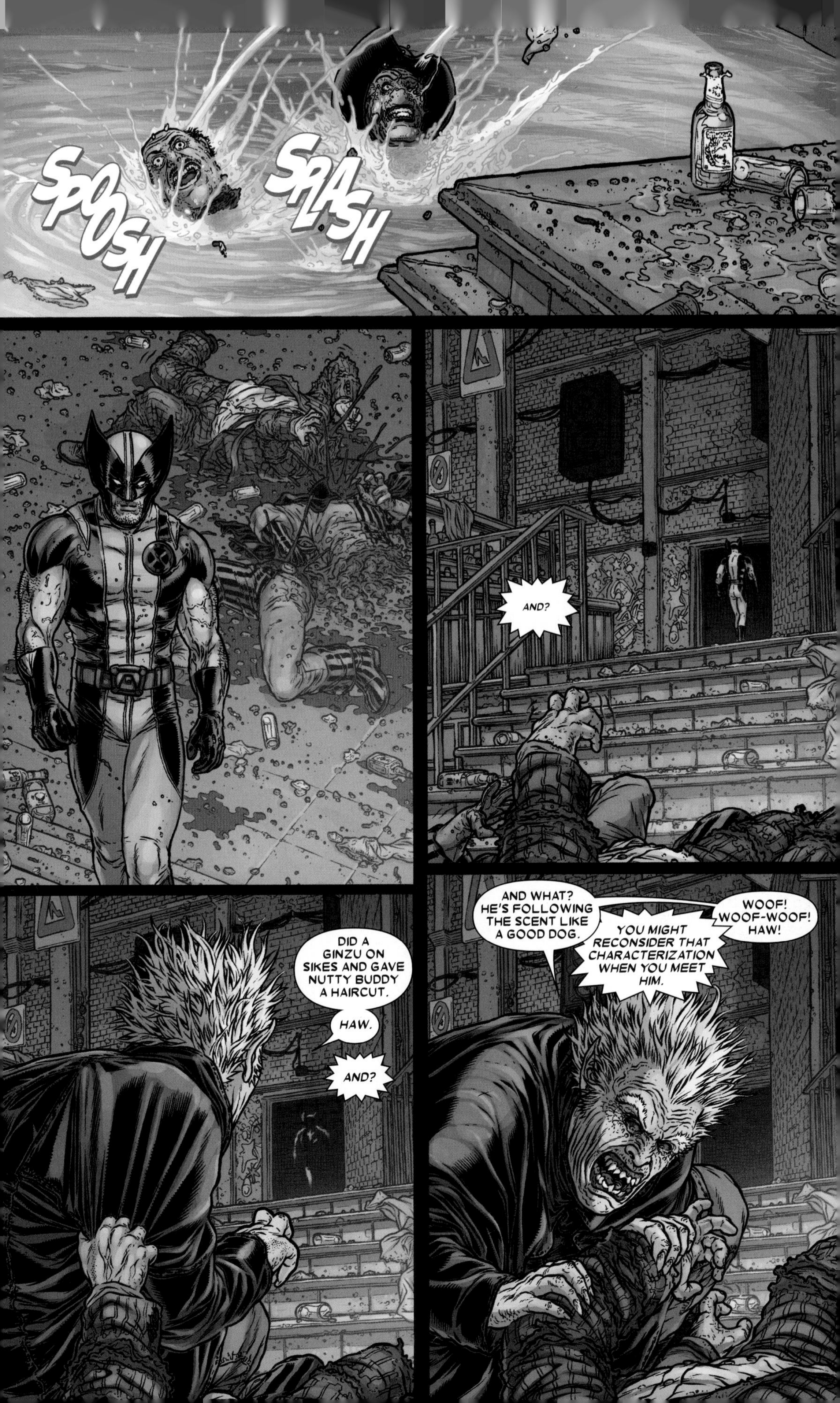
SPOOSH
SPLASH
AND?
DID A GINZU ON SIKES AND GAVE NUTTY BUDDY A HAIRCUT.
HAW.
AND?
AND WHAT? HE'S FOLLOWING THE SCENT LIKE A GOOD DOG.
WOOF! WOOF-WOOF! HAW!
YOU MIGHT RECONSIDER THAT CHARACTERIZATION WHEN YOU MEET HIM.

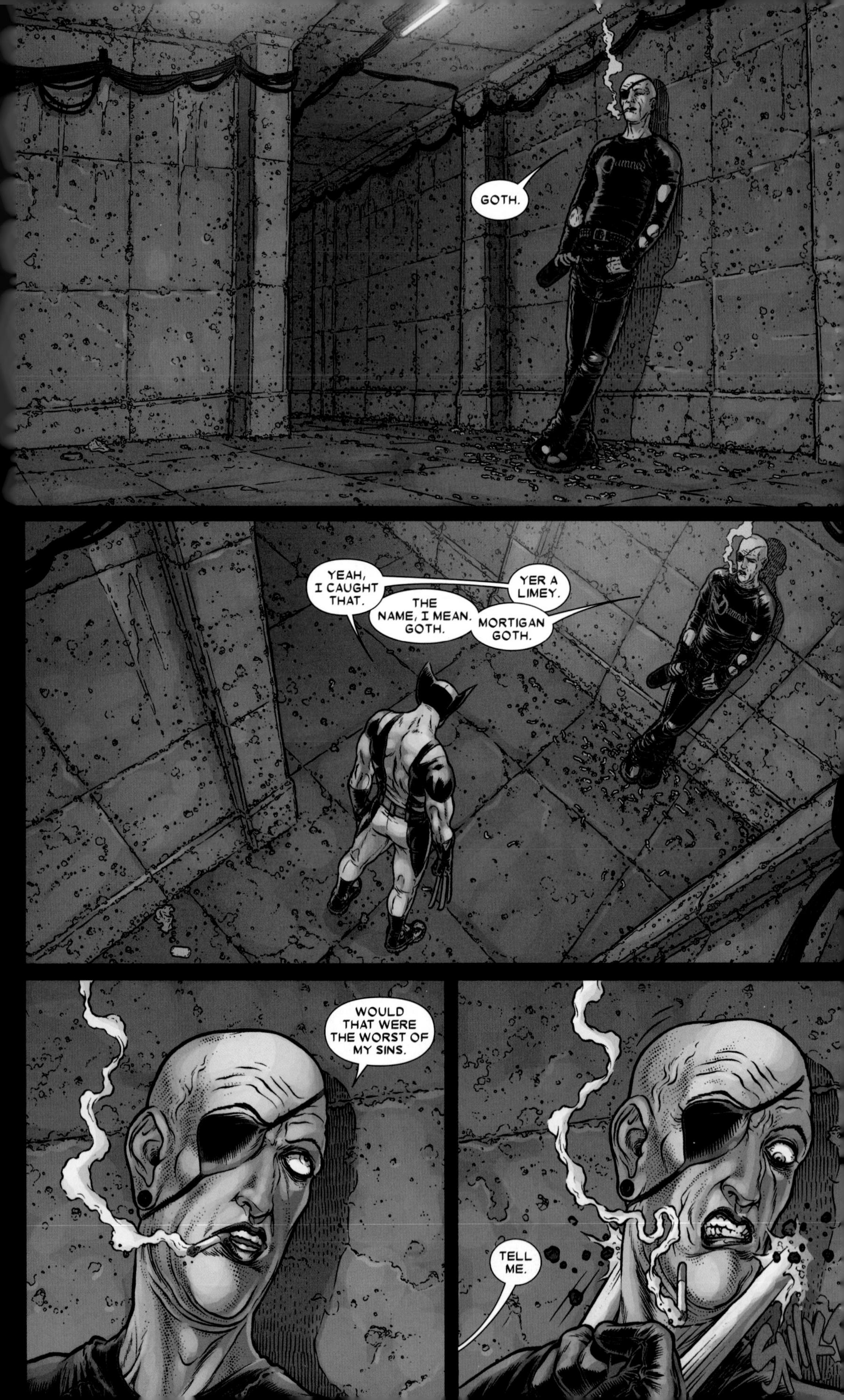
GOTH.
YER A LIMEY.
MORTIGAN GOTH.
THE NAME, I MEAN. GOTH.
YEAH, I CAUGHT THAT.
WOULD THAT WERE THE WORST OF MY SINS.
TELL ME.
SNIKT

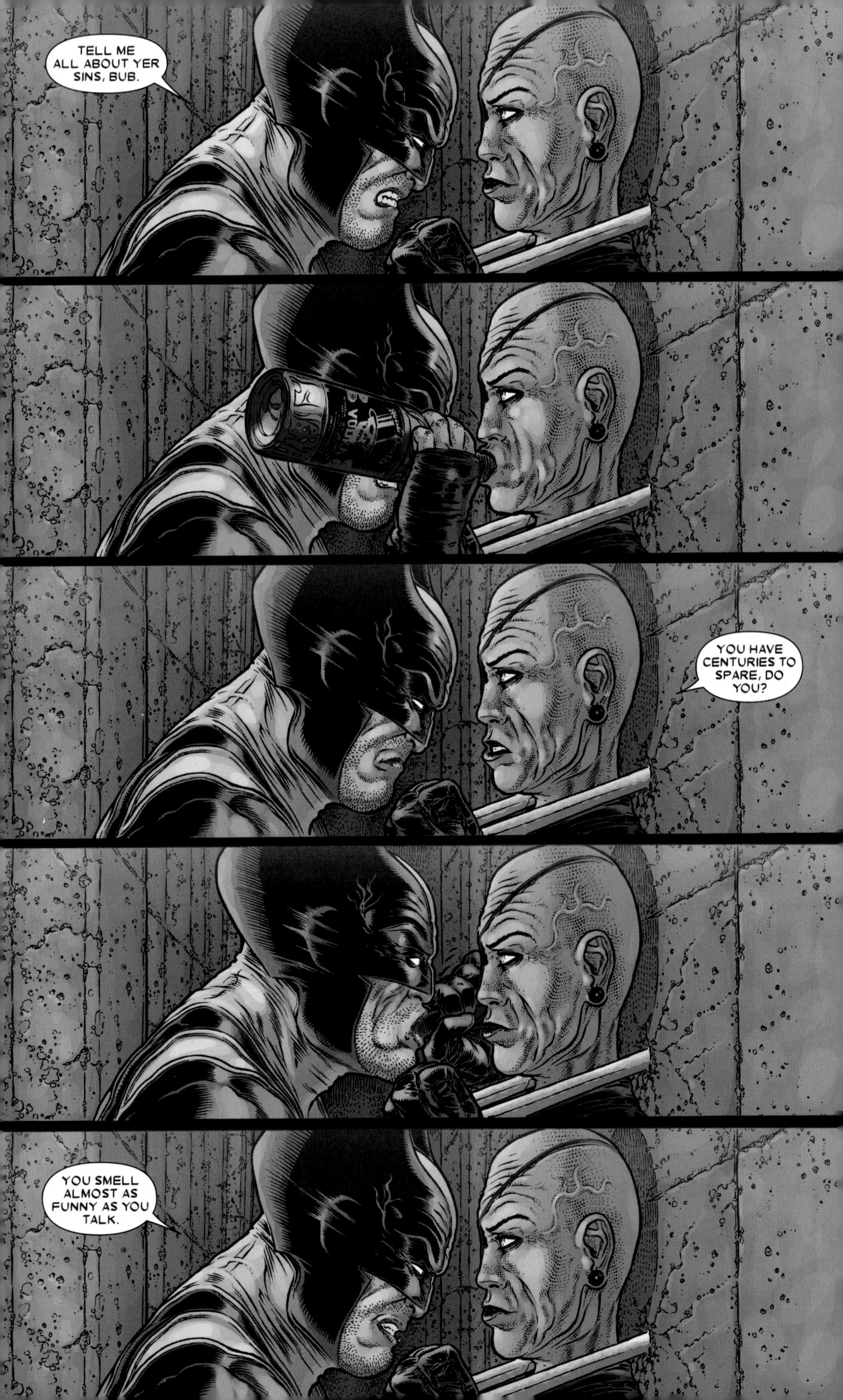
TELL ME ALL ABOUT YER SINS, BUB.
YOU HAVE CENTURIES TO SPARE, DO YOU?
YOU SMELL ALMOST AS FUNNY AS YOU TALK.

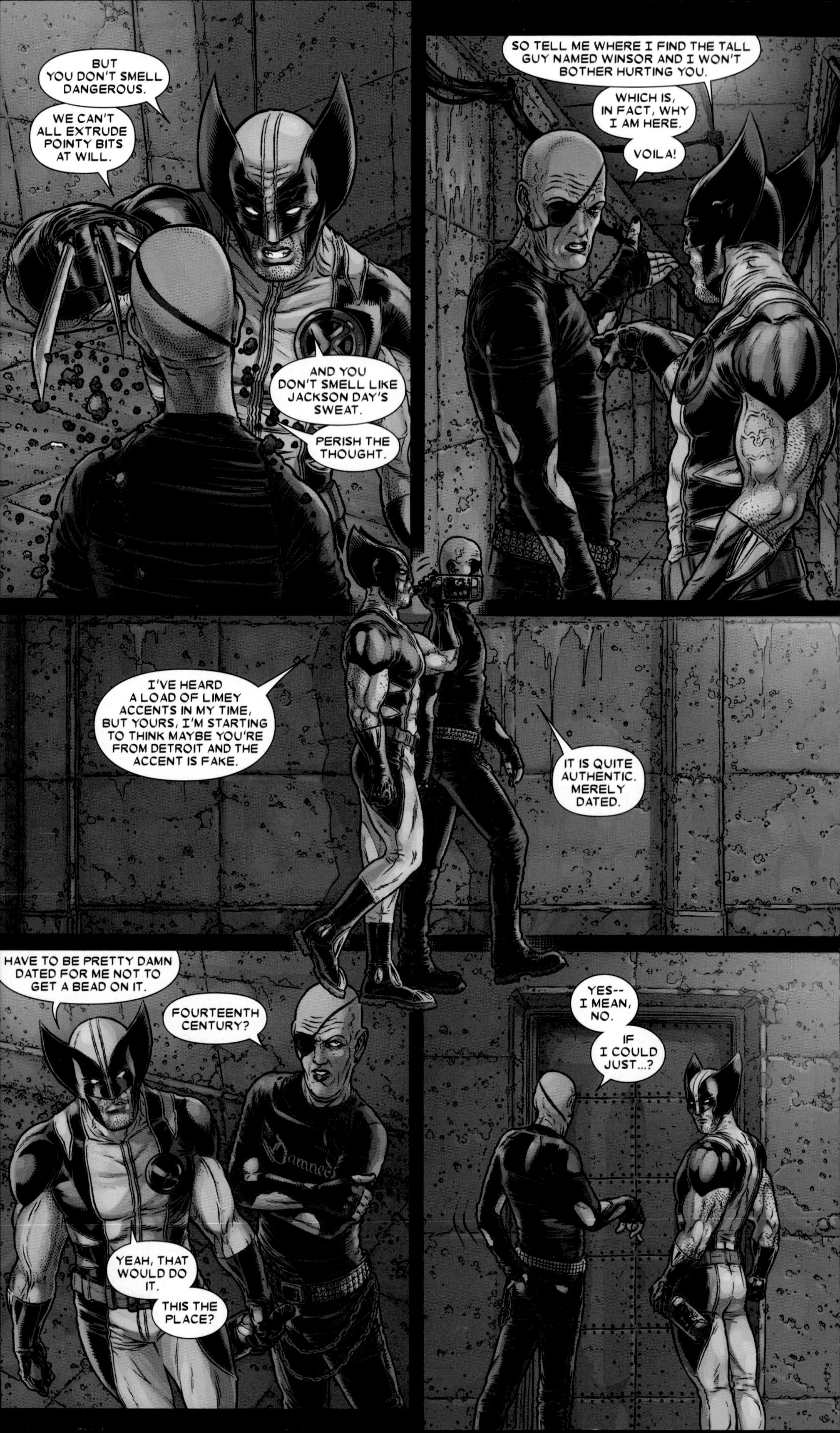

BUT YOU DON'T SMELL DANGEROUS.
WE CAN'T ALL EXTRUDE POINTY BITS AT WILL.
AND YOU DON'T SMELL LIKE JACKSON DAY'S SWEAT.
PERISH THE THOUGHT.
SO TELL ME WHERE I FIND THE TALL GUY NAMED WINSOR AND I WON'T BOTHER HURTING YOU.
WHICH IS, IN FACT, WHY I AM HERE.
VOILA!
I'VE HEARD A LOAD OF LIMEY ACCENTS IN MY TIME, BUT YOURS, I'M STARTING TO THINK MAYBE YOU'RE FROM DETROIT AND THE ACCENT IS FAKE.
IT IS QUITE AUTHENTIC. MERELY DATED.
HAVE TO BE PRETTY DAMN DATED FOR ME NOT TO GET A BEAD ON IT.
FOURTEENTH CENTURY?
YEAH, THAT WOULD DO IT.
THIS THE PLACE?
YES-- I MEAN, NO.
IF I COULD JUST...?

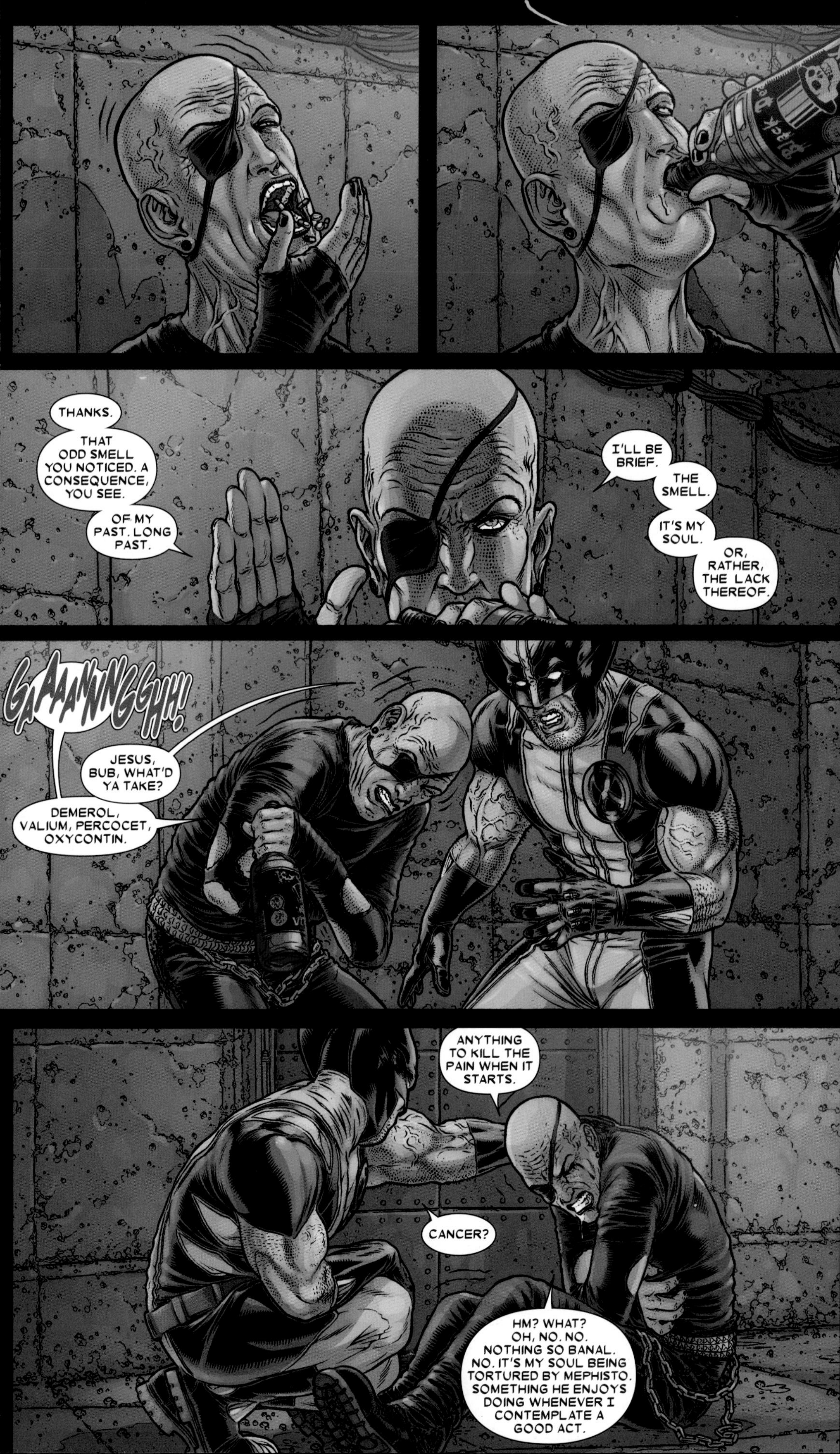
THANKS.
THAT ODD SMELL YOU NOTICED. A CONSEQUENCE, YOU SEE.
OF MY PAST. LONG PAST.
I'LL BE BRIEF.
THE SMELL.
IT'S MY SOUL.
OR, RATHER, THE LACK THEREOF.
GAAAANNGGHH!
JESUS, BUB, WHAT'D YA TAKE?
DEMEROL, VALIUM, PERCOCET, OXYCONTIN.
ANYTHING TO KILL THE PAIN WHEN IT STARTS.
CANCER?
HM? WHAT? OH, NO. NO. NOTHING SO BANAL. NO. IT'S MY SOUL BEING TORTURED BY MEPHISTO. SOMETHING HE ENJOYS DOING WHENEVER I CONTEMPLATE A GOOD ACT.

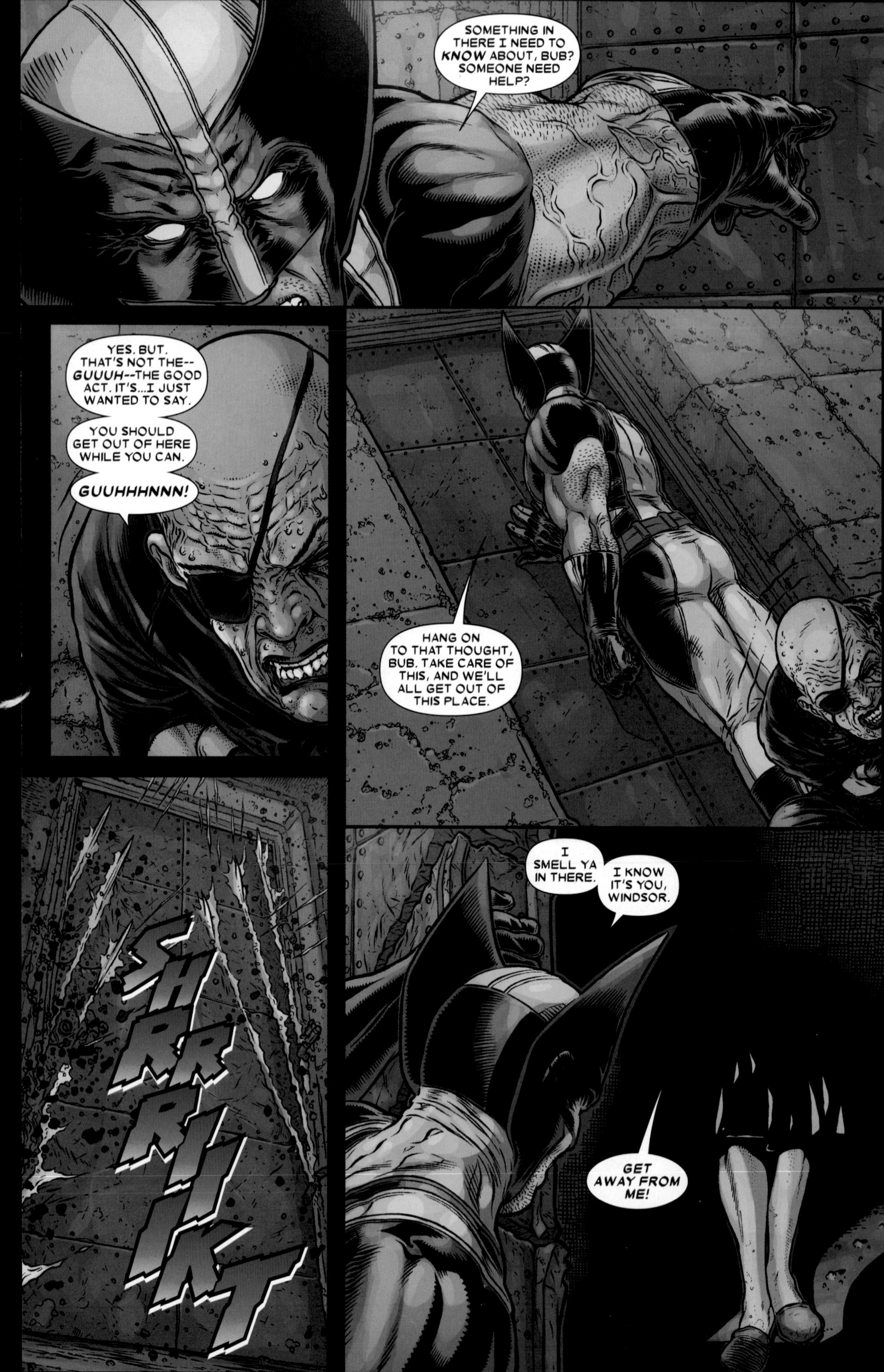
SOMETHING IN THERE I NEED TO KNOW ABOUT, BUB? SOMEONE NEED HELP?
YES. BUT. THAT'S NOT THE-- GUUUH--THE GOOD ACT. IT'S...I JUST WANTED TO SAY.
YOU SHOULD GET OUT OF HERE WHILE YOU CAN.
GUUHHHNNN!
HANG ON TO THAT THOUGHT, BUB. TAKE CARE OF THIS, AND WE'LL ALL GET OUT OF THIS PLACE.
SHRRRIIKT
I SMELL YA IN THERE.
I KNOW IT'S YOU, WINDSOR.
GET AWAY FROM ME!

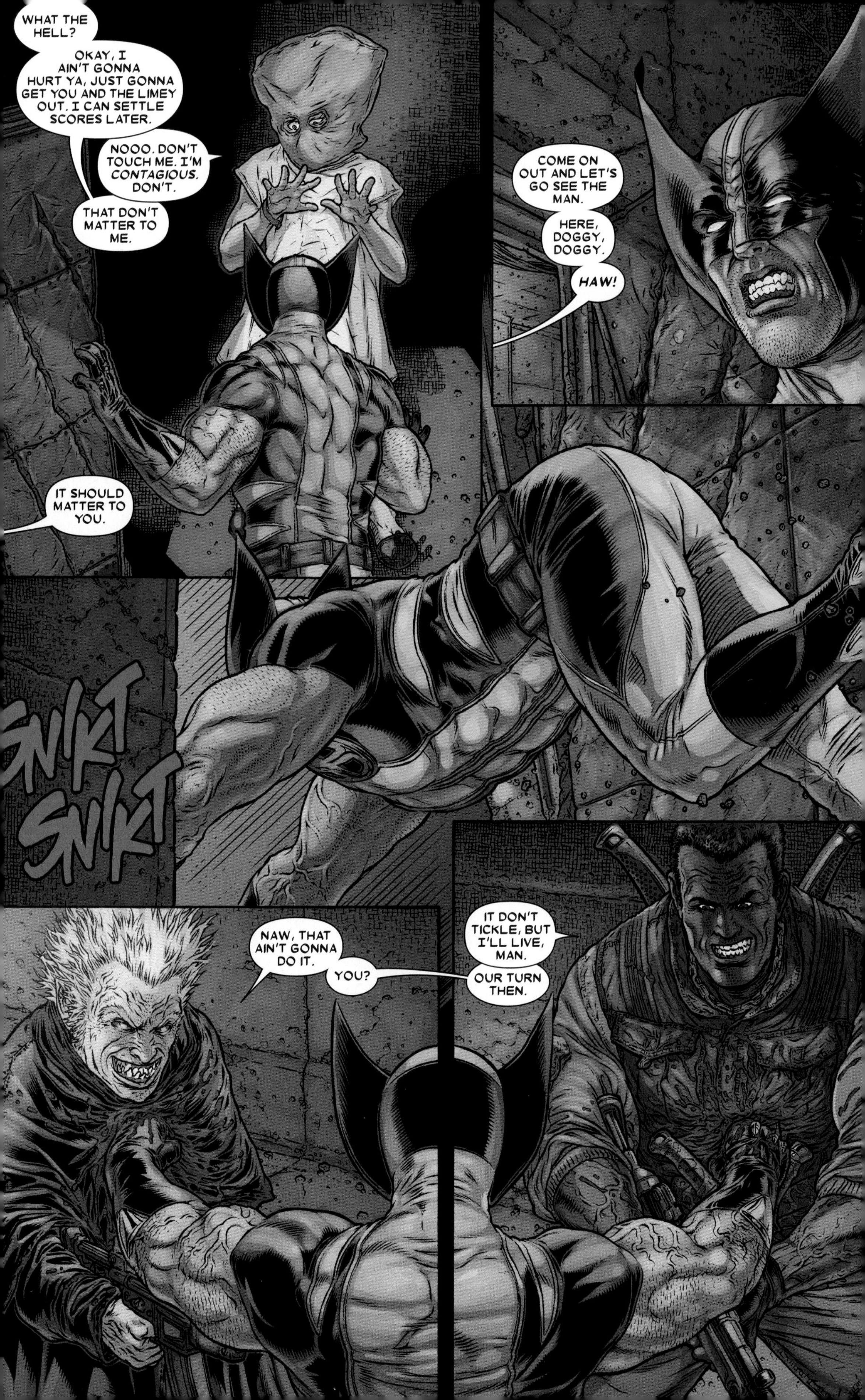
WHAT THE HELL?
OKAY, I AIN'T GONNA HURT YA, JUST GONNA GET YOU AND THE LIMEY OUT. I CAN SETTLE SCORES LATER.
NOOO. DON'T TOUCH ME. I'M *CONTAGIOUS.* DON'T.
THAT DON'T MATTER TO ME.
COME ON OUT AND LET'S GO SEE THE MAN.
HERE, DOGGY, DOGGY.
HAW!
IT SHOULD MATTER TO YOU.
SNIKT
SNIKT
NAW, THAT AIN'T GONNA DO IT.
YOU?
IT DON'T TICKLE, BUT I'LL LIVE, MAN.
OUR TURN THEN.

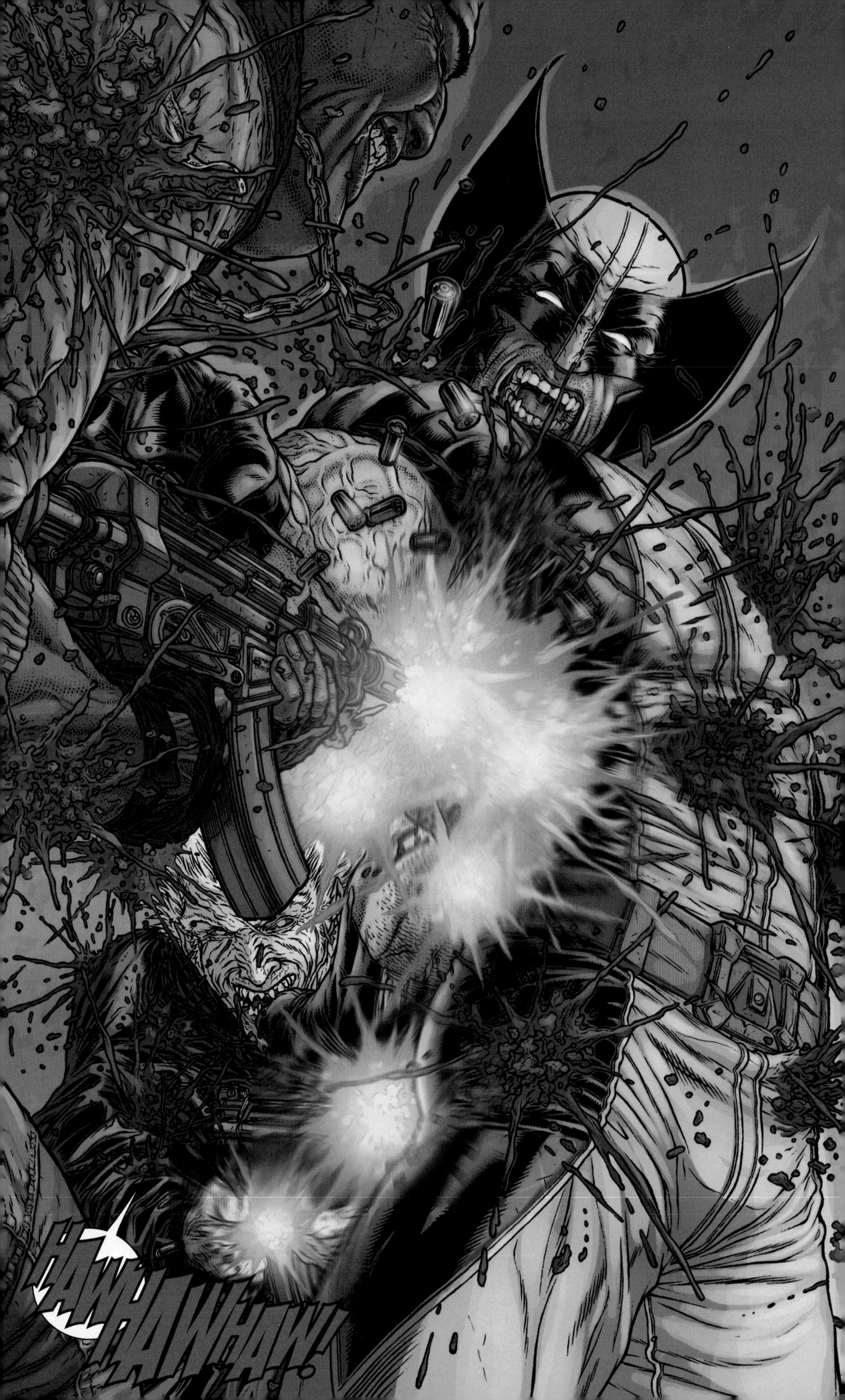
HAWHAWHAW!

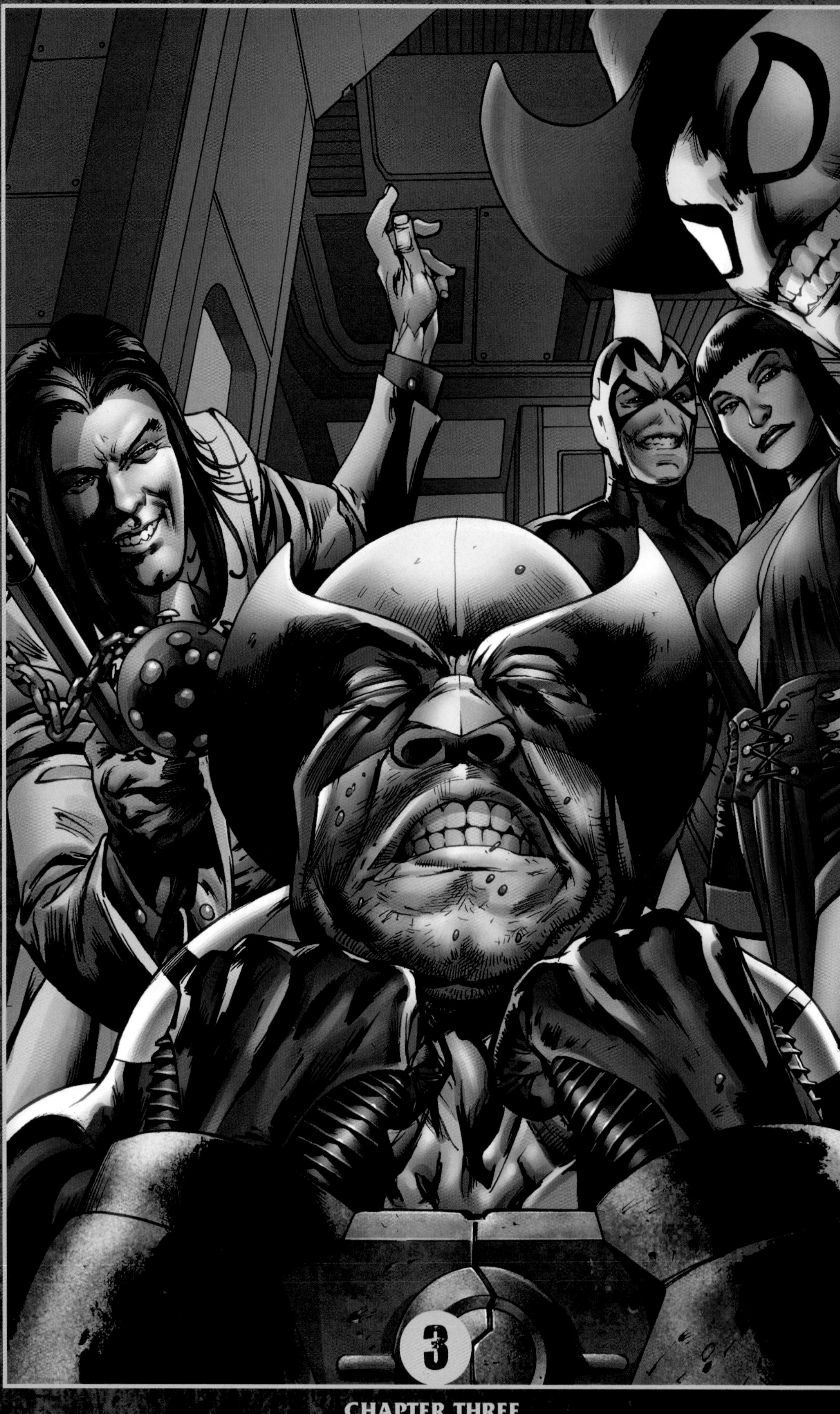
3

CHAPTER THREE

SOMEONE THEY CAN HATE

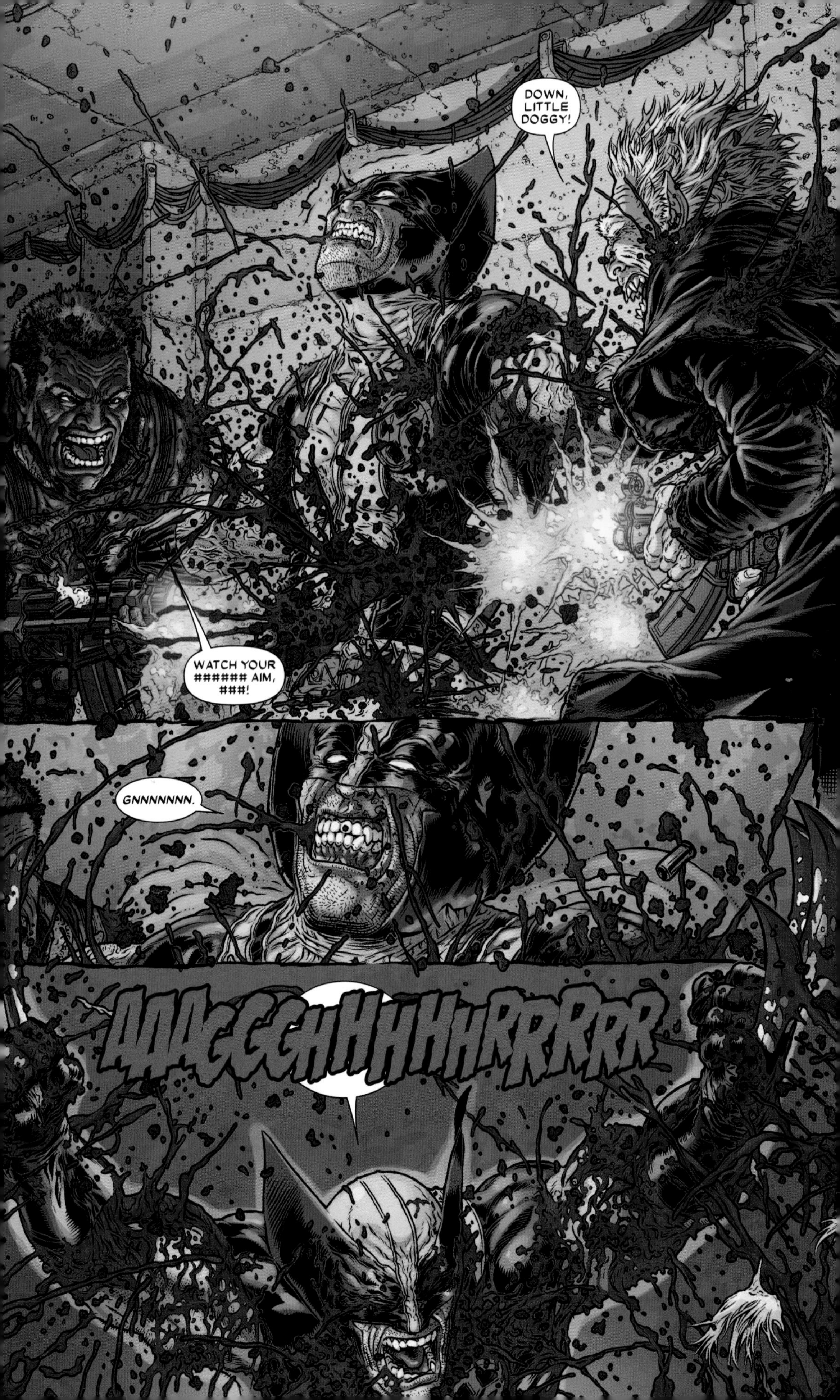
DOWN, LITTLE DOGGY!
WATCH YOUR ###### AIM, ###!
GNNNNNNN.
AAAGGHHHHHHRRRRRR

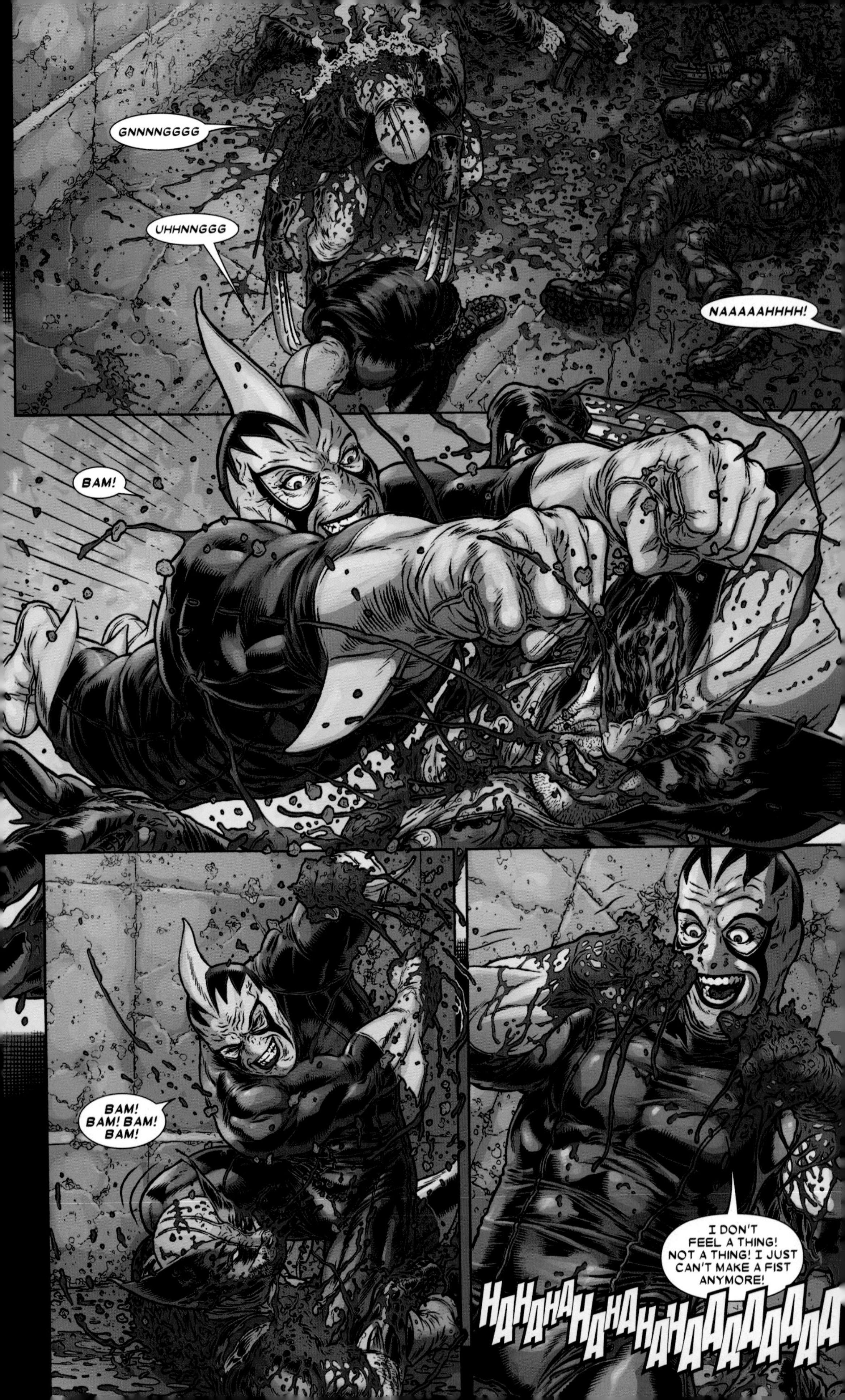
GNNNNGGGG
UHHNNGGG
NAAAAAHHHH!
BAM!
BAM! BAM! BAM! BAM!
I DON'T FEEL A THING! NOT A THING! I JUST CAN'T MAKE A FIST ANYMORE!
HAHAHAHAHAHAHAHAHAAAAAAAAA

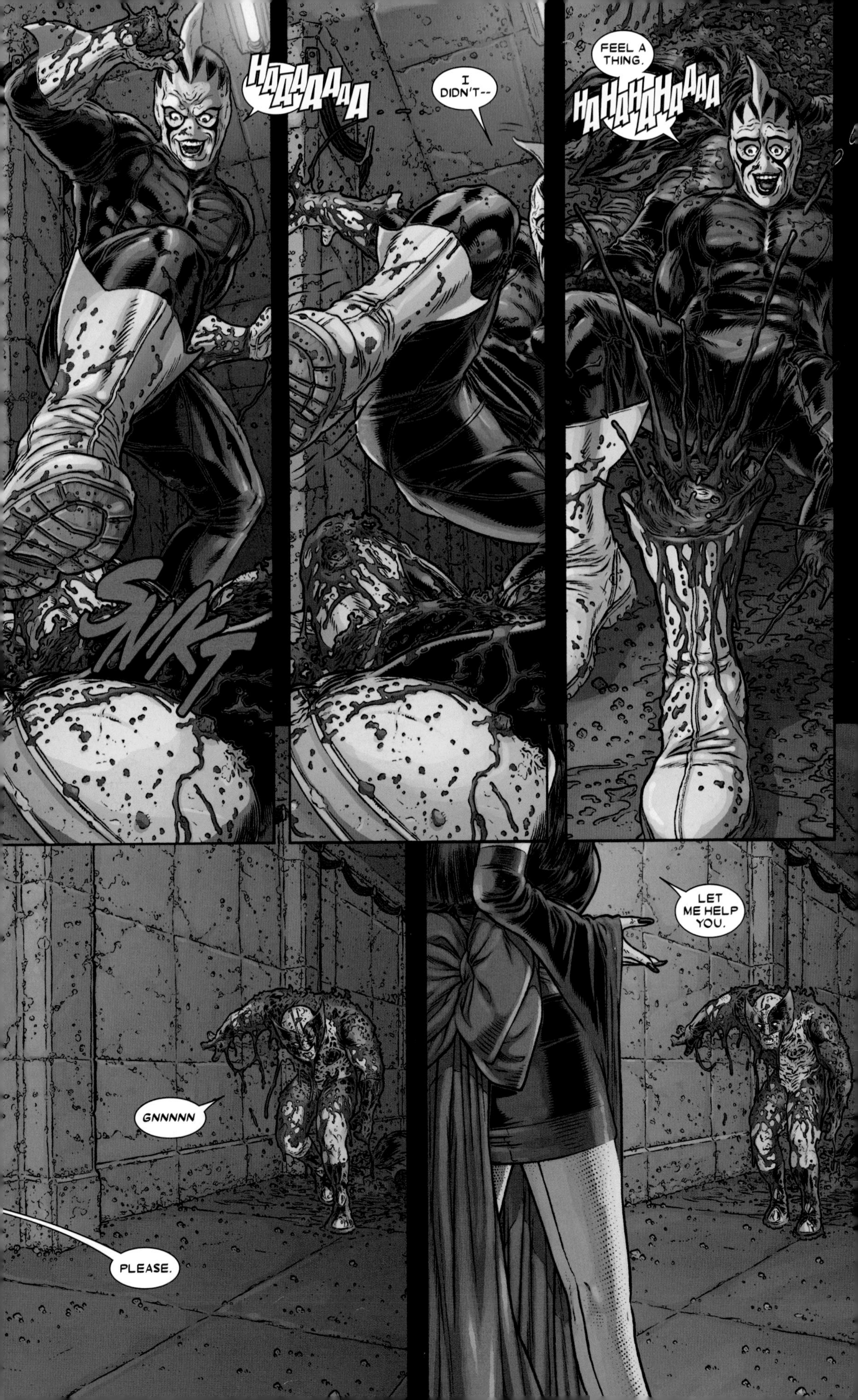
HAAAAAAA
SNIKT
I DIDN'T--
FEEL A THING.
HAHAHAHAAAA
GNNNNN
PLEASE.
LET ME HELP YOU.

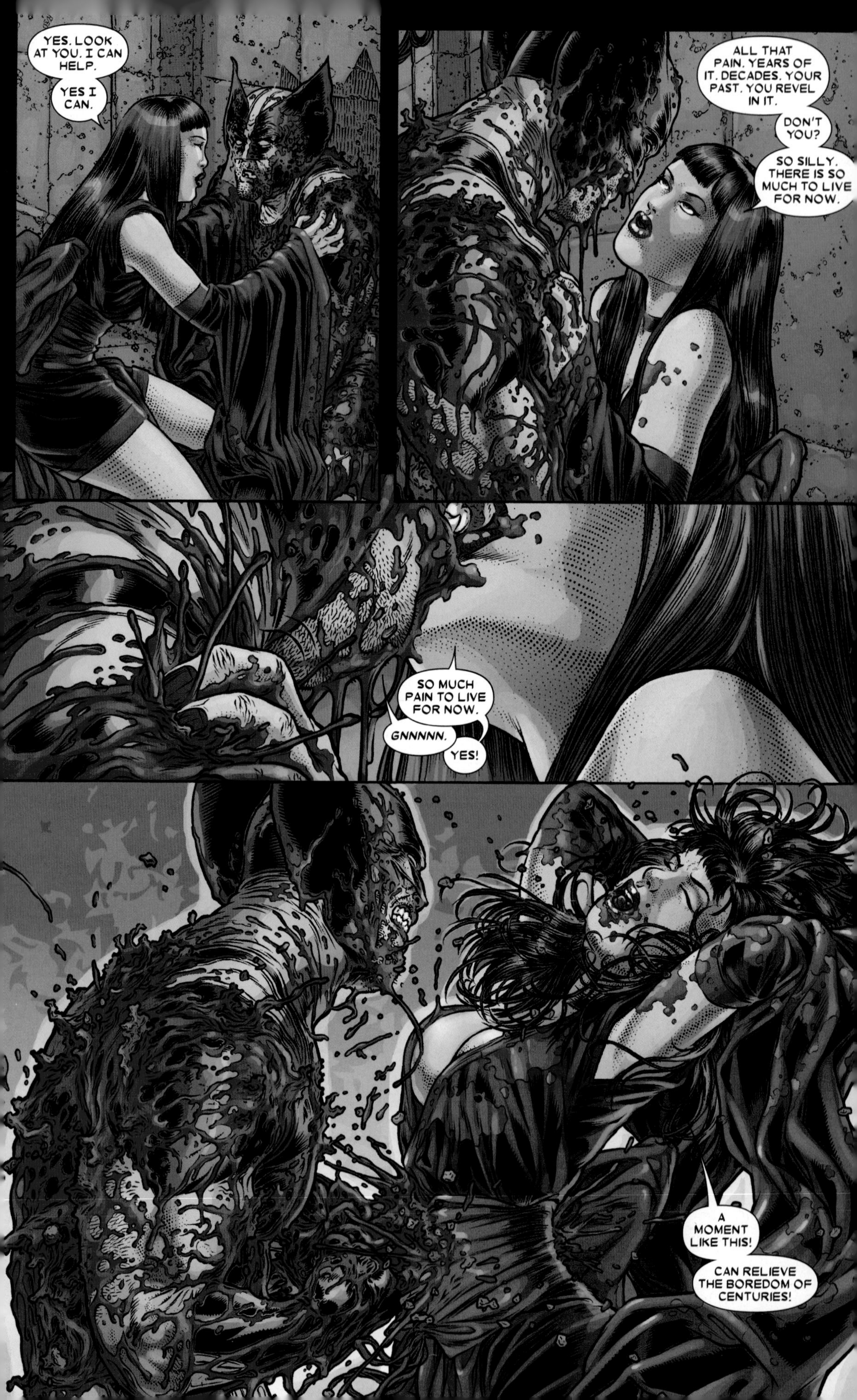
YES. LOOK AT YOU. I CAN HELP.
YES I CAN.
ALL THAT PAIN. YEARS OF IT. DECADES. YOUR PAST. YOU REVEL IN IT.
DON'T YOU?
SO SILLY. THERE IS SO MUCH TO LIVE FOR NOW.
SO MUCH PAIN TO LIVE FOR NOW.
GNNNNN.
YES!
A MOMENT LIKE THIS!
CAN RELIEVE THE BOREDOM OF CENTURIES!

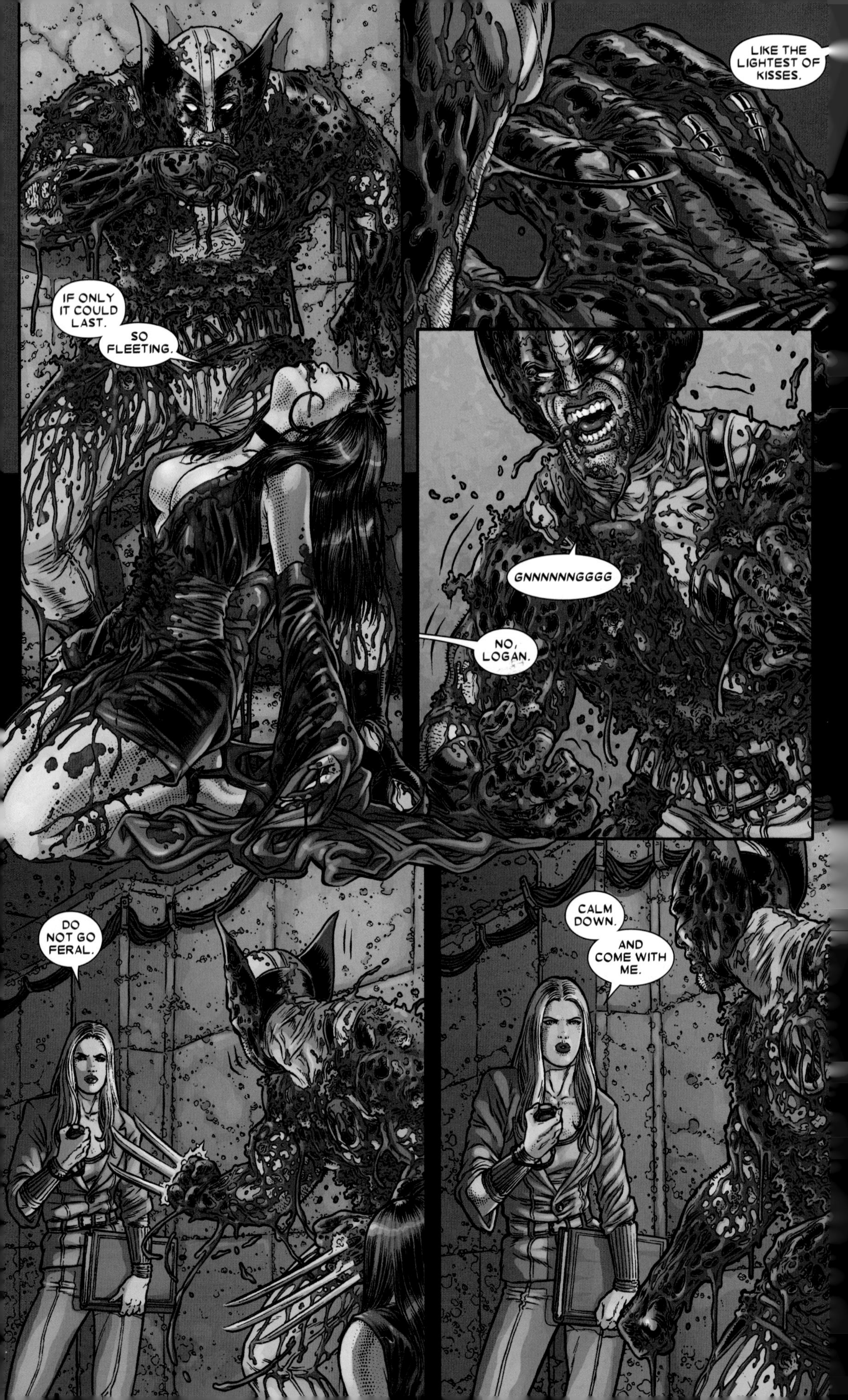
IF ONLY IT COULD LAST.
SO FLEETING.
LIKE THE LIGHTEST OF KISSES.
GNNNNNNGGGG
NO, LOGAN.
DO NOT GO FERAL.
CALM DOWN.
AND COME WITH ME.

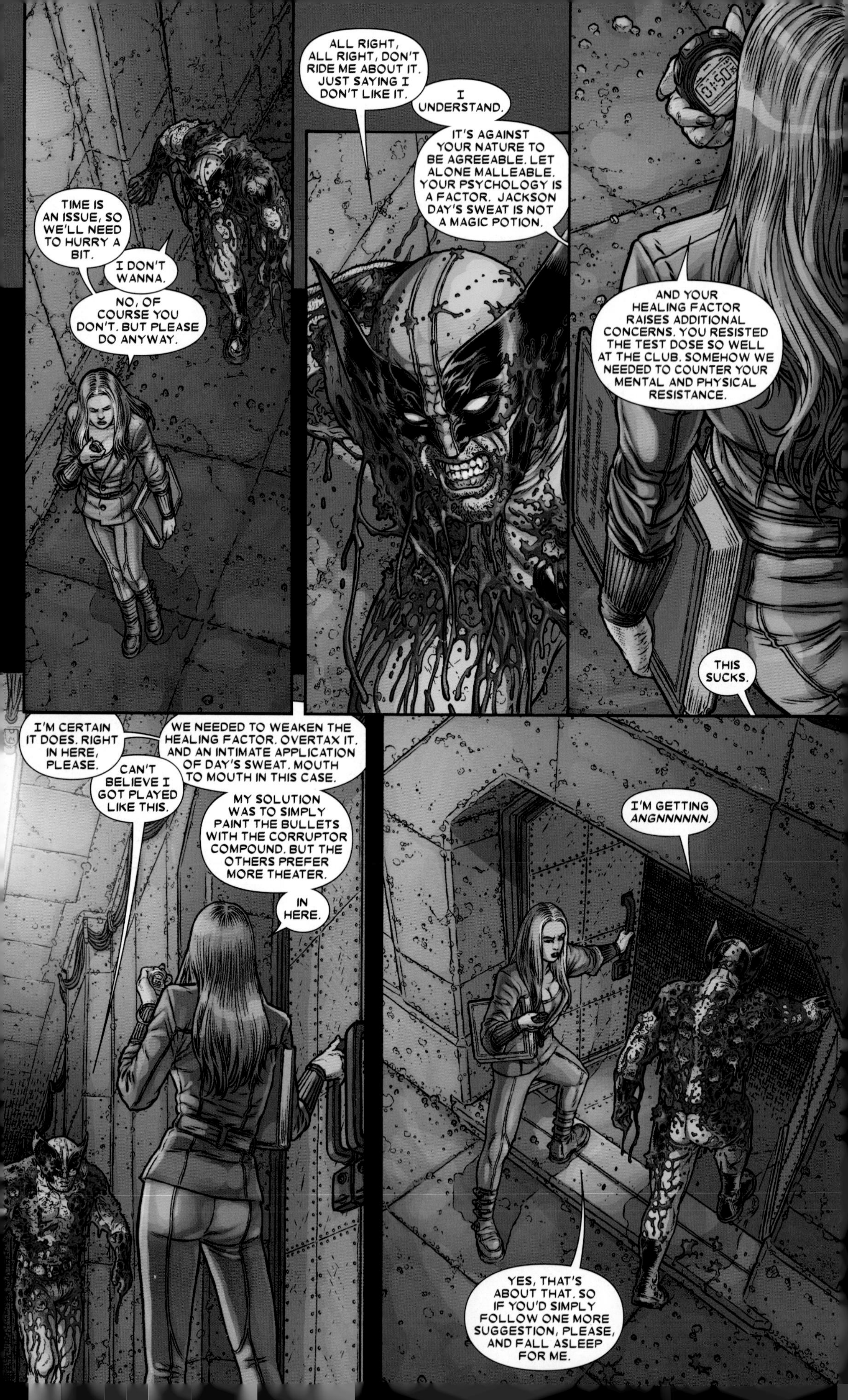

TIME IS AN ISSUE, SO WE'LL NEED TO HURRY A BIT.
I DON'T WANNA.
NO, OF COURSE YOU DON'T. BUT PLEASE DO ANYWAY.
ALL RIGHT, ALL RIGHT, DON'T RIDE ME ABOUT IT. JUST SAYING I DON'T LIKE IT.
I UNDERSTAND.
IT'S AGAINST YOUR NATURE TO BE AGREEABLE. LET ALONE MALLEABLE. YOUR PSYCHOLOGY IS A FACTOR. JACKSON DAY'S SWEAT IS NOT A MAGIC POTION.
AND YOUR HEALING FACTOR RAISES ADDITIONAL CONCERNS. YOU RESISTED THE TEST DOSE SO WELL AT THE CLUB. SOMEHOW WE NEEDED TO COUNTER YOUR MENTAL AND PHYSICAL RESISTANCE.
THIS SUCKS.
I'M CERTAIN IT DOES. RIGHT IN HERE, PLEASE.
CAN'T BELIEVE I GOT PLAYED LIKE THIS.
WE NEEDED TO WEAKEN THE HEALING FACTOR. OVERTAX IT. AND AN INTIMATE APPLICATION OF DAY'S SWEAT. MOUTH TO MOUTH IN THIS CASE.
MY SOLUTION WAS TO SIMPLY PAINT THE BULLETS WITH THE CORRUPTOR COMPOUND. BUT THE OTHERS PREFER MORE THEATER.
IN HERE.
I'M GETTING ANGNNNNNN.
YES, THAT'S ABOUT THAT. SO IF YOU'D SIMPLY FOLLOW ONE MORE SUGGESTION, PLEASE, AND FALL ASLEEP FOR ME.

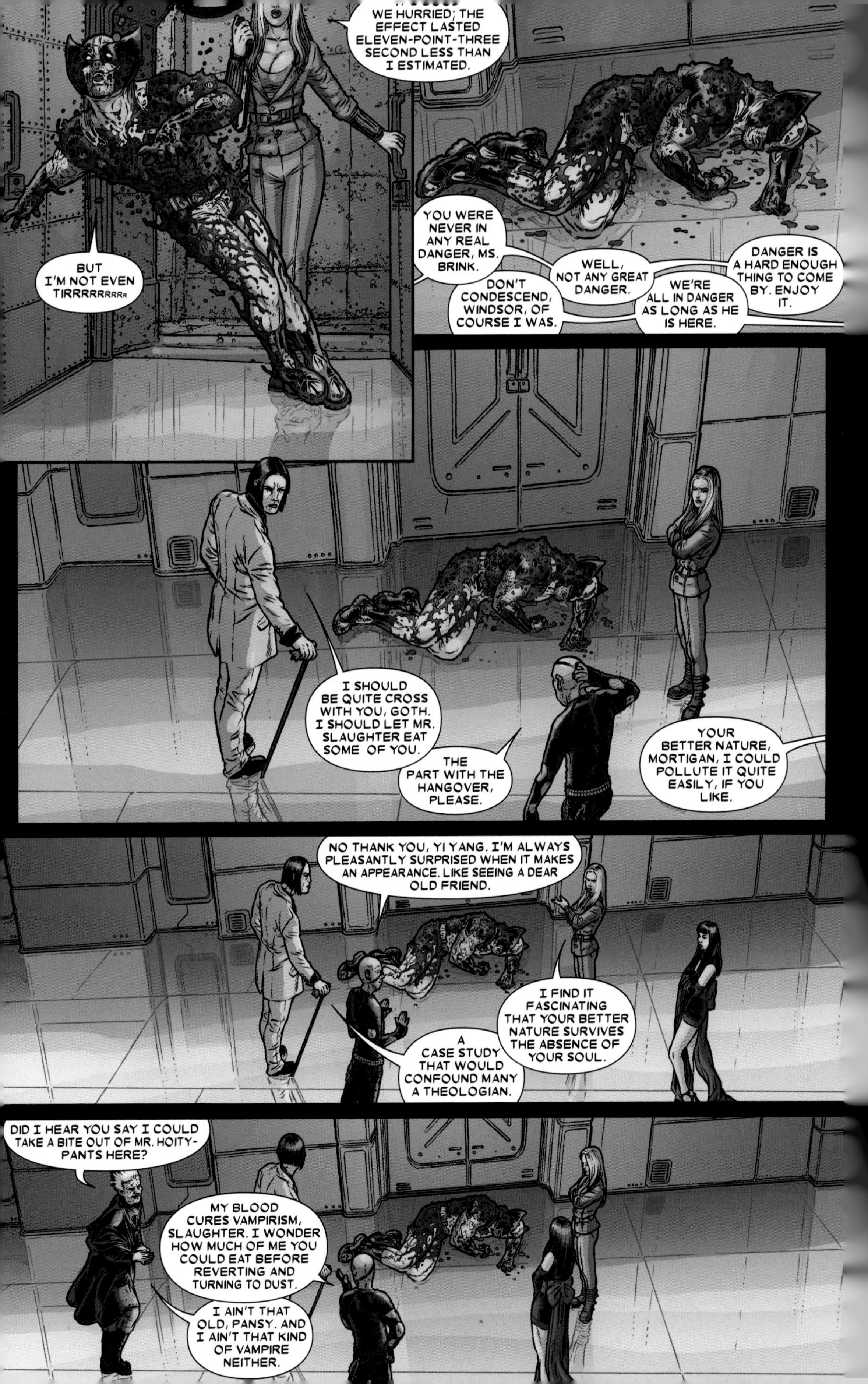
WE HURRIED; THE EFFECT LASTED ELEVEN-POINT-THREE SECOND LESS THAN I ESTIMATED.
BUT I'M NOT EVEN TIRRRRRRRRR
YOU WERE NEVER IN ANY REAL DANGER, MS. BRINK.
DON'T CONDESCEND, WINDSOR, OF COURSE I WAS.
WELL, NOT ANY GREAT DANGER.
WE'RE ALL IN DANGER AS LONG AS HE IS HERE.
DANGER IS A HARD ENOUGH THING TO COME BY. ENJOY IT.
I SHOULD BE QUITE CROSS WITH YOU, GOTH. I SHOULD LET MR. SLAUGHTER EAT SOME OF YOU.
THE PART WITH THE HANGOVER, PLEASE.
YOUR BETTER NATURE, MORTIGAN, I COULD POLLUTE IT QUITE EASILY, IF YOU LIKE.
NO THANK YOU, YI YANG. I'M ALWAYS PLEASANTLY SURPRISED WHEN IT MAKES AN APPEARANCE. LIKE SEEING A DEAR OLD FRIEND.
I FIND IT FASCINATING THAT YOUR BETTER NATURE SURVIVES THE ABSENCE OF YOUR SOUL.
A CASE STUDY THAT WOULD CONFOUND MANY A THEOLOGIAN.
DID I HEAR YOU SAY I COULD TAKE A BITE OUT OF MR. HOITY-PANTS HERE?
MY BLOOD CURES VAMPIRISM, SLAUGHTER. I WONDER HOW MUCH OF ME YOU COULD EAT BEFORE REVERTING AND TURNING TO DUST.
I AIN'T THAT OLD, PANSY. AND I AIN'T THAT KIND OF VAMPIRE NEITHER.

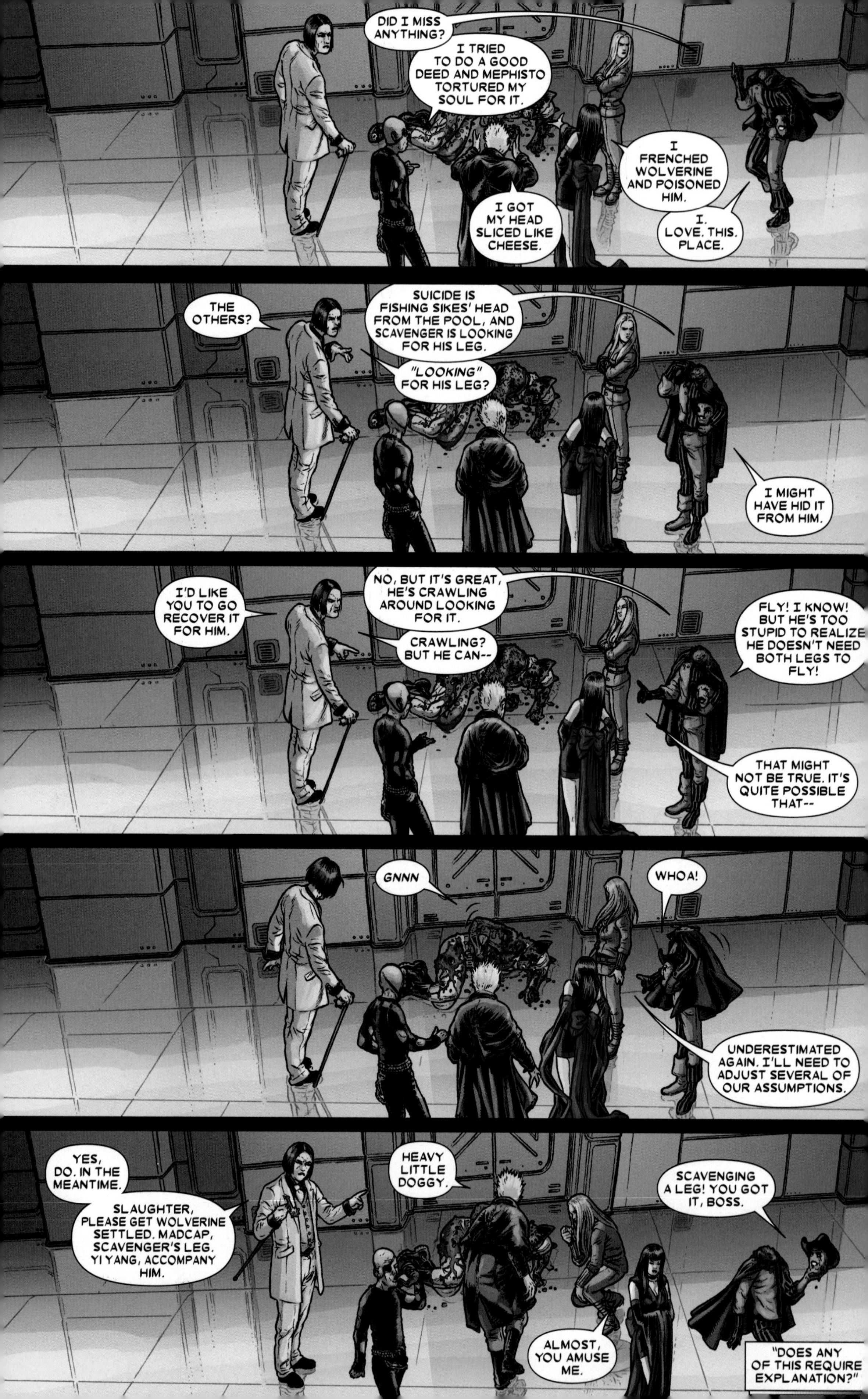
DID I MISS ANYTHING?
I TRIED TO DO A GOOD DEED AND MEPHISTO TORTURED MY SOUL FOR IT.
I FRENCHED WOLVERINE AND POISONED HIM.
I GOT MY HEAD SLICED LIKE CHEESE.
I. LOVE. THIS. PLACE.
THE OTHERS?
SUICIDE IS FISHING SIKES' HEAD FROM THE POOL, AND SCAVENGER IS LOOKING FOR HIS LEG.
"LOOKING" FOR HIS LEG?
I MIGHT HAVE HID IT FROM HIM.
I'D LIKE YOU TO GO RECOVER IT FOR HIM.
NO, BUT IT'S GREAT, HE'S CRAWLING AROUND LOOKING FOR IT.
CRAWLING? BUT HE CAN--
FLY! I KNOW! BUT HE'S TOO STUPID TO REALIZE HE DOESN'T NEED BOTH LEGS TO FLY!
THAT MIGHT NOT BE TRUE. IT'S QUITE POSSIBLE THAT--
GNNN
WHOA!
UNDERESTIMATED AGAIN. I'LL NEED TO ADJUST SEVERAL OF OUR ASSUMPTIONS.
YES, DO. IN THE MEANTIME.
SLAUGHTER, PLEASE GET WOLVERINE SETTLED. MADCAP, SCAVENGER'S LEG. YI YANG, ACCOMPANY HIM.
HEAVY LITTLE DOGGY.
SCAVENGING A LEG! YOU GOT IT, BOSS.
ALMOST, YOU AMUSE ME.
"DOES ANY OF THIS REQUIRE EXPLANATION?"

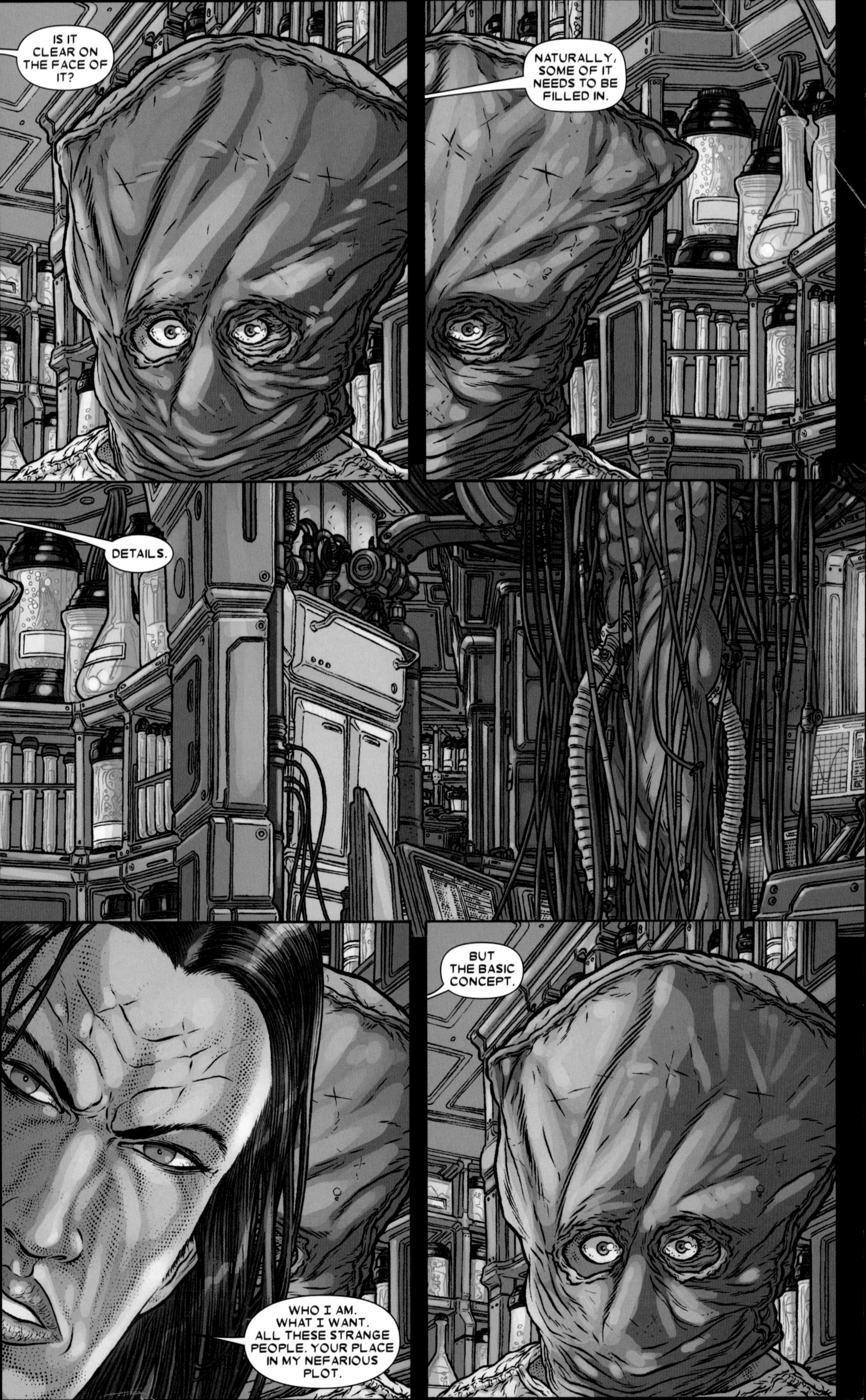
IS IT CLEAR ON THE FACE OF IT?
NATURALLY, SOME OF IT NEEDS TO BE FILLED IN.
DETAILS.
WHO I AM. WHAT I WANT. ALL THESE STRANGE PEOPLE. YOUR PLACE IN MY NEFARIOUS PLOT.
BUT THE BASIC CONCEPT.

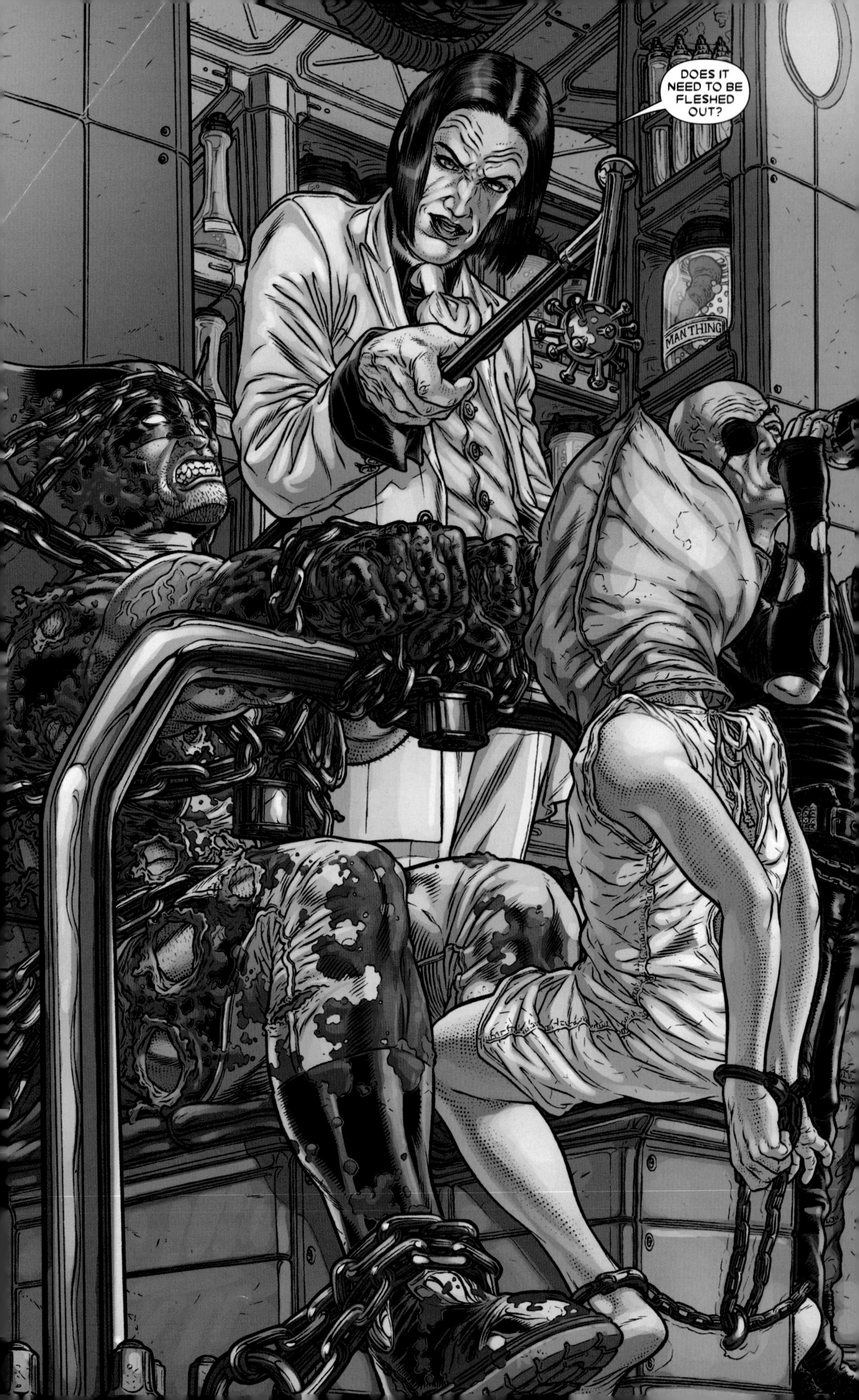
DOES IT NEED TO BE FLESHED OUT?
MAN THING

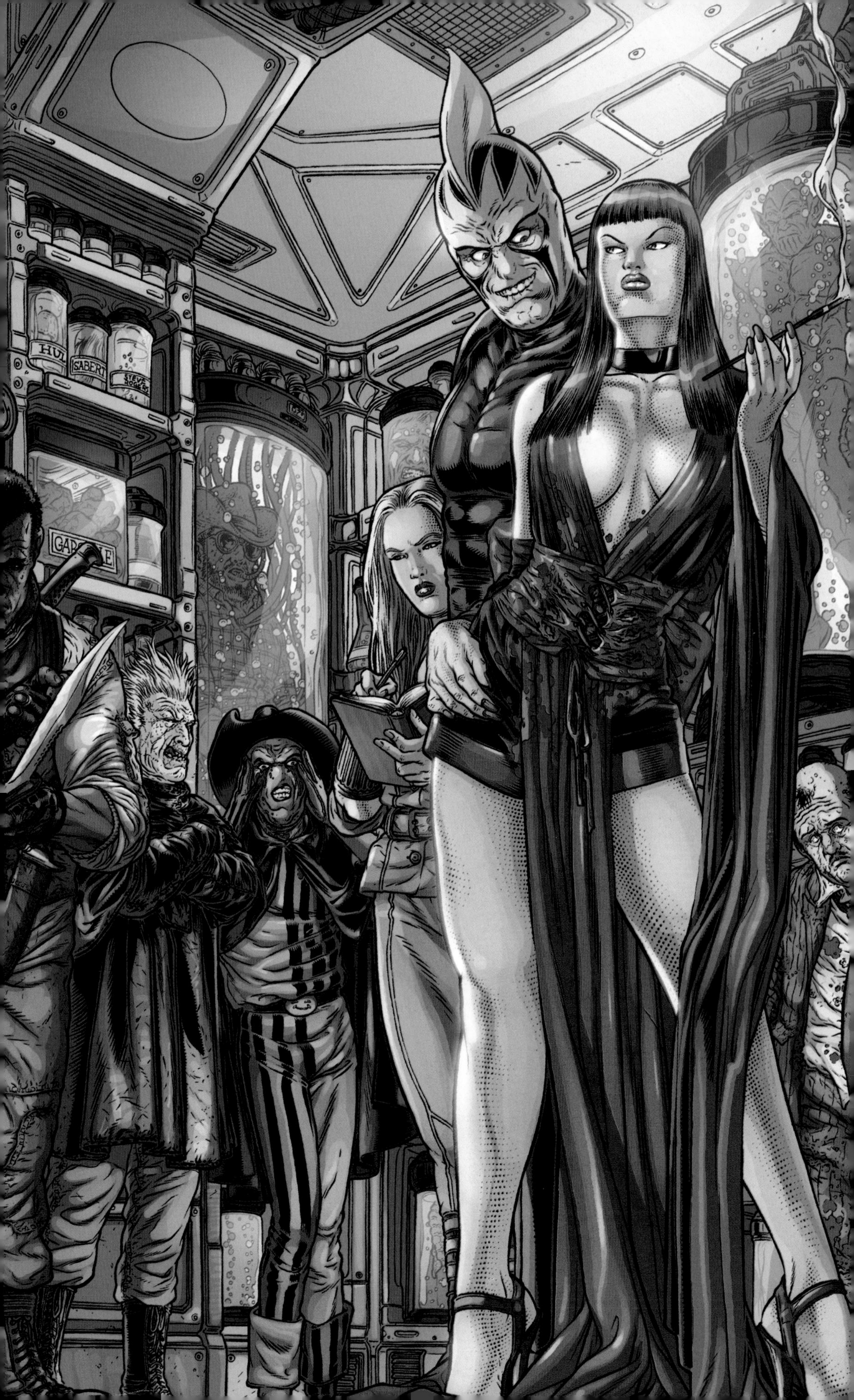
STEVE ROGERS

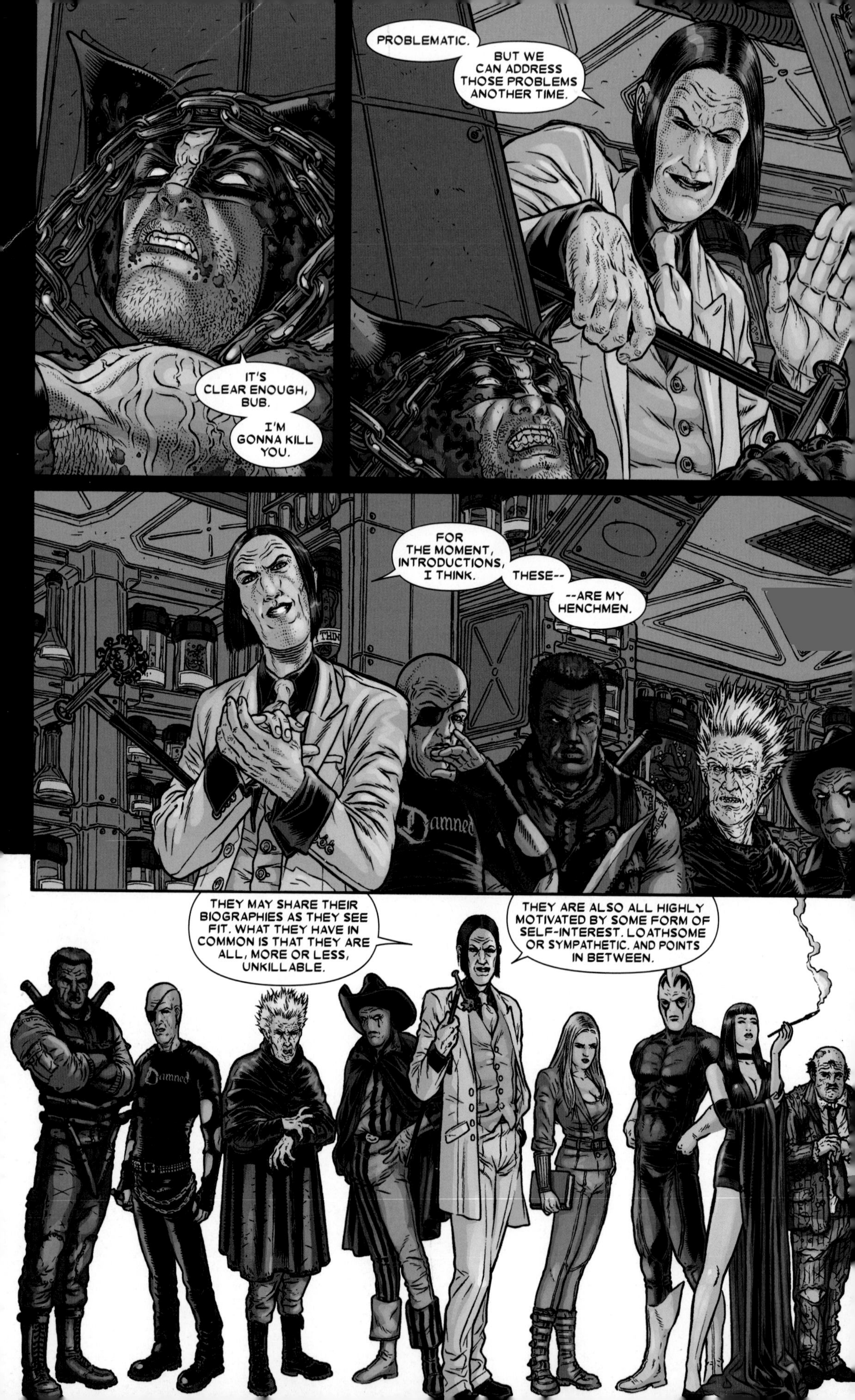
IT'S CLEAR ENOUGH, BUB.
I'M GONNA KILL YOU.
PROBLEMATIC.
BUT WE CAN ADDRESS THOSE PROBLEMS ANOTHER TIME.
FOR THE MOMENT, INTRODUCTIONS, I THINK.
THESE--
--ARE MY HENCHMEN.
THEY MAY SHARE THEIR BIOGRAPHIES AS THEY SEE FIT. WHAT THEY HAVE IN COMMON IS THAT THEY ARE ALL, MORE OR LESS, UNKILLABLE.
THEY ARE ALSO ALL HIGHLY MOTIVATED BY SOME FORM OF SELF-INTEREST. LOATHSOME OR SYMPATHETIC. AND POINTS IN BETWEEN.

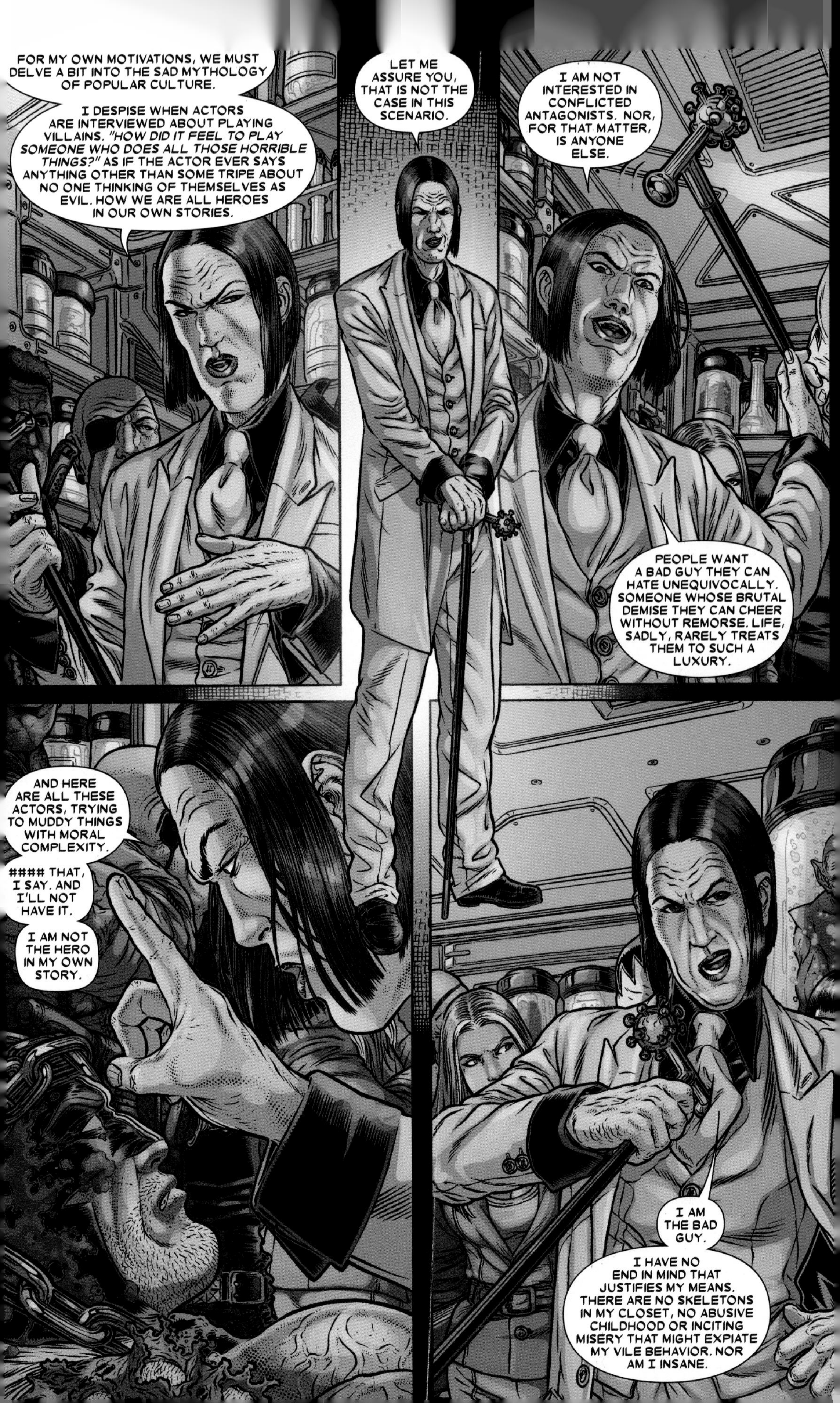
FOR MY OWN MOTIVATIONS, WE MUST DELVE A BIT INTO THE SAD MYTHOLOGY OF POPULAR CULTURE.
I DESPISE WHEN ACTORS ARE INTERVIEWED ABOUT PLAYING VILLAINS. "HOW DID IT FEEL TO PLAY SOMEONE WHO DOES ALL THOSE HORRIBLE THINGS?" AS IF THE ACTOR EVER SAYS ANYTHING OTHER THAN SOME TRIPE ABOUT NO ONE THINKING OF THEMSELVES AS EVIL. HOW WE ARE ALL HEROES IN OUR OWN STORIES.
LET ME ASSURE YOU, THAT IS NOT THE CASE IN THIS SCENARIO.
I AM NOT INTERESTED IN CONFLICTED ANTAGONISTS. NOR, FOR THAT MATTER, IS ANYONE ELSE.
PEOPLE WANT A BAD GUY THEY CAN HATE UNEQUIVOCALLY. SOMEONE WHOSE BRUTAL DEMISE THEY CAN CHEER WITHOUT REMORSE. LIFE, SADLY, RARELY TREATS THEM TO SUCH A LUXURY.
AND HERE ARE ALL THESE ACTORS, TRYING TO MUDDY THINGS WITH MORAL COMPLEXITY.
THAT, I SAY. AND I'LL NOT HAVE IT.
I AM NOT THE HERO IN MY OWN STORY.
I AM THE BAD GUY.
I HAVE NO END IN MIND THAT JUSTIFIES MY MEANS. THERE ARE NO SKELETONS IN MY CLOSET, NO ABUSIVE CHILDHOOD OR INCITING MISERY THAT MIGHT EXPIATE MY VILE BEHAVIOR. NOR AM I INSANE.

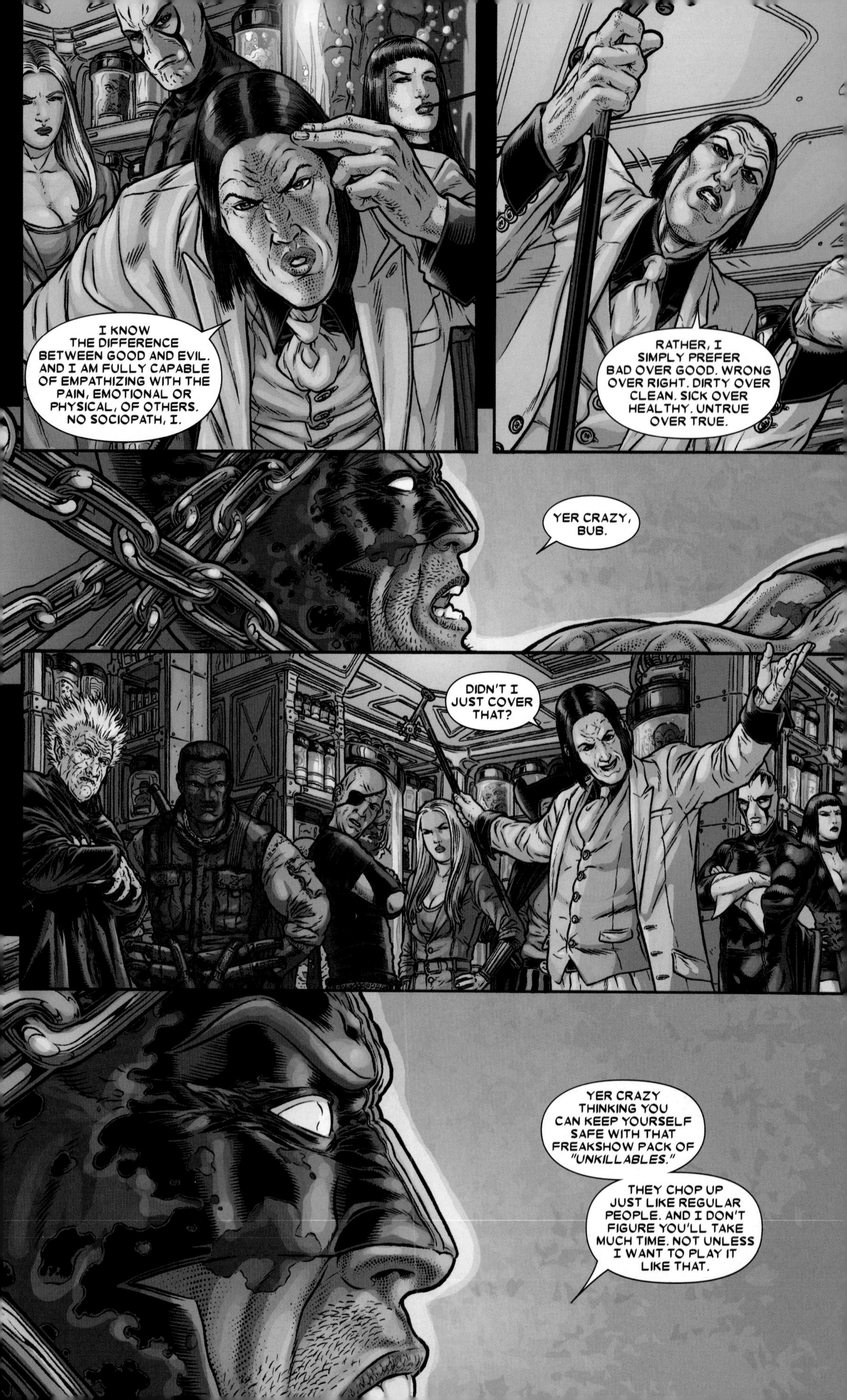
I KNOW THE DIFFERENCE BETWEEN GOOD AND EVIL. AND I AM FULLY CAPABLE OF EMPATHIZING WITH THE PAIN, EMOTIONAL OR PHYSICAL, OF OTHERS. NO SOCIOPATH, I.
RATHER, I SIMPLY PREFER BAD OVER GOOD. WRONG OVER RIGHT. DIRTY OVER CLEAN. SICK OVER HEALTHY. UNTRUE OVER TRUE.
YER CRAZY, BUB.
DIDN'T I JUST COVER THAT?
YER CRAZY THINKING YOU CAN KEEP YOURSELF SAFE WITH THAT FREAKSHOW PACK OF *"UNKILLABLES."*
THEY CHOP UP JUST LIKE REGULAR PEOPLE. AND I DON'T FIGURE YOU'LL TAKE MUCH TIME. NOT UNLESS I WANT TO PLAY IT LIKE THAT.

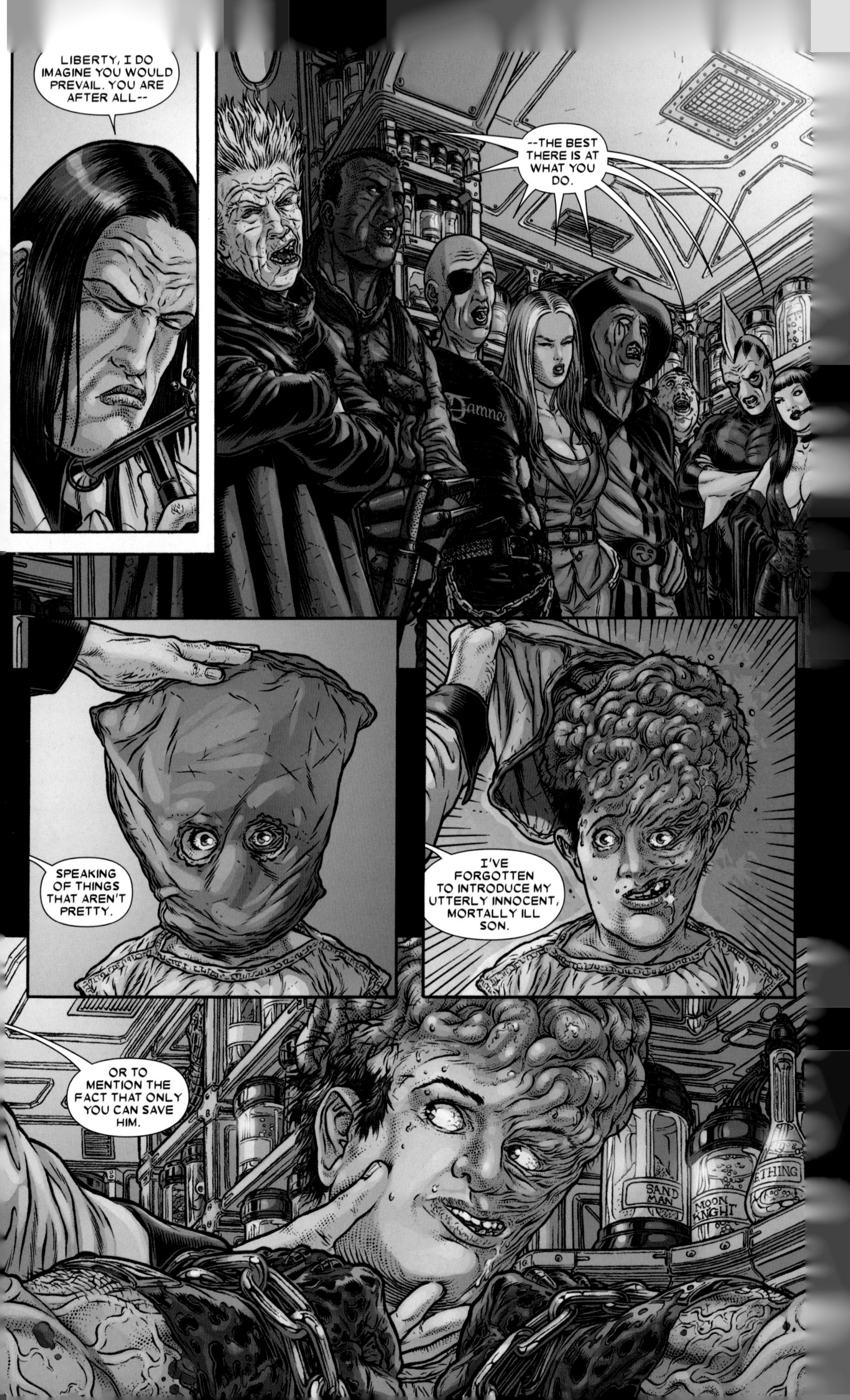
LIBERTY, I DO IMAGINE YOU WOULD PREVAIL. YOU ARE AFTER ALL--
--THE BEST THERE IS AT WHAT YOU DO.
SPEAKING OF THINGS THAT AREN'T PRETTY.
I'VE FORGOTTEN TO INTRODUCE MY UTTERLY INNOCENT, MORTALLY ILL SON.
OR TO MENTION THE FACT THAT ONLY YOU CAN SAVE HIM.
SAND MAN
MOON KNIGHT

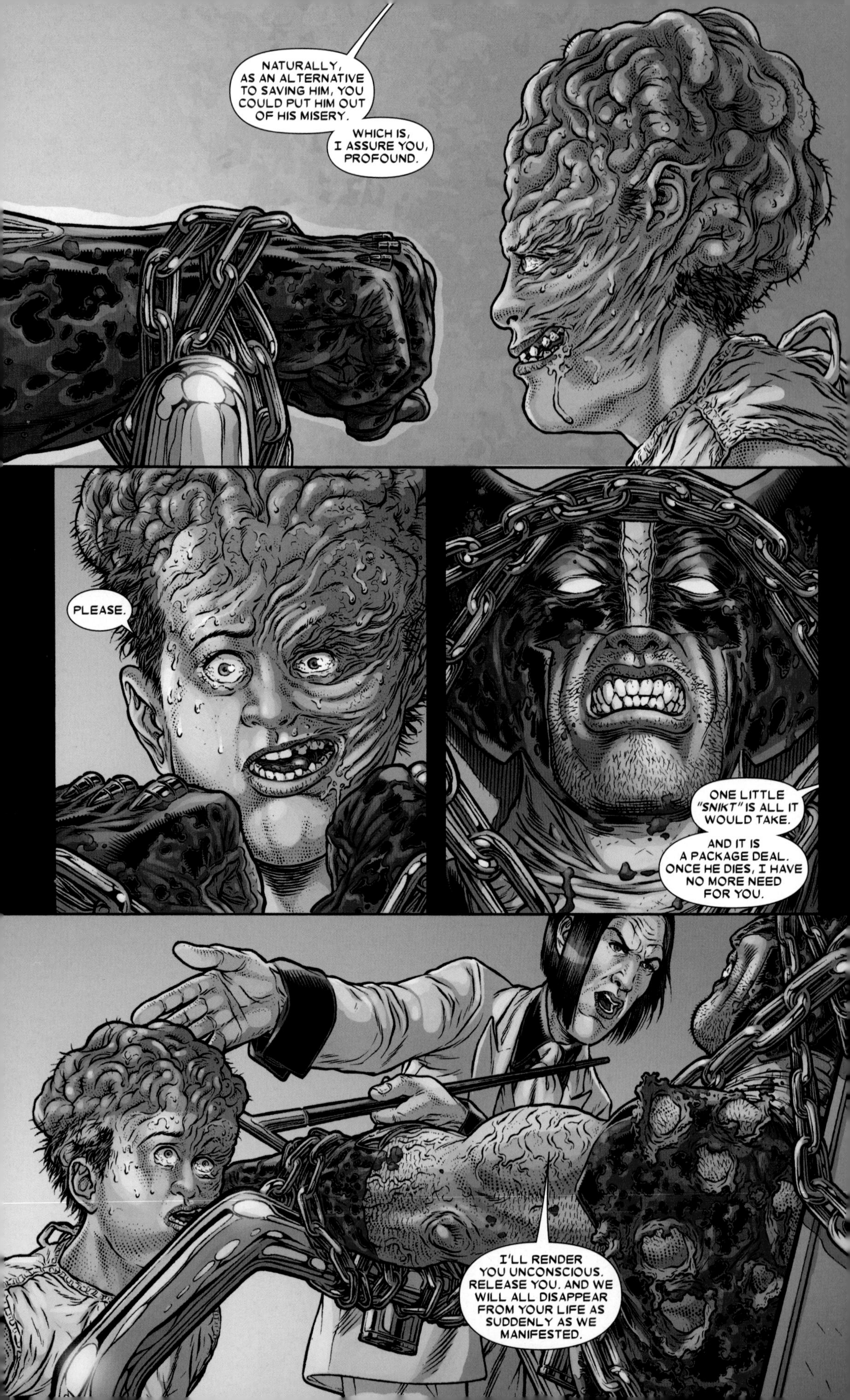
NATURALLY, AS AN ALTERNATIVE TO SAVING HIM, YOU COULD PUT HIM OUT OF HIS MISERY.
WHICH IS, I ASSURE YOU, PROFOUND.
PLEASE.
ONE LITTLE "SNIKT" IS ALL IT WOULD TAKE.
AND IT IS A PACKAGE DEAL. ONCE HE DIES, I HAVE NO MORE NEED FOR YOU.
I'LL RENDER YOU UNCONSCIOUS. RELEASE YOU. AND WE WILL ALL DISAPPEAR FROM YOUR LIFE AS SUDDENLY AS WE MANIFESTED.

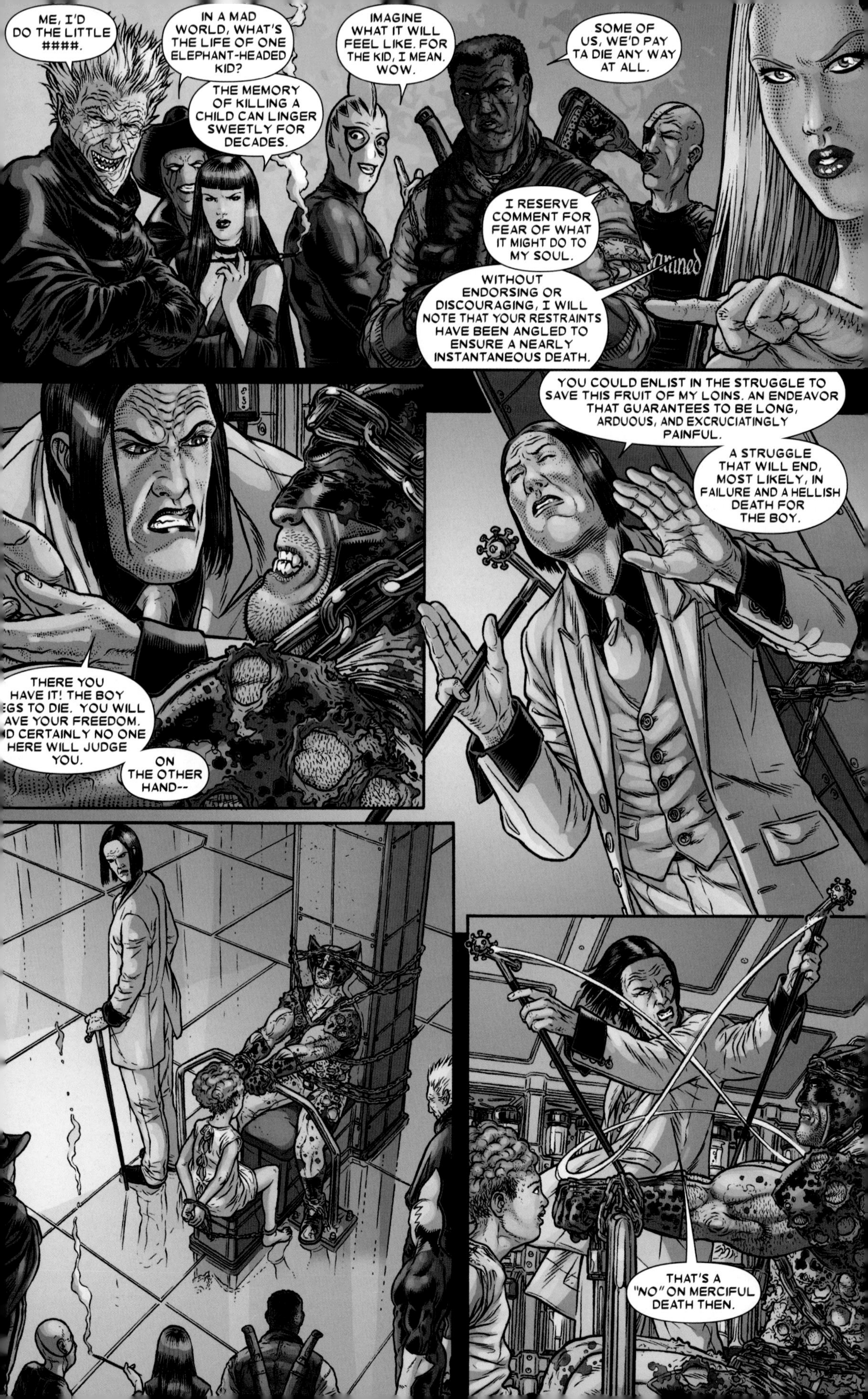
ME, I'D DO THE LITTLE ####.
IN A MAD WORLD, WHAT'S THE LIFE OF ONE ELEPHANT-HEADED KID?
THE MEMORY OF KILLING A CHILD CAN LINGER SWEETLY FOR DECADES.
IMAGINE WHAT IT WILL FEEL LIKE. FOR THE KID, I MEAN. WOW.
SOME OF US, WE'D PAY TA DIE ANY WAY AT ALL.
I RESERVE COMMENT FOR FEAR OF WHAT IT MIGHT DO TO MY SOUL.
WITHOUT ENDORSING OR DISCOURAGING, I WILL NOTE THAT YOUR RESTRAINTS HAVE BEEN ANGLED TO ENSURE A NEARLY INSTANTANEOUS DEATH.
THERE YOU HAVE IT! THE BOY EGS TO DIE. YOU WILL AVE YOUR FREEDOM. D CERTAINLY NO ONE HERE WILL JUDGE YOU.
ON THE OTHER HAND--
YOU COULD ENLIST IN THE STRUGGLE TO SAVE THIS FRUIT OF MY LOINS. AN ENDEAVOR THAT GUARANTEES TO BE LONG, ARDUOUS, AND EXCRUCIATINGLY PAINFUL.
A STRUGGLE THAT WILL END, MOST LIKELY, IN FAILURE AND A HELLISH DEATH FOR THE BOY.
THAT'S A "NO" ON MERCIFUL DEATH THEN.

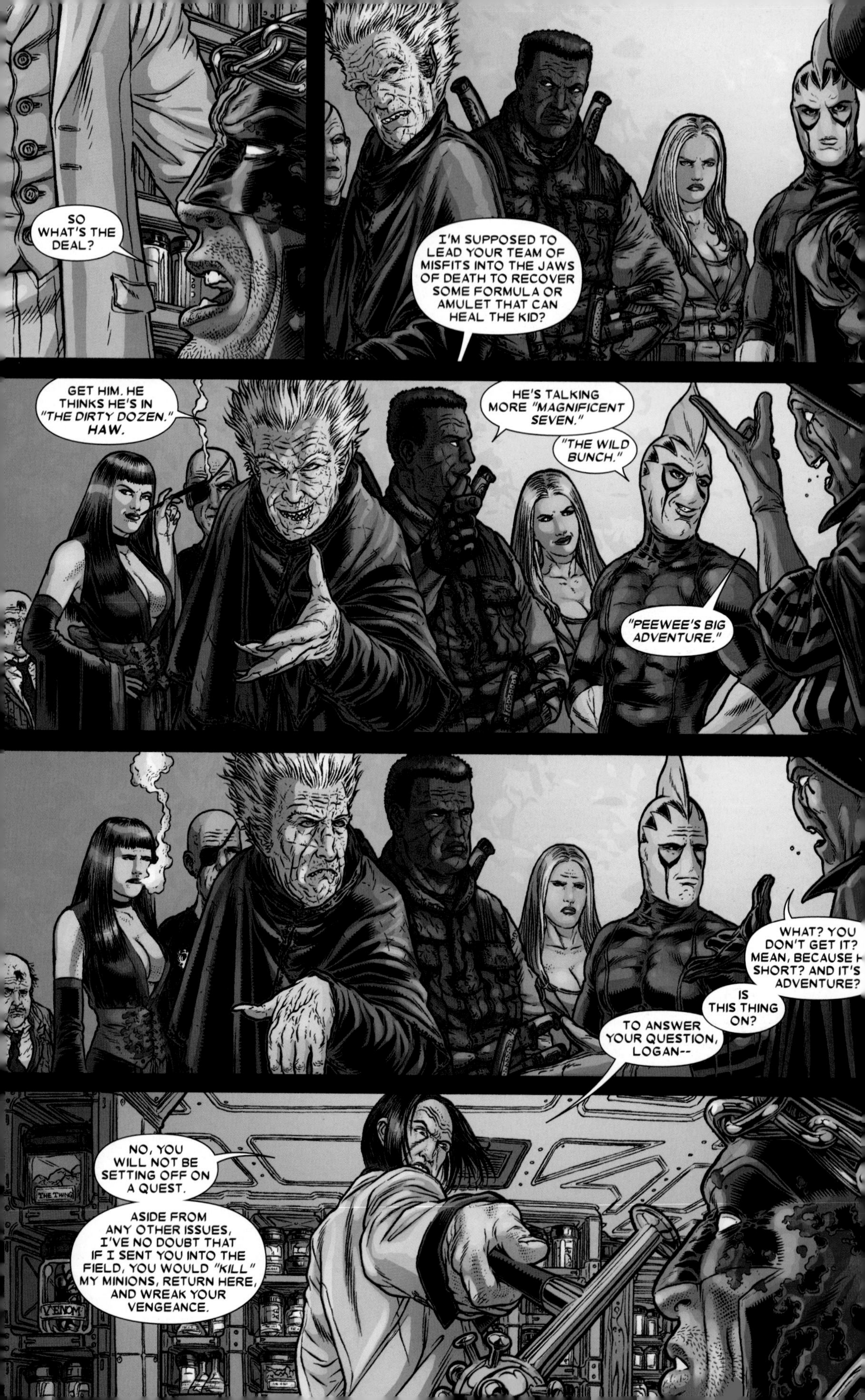

SO WHAT'S THE DEAL?
I'M SUPPOSED TO LEAD YOUR TEAM OF MISFITS INTO THE JAWS OF DEATH TO RECOVER SOME FORMULA OR AMULET THAT CAN HEAL THE KID?
GET HIM. HE THINKS HE'S IN "THE DIRTY DOZEN." HAW.
HE'S TALKING MORE "MAGNIFICENT SEVEN."
"THE WILD BUNCH."
"PEEWEE'S BIG ADVENTURE."
IS THIS THING ON?
TO ANSWER YOUR QUESTION, LOGAN--
NO, YOU WILL NOT BE SETTING OFF ON A QUEST.
ASIDE FROM ANY OTHER ISSUES, I'VE NO DOUBT THAT IF I SENT YOU INTO THE FIELD, YOU WOULD "KILL" MY MINIONS, RETURN HERE, AND WREAK YOUR VENGEANCE.
THE THING
VENOM

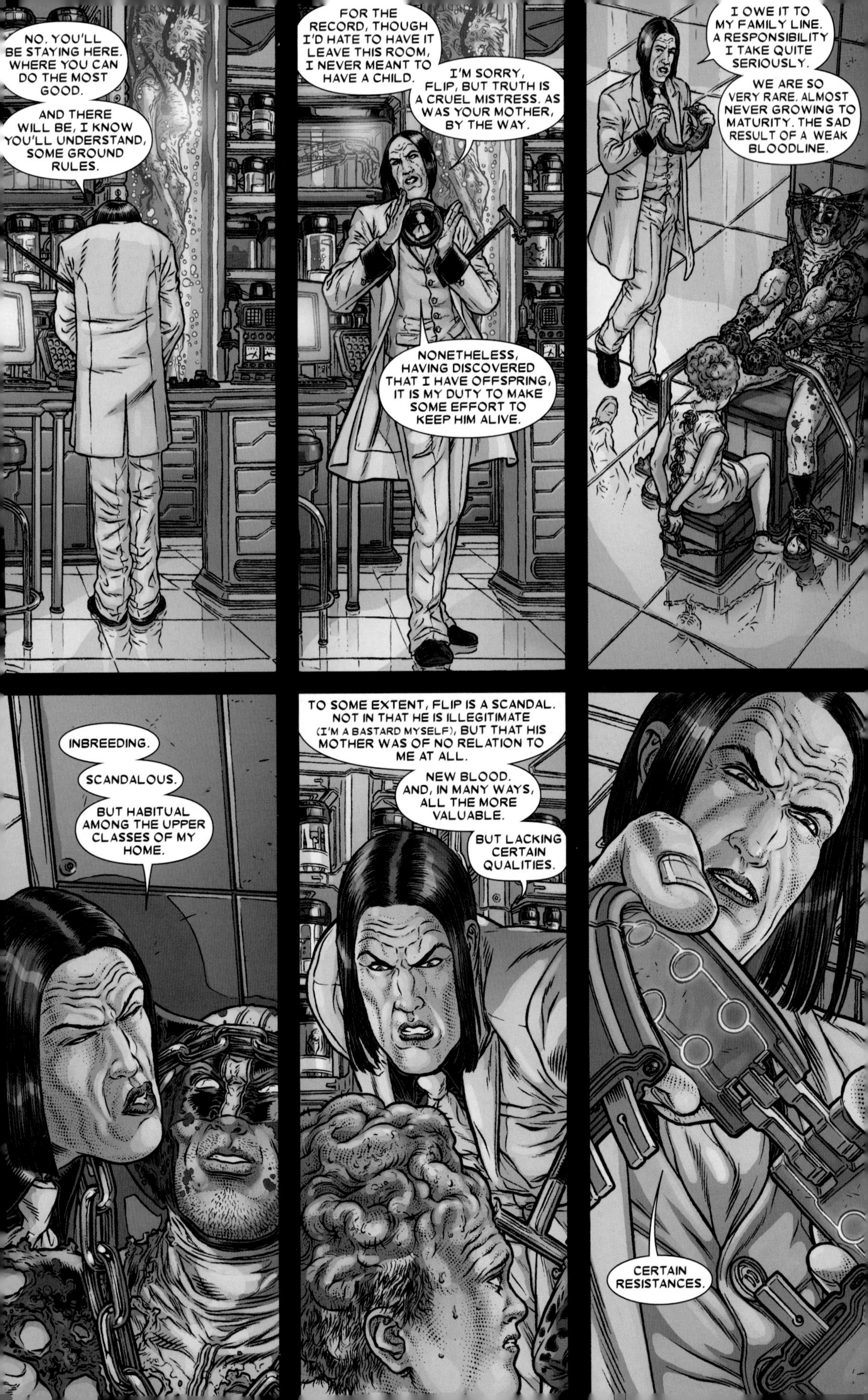

NO. YOU'LL BE STAYING HERE. WHERE YOU CAN DO THE MOST GOOD.
AND THERE WILL BE, I KNOW YOU'LL UNDERSTAND, SOME GROUND RULES.
FOR THE RECORD, THOUGH I'D HATE TO HAVE IT LEAVE THIS ROOM, I NEVER MEANT TO HAVE A CHILD.
I'M SORRY, FLIP, BUT TRUTH IS A CRUEL MISTRESS. AS WAS YOUR MOTHER, BY THE WAY.
NONETHELESS, HAVING DISCOVERED THAT I HAVE OFFSPRING, IT IS MY DUTY TO MAKE SOME EFFORT TO KEEP HIM ALIVE.
I OWE IT TO MY FAMILY LINE. A RESPONSIBILITY I TAKE QUITE SERIOUSLY.
WE ARE SO VERY RARE. ALMOST NEVER GROWING TO MATURITY. THE SAD RESULT OF A WEAK BLOODLINE.
INBREEDING.
SCANDALOUS.
BUT HABITUAL AMONG THE UPPER CLASSES OF MY HOME.
TO SOME EXTENT, FLIP IS A SCANDAL. NOT IN THAT HE IS ILLEGITIMATE (I'M A BASTARD MYSELF), BUT THAT HIS MOTHER WAS OF NO RELATION TO ME AT ALL.
NEW BLOOD. AND, IN MANY WAYS, ALL THE MORE VALUABLE.
BUT LACKING CERTAIN QUALITIES.
CERTAIN RESISTANCES.

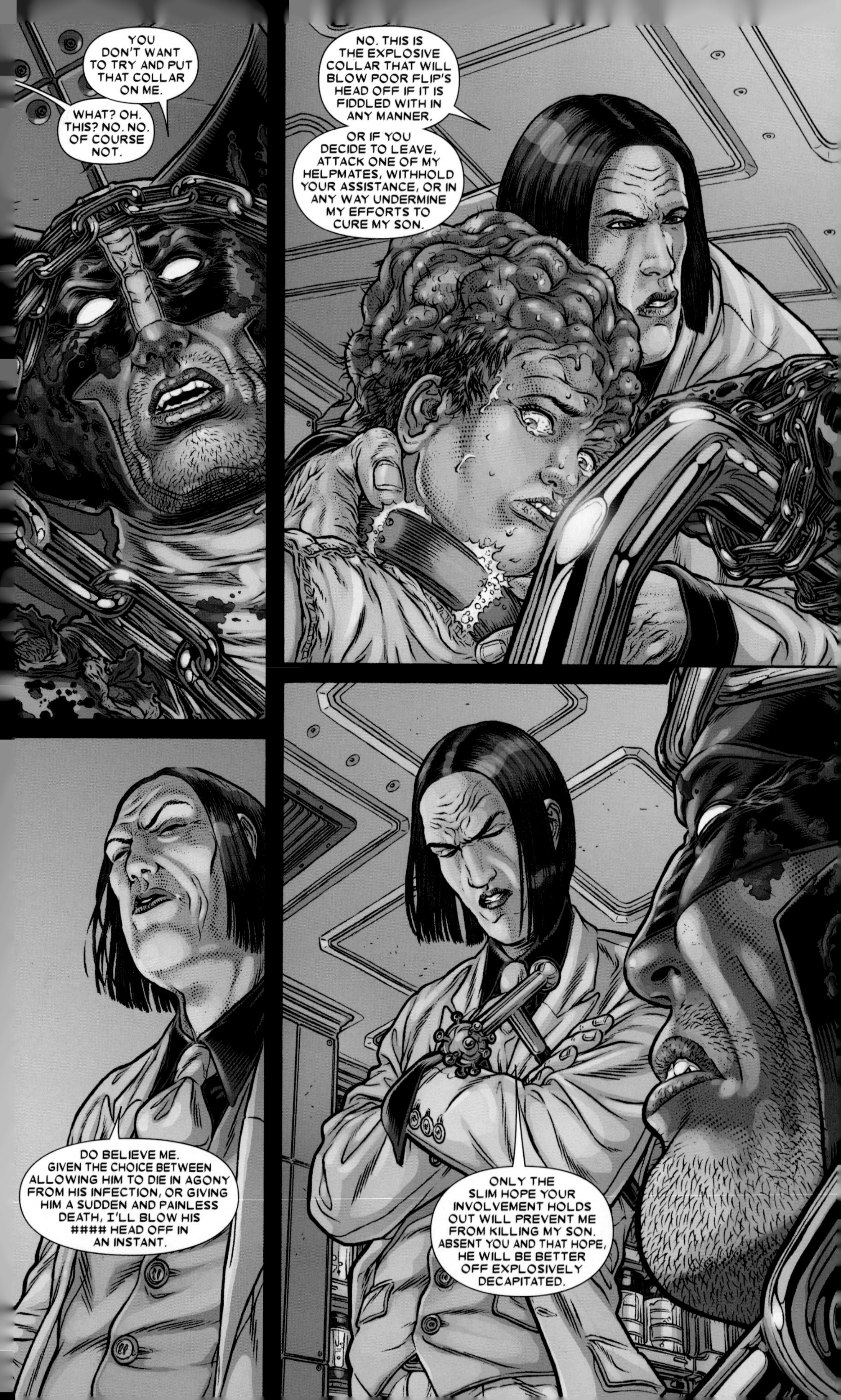
YOU DON'T WANT TO TRY AND PUT THAT COLLAR ON ME.
WHAT? OH. THIS? NO. NO. OF COURSE NOT.
NO. THIS IS THE EXPLOSIVE COLLAR THAT WILL BLOW POOR FLIP'S HEAD OFF IF IT IS FIDDLED WITH IN ANY MANNER.
OR IF YOU DECIDE TO LEAVE, ATTACK ONE OF MY HELPMATES, WITHHOLD YOUR ASSISTANCE, OR IN ANY WAY UNDERMINE MY EFFORTS TO CURE MY SON.
DO BELIEVE ME. GIVEN THE CHOICE BETWEEN ALLOWING HIM TO DIE IN AGONY FROM HIS INFECTION, OR GIVING HIM A SUDDEN AND PAINLESS DEATH, I'LL BLOW HIS #### HEAD OFF IN AN INSTANT.
ONLY THE SLIM HOPE YOUR INVOLVEMENT HOLDS OUT WILL PREVENT ME FROM KILLING MY SON. ABSENT YOU AND THAT HOPE, HE WILL BE BETTER OFF EXPLOSIVELY DECAPITATED.

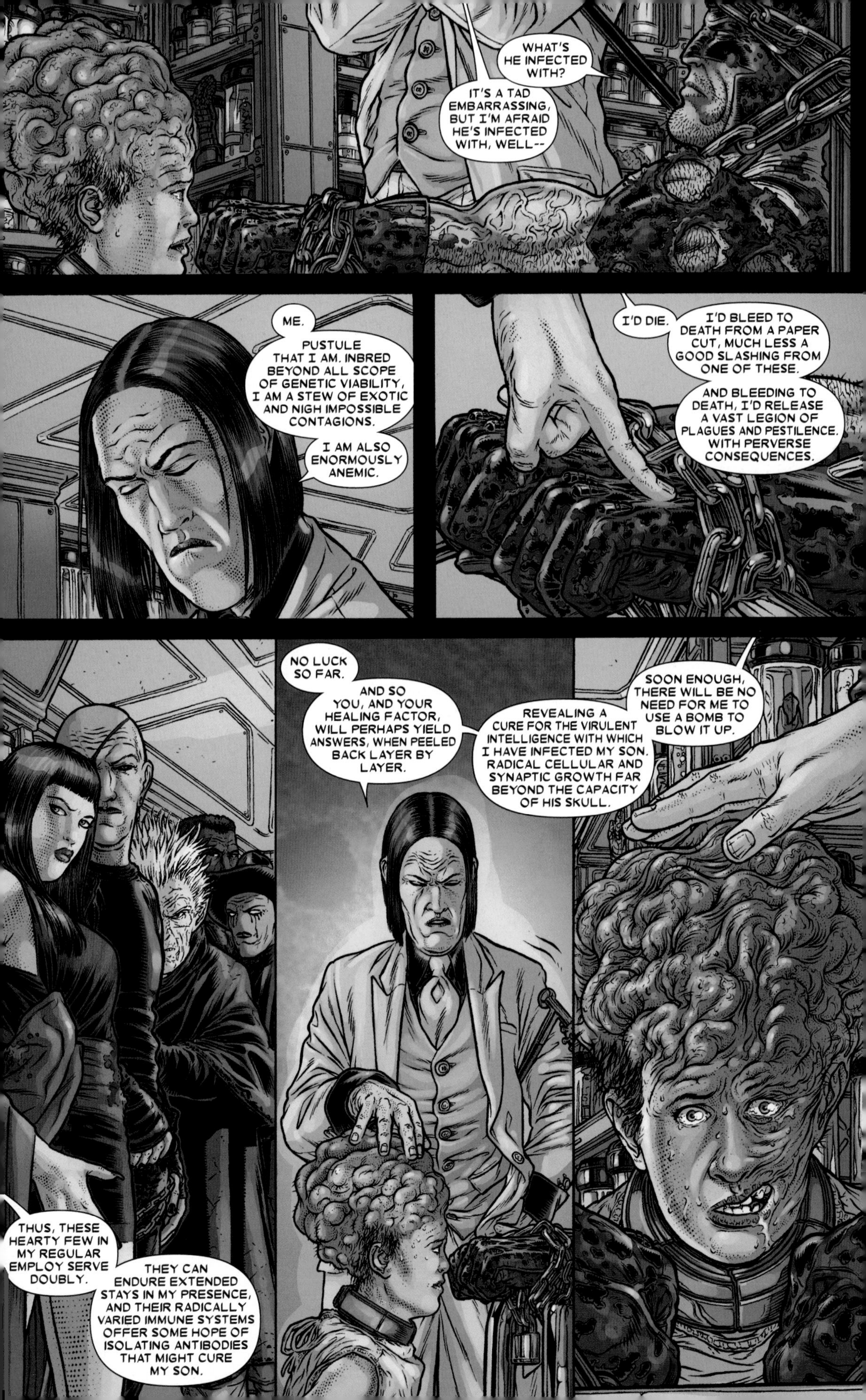
WHAT'S HE INFECTED WITH?
IT'S A TAD EMBARRASSING, BUT I'M AFRAID HE'S INFECTED WITH, WELL--
ME.
PUSTULE THAT I AM. INBRED BEYOND ALL SCOPE OF GENETIC VIABILITY, I AM A STEW OF EXOTIC AND NIGH IMPOSSIBLE CONTAGIONS.
I AM ALSO ENORMOUSLY ANEMIC.
I'D DIE.
I'D BLEED TO DEATH FROM A PAPER CUT, MUCH LESS A GOOD SLASHING FROM ONE OF THESE.
AND BLEEDING TO DEATH, I'D RELEASE A VAST LEGION OF PLAGUES AND PESTILENCE. WITH PERVERSE CONSEQUENCES.
THUS, THESE HEARTY FEW IN MY REGULAR EMPLOY SERVE DOUBLY.
THEY CAN ENDURE EXTENDED STAYS IN MY PRESENCE, AND THEIR RADICALLY VARIED IMMUNE SYSTEMS OFFER SOME HOPE OF ISOLATING ANTIBODIES THAT MIGHT CURE MY SON.
NO LUCK SO FAR.
AND SO YOU, AND YOUR HEALING FACTOR, WILL PERHAPS YIELD ANSWERS, WHEN PEELED BACK LAYER BY LAYER.
REVEALING A CURE FOR THE VIRULENT INTELLIGENCE WITH WHICH I HAVE INFECTED MY SON. RADICAL CELLULAR AND SYNAPTIC GROWTH FAR BEYOND THE CAPACITY OF HIS SKULL.
SOON ENOUGH, THERE WILL BE NO NEED FOR ME TO USE A BOMB TO BLOW IT UP.

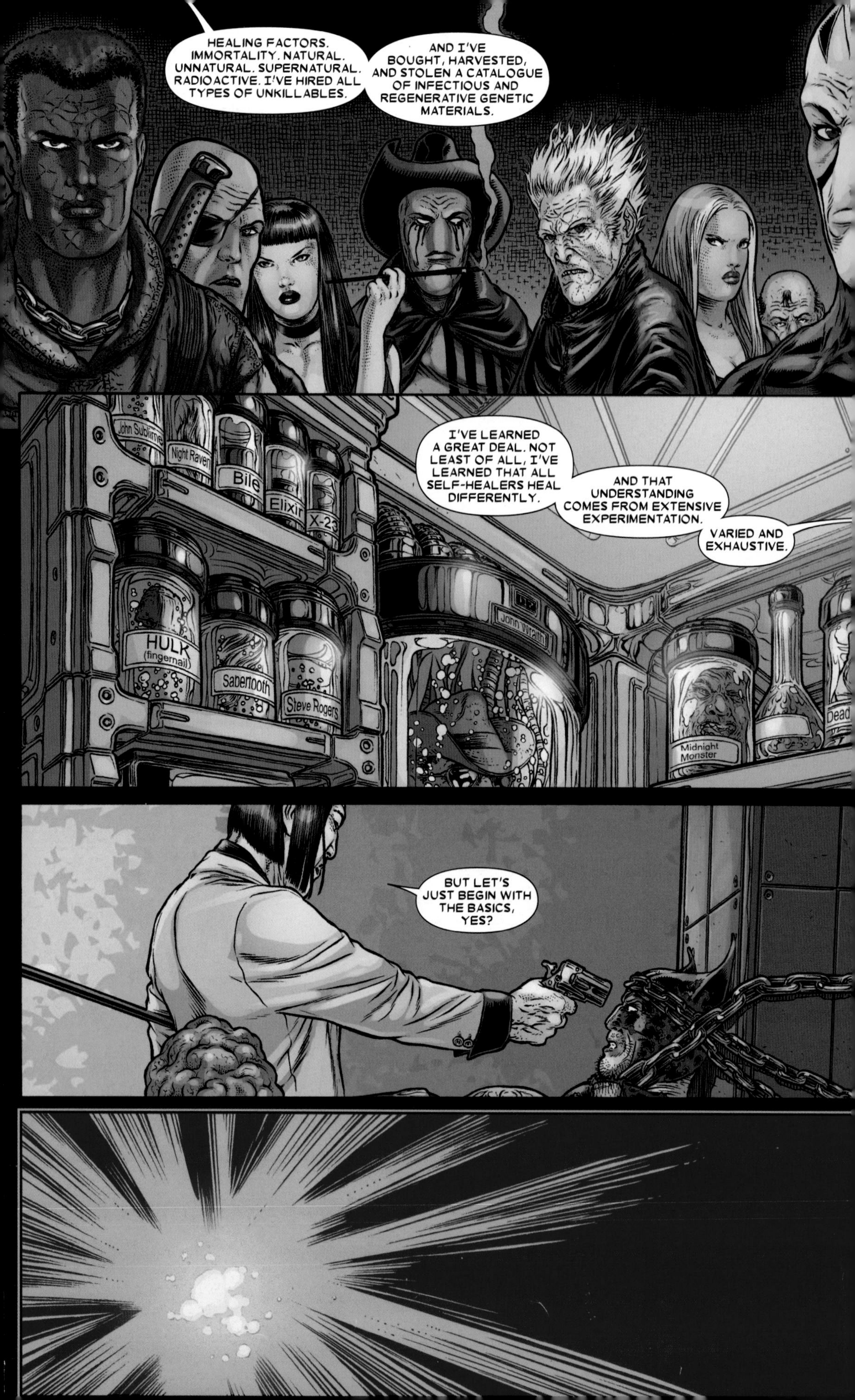
HEALING FACTORS. IMMORTALITY. NATURAL. UNNATURAL. SUPERNATURAL. RADIOACTIVE. I'VE HIRED ALL TYPES OF UNKILLABLES.
AND I'VE BOUGHT, HARVESTED, AND STOLEN A CATALOGUE OF INFECTIOUS AND REGENERATIVE GENETIC MATERIALS.
John Sublime
Night Raven
Bile
Elixir
X-23
HULK (fingernail)
Sabertooth
Steve Rogers
John Wraith
Midnight Monster
I'VE LEARNED A GREAT DEAL. NOT LEAST OF ALL, I'VE LEARNED THAT ALL SELF-HEALERS HEAL DIFFERENTLY.
AND THAT UNDERSTANDING COMES FROM EXTENSIVE EXPERIMENTATION.
VARIED AND EXHAUSTIVE.
BUT LET'S JUST BEGIN WITH THE BASICS, YES?

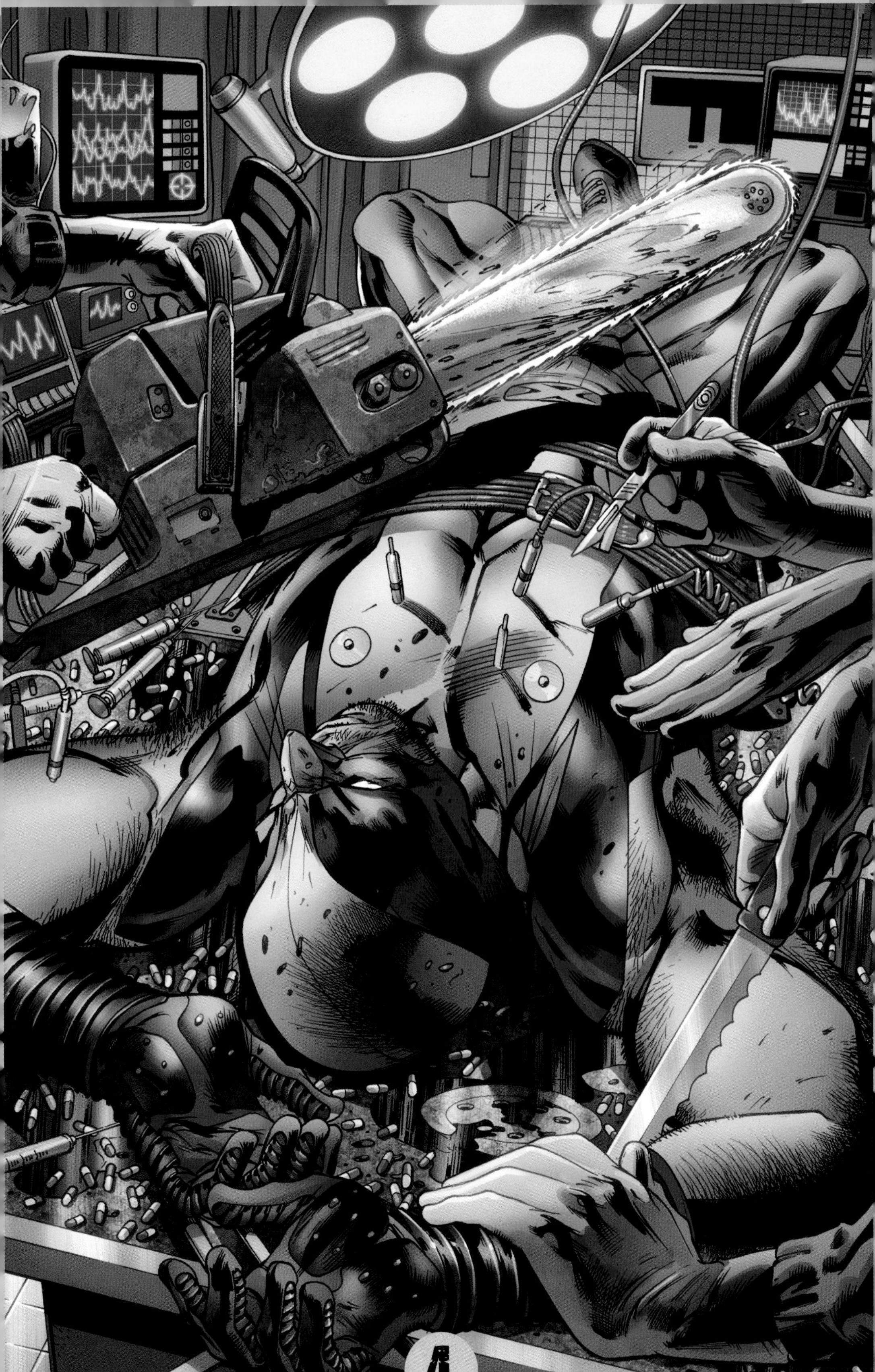
4

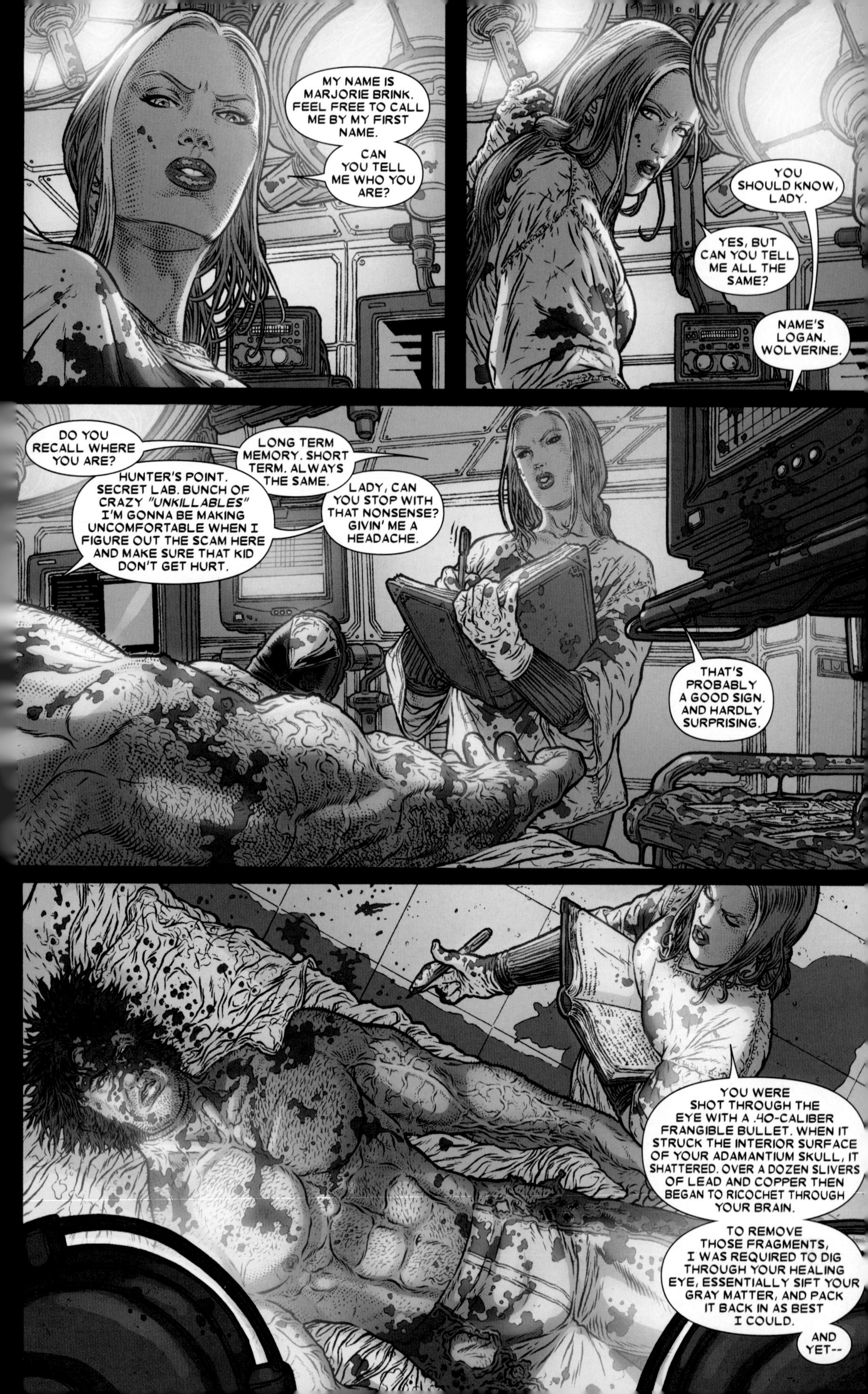
MY NAME IS MARJORIE BRINK. FEEL FREE TO CALL ME BY MY FIRST NAME.
CAN YOU TELL ME WHO YOU ARE?
YOU SHOULD KNOW, LADY.
YES, BUT CAN YOU TELL ME ALL THE SAME?
NAME'S LOGAN. WOLVERINE.
DO YOU RECALL WHERE YOU ARE?
HUNTER'S POINT. SECRET LAB. BUNCH OF CRAZY "UNKILLABLES" I'M GONNA BE MAKING UNCOMFORTABLE WHEN I FIGURE OUT THE SCAM HERE AND MAKE SURE THAT KID DON'T GET HURT.
LONG TERM MEMORY. SHORT TERM. ALWAYS THE SAME.
LADY, CAN YOU STOP WITH THAT NONSENSE? GIVIN' ME A HEADACHE.
THAT'S PROBABLY A GOOD SIGN. AND HARDLY SURPRISING.
YOU WERE SHOT THROUGH THE EYE WITH A .40-CALIBER FRANGIBLE BULLET. WHEN IT STRUCK THE INTERIOR SURFACE OF YOUR ADAMANTIUM SKULL, IT SHATTERED. OVER A DOZEN SLIVERS OF LEAD AND COPPER THEN BEGAN TO RICOCHET THROUGH YOUR BRAIN.
TO REMOVE THOSE FRAGMENTS, I WAS REQUIRED TO DIG THROUGH YOUR HEALING EYE, ESSENTIALLY SIFT YOUR GRAY MATTER, AND PACK IT BACK IN AS BEST I COULD.
AND YET--

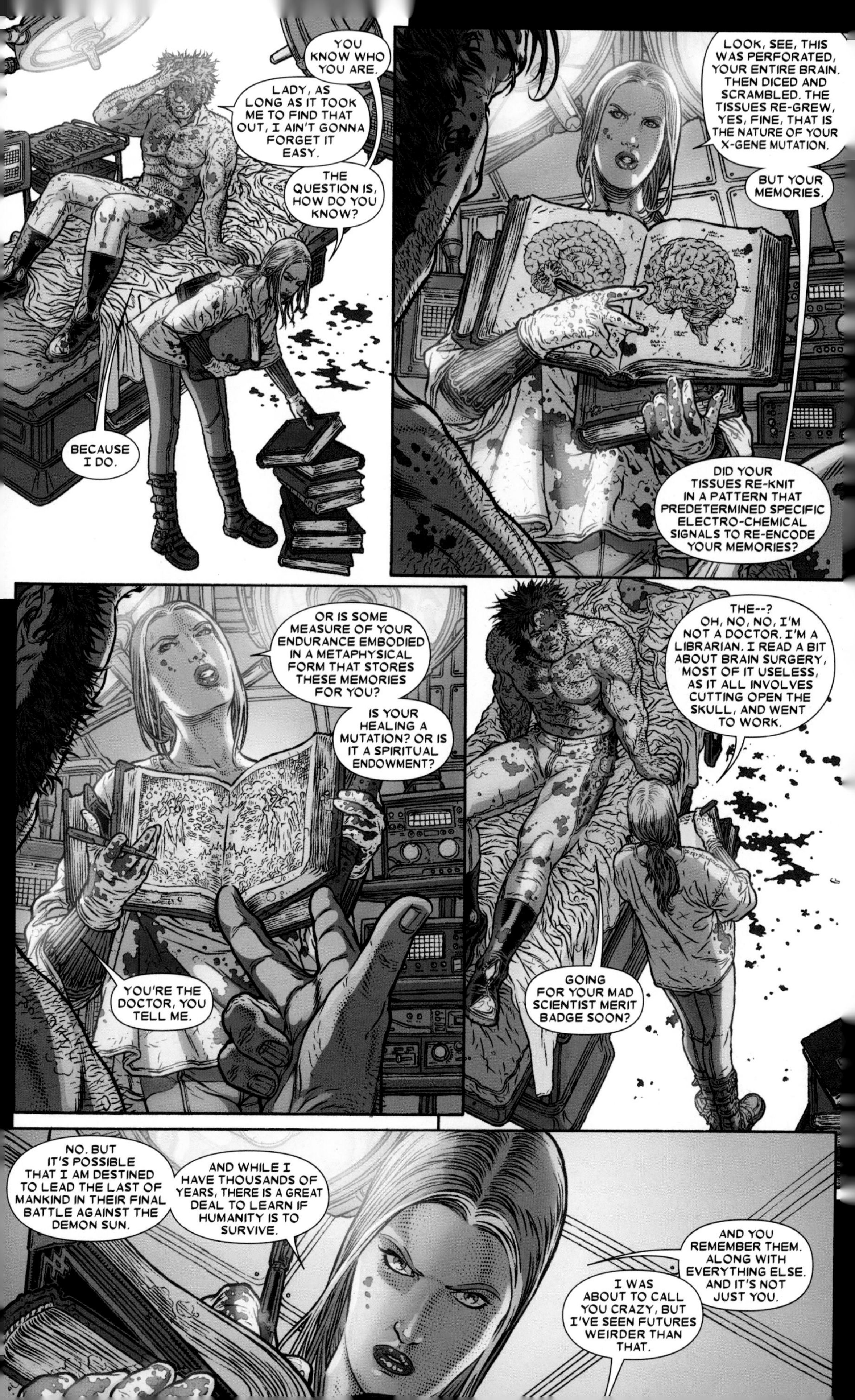
YOU KNOW WHO YOU ARE.
LADY, AS LONG AS IT TOOK ME TO FIND THAT OUT, I AIN'T GONNA FORGET IT EASY.
THE QUESTION IS, HOW DO YOU KNOW?
BECAUSE I DO.
LOOK, SEE, THIS WAS PERFORATED, YOUR ENTIRE BRAIN. THEN DICED AND SCRAMBLED. THE TISSUES RE-GREW, YES, FINE, THAT IS THE NATURE OF YOUR X-GENE MUTATION.
BUT YOUR MEMORIES.
DID YOUR TISSUES RE-KNIT IN A PATTERN THAT PREDETERMINED SPECIFIC ELECTRO-CHEMICAL SIGNALS TO RE-ENCODE YOUR MEMORIES?
OR IS SOME MEASURE OF YOUR ENDURANCE EMBODIED IN A METAPHYSICAL FORM THAT STORES THESE MEMORIES FOR YOU?
IS YOUR HEALING A MUTATION? OR IS IT A SPIRITUAL ENDOWMENT?
YOU'RE THE DOCTOR, YOU TELL ME.
THE--? OH, NO, NO, I'M NOT A DOCTOR. I'M A LIBRARIAN. I READ A BIT ABOUT BRAIN SURGERY, MOST OF IT USELESS, AS IT ALL INVOLVES CUTTING OPEN THE SKULL, AND WENT TO WORK.
GOING FOR YOUR MAD SCIENTIST MERIT BADGE SOON?
NO. BUT IT'S POSSIBLE THAT I AM DESTINED TO LEAD THE LAST OF MANKIND IN THEIR FINAL BATTLE AGAINST THE DEMON SUN.
AND WHILE I HAVE THOUSANDS OF YEARS, THERE IS A GREAT DEAL TO LEARN IF HUMANITY IS TO SURVIVE.
I WAS ABOUT TO CALL YOU CRAZY, BUT I'VE SEEN FUTURES WEIRDER THAN THAT.
AND YOU REMEMBER THEM. ALONG WITH EVERYTHING ELSE. AND IT'S NOT JUST YOU.

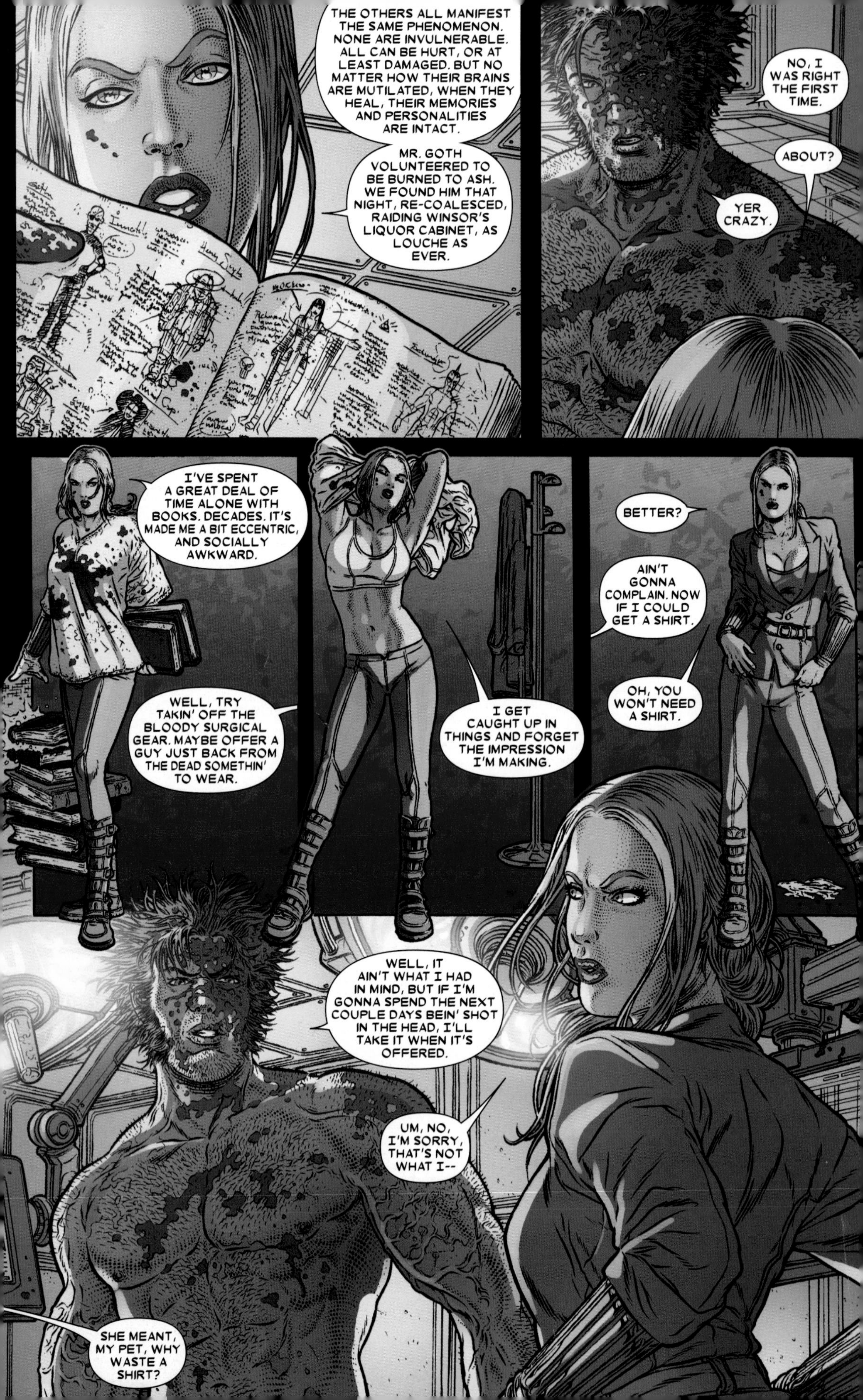
THE OTHERS ALL MANIFEST THE SAME PHENOMENON. NONE ARE INVULNERABLE. ALL CAN BE HURT, OR AT LEAST DAMAGED. BUT NO MATTER HOW THEIR BRAINS ARE MUTILATED, WHEN THEY HEAL, THEIR MEMORIES AND PERSONALITIES ARE INTACT.
MR. GOTH VOLUNTEERED TO BE BURNED TO ASH. WE FOUND HIM THAT NIGHT, RE-COALESCED, RAIDING WINSOR'S LIQUOR CABINET, AS LOUCHE AS EVER.
YER CRAZY.
ABOUT?
NO, I WAS RIGHT THE FIRST TIME.
I'VE SPENT A GREAT DEAL OF TIME ALONE WITH BOOKS. DECADES. IT'S MADE ME A BIT ECCENTRIC, AND SOCIALLY AWKWARD.
WELL, TRY TAKIN' OFF THE BLOODY SURGICAL GEAR. MAYBE OFFER A GUY JUST BACK FROM THE DEAD SOMETHIN' TO WEAR.
I GET CAUGHT UP IN THINGS AND FORGET THE IMPRESSION I'M MAKING.
BETTER?
AIN'T GONNA COMPLAIN. NOW IF I COULD GET A SHIRT.
OH, YOU WON'T NEED A SHIRT.
WELL, IT AIN'T WHAT I HAD IN MIND, BUT IF I'M GONNA SPEND THE NEXT COUPLE DAYS BEIN' SHOT IN THE HEAD, I'LL TAKE IT WHEN IT'S OFFERED.
UM, NO, I'M SORRY, THAT'S NOT WHAT I--
SHE MEANT, MY PET, WHY WASTE A SHIRT?

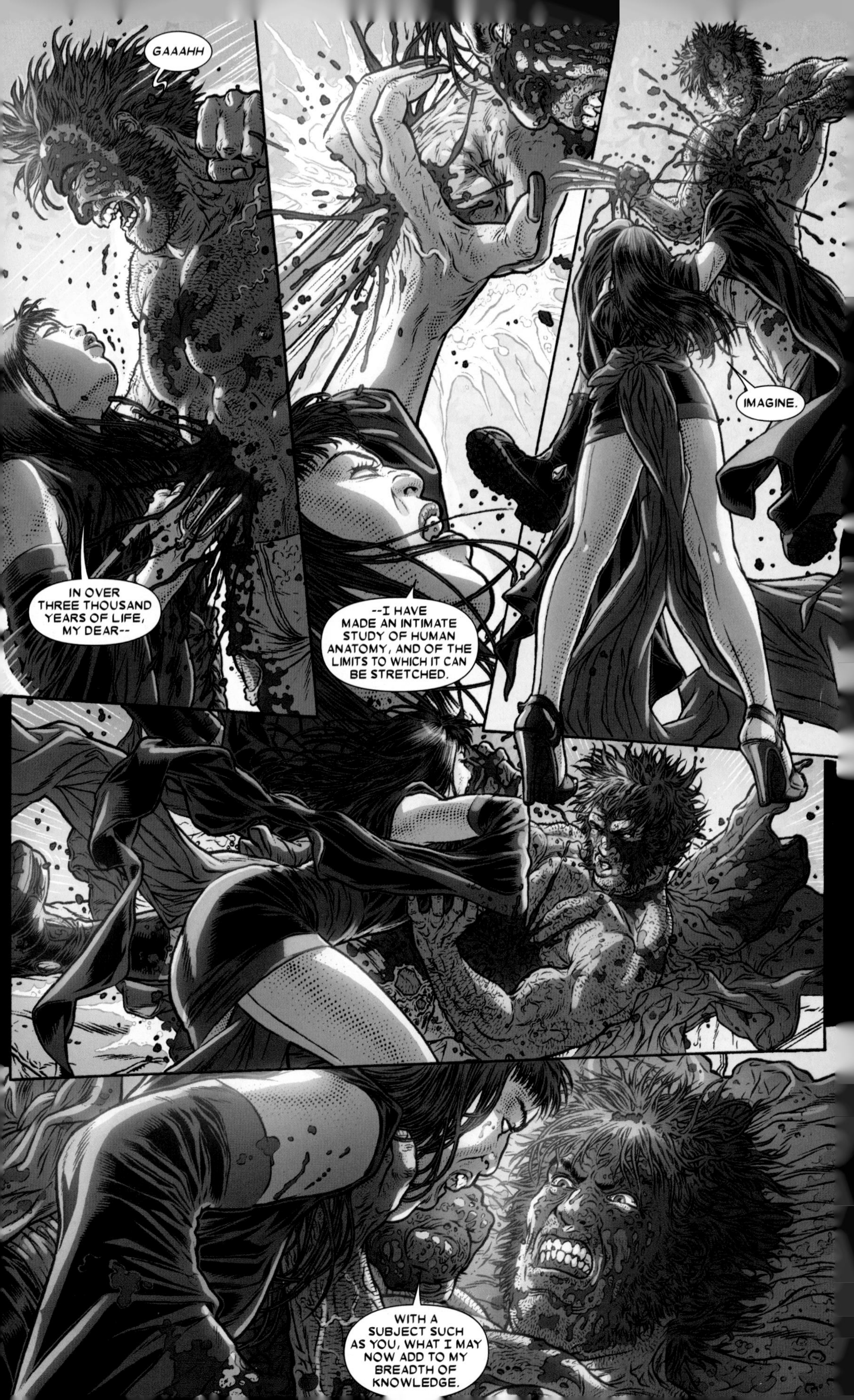
GAAAHH
IN OVER THREE THOUSAND YEARS OF LIFE, MY DEAR--
--I HAVE MADE AN INTIMATE STUDY OF HUMAN ANATOMY, AND OF THE LIMITS TO WHICH IT CAN BE STRETCHED.
IMAGINE.
WITH A SUBJECT SUCH AS YOU, WHAT I MAY NOW ADD TO MY BREADTH OF KNOWLEDGE.

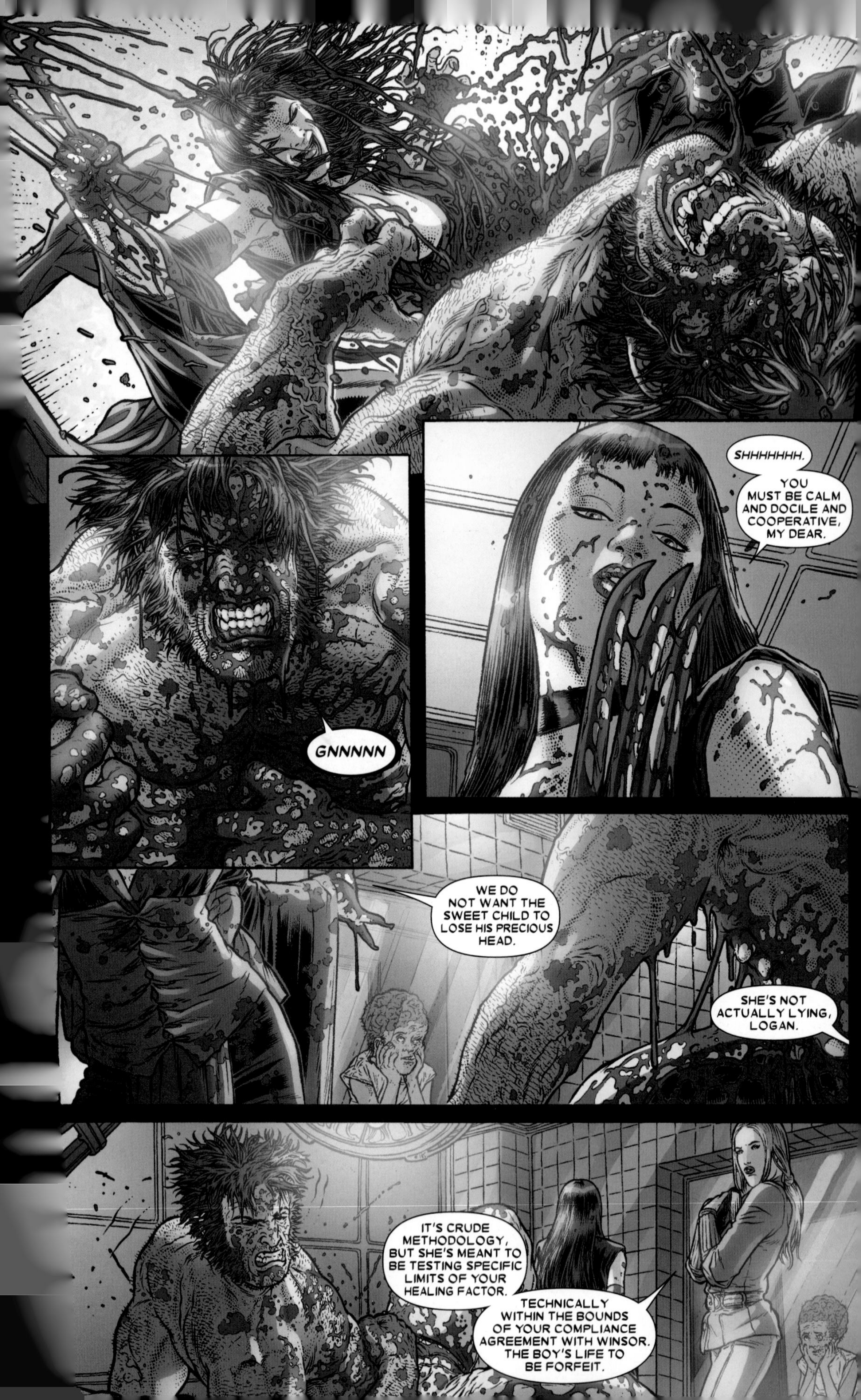
GNNNNN
SHHHHHHH.
YOU MUST BE CALM AND DOCILE AND COOPERATIVE, MY DEAR.
WE DO NOT WANT THE SWEET CHILD TO LOSE HIS PRECIOUS HEAD.
SHE'S NOT ACTUALLY LYING, LOGAN.
IT'S CRUDE METHODOLOGY, BUT SHE'S MEANT TO BE TESTING SPECIFIC LIMITS OF YOUR HEALING FACTOR.
TECHNICALLY WITHIN THE BOUNDS OF YOUR COMPLIANCE AGREEMENT WITH WINSOR. THE BOY'S LIFE TO BE FORFEIT.

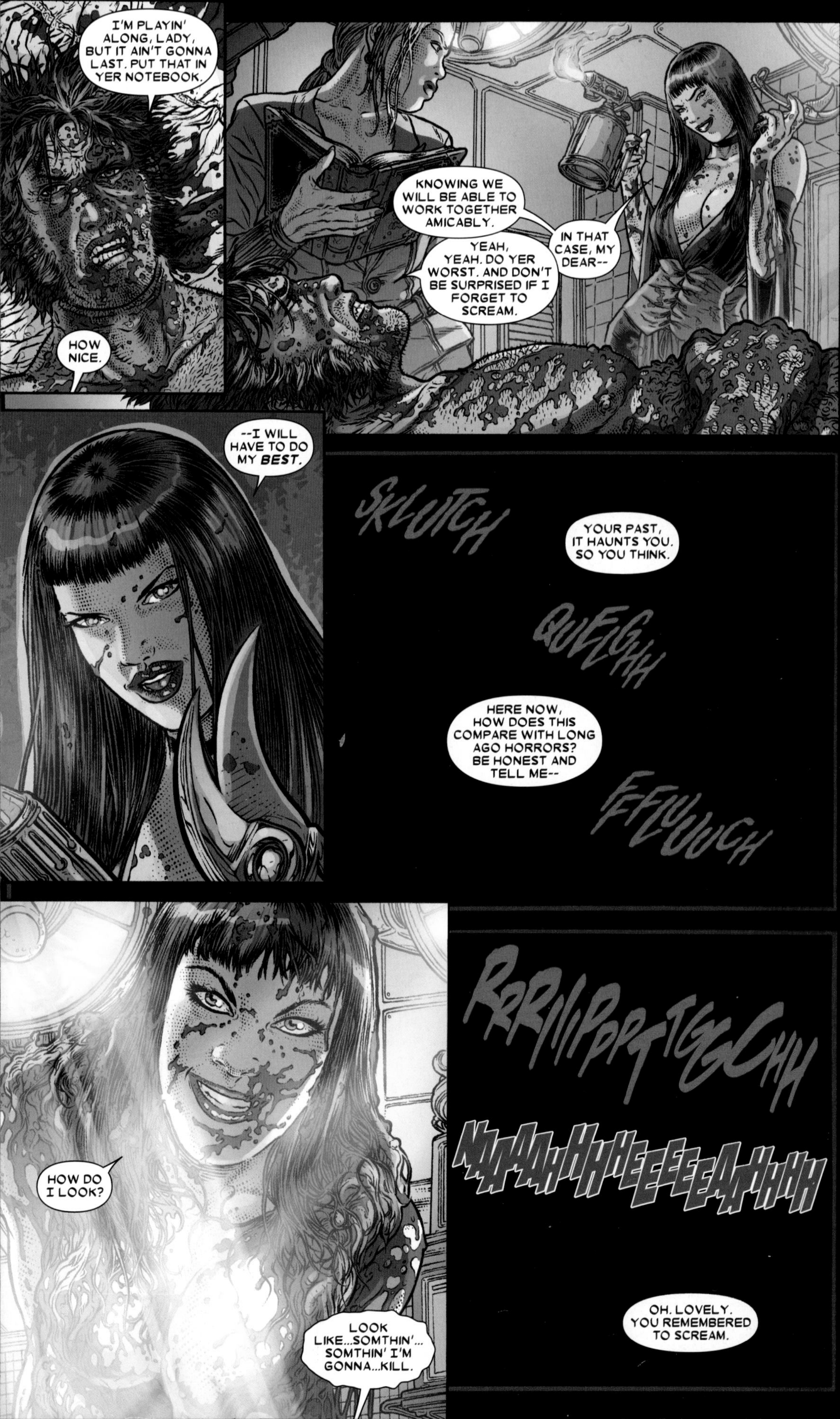
I'M PLAYIN' ALONG, LADY, BUT IT AIN'T GONNA LAST. PUT THAT IN YER NOTEBOOK.
HOW NICE.
KNOWING WE WILL BE ABLE TO WORK TOGETHER AMICABLY.
YEAH, YEAH. DO YER WORST. AND DON'T BE SURPRISED IF I FORGET TO SCREAM.
IN THAT CASE, MY DEAR--
--I WILL HAVE TO DO MY *BEST*.
SKLUTCH
YOUR PAST, IT HAUNTS YOU. SO YOU THINK.
QUELGHH
HERE NOW, HOW DOES THIS COMPARE WITH LONG AGO HORRORS? BE HONEST AND TELL ME--
FFFLUUUCH
RRRIIPPPTTGGCHH
NAAAHHHHEEEEEAAHHHH
HOW DO I LOOK?
LOOK LIKE...SOMTHIN'... SOMTHIN' I'M GONNA...KILL.
OH. LOVELY. YOU REMEMBERED TO SCREAM.

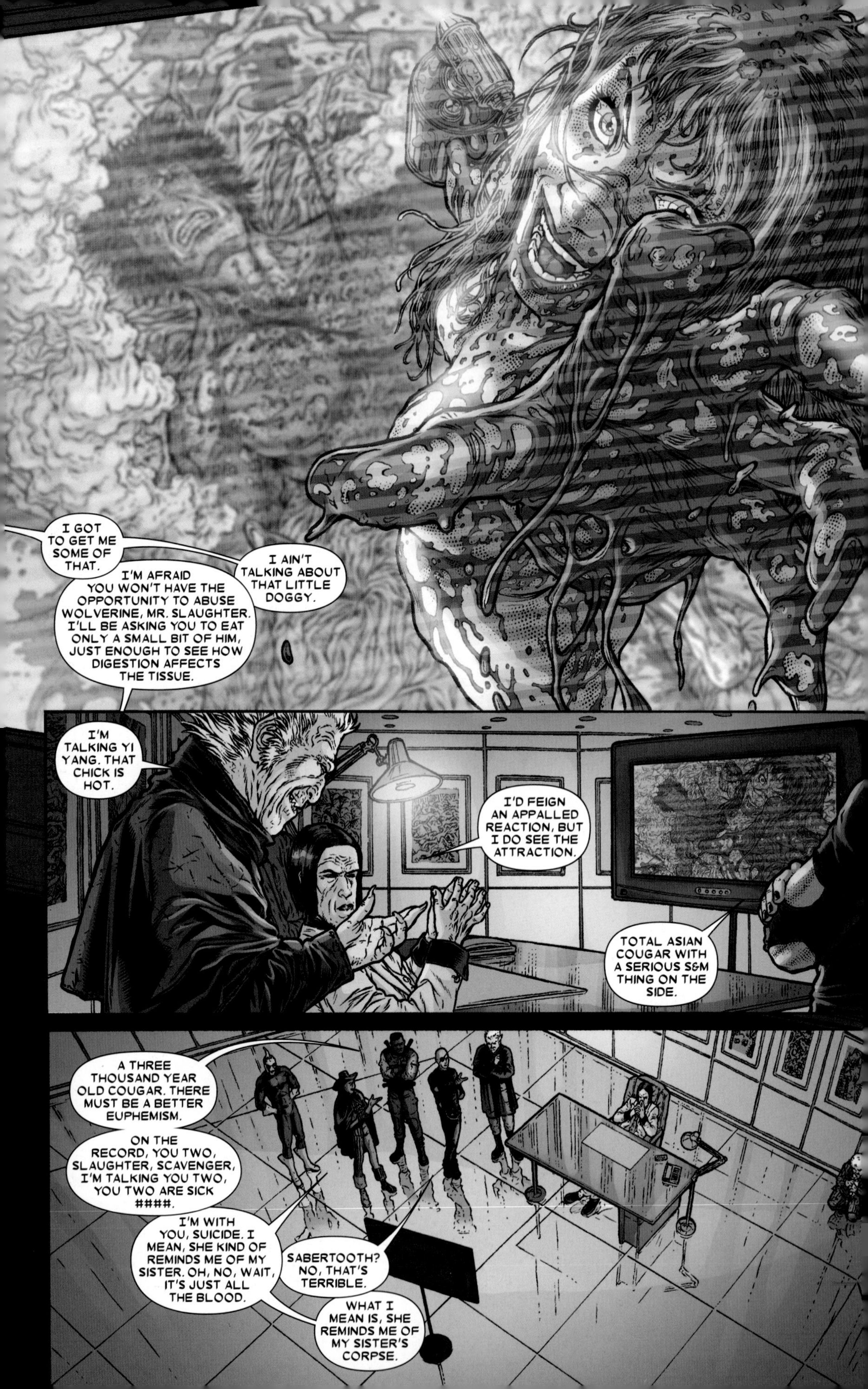
I GOT TO GET ME SOME OF THAT.
I AIN'T TALKING ABOUT THAT LITTLE DOGGY.
I'M AFRAID YOU WON'T HAVE THE OPPORTUNITY TO ABUSE WOLVERINE, MR. SLAUGHTER. I'LL BE ASKING YOU TO EAT ONLY A SMALL BIT OF HIM, JUST ENOUGH TO SEE HOW DIGESTION AFFECTS THE TISSUE.
I'M TALKING YI YANG. THAT CHICK IS HOT.
I'D FEIGN AN APPALLED REACTION, BUT I DO SEE THE ATTRACTION.
TOTAL ASIAN COUGAR WITH A SERIOUS S&M THING ON THE SIDE.
A THREE THOUSAND YEAR OLD COUGAR. THERE MUST BE A BETTER EUPHEMISM.
ON THE RECORD, YOU TWO, SLAUGHTER, SCAVENGER, I'M TALKING YOU TWO, YOU TWO ARE SICK ####.
I'M WITH YOU, SUICIDE. I MEAN, SHE KIND OF REMINDS ME OF MY SISTER. OH, NO, WAIT, IT'S JUST ALL THE BLOOD.
SABERTOOTH? NO, THAT'S TERRIBLE.
WHAT I MEAN IS, SHE REMINDS ME OF MY SISTER'S CORPSE.

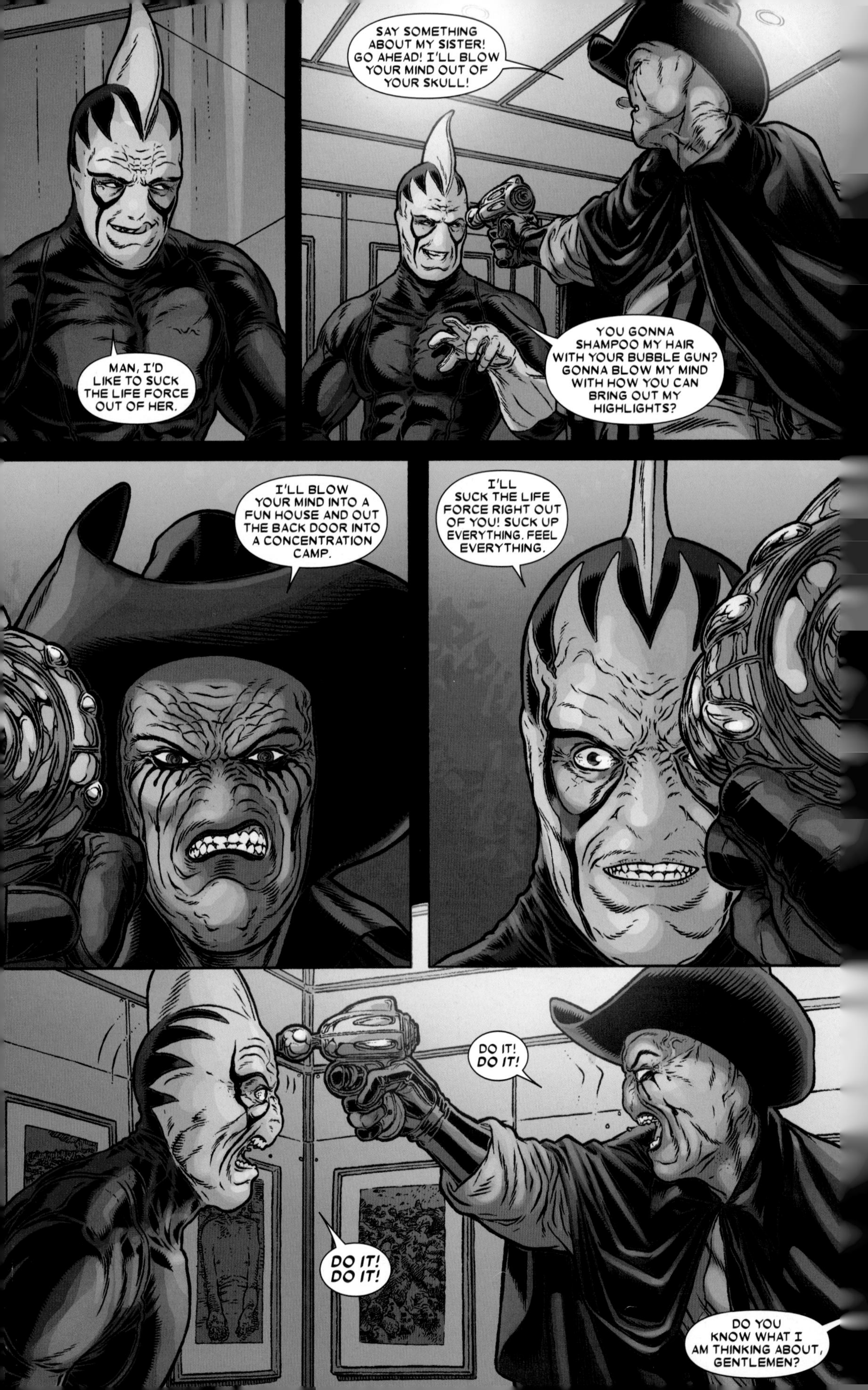
MAN, I'D LIKE TO SUCK THE LIFE FORCE OUT OF HER.
SAY SOMETHING ABOUT MY SISTER! GO AHEAD! I'LL BLOW YOUR MIND OUT OF YOUR SKULL!
YOU GONNA SHAMPOO MY HAIR WITH YOUR BUBBLE GUN? GONNA BLOW MY MIND WITH HOW YOU CAN BRING OUT MY HIGHLIGHTS?
I'LL BLOW YOUR MIND INTO A FUN HOUSE AND OUT THE BACK DOOR INTO A CONCENTRATION CAMP.
I'LL SUCK THE LIFE FORCE RIGHT OUT OF YOU! SUCK UP EVERYTHING. FEEL EVERYTHING.
DO IT! DO IT!
DO IT! DO IT!
DO YOU KNOW WHAT I AM THINKING ABOUT, GENTLEMEN?

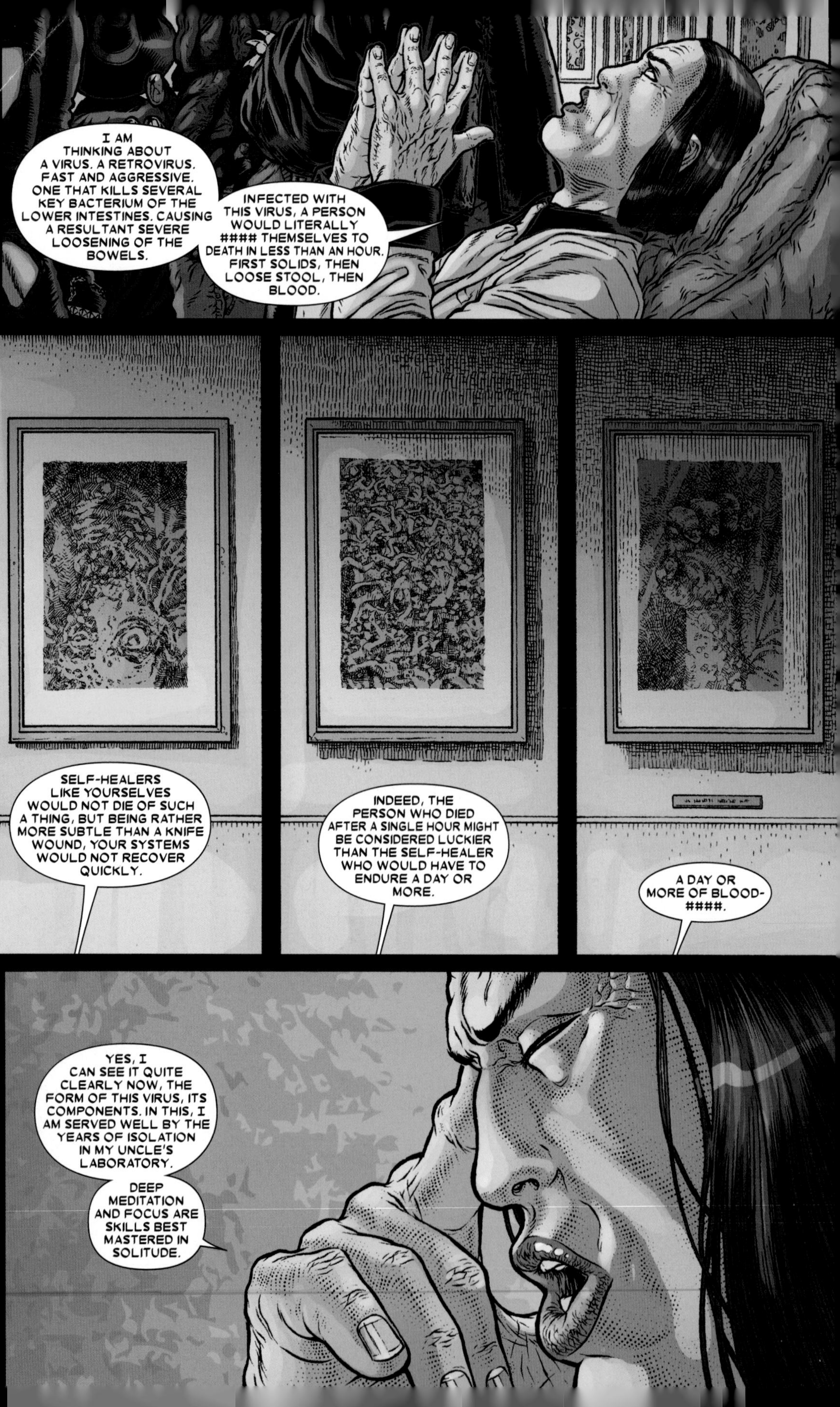

I AM THINKING ABOUT A VIRUS. A RETROVIRUS. FAST AND AGGRESSIVE. ONE THAT KILLS SEVERAL KEY BACTERIUM OF THE LOWER INTESTINES. CAUSING A RESULTANT SEVERE LOOSENING OF THE BOWELS.
INFECTED WITH THIS VIRUS, A PERSON WOULD LITERALLY #### THEMSELVES TO DEATH IN LESS THAN AN HOUR. FIRST SOLIDS, THEN LOOSE STOOL, THEN BLOOD.
SELF-HEALERS LIKE YOURSELVES WOULD NOT DIE OF SUCH A THING, BUT BEING RATHER MORE SUBTLE THAN A KNIFE WOUND, YOUR SYSTEMS WOULD NOT RECOVER QUICKLY.
INDEED, THE PERSON WHO DIED AFTER A SINGLE HOUR MIGHT BE CONSIDERED LUCKIER THAN THE SELF-HEALER WHO WOULD HAVE TO ENDURE A DAY OR MORE.
A DAY OR MORE OF BLOOD-####.
YES, I CAN SEE IT QUITE CLEARLY NOW, THE FORM OF THIS VIRUS, ITS COMPONENTS. IN THIS, I AM SERVED WELL BY THE YEARS OF ISOLATION IN MY UNCLE'S LABORATORY.
DEEP MEDITATION AND FOCUS ARE SKILLS BEST MASTERED IN SOLITUDE.

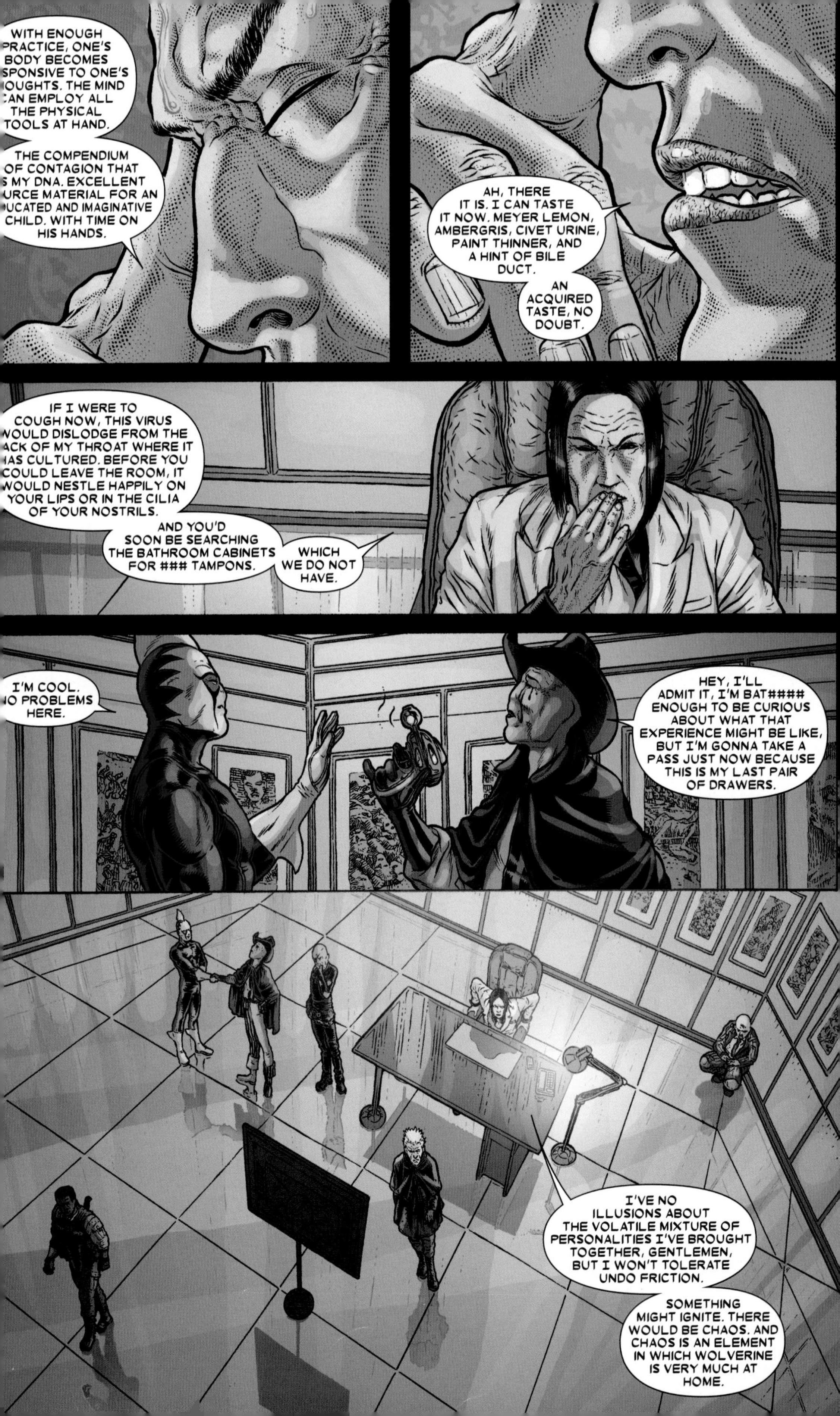
WITH ENOUGH PRACTICE, ONE'S BODY BECOMES SPONSIVE TO ONE'S OUGHTS. THE MIND CAN EMPLOY ALL THE PHYSICAL TOOLS AT HAND.
THE COMPENDIUM OF CONTAGION THAT S MY DNA. EXCELLENT URCE MATERIAL FOR AN UCATED AND IMAGINATIVE CHILD. WITH TIME ON HIS HANDS.
AH, THERE IT IS. I CAN TASTE IT NOW. MEYER LEMON, AMBERGRIS, CIVET URINE, PAINT THINNER, AND A HINT OF BILE DUCT.
AN ACQUIRED TASTE, NO DOUBT.
IF I WERE TO COUGH NOW, THIS VIRUS WOULD DISLODGE FROM THE ACK OF MY THROAT WHERE IT HAS CULTURED. BEFORE YOU COULD LEAVE THE ROOM, IT WOULD NESTLE HAPPILY ON YOUR LIPS OR IN THE CILIA OF YOUR NOSTRILS.
AND YOU'D SOON BE SEARCHING THE BATHROOM CABINETS FOR ### TAMPONS.
WHICH WE DO NOT HAVE.
I'M COOL. NO PROBLEMS HERE.
HEY, I'LL ADMIT IT, I'M BAT#### ENOUGH TO BE CURIOUS ABOUT WHAT THAT EXPERIENCE MIGHT BE LIKE, BUT I'M GONNA TAKE A PASS JUST NOW BECAUSE THIS IS MY LAST PAIR OF DRAWERS.
I'VE NO ILLUSIONS ABOUT THE VOLATILE MIXTURE OF PERSONALITIES I'VE BROUGHT TOGETHER, GENTLEMEN, BUT I WON'T TOLERATE UNDO FRICTION.
SOMETHING MIGHT IGNITE. THERE WOULD BE CHAOS. AND CHAOS IS AN ELEMENT IN WHICH WOLVERINE IS VERY MUCH AT HOME.

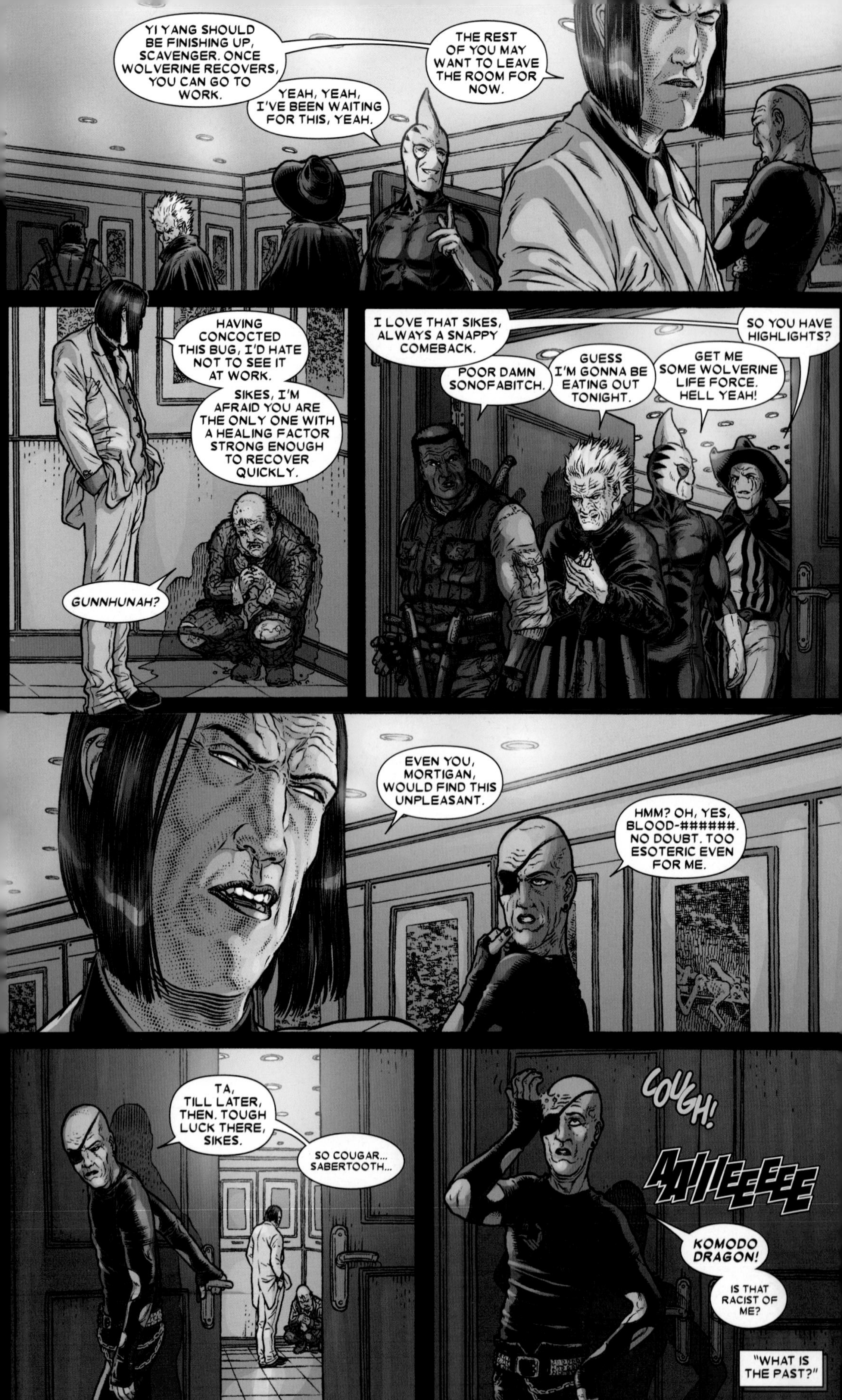
YI YANG SHOULD BE FINISHING UP, SCAVENGER. ONCE WOLVERINE RECOVERS, YOU CAN GO TO WORK.
THE REST OF YOU MAY WANT TO LEAVE THE ROOM FOR NOW.
YEAH, YEAH, I'VE BEEN WAITING FOR THIS, YEAH.
HAVING CONCOCTED THIS BUG, I'D HATE NOT TO SEE IT AT WORK.
SIKES, I'M AFRAID YOU ARE THE ONLY ONE WITH A HEALING FACTOR STRONG ENOUGH TO RECOVER QUICKLY.
GUNNHUNAH?
I LOVE THAT SIKES, ALWAYS A SNAPPY COMEBACK.
SO YOU HAVE HIGHLIGHTS?
POOR DAMN SONOFABITCH.
GUESS I'M GONNA BE EATING OUT TONIGHT.
GET ME SOME WOLVERINE LIFE FORCE. HELL YEAH!
EVEN YOU, MORTIGAN, WOULD FIND THIS UNPLEASANT.
HMM? OH, YES, BLOOD-######. NO DOUBT. TOO ESOTERIC EVEN FOR ME.
TA, TILL LATER, THEN. TOUGH LUCK THERE, SIKES.
SO COUGAR... SABERTOOTH...
COUGH!
AAIIEEEEE
KOMODO DRAGON!
IS THAT RACIST OF ME?
"WHAT IS THE PAST?"

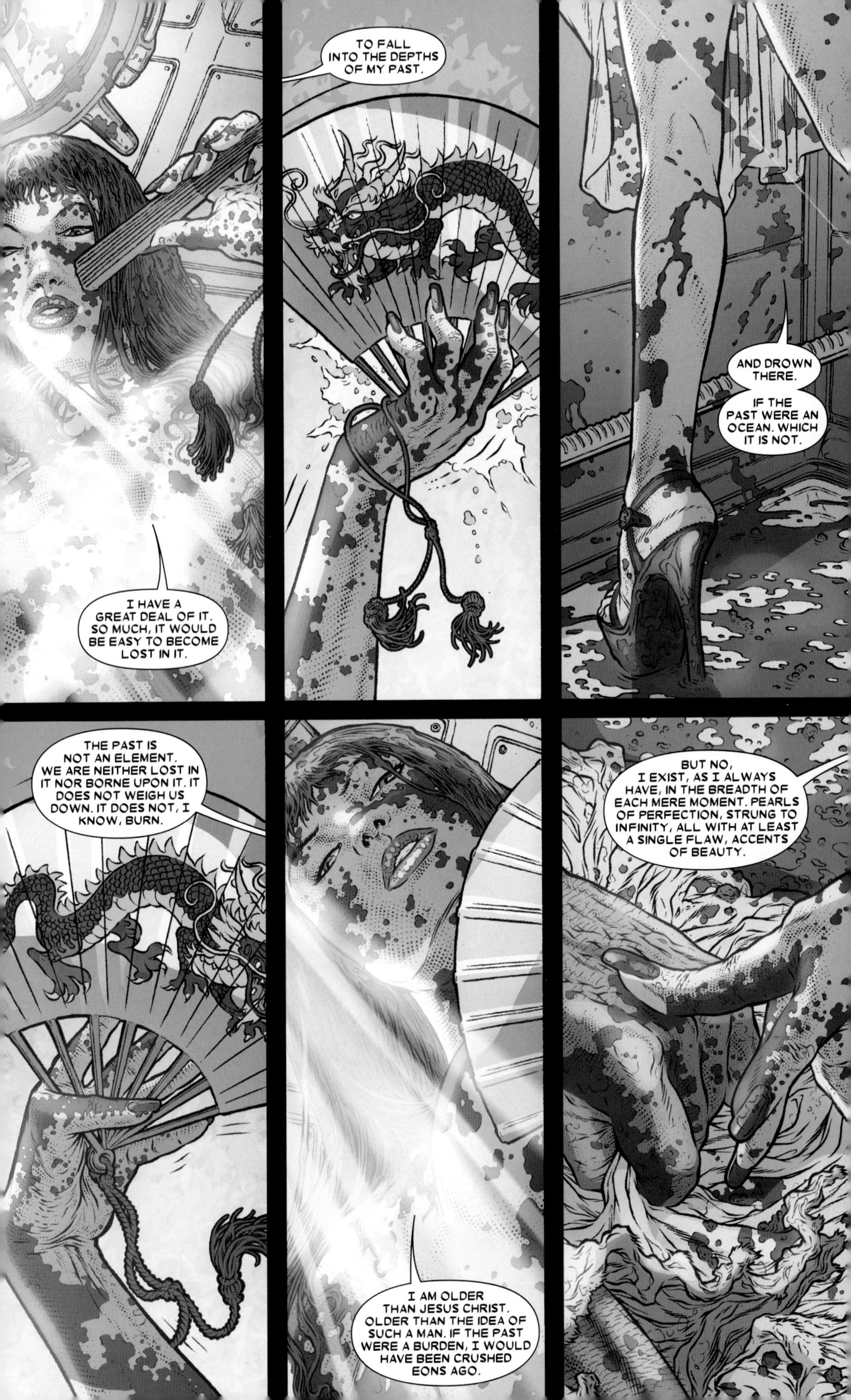
I HAVE A GREAT DEAL OF IT. SO MUCH, IT WOULD BE EASY TO BECOME LOST IN IT.
TO FALL INTO THE DEPTHS OF MY PAST.
AND DROWN THERE.
IF THE PAST WERE AN OCEAN. WHICH IT IS NOT.
THE PAST IS NOT AN ELEMENT. WE ARE NEITHER LOST IN IT NOR BORNE UPON IT. IT DOES NOT WEIGH US DOWN. IT DOES NOT, I KNOW, BURN.
I AM OLDER THAN JESUS CHRIST. OLDER THAN THE IDEA OF SUCH A MAN. IF THE PAST WERE A BURDEN, I WOULD HAVE BEEN CRUSHED EONS AGO.
BUT NO, I EXIST, AS I ALWAYS HAVE, IN THE BREADTH OF EACH MERE MOMENT. PEARLS OF PERFECTION, STRUNG TO INFINITY, ALL WITH AT LEAST A SINGLE FLAW, ACCENTS OF BEAUTY.

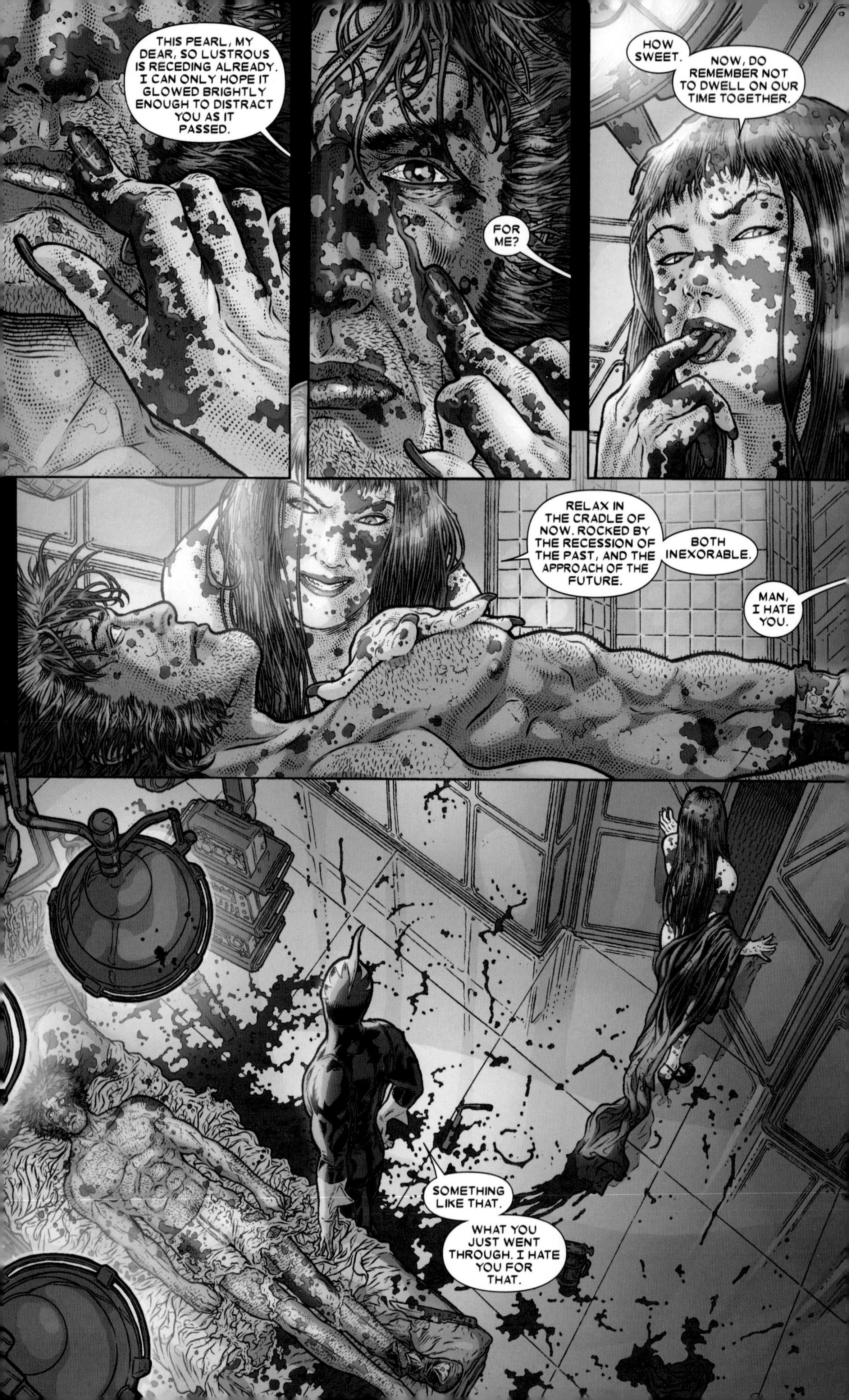
THIS PEARL, MY DEAR, SO LUSTROUS IS RECEDING ALREADY. I CAN ONLY HOPE IT GLOWED BRIGHTLY ENOUGH TO DISTRACT YOU AS IT PASSED.
FOR ME?
HOW SWEET.
NOW, DO REMEMBER NOT TO DWELL ON OUR TIME TOGETHER.
RELAX IN THE CRADLE OF NOW. ROCKED BY THE RECESSION OF THE PAST, AND THE APPROACH OF THE FUTURE.
BOTH INEXORABLE.
MAN, I HATE YOU.
SOMETHING LIKE THAT.
WHAT YOU JUST WENT THROUGH. I HATE YOU FOR THAT.

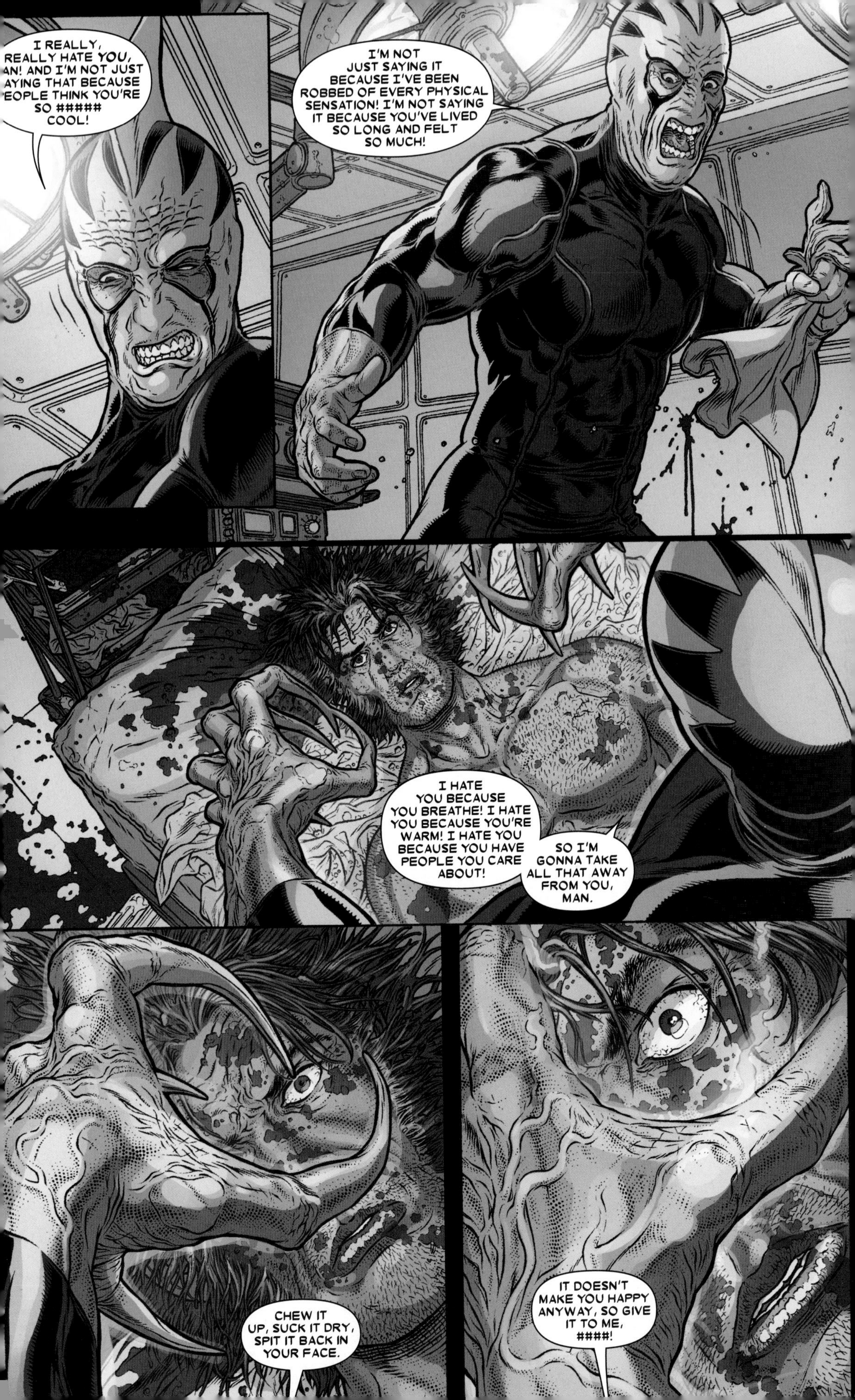
I REALLY, REALLY HATE YOU, AN! AND I'M NOT JUST AYING THAT BECAUSE EOPLE THINK YOU'RE SO ##### COOL!
I'M NOT JUST SAYING IT BECAUSE I'VE BEEN ROBBED OF EVERY PHYSICAL SENSATION! I'M NOT SAYING IT BECAUSE YOU'VE LIVED SO LONG AND FELT SO MUCH!
I HATE YOU BECAUSE YOU BREATHE! I HATE YOU BECAUSE YOU'RE WARM! I HATE YOU BECAUSE YOU HAVE PEOPLE YOU CARE ABOUT!
SO I'M GONNA TAKE ALL THAT AWAY FROM YOU, MAN.
CHEW IT UP, SUCK IT DRY, SPIT IT BACK IN YOUR FACE.
IT DOESN'T MAKE YOU HAPPY ANYWAY, SO GIVE IT TO ME, ####!

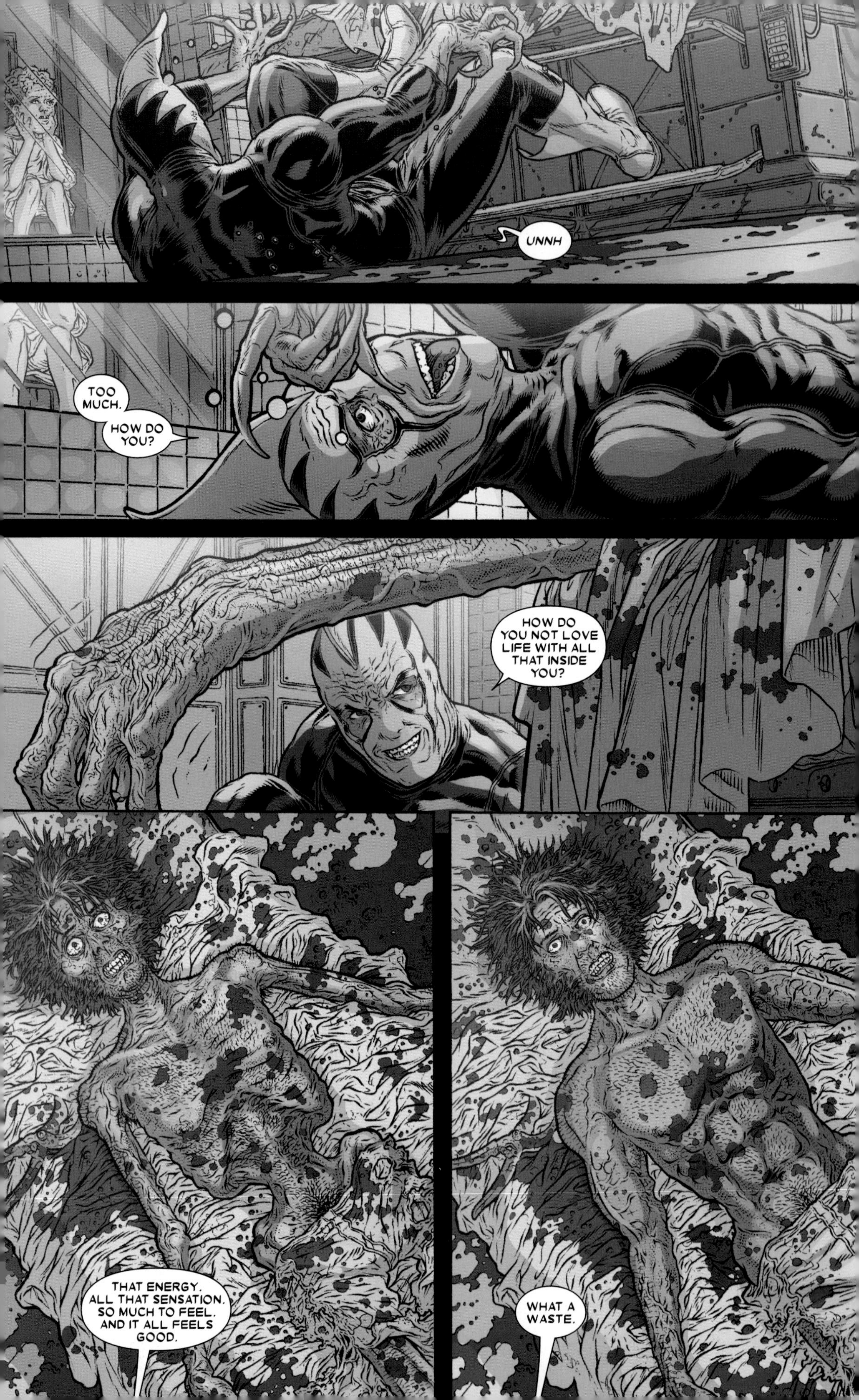
UNNH
TOO MUCH.
HOW DO YOU?
HOW DO YOU NOT LOVE LIFE WITH ALL THAT INSIDE YOU?
THAT ENERGY. ALL THAT SENSATION. SO MUCH TO FEEL. AND IT ALL FEELS GOOD.
WHAT A WASTE.

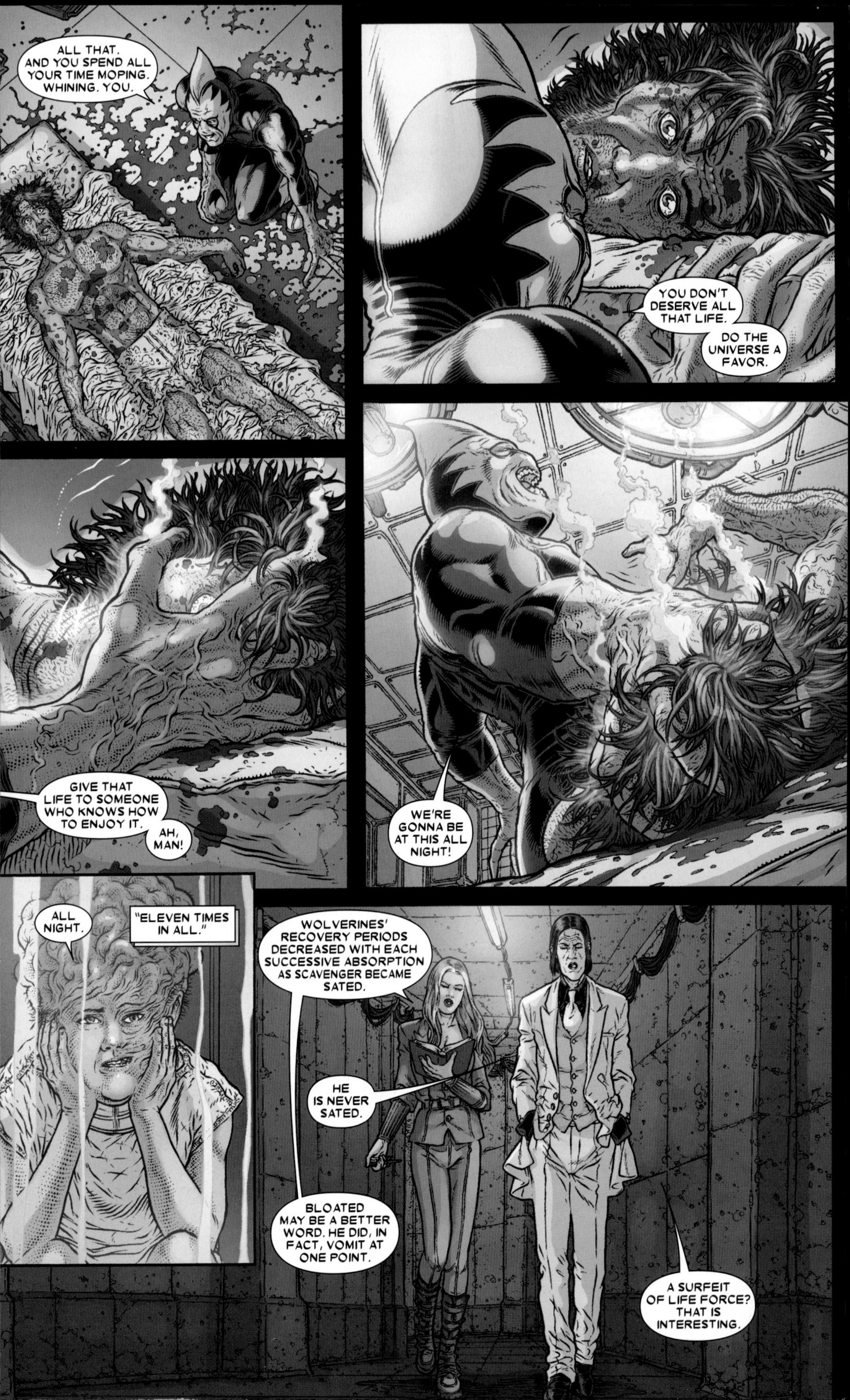
ALL THAT. AND YOU SPEND ALL YOUR TIME MOPING. WHINING. YOU.
YOU DON'T DESERVE ALL THAT LIFE.
DO THE UNIVERSE A FAVOR.
GIVE THAT LIFE TO SOMEONE WHO KNOWS HOW TO ENJOY IT.
AH, MAN!
WE'RE GONNA BE AT THIS ALL NIGHT!
ALL NIGHT.
"ELEVEN TIMES IN ALL."
WOLVERINES' RECOVERY PERIODS DECREASED WITH EACH SUCCESSIVE ABSORPTION AS SCAVENGER BECAME SATED.
HE IS NEVER SATED.
BLOATED MAY BE A BETTER WORD. HE DID, IN FACT, VOMIT AT ONE POINT.
A SURFEIT OF LIFE FORCE? THAT IS INTERESTING.

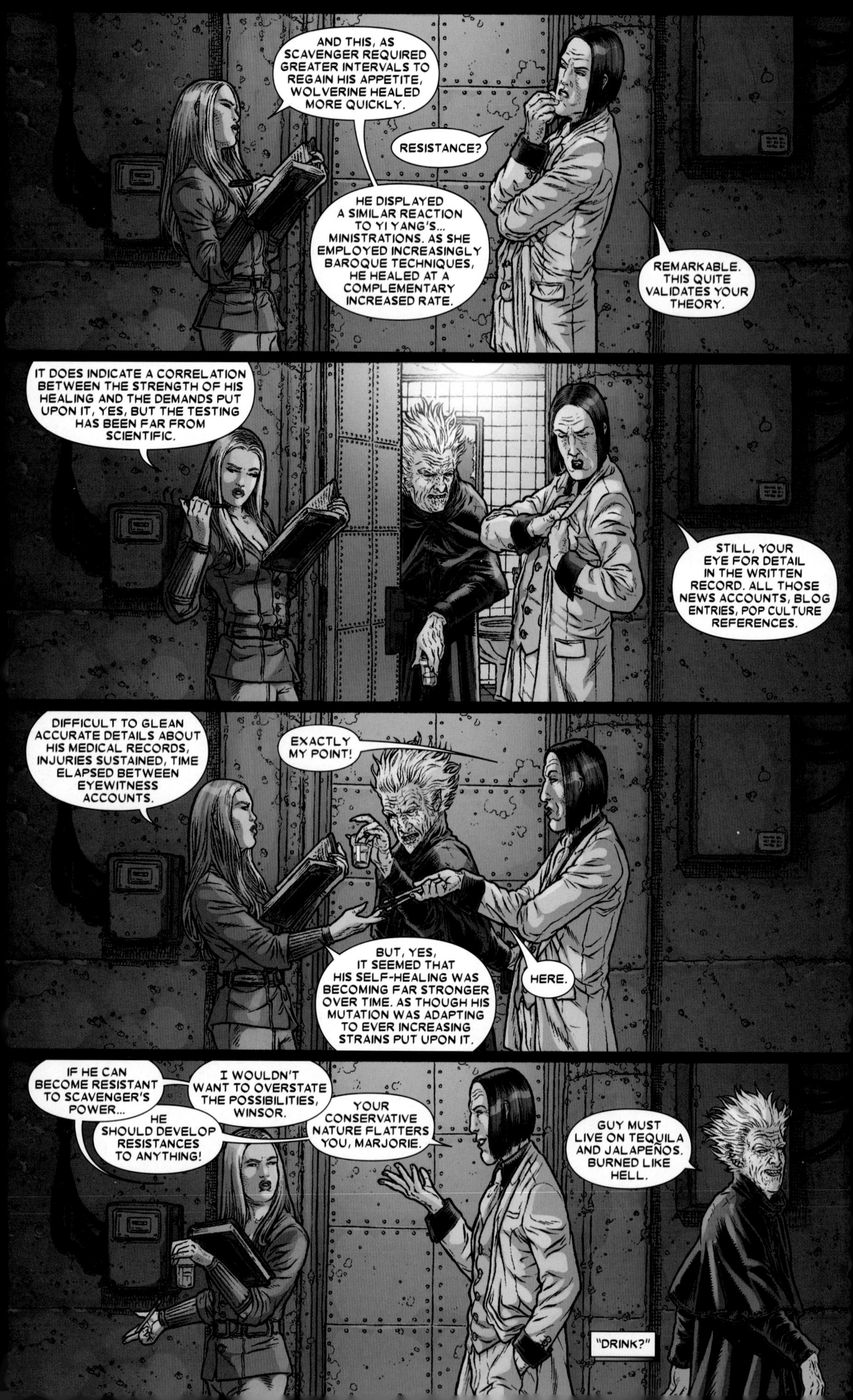
AND THIS, AS SCAVENGER REQUIRED GREATER INTERVALS TO REGAIN HIS APPETITE, WOLVERINE HEALED MORE QUICKLY.
RESISTANCE?
HE DISPLAYED A SIMILAR REACTION TO YI YANG'S... MINISTRATIONS. AS SHE EMPLOYED INCREASINGLY BAROQUE TECHNIQUES, HE HEALED AT A COMPLEMENTARY INCREASED RATE.
REMARKABLE. THIS QUITE VALIDATES YOUR THEORY.
IT DOES INDICATE A CORRELATION BETWEEN THE STRENGTH OF HIS HEALING AND THE DEMANDS PUT UPON IT, YES, BUT THE TESTING HAS BEEN FAR FROM SCIENTIFIC.
STILL, YOUR EYE FOR DETAIL IN THE WRITTEN RECORD. ALL THOSE NEWS ACCOUNTS, BLOG ENTRIES, POP CULTURE REFERENCES.
DIFFICULT TO GLEAN ACCURATE DETAILS ABOUT HIS MEDICAL RECORDS, INJURIES SUSTAINED, TIME ELAPSED BETWEEN EYEWITNESS ACCOUNTS.
EXACTLY MY POINT!
BUT, YES, IT SEEMED THAT HIS SELF-HEALING WAS BECOMING FAR STRONGER OVER TIME. AS THOUGH HIS MUTATION WAS ADAPTING TO EVER INCREASING STRAINS PUT UPON IT.
HERE.
IF HE CAN BECOME RESISTANT TO SCAVENGER'S POWER...
I WOULDN'T WANT TO OVERSTATE THE POSSIBILITIES, WINSOR.
HE SHOULD DEVELOP RESISTANCES TO ANYTHING!
YOUR CONSERVATIVE NATURE FLATTERS YOU, MARJORIE.
GUY MUST LIVE ON TEQUILA AND JALAPEÑOS. BURNED LIKE HELL.
"DRINK?"

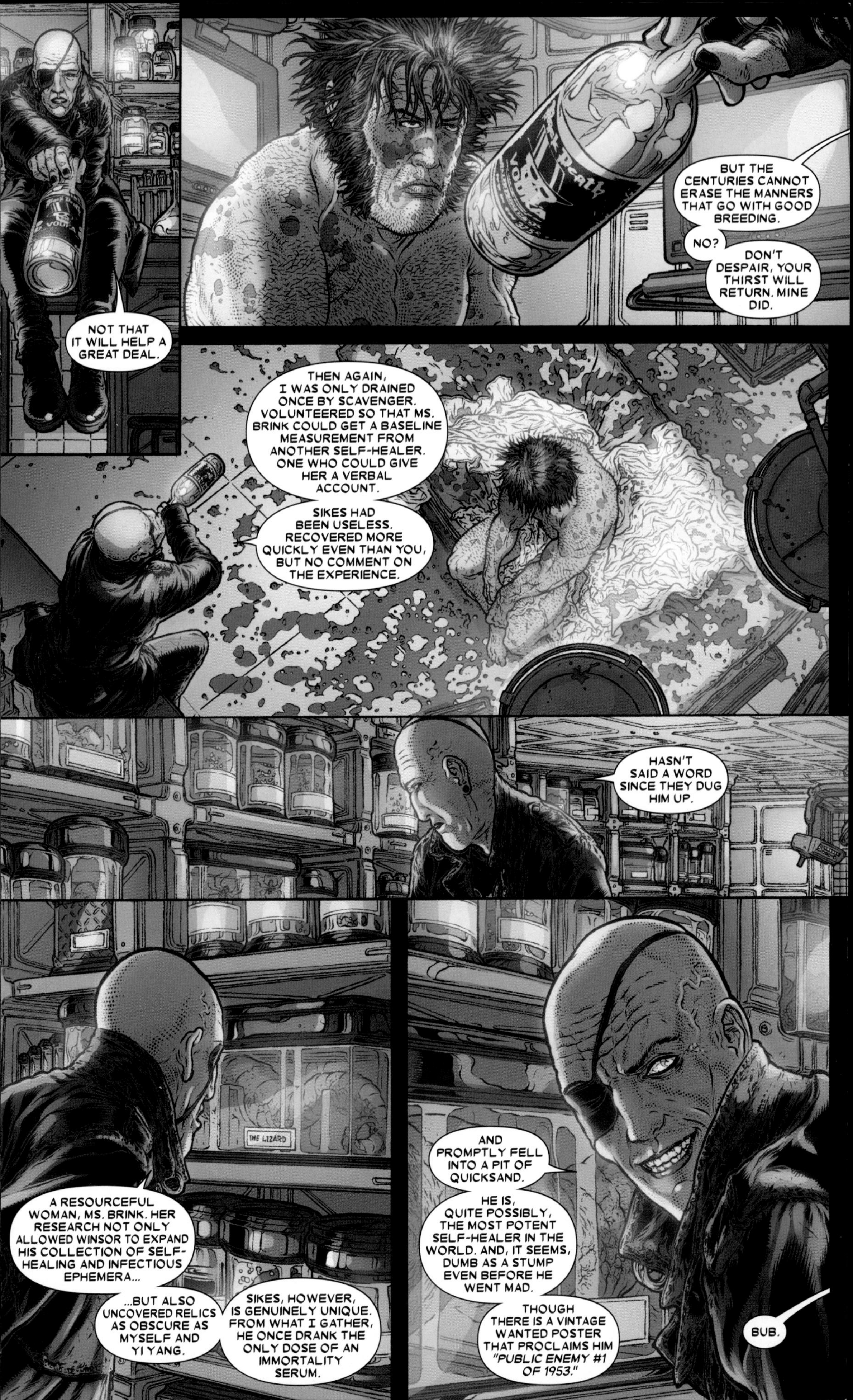
BUT THE CENTURIES CANNOT ERASE THE MANNERS THAT GO WITH GOOD BREEDING.
NO?
DON'T DESPAIR, YOUR THIRST WILL RETURN. MINE DID.
NOT THAT IT WILL HELP A GREAT DEAL.
THEN AGAIN, I WAS ONLY DRAINED ONCE BY SCAVENGER. VOLUNTEERED SO THAT MS. BRINK COULD GET A BASELINE MEASUREMENT FROM ANOTHER SELF-HEALER. ONE WHO COULD GIVE HER A VERBAL ACCOUNT.
SIKES HAD BEEN USELESS. RECOVERED MORE QUICKLY EVEN THAN YOU, BUT NO COMMENT ON THE EXPERIENCE.
HASN'T SAID A WORD SINCE THEY DUG HIM UP.
THE LIZARD
A RESOURCEFUL WOMAN, MS. BRINK. HER RESEARCH NOT ONLY ALLOWED WINSOR TO EXPAND HIS COLLECTION OF SELF-HEALING AND INFECTIOUS EPHEMERA...
...BUT ALSO UNCOVERED RELICS AS OBSCURE AS MYSELF AND YI YANG.
SIKES, HOWEVER, IS GENUINELY UNIQUE. FROM WHAT I GATHER, HE ONCE DRANK THE ONLY DOSE OF AN IMMORTALITY SERUM.
AND PROMPTLY FELL INTO A PIT OF QUICKSAND.
HE IS, QUITE POSSIBLY, THE MOST POTENT SELF-HEALER IN THE WORLD. AND, IT SEEMS, DUMB AS A STUMP EVEN BEFORE HE WENT MAD.
THOUGH THERE IS A VINTAGE WANTED POSTER THAT PROCLAIMS HIM *"PUBLIC ENEMY #1 OF 1953."*
BUB.

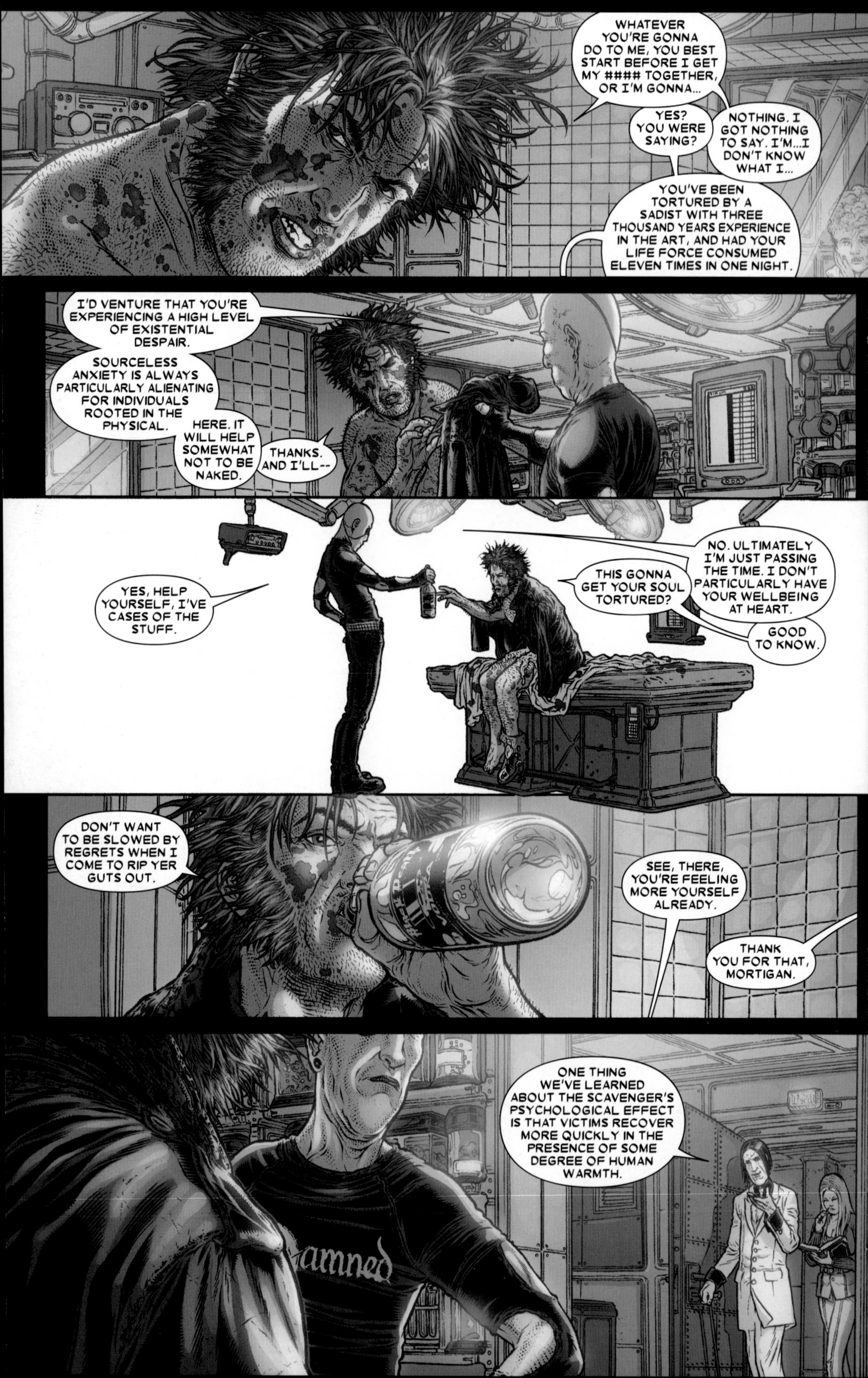
WHATEVER YOU'RE GONNA DO TO ME, YOU BEST START BEFORE I GET MY #### TOGETHER, OR I'M GONNA...
YES? YOU WERE SAYING?
NOTHING. I GOT NOTHING TO SAY. I'M...I DON'T KNOW WHAT I...
YOU'VE BEEN TORTURED BY A SADIST WITH THREE THOUSAND YEARS EXPERIENCE IN THE ART, AND HAD YOUR LIFE FORCE CONSUMED ELEVEN TIMES IN ONE NIGHT.
I'D VENTURE THAT YOU'RE EXPERIENCING A HIGH LEVEL OF EXISTENTIAL DESPAIR.
SOURCELESS ANXIETY IS ALWAYS PARTICULARLY ALIENATING FOR INDIVIDUALS ROOTED IN THE PHYSICAL.
HERE. IT WILL HELP SOMEWHAT NOT TO BE NAKED.
THANKS. AND I'LL--
YES, HELP YOURSELF, I'VE CASES OF THE STUFF.
THIS GONNA GET YOUR SOUL TORTURED?
NO. ULTIMATELY I'M JUST PASSING THE TIME. I DON'T PARTICULARLY HAVE YOUR WELLBEING AT HEART.
GOOD TO KNOW.
DON'T WANT TO BE SLOWED BY REGRETS WHEN I COME TO RIP YER GUTS OUT.
SEE, THERE, YOU'RE FEELING MORE YOURSELF ALREADY.
THANK YOU FOR THAT, MORTIGAN.
ONE THING WE'VE LEARNED ABOUT THE SCAVENGER'S PSYCHOLOGICAL EFFECT IS THAT VICTIMS RECOVER MORE QUICKLY IN THE PRESENCE OF SOME DEGREE OF HUMAN WARMTH.

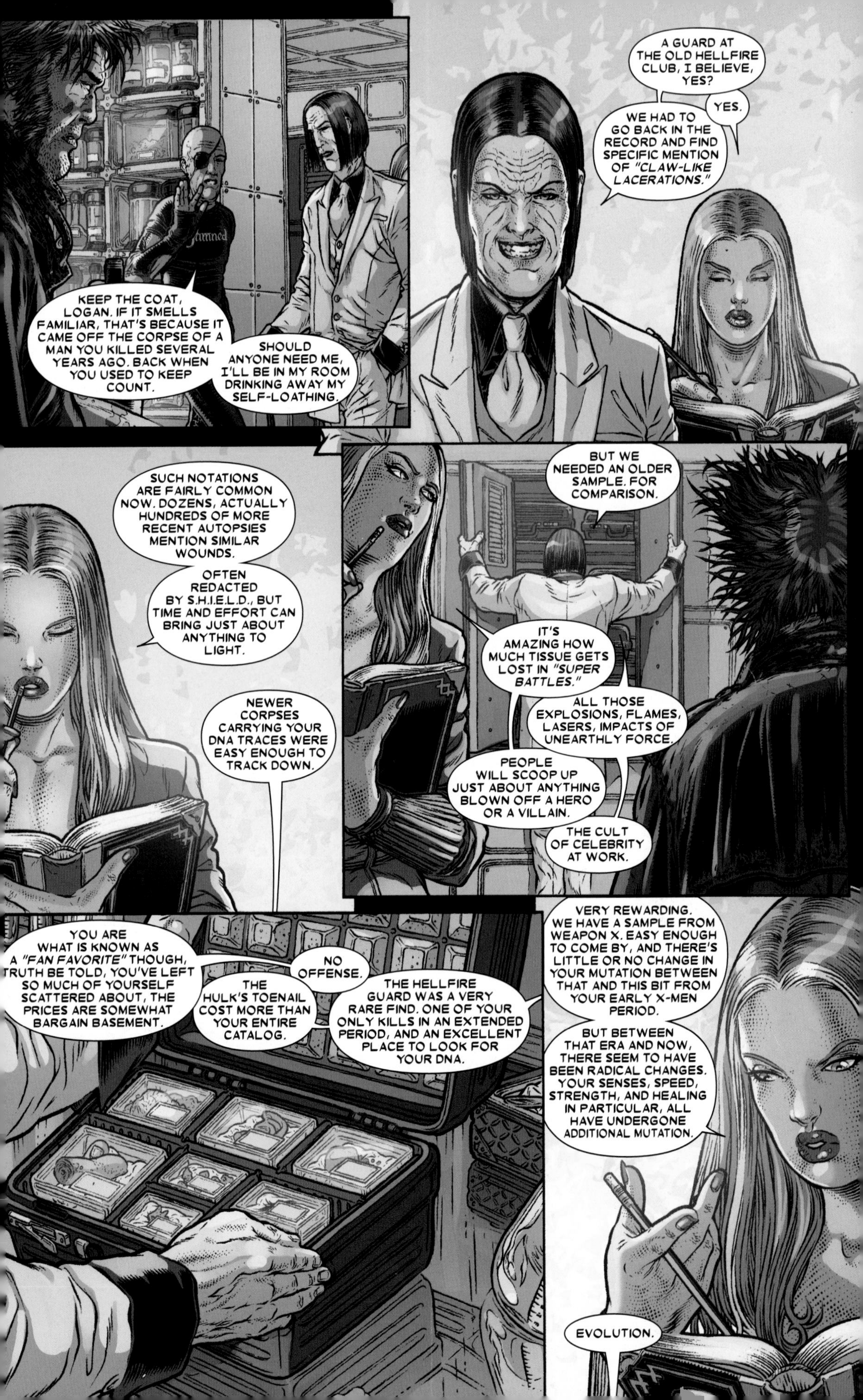

KEEP THE COAT, LOGAN. IF IT SMELLS FAMILIAR, THAT'S BECAUSE IT CAME OFF THE CORPSE OF A MAN YOU KILLED SEVERAL YEARS AGO. BACK WHEN YOU USED TO KEEP COUNT.
SHOULD ANYONE NEED ME, I'LL BE IN MY ROOM DRINKING AWAY MY SELF-LOATHING.
A GUARD AT THE OLD HELLFIRE CLUB, I BELIEVE, YES?
YES.
WE HAD TO GO BACK IN THE RECORD AND FIND SPECIFIC MENTION OF "CLAW-LIKE LACERATIONS."
SUCH NOTATIONS ARE FAIRLY COMMON NOW. DOZENS, ACTUALLY HUNDREDS OF MORE RECENT AUTOPSIES MENTION SIMILAR WOUNDS.
OFTEN REDACTED BY S.H.I.E.L.D., BUT TIME AND EFFORT CAN BRING JUST ABOUT ANYTHING TO LIGHT.
NEWER CORPSES CARRYING YOUR DNA TRACES WERE EASY ENOUGH TO TRACK DOWN.
BUT WE NEEDED AN OLDER SAMPLE. FOR COMPARISON.
IT'S AMAZING HOW MUCH TISSUE GETS LOST IN "SUPER BATTLES."
ALL THOSE EXPLOSIONS, FLAMES, LASERS, IMPACTS OF UNEARTHLY FORCE.
PEOPLE WILL SCOOP UP JUST ABOUT ANYTHING BLOWN OFF A HERO OR A VILLAIN.
THE CULT OF CELEBRITY AT WORK.
YOU ARE WHAT IS KNOWN AS A "FAN FAVORITE" THOUGH, TRUTH BE TOLD, YOU'VE LEFT SO MUCH OF YOURSELF SCATTERED ABOUT, THE PRICES ARE SOMEWHAT BARGAIN BASEMENT.
NO OFFENSE.
THE HULK'S TOENAIL COST MORE THAN YOUR ENTIRE CATALOG.
THE HELLFIRE GUARD WAS A VERY RARE FIND. ONE OF YOUR ONLY KILLS IN AN EXTENDED PERIOD, AND AN EXCELLENT PLACE TO LOOK FOR YOUR DNA.
VERY REWARDING. WE HAVE A SAMPLE FROM WEAPON X. EASY ENOUGH TO COME BY, AND THERE'S LITTLE OR NO CHANGE IN YOUR MUTATION BETWEEN THAT AND THIS BIT FROM YOUR EARLY X-MEN PERIOD.
BUT BETWEEN THAT ERA AND NOW, THERE SEEM TO HAVE BEEN RADICAL CHANGES. YOUR SENSES, SPEED, STRENGTH, AND HEALING IN PARTICULAR, ALL HAVE UNDERGONE ADDITIONAL MUTATION.
EVOLUTION.

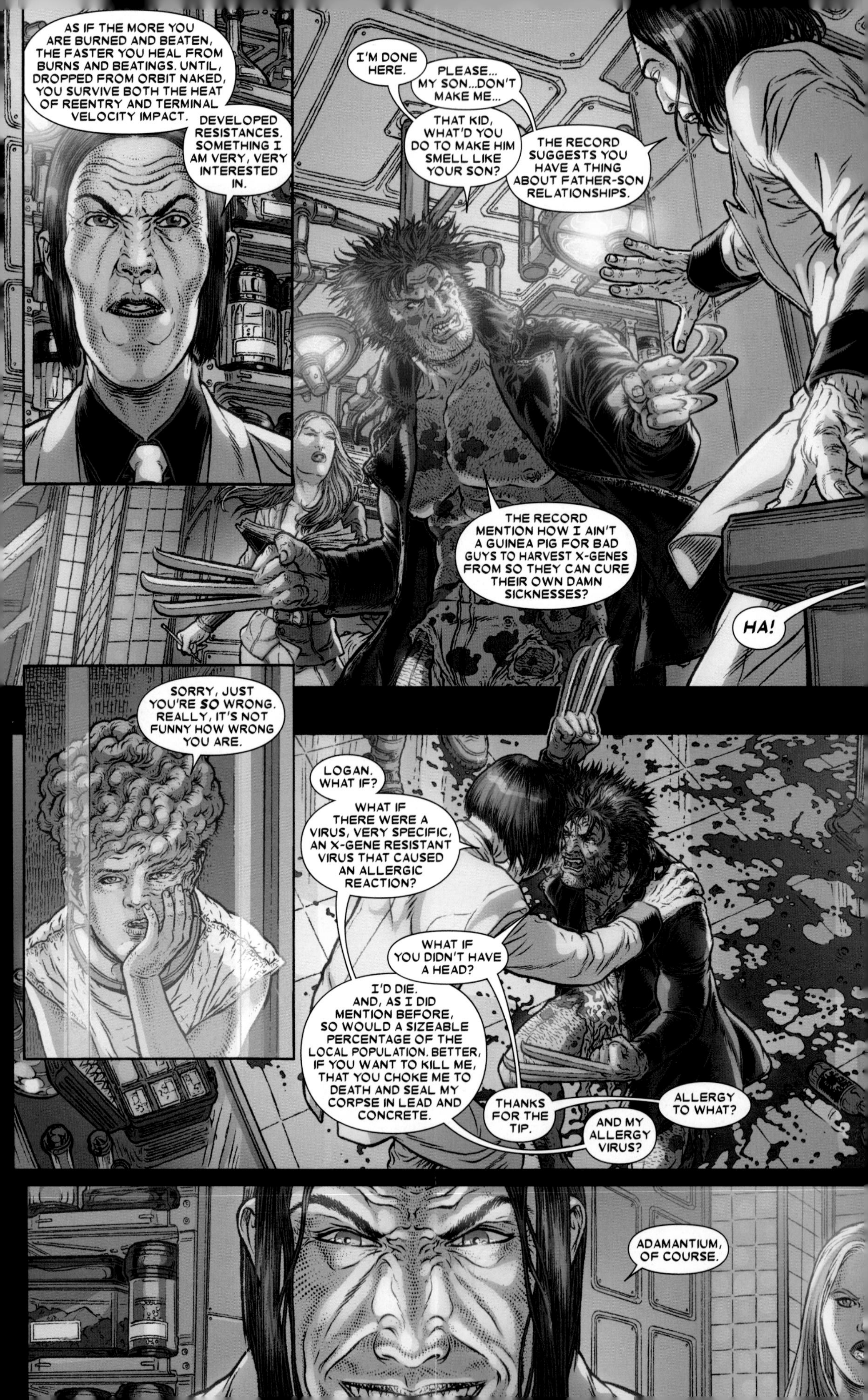
AS IF THE MORE YOU ARE BURNED AND BEATEN, THE FASTER YOU HEAL FROM BURNS AND BEATINGS. UNTIL, DROPPED FROM ORBIT NAKED, YOU SURVIVE BOTH THE HEAT OF REENTRY AND TERMINAL VELOCITY IMPACT.
DEVELOPED RESISTANCES. SOMETHING I AM VERY, VERY INTERESTED IN.
I'M DONE HERE.
PLEASE... MY SON...DON'T MAKE ME...
THAT KID, WHAT'D YOU DO TO MAKE HIM SMELL LIKE YOUR SON?
THE RECORD SUGGESTS YOU HAVE A THING ABOUT FATHER-SON RELATIONSHIPS.
THE RECORD MENTION HOW I AIN'T A GUINEA PIG FOR BAD GUYS TO HARVEST X-GENES FROM SO THEY CAN CURE THEIR OWN DAMN SICKNESSES?
HA!
SORRY, JUST YOU'RE SO WRONG. REALLY, IT'S NOT FUNNY HOW WRONG YOU ARE.
LOGAN. WHAT IF?
WHAT IF THERE WERE A VIRUS, VERY SPECIFIC, AN X-GENE RESISTANT VIRUS THAT CAUSED AN ALLERGIC REACTION?
WHAT IF YOU DIDN'T HAVE A HEAD?
I'D DIE. AND, AS I DID MENTION BEFORE, SO WOULD A SIZEABLE PERCENTAGE OF THE LOCAL POPULATION. BETTER, IF YOU WANT TO KILL ME, THAT YOU CHOKE ME TO DEATH AND SEAL MY CORPSE IN LEAD AND CONCRETE.
THANKS FOR THE TIP.
AND MY ALLERGY VIRUS?
ALLERGY TO WHAT?
ADAMANTIUM, OF COURSE.

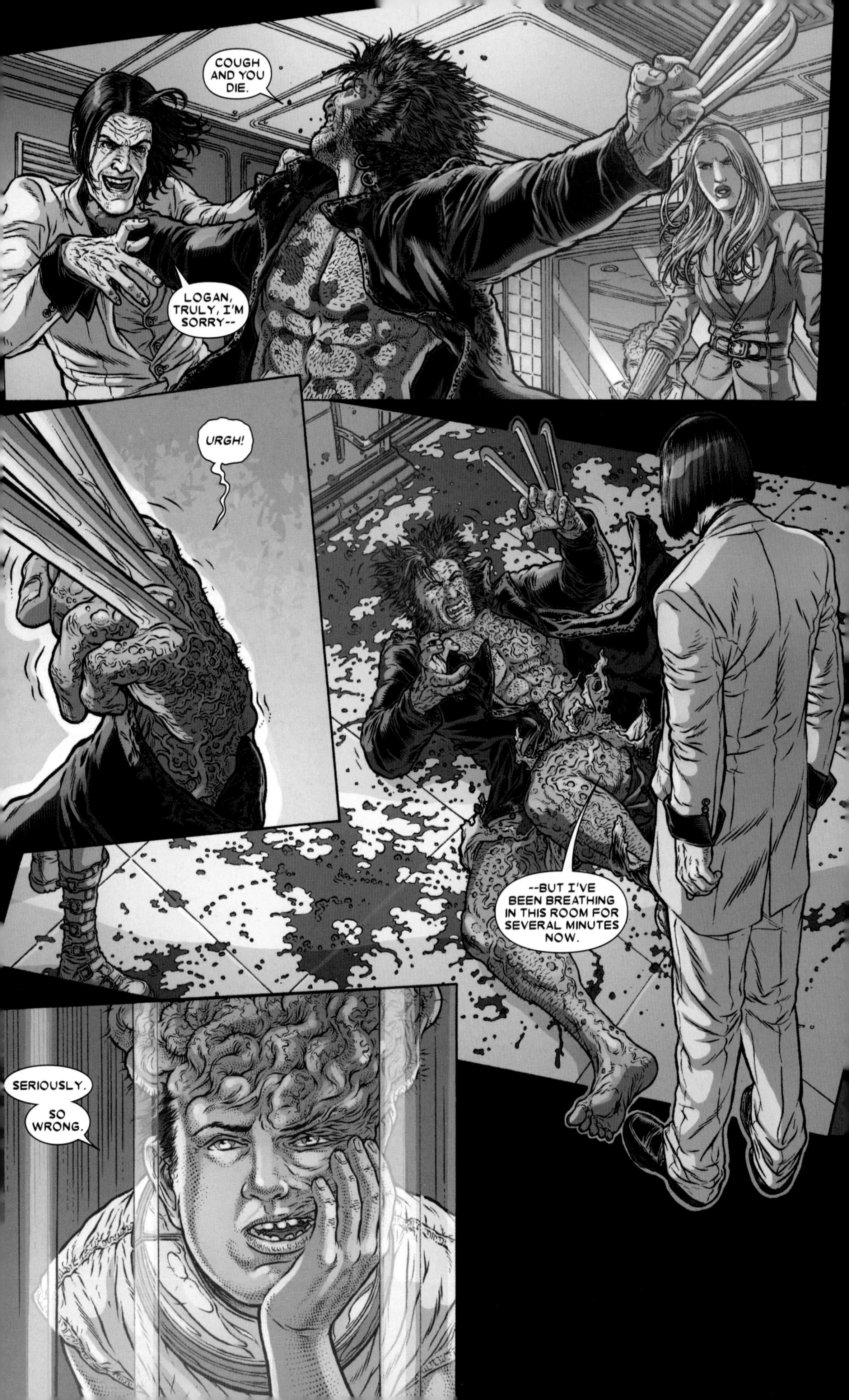
COUGH AND YOU DIE.
LOGAN, TRULY, I'M SORRY--
URGH!
--BUT I'VE BEEN BREATHING IN THIS ROOM FOR SEVERAL MINUTES NOW.
SERIOUSLY.
SO WRONG.

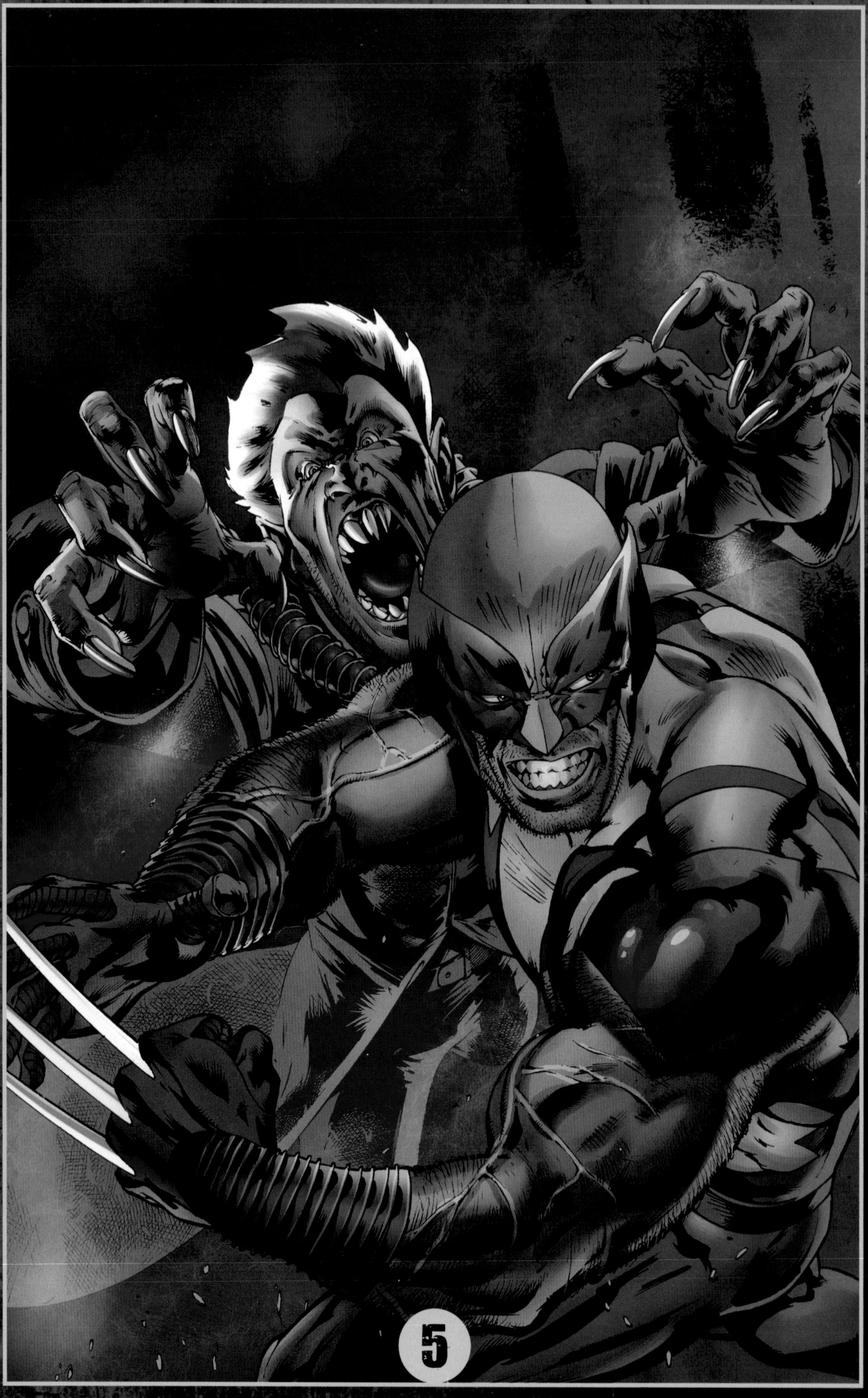
5

CHAPTER FIVE

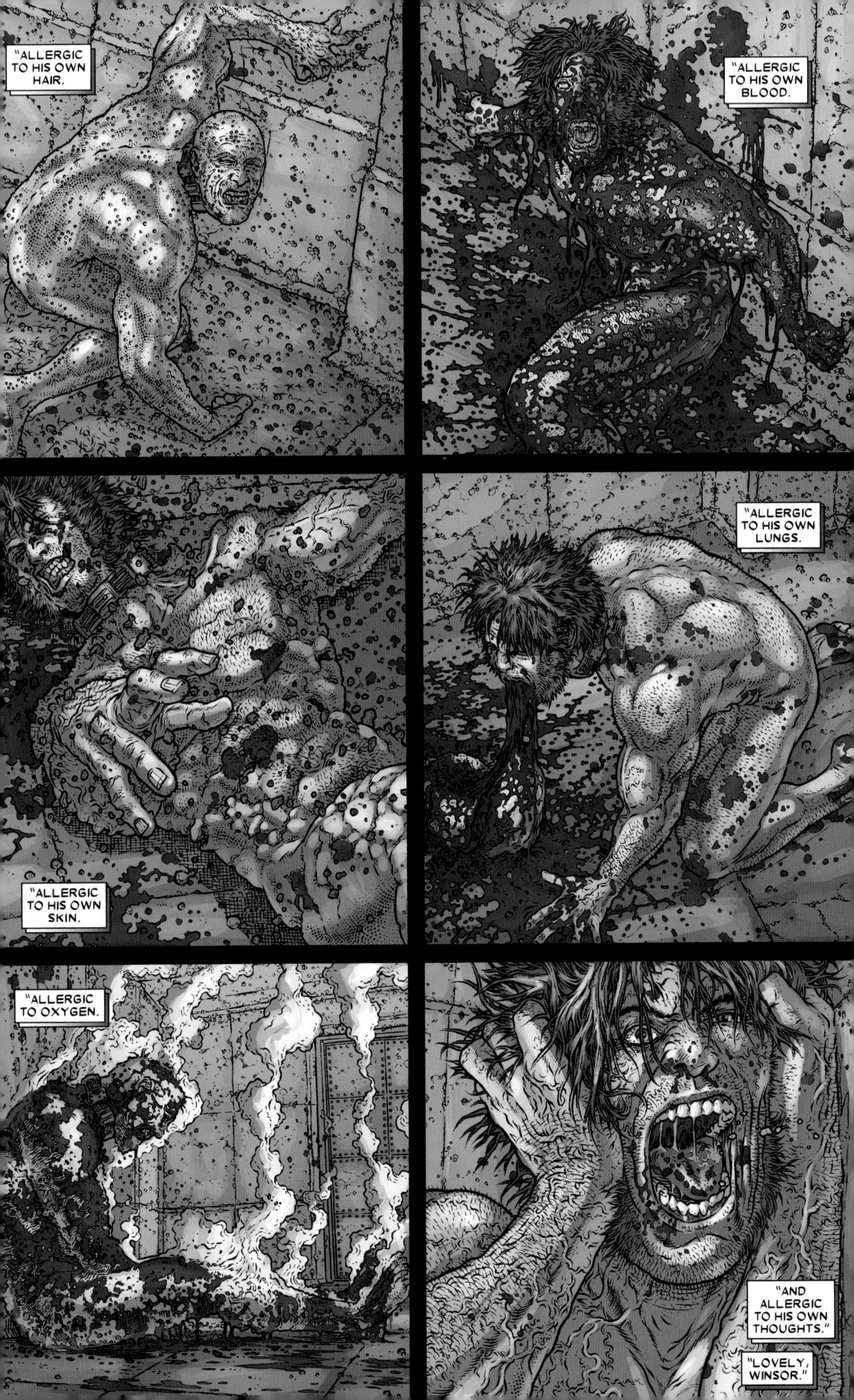
"ALLERGIC TO HIS OWN HAIR.
"ALLERGIC TO HIS OWN BLOOD.
"ALLERGIC TO HIS OWN SKIN.
"ALLERGIC TO HIS OWN LUNGS.
"ALLERGIC TO OXYGEN.
"AND ALLERGIC TO HIS OWN THOUGHTS."
"LOVELY, WINSOR."

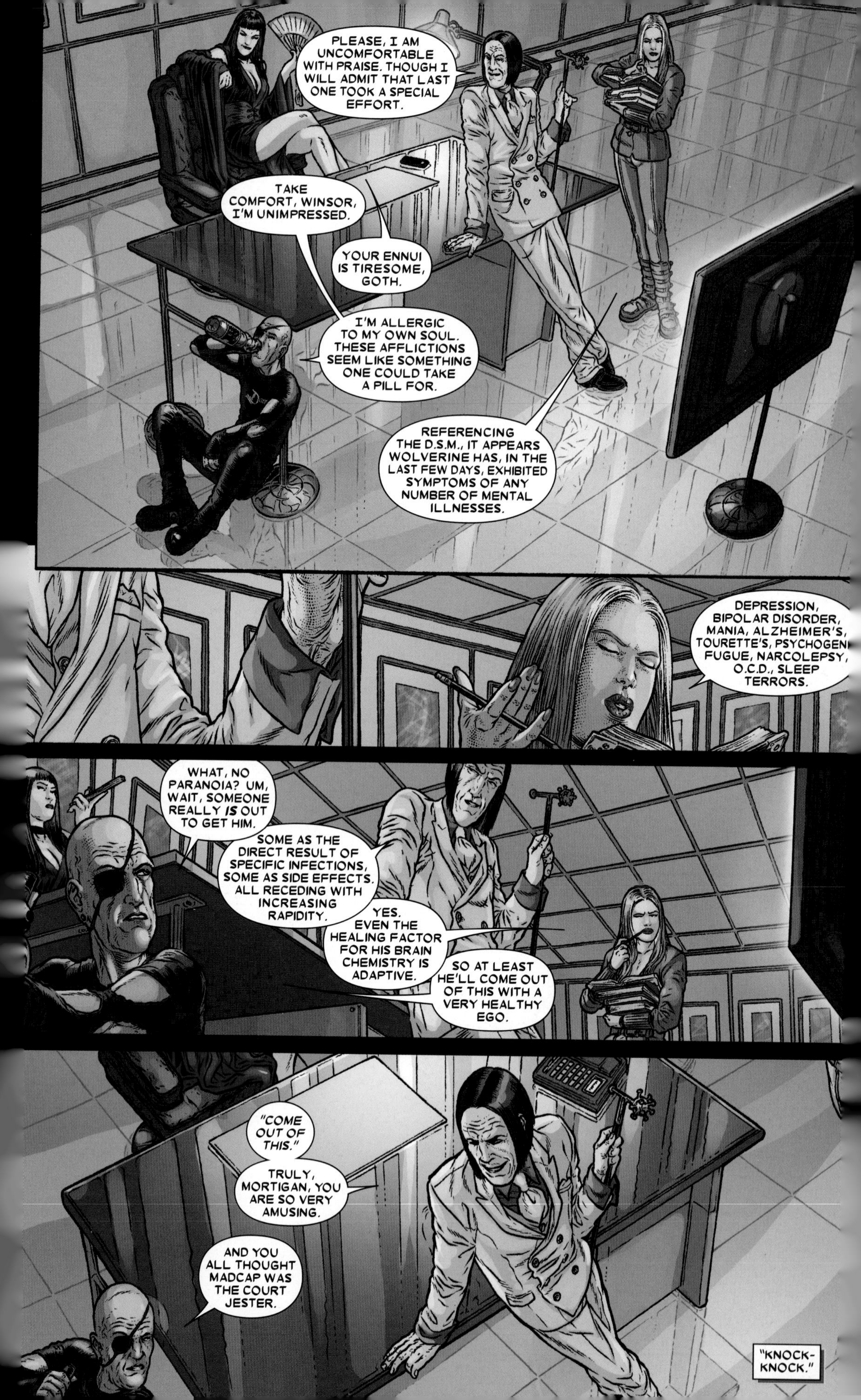
PLEASE, I AM UNCOMFORTABLE WITH PRAISE. THOUGH I WILL ADMIT THAT LAST ONE TOOK A SPECIAL EFFORT.
TAKE COMFORT, WINSOR, I'M UNIMPRESSED.
YOUR ENNUI IS TIRESOME, GOTH.
I'M ALLERGIC TO MY OWN SOUL. THESE AFFLICTIONS SEEM LIKE SOMETHING ONE COULD TAKE A PILL FOR.
REFERENCING THE D.S.M., IT APPEARS WOLVERINE HAS, IN THE LAST FEW DAYS, EXHIBITED SYMPTOMS OF ANY NUMBER OF MENTAL ILLNESSES.
DEPRESSION, BIPOLAR DISORDER, MANIA, ALZHEIMER'S, TOURETTE'S, PSYCHOGEN FUGUE, NARCOLEPSY, O.C.D., SLEEP TERRORS.
WHAT, NO PARANOIA? UM, WAIT, SOMEONE REALLY *IS* OUT TO GET HIM.
SOME AS THE DIRECT RESULT OF SPECIFIC INFECTIONS, SOME AS SIDE EFFECTS. ALL RECEDING WITH INCREASING RAPIDITY.
YES. EVEN THE HEALING FACTOR FOR HIS BRAIN CHEMISTRY IS ADAPTIVE.
SO AT LEAST HE'LL COME OUT OF THIS WITH A VERY HEALTHY EGO.
"COME OUT OF THIS."
TRULY, MORTIGAN, YOU ARE SO VERY AMUSING.
AND YOU ALL THOUGHT MADCAP WAS THE COURT JESTER.
"KNOCK-KNOCK."

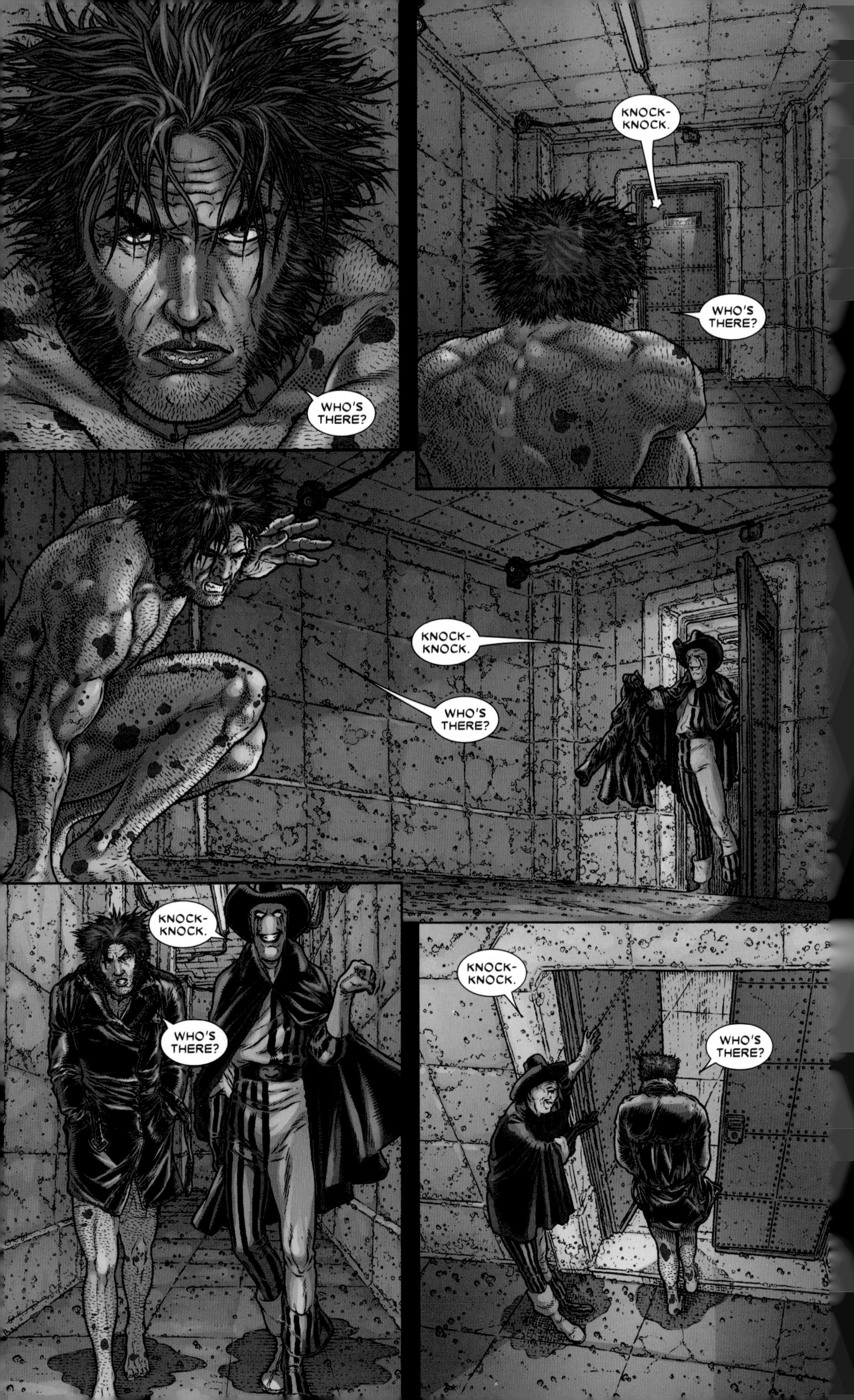
WHO'S THERE?
KNOCK-KNOCK.
WHO'S THERE?
KNOCK-KNOCK.
WHO'S THERE?
KNOCK-KNOCK.
WHO'S THERE?
KNOCK-KNOCK.
WHO'S THERE?

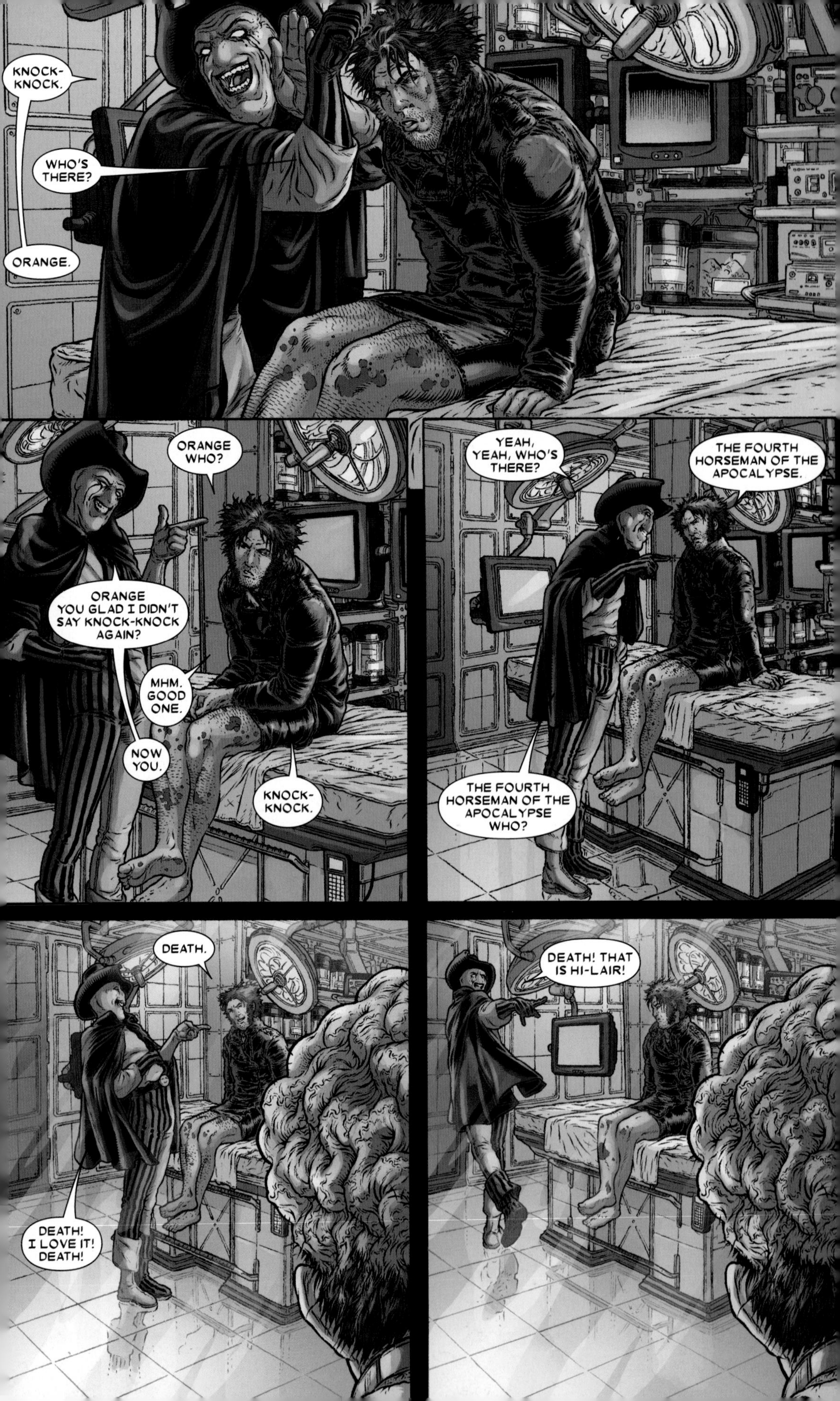
KNOCK-KNOCK.
WHO'S THERE?
ORANGE.
ORANGE WHO?
ORANGE YOU GLAD I DIDN'T SAY KNOCK-KNOCK AGAIN?
MHM. GOOD ONE.
NOW YOU.
KNOCK-KNOCK.
YEAH, YEAH, WHO'S THERE?
THE FOURTH HORSEMAN OF THE APOCALYPSE.
THE FOURTH HORSEMAN OF THE APOCALYPSE WHO?
DEATH.
DEATH! I LOVE IT! DEATH!
DEATH! THAT IS HI-LAIR!

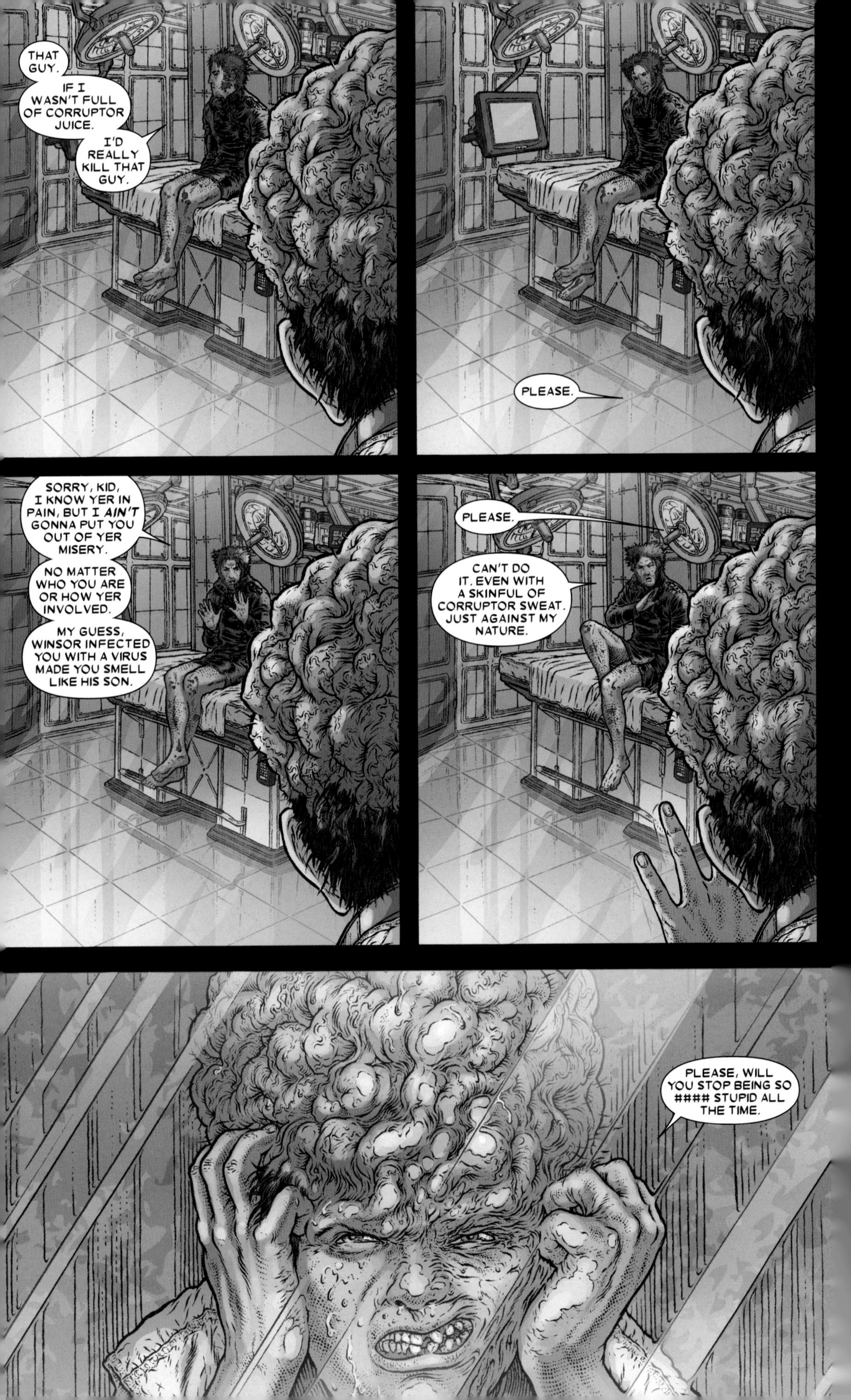
THAT GUY.
IF I WASN'T FULL OF CORRUPTOR JUICE.
I'D REALLY KILL THAT GUY.
PLEASE.
SORRY, KID, I KNOW YER IN PAIN, BUT I *AIN'T* GONNA PUT YOU OUT OF YER MISERY.
NO MATTER WHO YOU ARE OR HOW YER INVOLVED.
MY GUESS, WINSOR INFECTED YOU WITH A VIRUS MADE YOU SMELL LIKE HIS SON.
PLEASE.
CAN'T DO IT. EVEN WITH A SKINFUL OF CORRUPTOR SWEAT. JUST AGAINST MY NATURE.
PLEASE, WILL YOU STOP BEING SO #### STUPID ALL THE TIME.

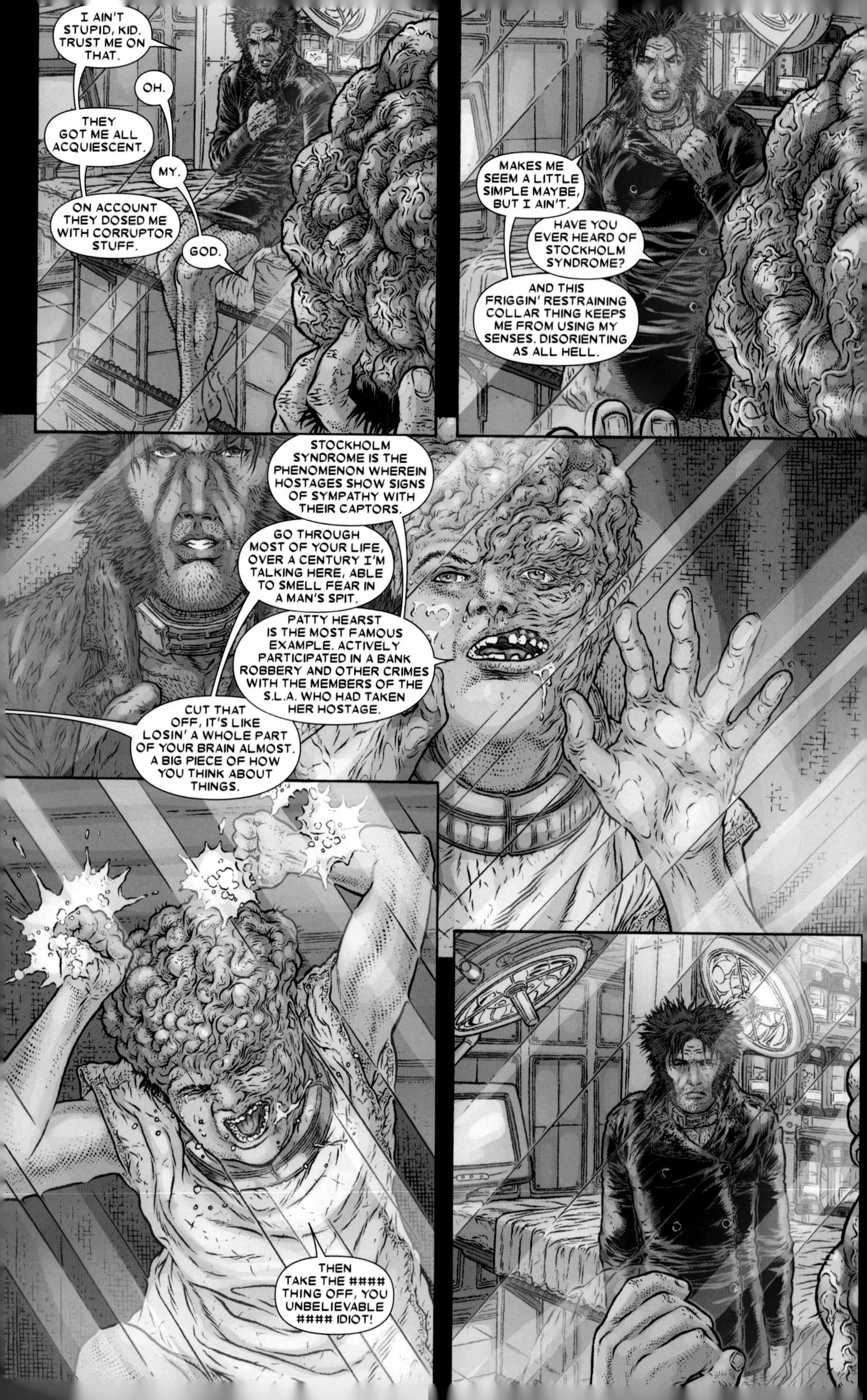
I AIN'T STUPID, KID. TRUST ME ON THAT.
OH.
THEY GOT ME ALL ACQUIESCENT.
MY.
ON ACCOUNT THEY DOSED ME WITH CORRUPTOR STUFF.
GOD.
MAKES ME SEEM A LITTLE SIMPLE MAYBE, BUT I AIN'T.
HAVE YOU EVER HEARD OF STOCKHOLM SYNDROME?
AND THIS FRIGGIN' RESTRAINING COLLAR THING KEEPS ME FROM USING MY SENSES. DISORIENTING AS ALL HELL.
STOCKHOLM SYNDROME IS THE PHENOMENON WHEREIN HOSTAGES SHOW SIGNS OF SYMPATHY WITH THEIR CAPTORS.
GO THROUGH MOST OF YOUR LIFE, OVER A CENTURY I'M TALKING HERE, ABLE TO SMELL FEAR IN A MAN'S SPIT.
PATTY HEARST IS THE MOST FAMOUS EXAMPLE. ACTIVELY PARTICIPATED IN A BANK ROBBERY AND OTHER CRIMES WITH THE MEMBERS OF THE S.L.A. WHO HAD TAKEN HER HOSTAGE.
CUT THAT OFF, IT'S LIKE LOSIN' A WHOLE PART OF YOUR BRAIN ALMOST. A BIG PIECE OF HOW YOU THINK ABOUT THINGS.
THEN TAKE THE #### THING OFF, YOU UNBELIEVABLE #### IDIOT!

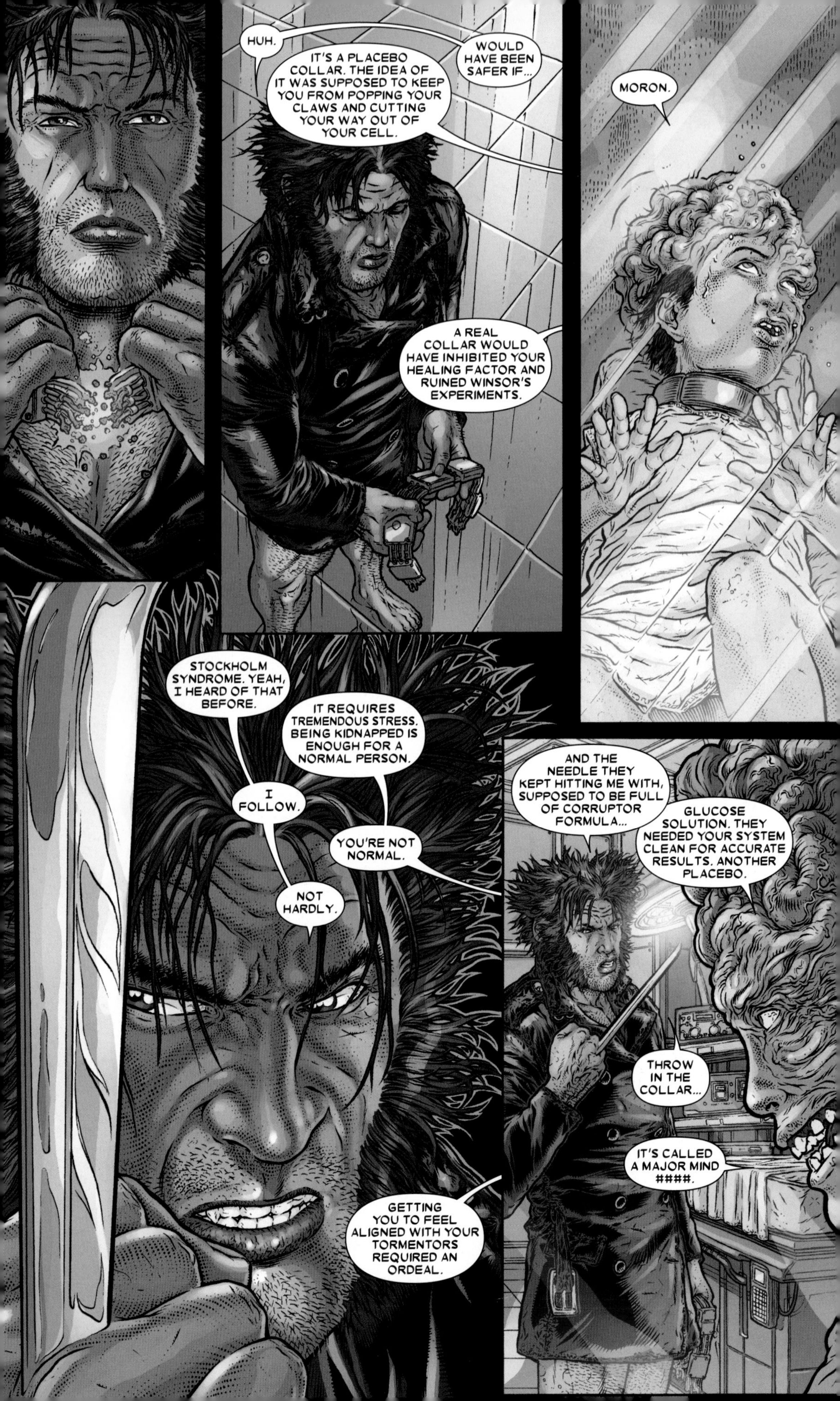
HUH.
IT'S A PLACEBO COLLAR. THE IDEA OF IT WAS SUPPOSED TO KEEP YOU FROM POPPING YOUR CLAWS AND CUTTING YOUR WAY OUT OF YOUR CELL.
WOULD HAVE BEEN SAFER IF...
A REAL COLLAR WOULD HAVE INHIBITED YOUR HEALING FACTOR AND RUINED WINSOR'S EXPERIMENTS.
MORON.
STOCKHOLM SYNDROME. YEAH, I HEARD OF THAT BEFORE.
IT REQUIRES TREMENDOUS STRESS. BEING KIDNAPPED IS ENOUGH FOR A NORMAL PERSON.
I FOLLOW.
YOU'RE NOT NORMAL.
NOT HARDLY.
GETTING YOU TO FEEL ALIGNED WITH YOUR TORMENTORS REQUIRED AN ORDEAL.
AND THE NEEDLE THEY KEPT HITTING ME WITH, SUPPOSED TO BE FULL OF CORRUPTOR FORMULA...
GLUCOSE SOLUTION. THEY NEEDED YOUR SYSTEM CLEAN FOR ACCURATE RESULTS. ANOTHER PLACEBO.
THROW IN THE COLLAR...
IT'S CALLED A MAJOR MIND ####.

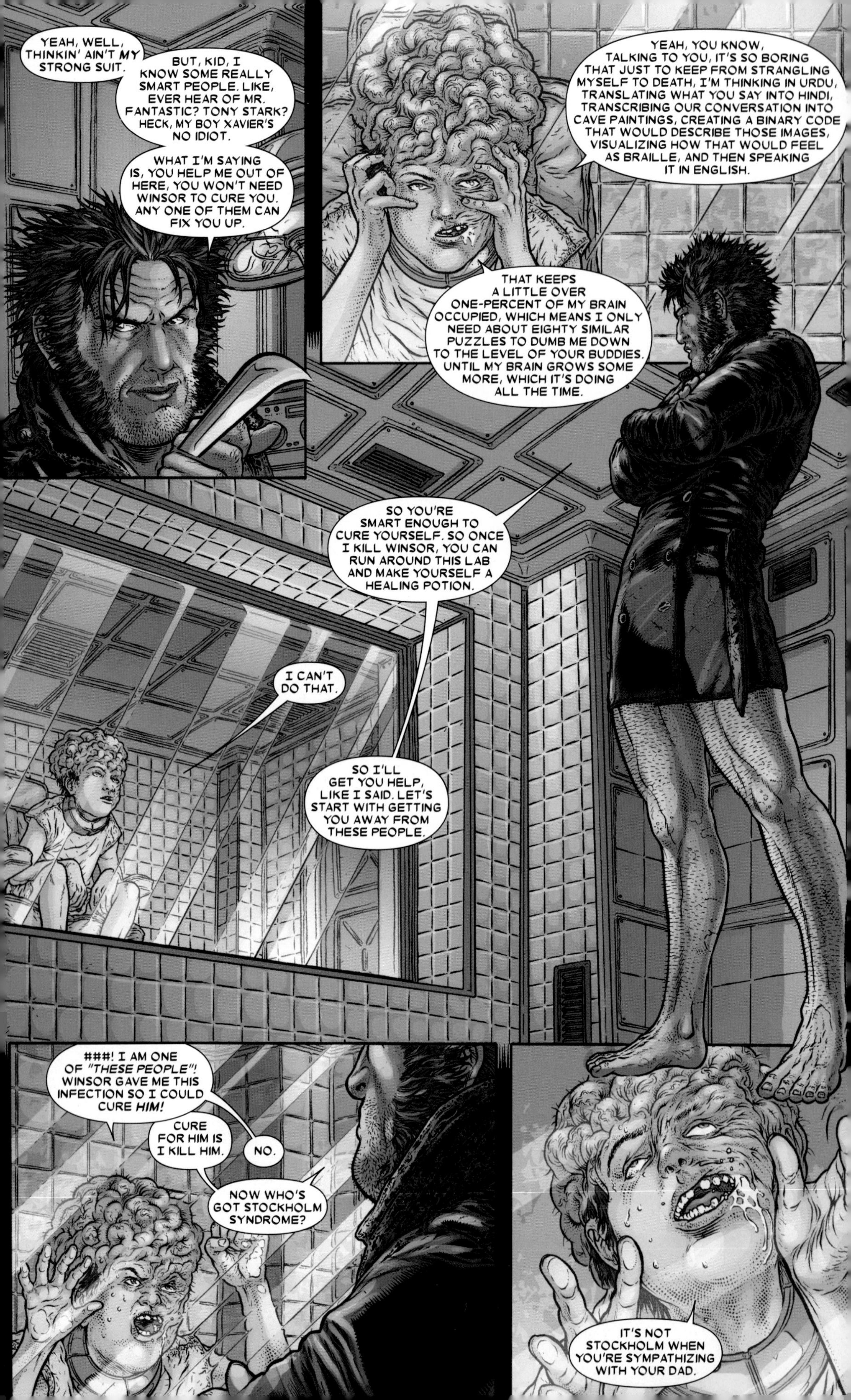
YEAH, WELL, THINKIN' AIN'T MY STRONG SUIT.
BUT, KID, I KNOW SOME REALLY SMART PEOPLE. LIKE, EVER HEAR OF MR. FANTASTIC? TONY STARK? HECK, MY BOY XAVIER'S NO IDIOT.
WHAT I'M SAYING IS, YOU HELP ME OUT OF HERE, YOU WON'T NEED WINSOR TO CURE YOU. ANY ONE OF THEM CAN FIX YOU UP.
YEAH, YOU KNOW, TALKING TO YOU, IT'S SO BORING THAT JUST TO KEEP FROM STRANGLING MYSELF TO DEATH, I'M THINKING IN URDU, TRANSLATING WHAT YOU SAY INTO HINDI, TRANSCRIBING OUR CONVERSATION INTO CAVE PAINTINGS, CREATING A BINARY CODE THAT WOULD DESCRIBE THOSE IMAGES, VISUALIZING HOW THAT WOULD FEEL AS BRAILLE, AND THEN SPEAKING IT IN ENGLISH.
THAT KEEPS A LITTLE OVER ONE-PERCENT OF MY BRAIN OCCUPIED, WHICH MEANS I ONLY NEED ABOUT EIGHTY SIMILAR PUZZLES TO DUMB ME DOWN TO THE LEVEL OF YOUR BUDDIES. UNTIL MY BRAIN GROWS SOME MORE, WHICH IT'S DOING ALL THE TIME.
SO YOU'RE SMART ENOUGH TO CURE YOURSELF. SO ONCE I KILL WINSOR, YOU CAN RUN AROUND THIS LAB AND MAKE YOURSELF A HEALING POTION.
I CAN'T DO THAT.
SO I'LL GET YOU HELP, LIKE I SAID. LET'S START WITH GETTING YOU AWAY FROM THESE PEOPLE.
###! I AM ONE OF "THESE PEOPLE"! WINSOR GAVE ME THIS INFECTION SO I COULD CURE HIM!
CURE FOR HIM IS I KILL HIM.
NO.
NOW WHO'S GOT STOCKHOLM SYNDROME?
IT'S NOT STOCKHOLM WHEN YOU'RE SYMPATHIZING WITH YOUR DAD.

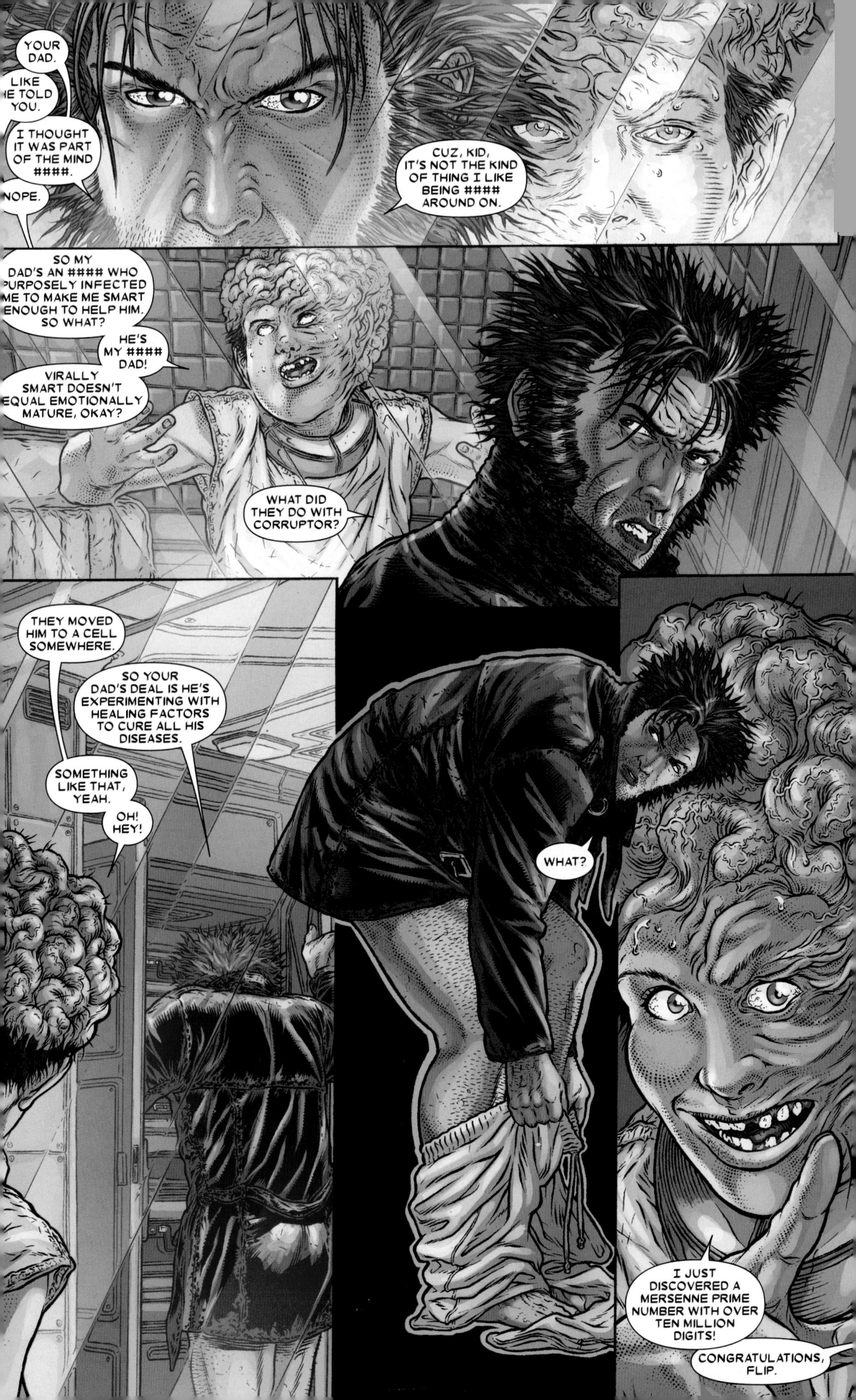
YOUR DAD.
LIKE HE TOLD YOU.
I THOUGHT IT WAS PART OF THE MIND ####.
NOPE.
CUZ, KID, IT'S NOT THE KIND OF THING I LIKE BEING #### AROUND ON.
SO MY DAD'S AN #### WHO PURPOSELY INFECTED ME TO MAKE ME SMART ENOUGH TO HELP HIM. SO WHAT?
HE'S MY #### DAD!
VIRALLY SMART DOESN'T EQUAL EMOTIONALLY MATURE, OKAY?
WHAT DID THEY DO WITH CORRUPTOR?
THEY MOVED HIM TO A CELL SOMEWHERE.
SO YOUR DAD'S DEAL IS HE'S EXPERIMENTING WITH HEALING FACTORS TO CURE ALL HIS DISEASES.
SOMETHING LIKE THAT, YEAH.
OH! HEY!
WHAT?
I JUST DISCOVERED A MERSENNE PRIME NUMBER WITH OVER TEN MILLION DIGITS!
CONGRATULATIONS, FLIP.

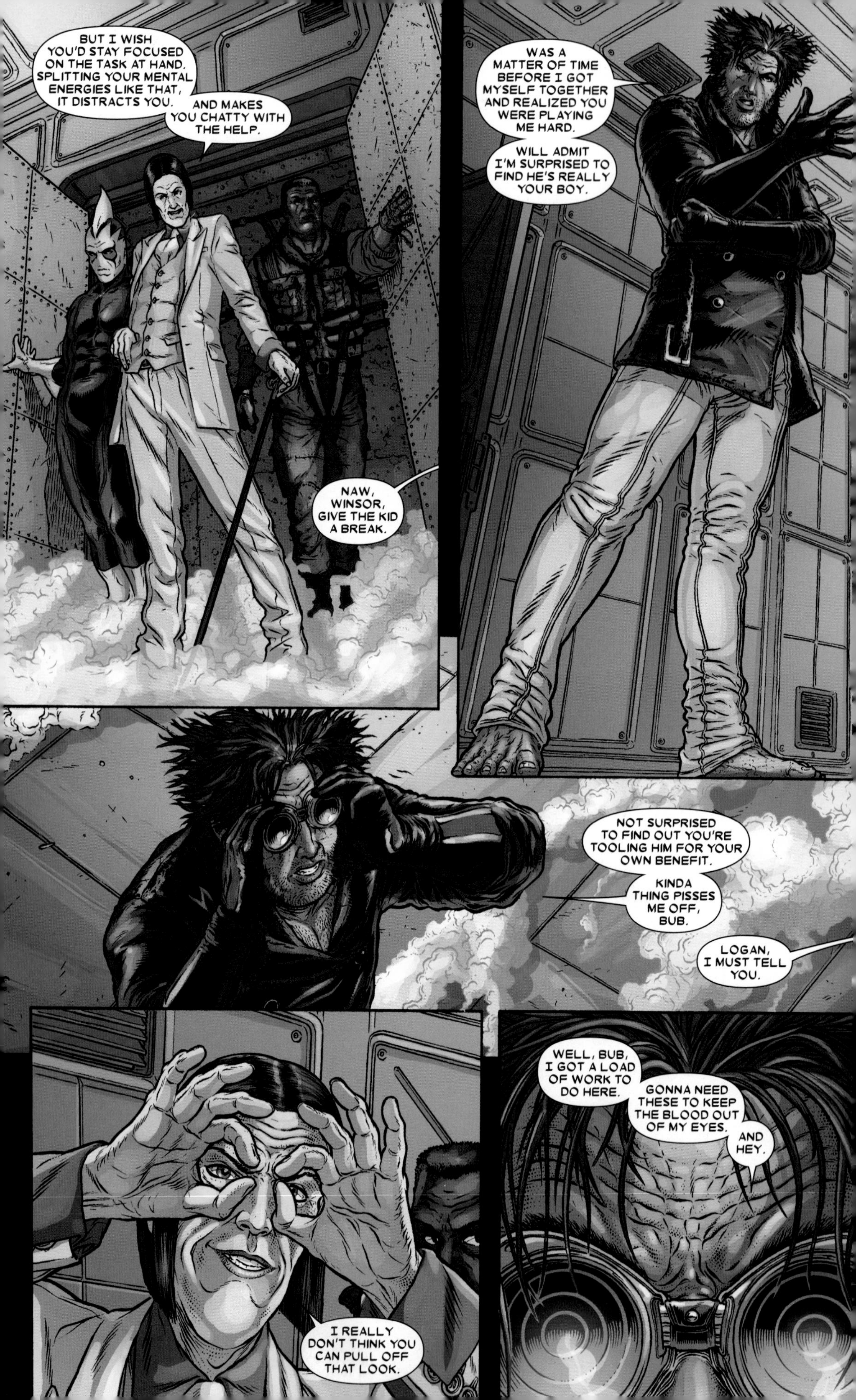
BUT I WISH YOU'D STAY FOCUSED ON THE TASK AT HAND. SPLITTING YOUR MENTAL ENERGIES LIKE THAT, IT DISTRACTS YOU.
AND MAKES YOU CHATTY WITH THE HELP.
NAW, WINSOR, GIVE THE KID A BREAK.
WAS A MATTER OF TIME BEFORE I GOT MYSELF TOGETHER AND REALIZED YOU WERE PLAYING ME HARD.
WILL ADMIT I'M SURPRISED TO FIND HE'S REALLY YOUR BOY.
NOT SURPRISED TO FIND OUT YOU'RE TOOLING HIM FOR YOUR OWN BENEFIT.
KINDA THING PISSES ME OFF, BUB.
LOGAN, I MUST TELL YOU.
I REALLY DON'T THINK YOU CAN PULL OFF THAT LOOK.
WELL, BUB, I GOT A LOAD OF WORK TO DO HERE.
GONNA NEED THESE TO KEEP THE BLOOD OUT OF MY EYES.
AND HEY.

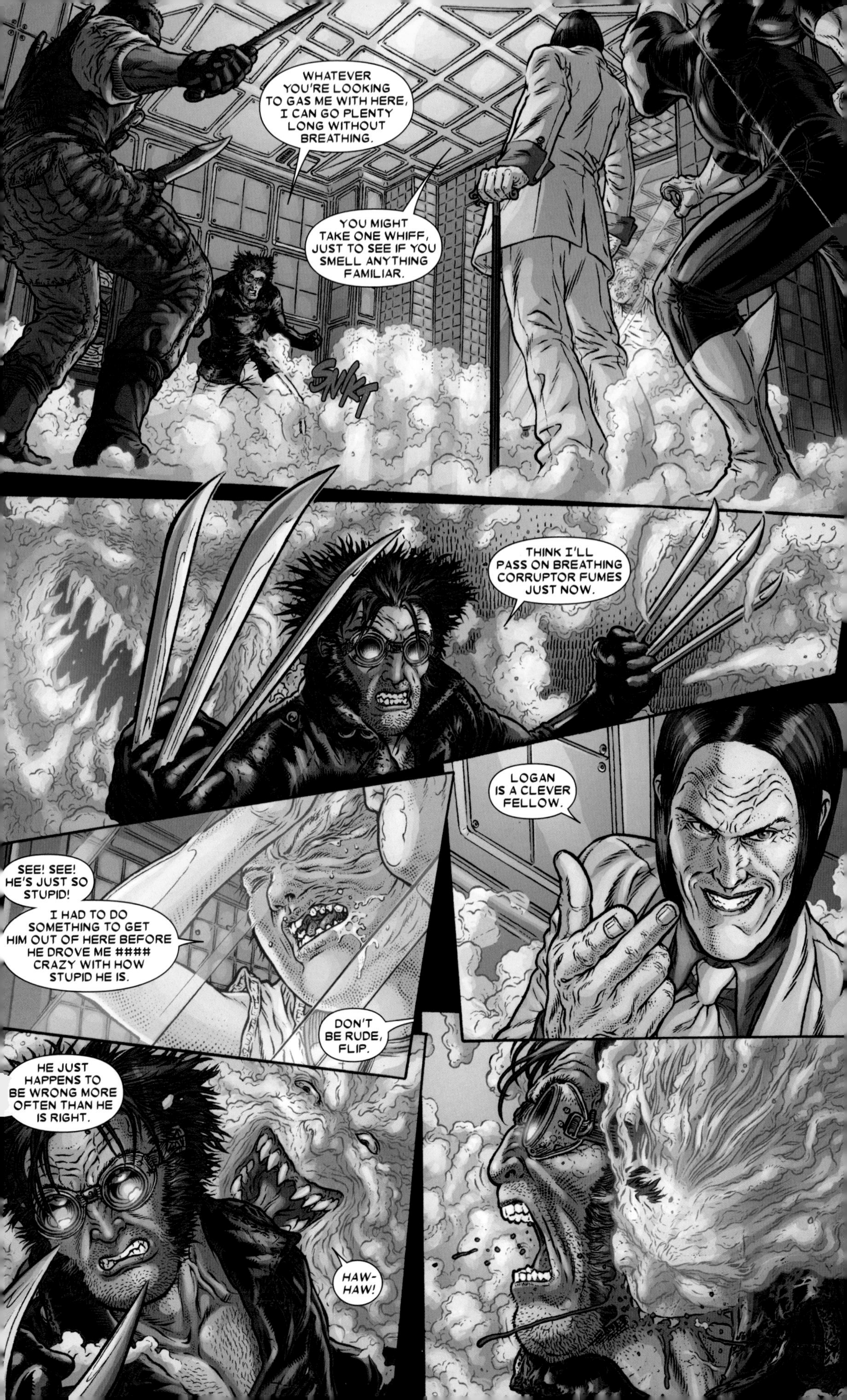
WHATEVER YOU'RE LOOKING TO GAS ME WITH HERE, I CAN GO PLENTY LONG WITHOUT BREATHING.
YOU MIGHT TAKE ONE WHIFF, JUST TO SEE IF YOU SMELL ANYTHING FAMILIAR.
SNIKT
THINK I'LL PASS ON BREATHING CORRUPTOR FUMES JUST NOW.
LOGAN IS A CLEVER FELLOW.
SEE! SEE! HE'S JUST SO STUPID!
I HAD TO DO SOMETHING TO GET HIM OUT OF HERE BEFORE HE DROVE ME #### CRAZY WITH HOW STUPID HE IS.
DON'T BE RUDE, FLIP.
HE JUST HAPPENS TO BE WRONG MORE OFTEN THAN HE IS RIGHT.
HAW-HAW!

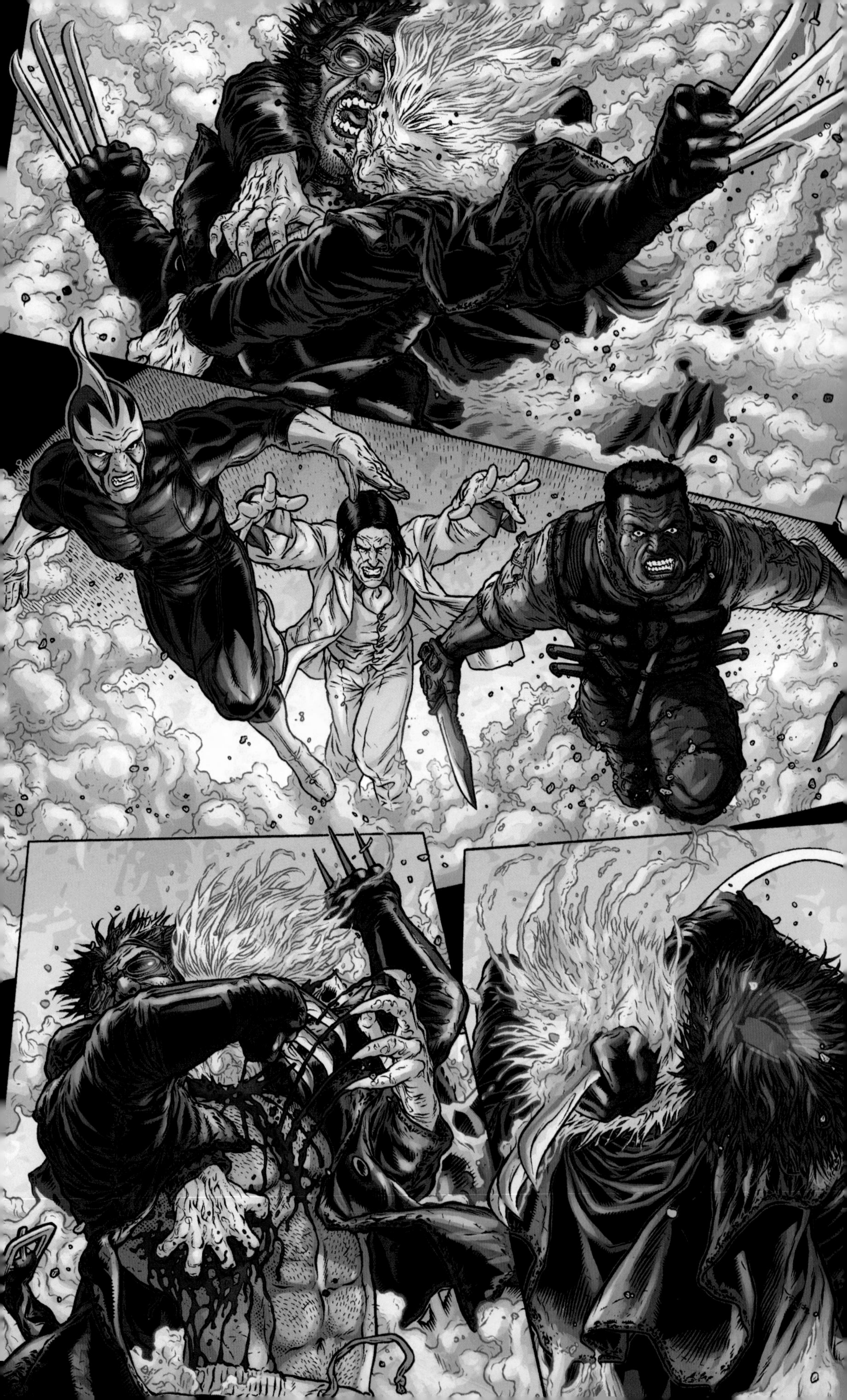

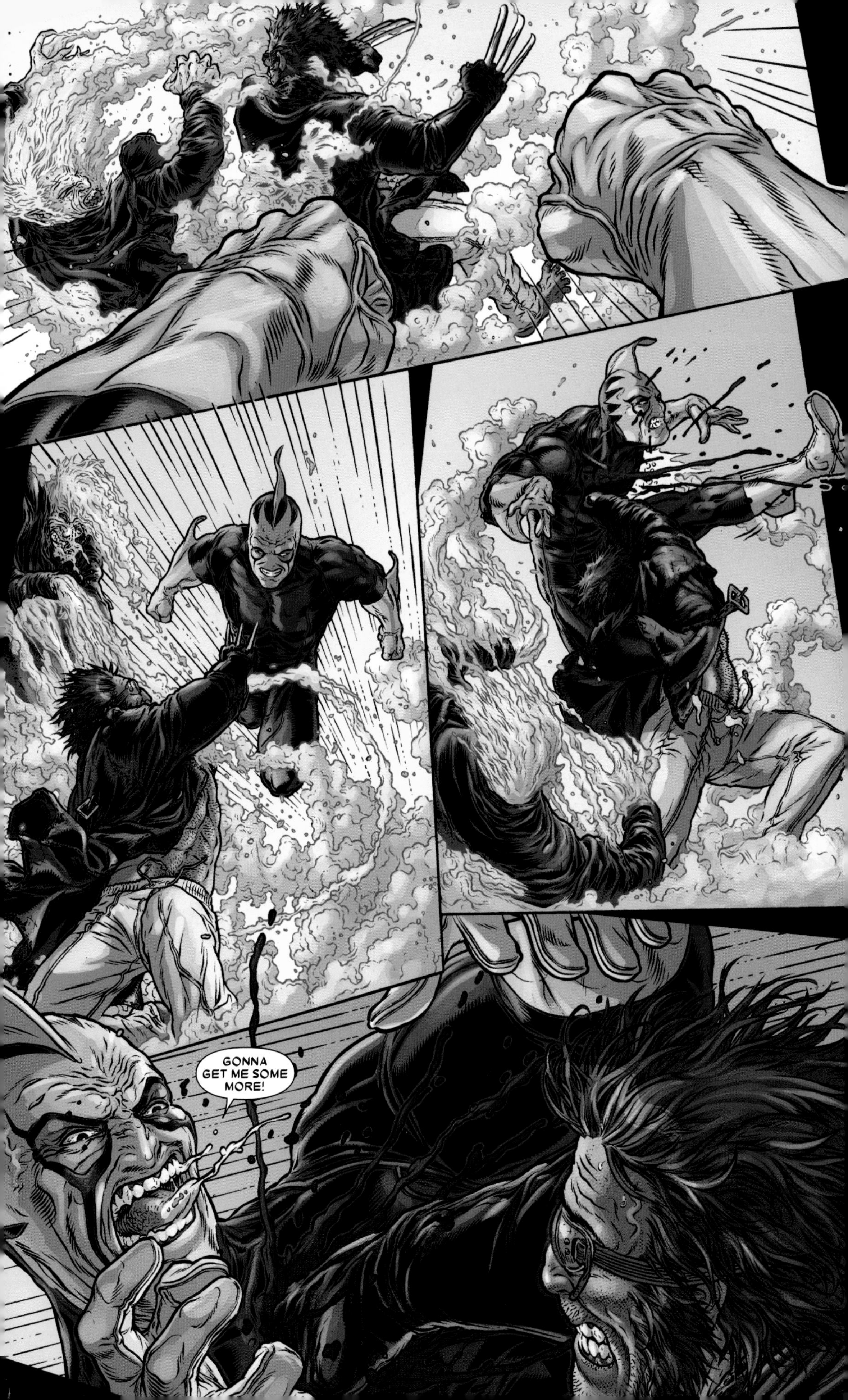
GONNA GET ME SOME MORE!

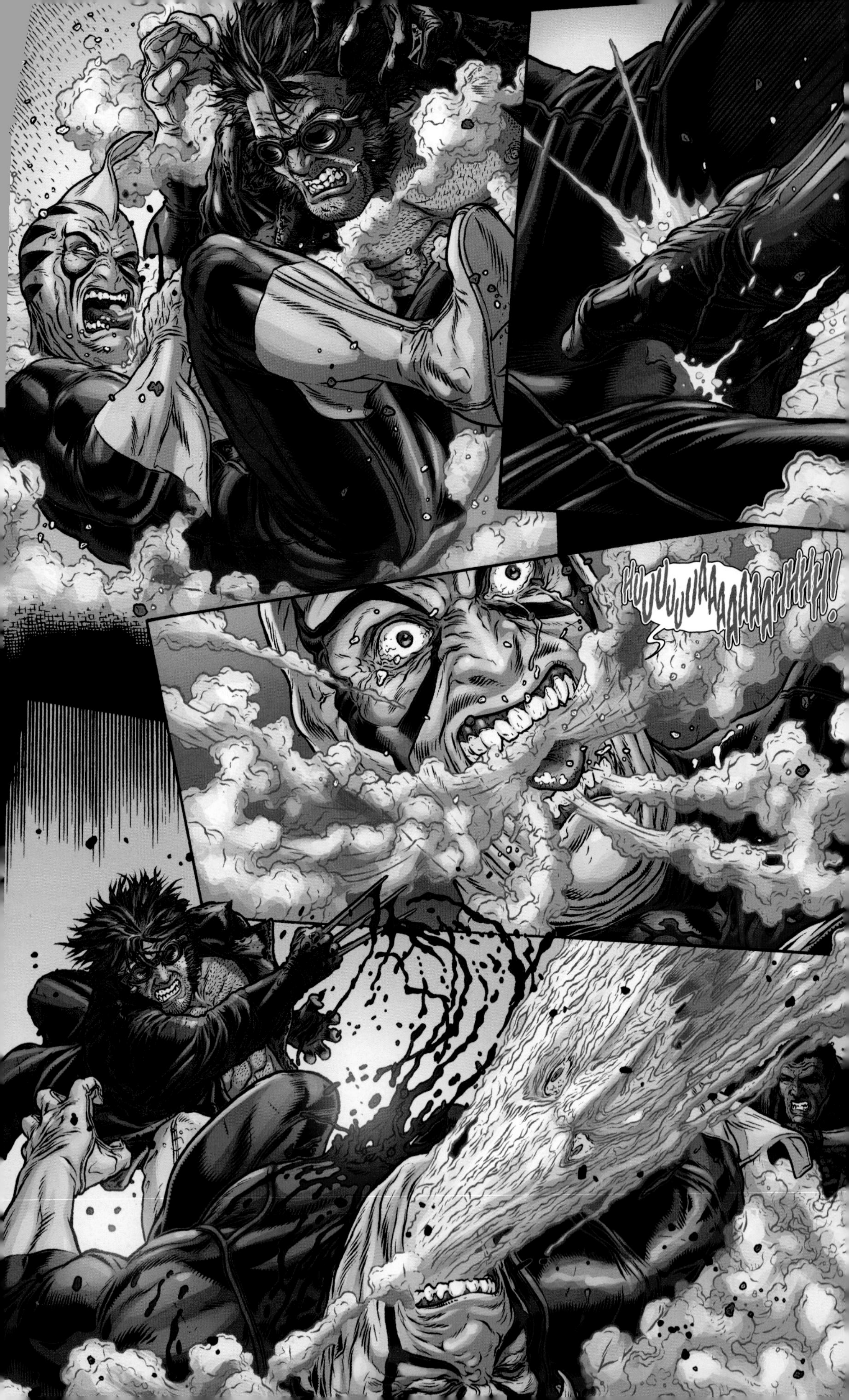
HUUUUUUAAAAAAAHHHH!

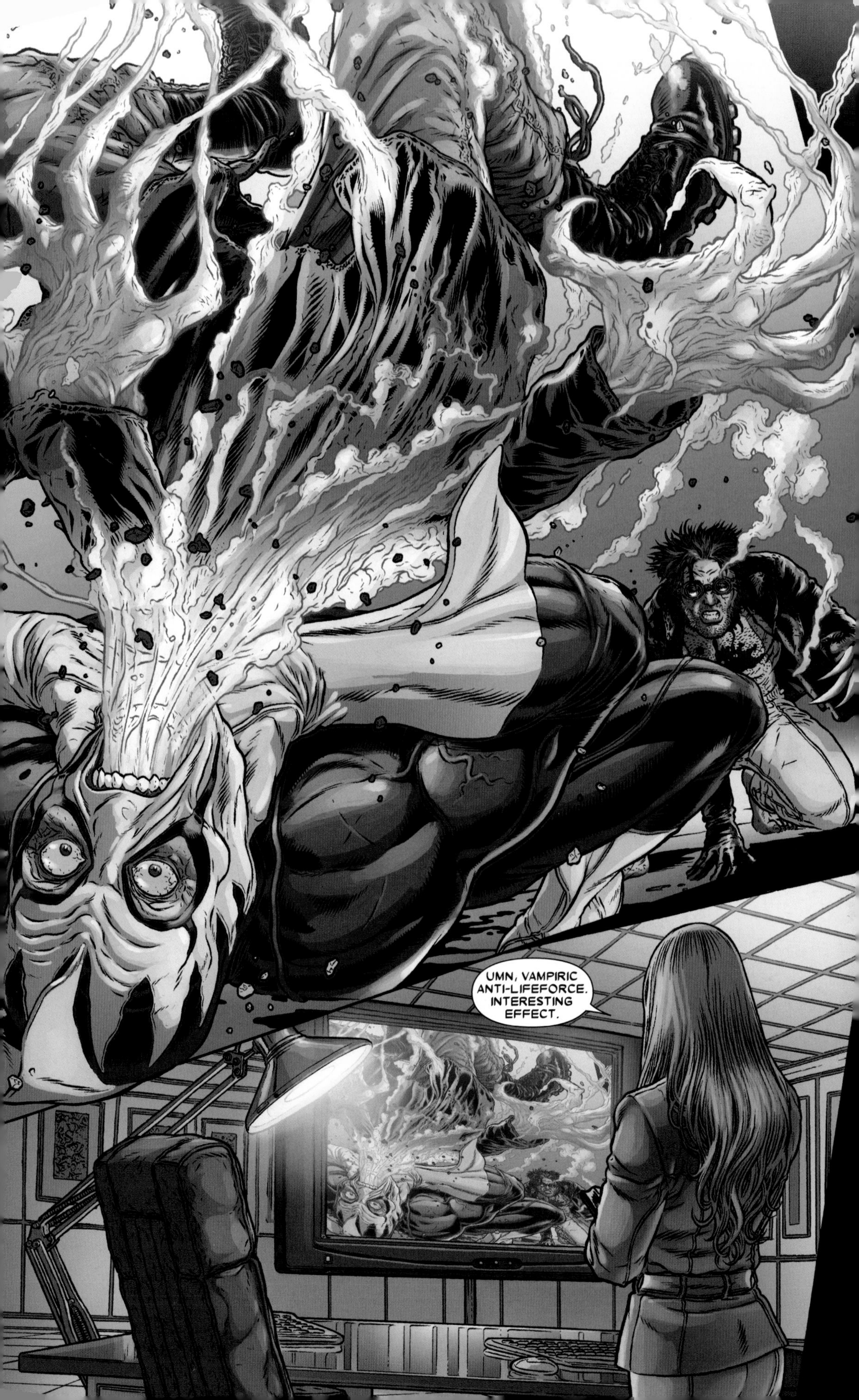
UMN, VAMPIRIC ANTI-LIFEFORCE. INTERESTING EFFECT.

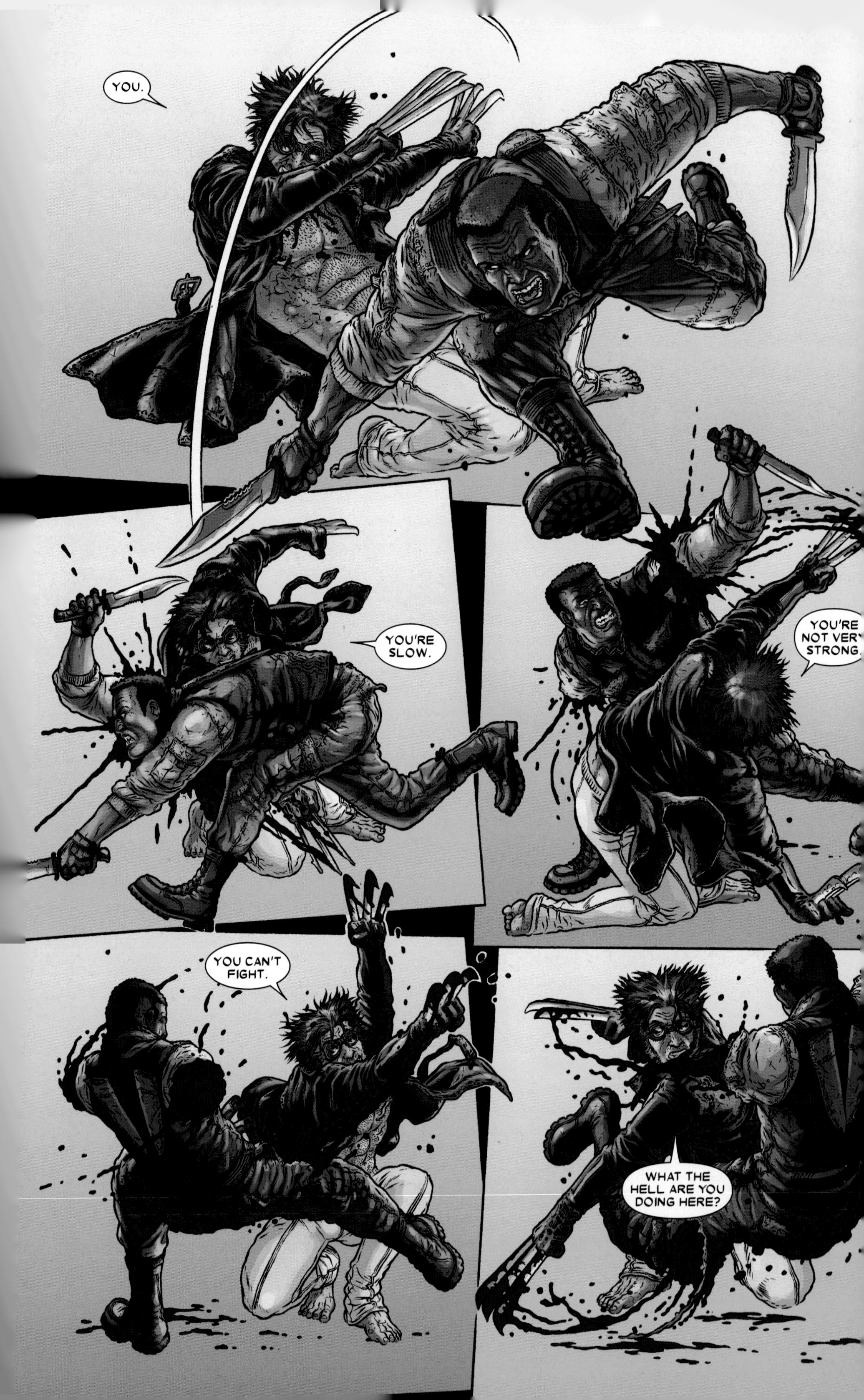
YOU.
YOU'RE SLOW.
YOU'RE NOT VER STRONG.
YOU CAN'T FIGHT.
WHAT THE HELL ARE YOU DOING HERE?

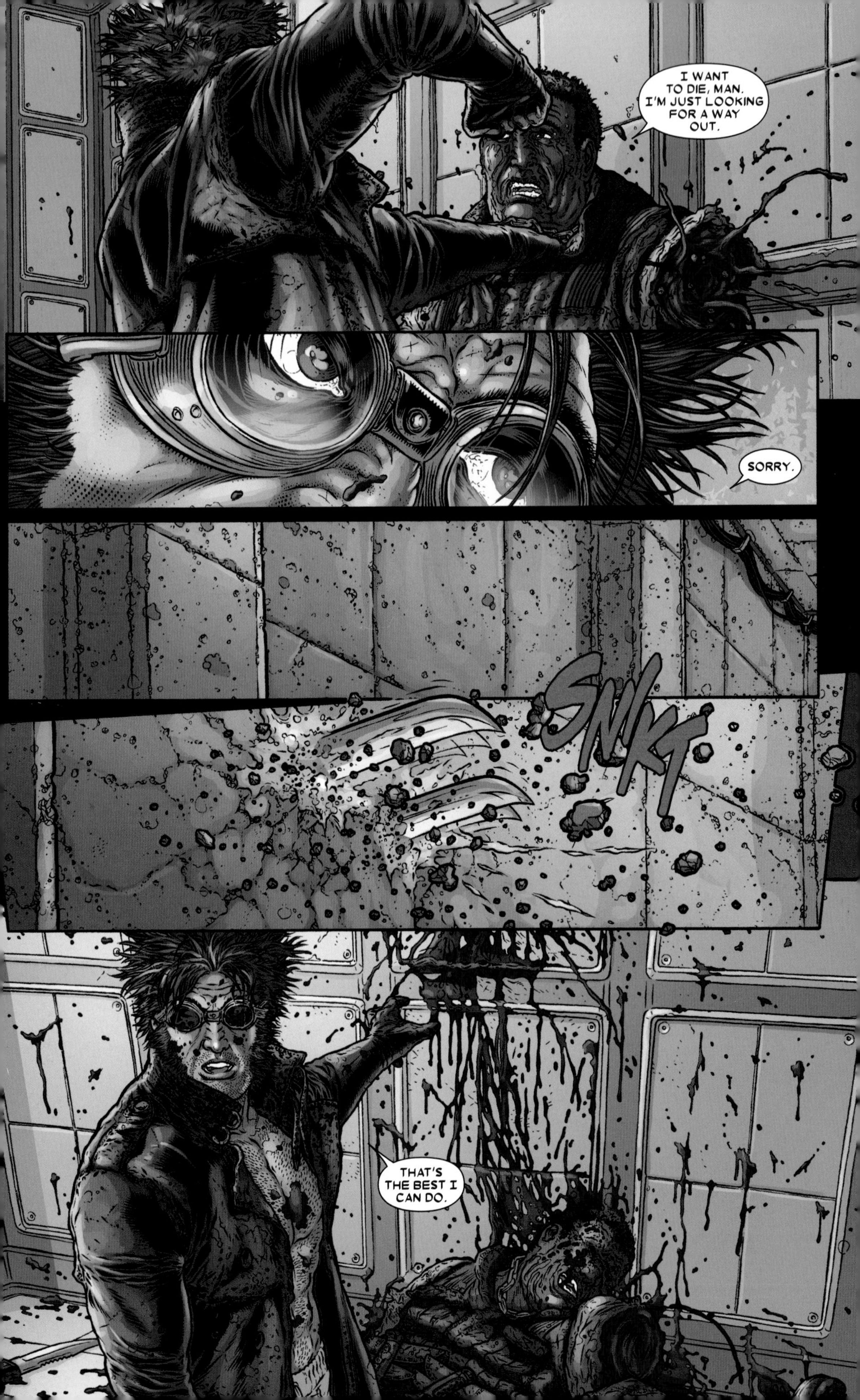
I WANT TO DIE, MAN. I'M JUST LOOKING FOR A WAY OUT.
SORRY.
SNKT
THAT'S THE BEST I CAN DO.

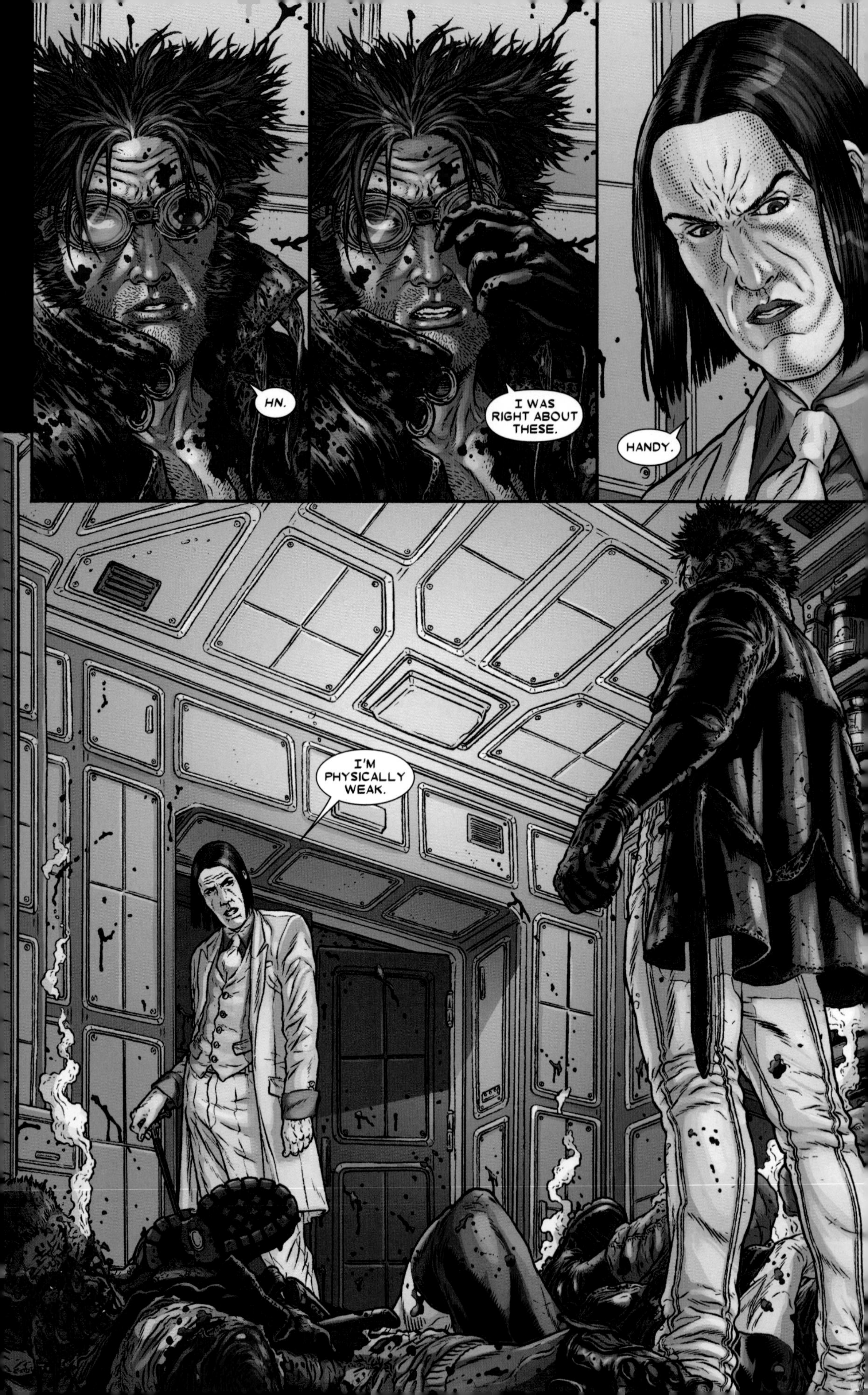
HN.
I WAS RIGHT ABOUT THESE.
HANDY.
I'M PHYSICALLY WEAK.

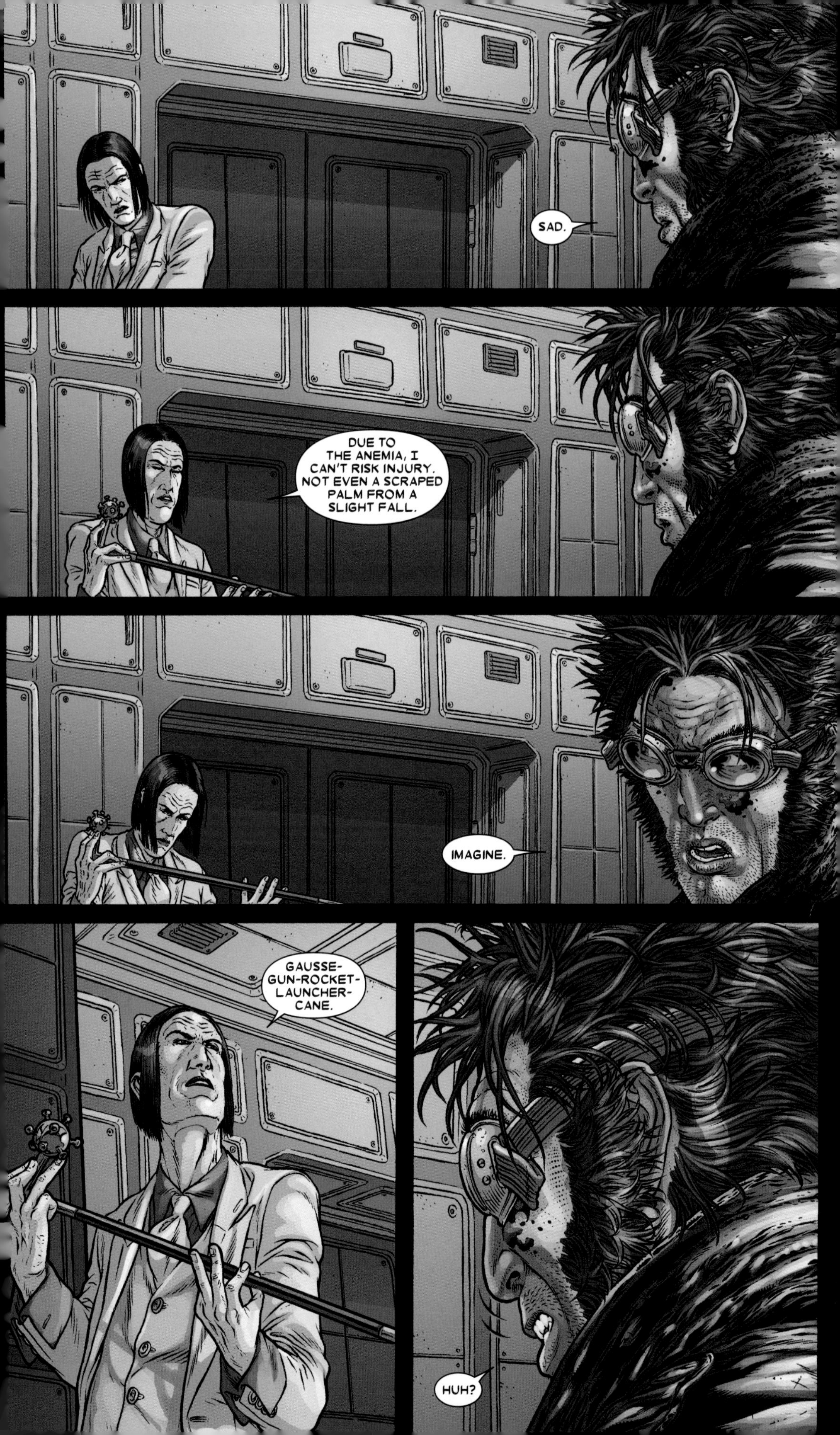
SAD.
DUE TO THE ANEMIA, I CAN'T RISK INJURY. NOT EVEN A SCRAPED PALM FROM A SLIGHT FALL.
IMAGINE.
GAUSSE-GUN-ROCKET-LAUNCHER-CANE.
HUH?

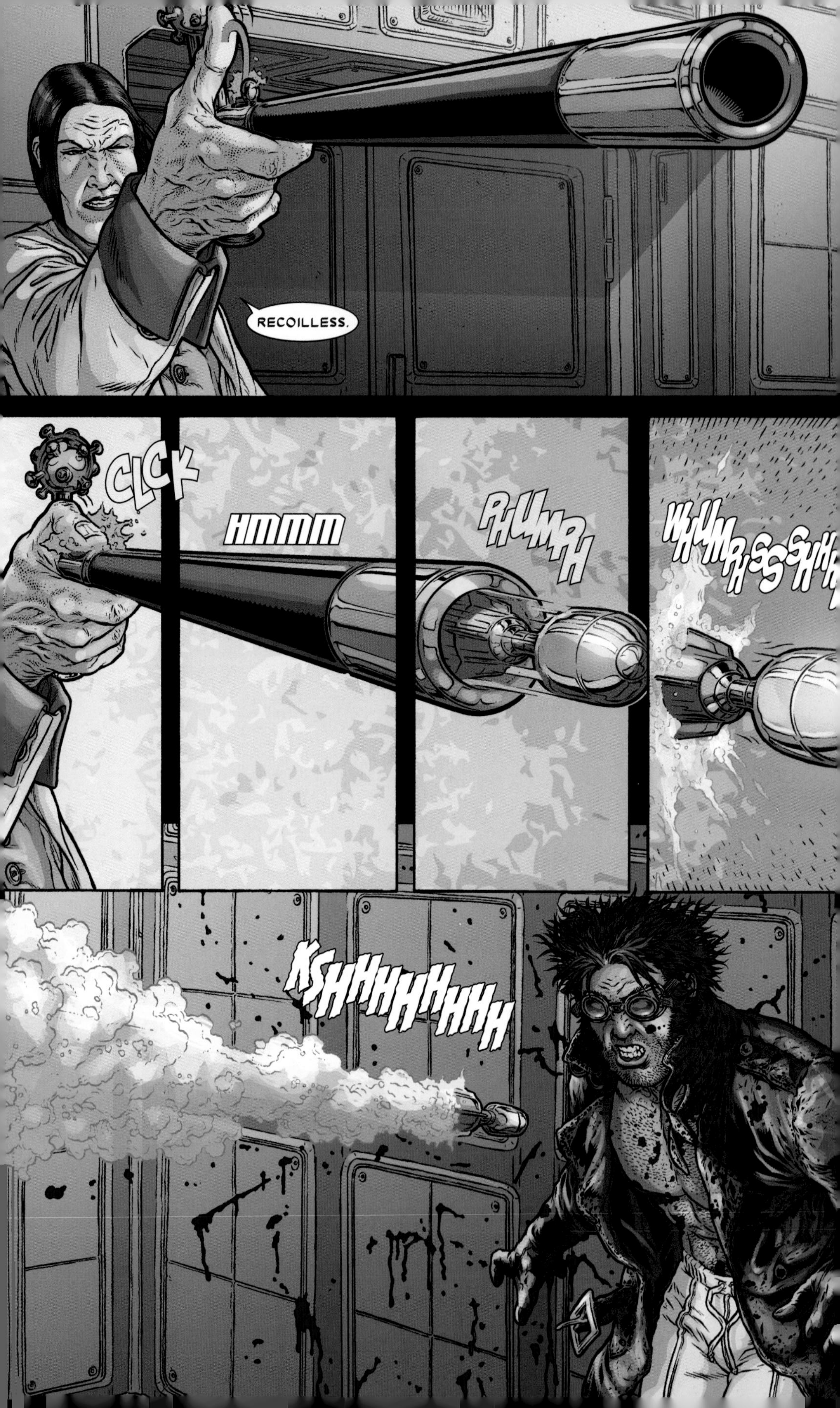
RECOILLESS.
CLCK
HMMM
PHUMPH
WHUMPHSSSHH
KSHHHHHHHHH

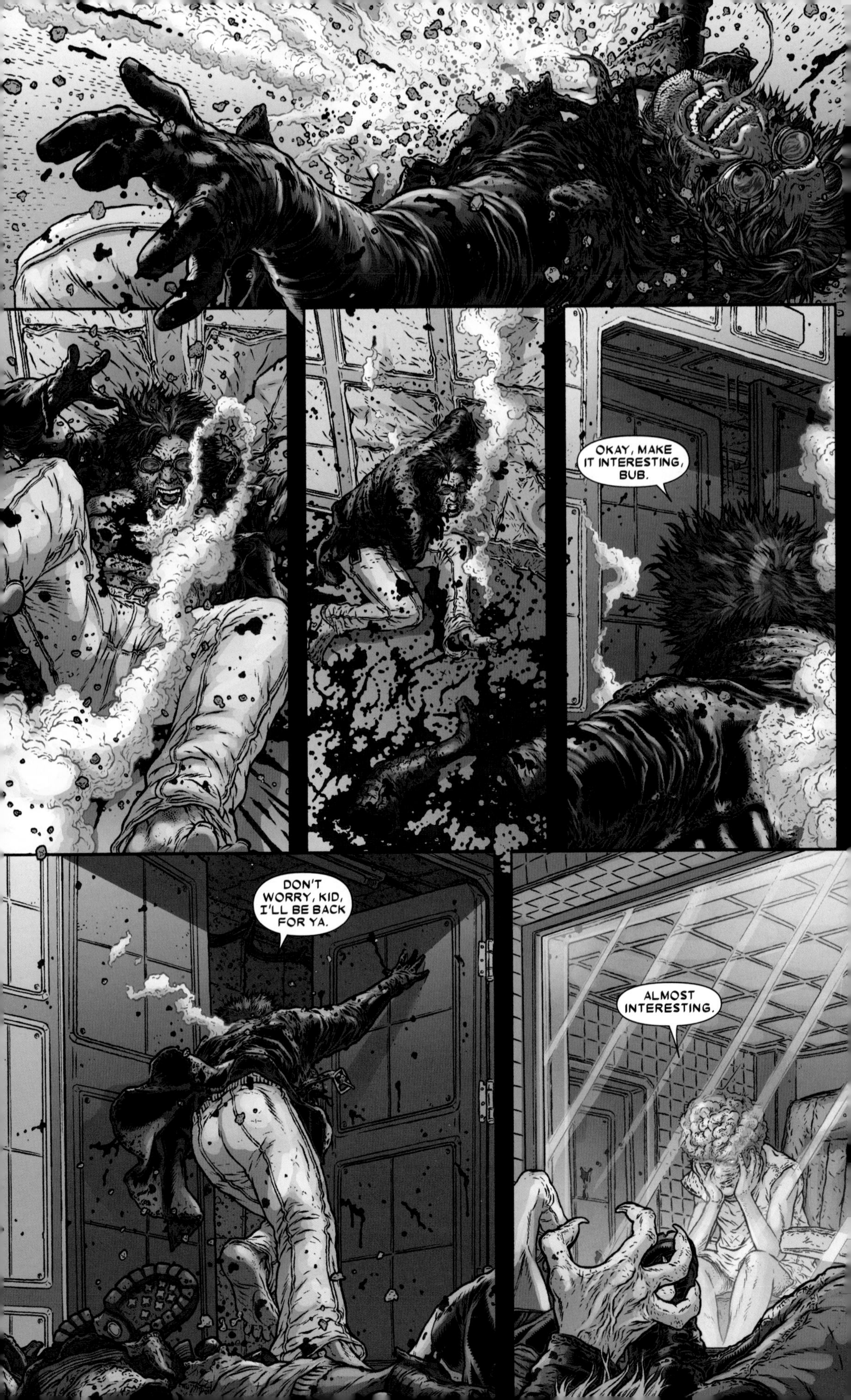
OKAY, MAKE IT INTERESTING, BUB.
DON'T WORRY, KID, I'LL BE BACK FOR YA.
ALMOST INTERESTING.

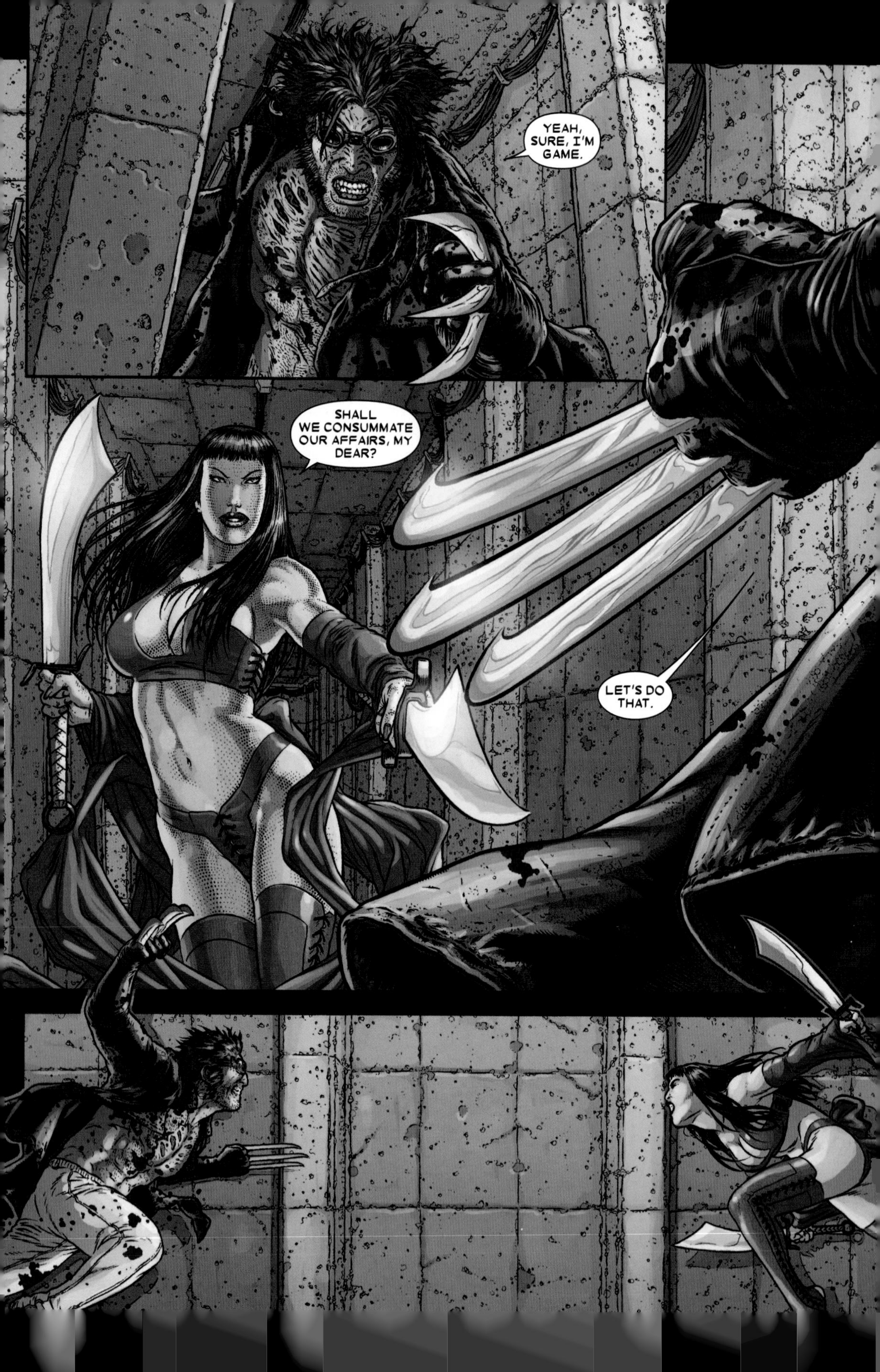
YEAH, SURE, I'M GAME.
SHALL WE CONSUMMATE OUR AFFAIRS, MY DEAR?
LET'S DO THAT.

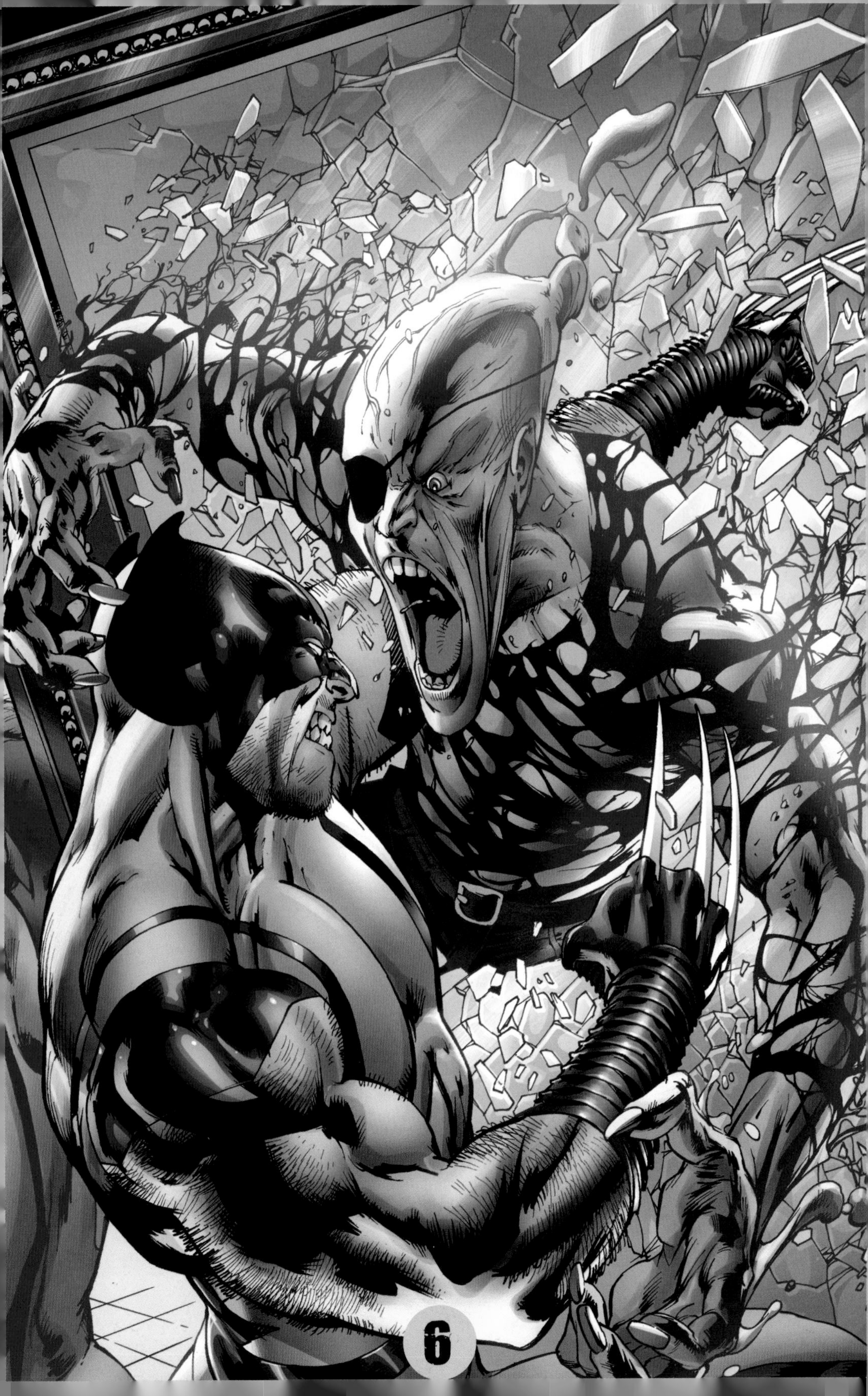
6

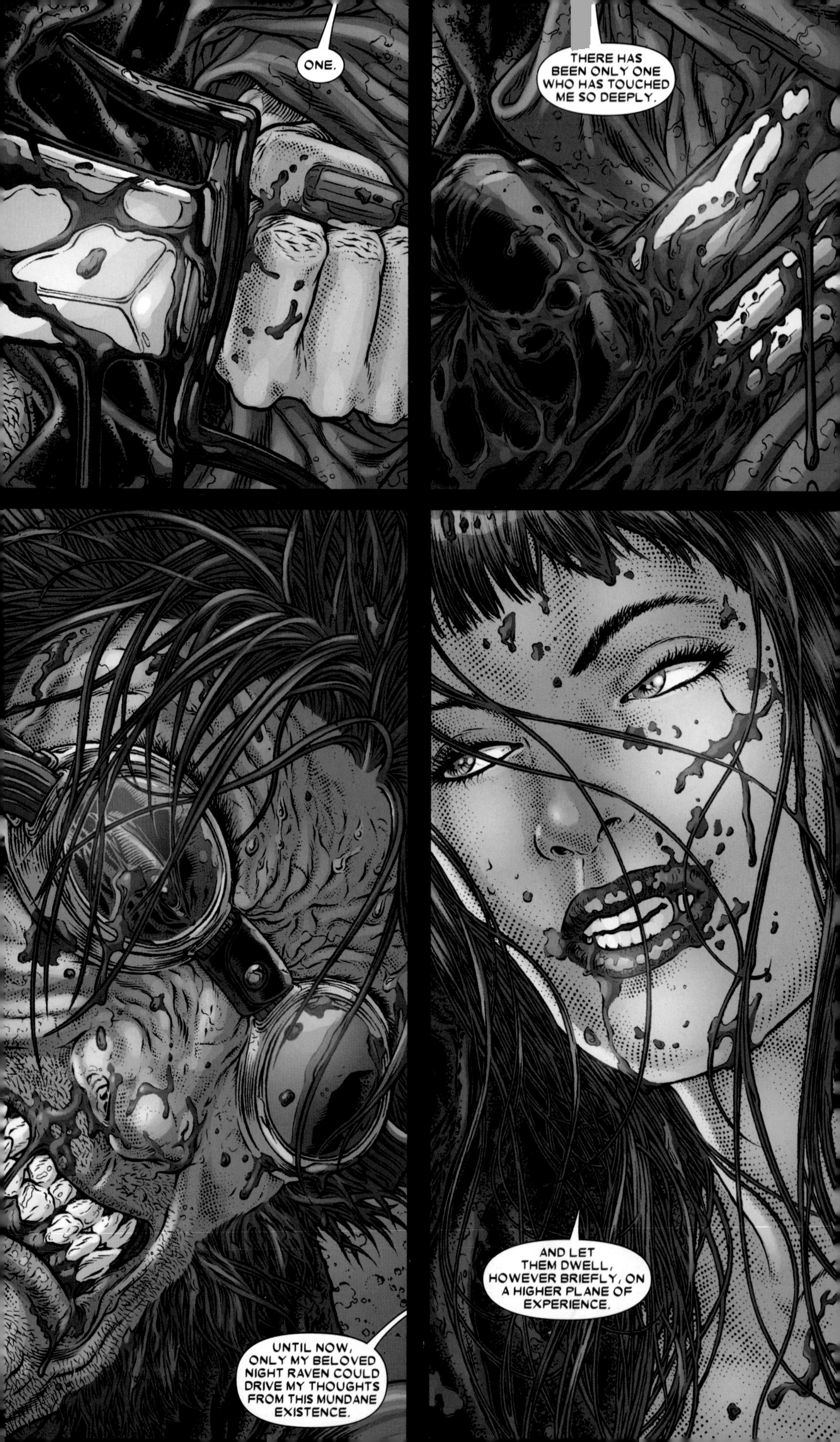
ONE.
THERE HAS BEEN ONLY ONE WHO HAS TOUCHED ME SO DEEPLY.
UNTIL NOW, ONLY MY BELOVED NIGHT RAVEN COULD DRIVE MY THOUGHTS FROM THIS MUNDANE EXISTENCE.
AND LET THEM DWELL, HOWEVER BRIEFLY, ON A HIGHER PLANE OF EXPERIENCE.

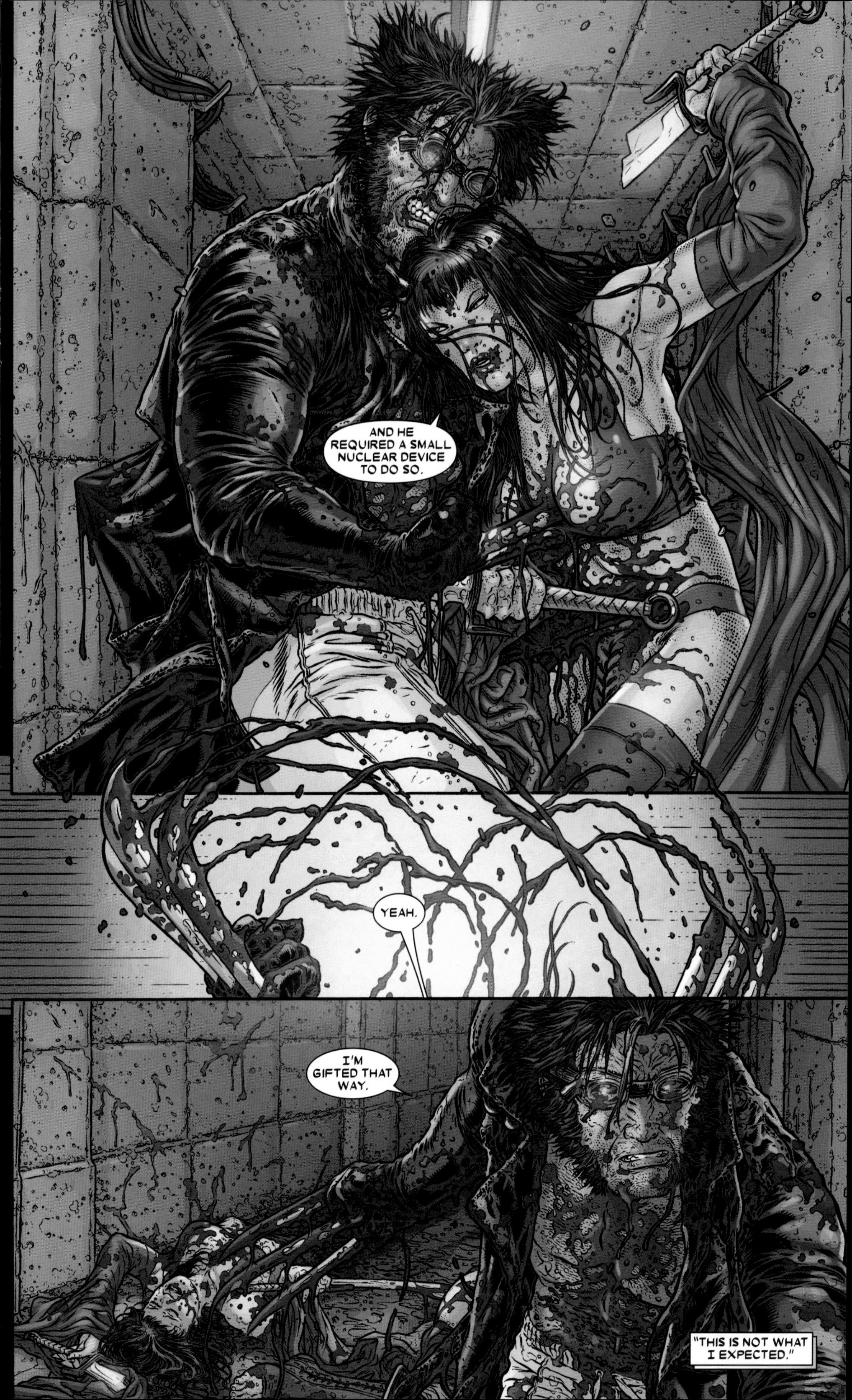
AND HE REQUIRED A SMALL NUCLEAR DEVICE TO DO SO.
YEAH.
I'M GIFTED THAT WAY.
"THIS IS NOT WHAT I EXPECTED."

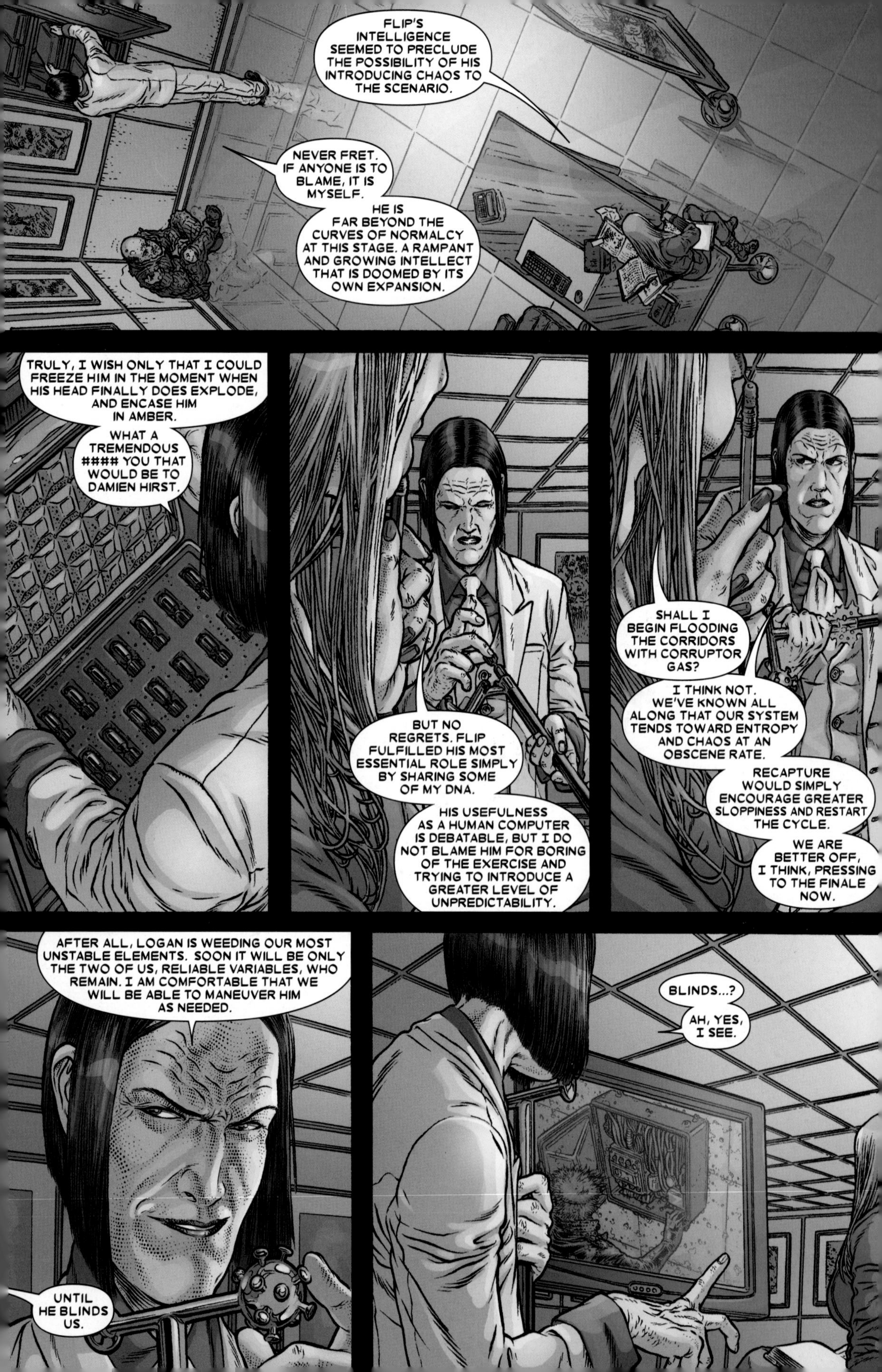
FLIP'S INTELLIGENCE SEEMED TO PRECLUDE THE POSSIBILITY OF HIS INTRODUCING CHAOS TO THE SCENARIO.
NEVER FRET. IF ANYONE IS TO BLAME, IT IS MYSELF.
HE IS FAR BEYOND THE CURVES OF NORMALCY AT THIS STAGE. A RAMPANT AND GROWING INTELLECT THAT IS DOOMED BY ITS OWN EXPANSION.
TRULY, I WISH ONLY THAT I COULD FREEZE HIM IN THE MOMENT WHEN HIS HEAD FINALLY DOES EXPLODE, AND ENCASE HIM IN AMBER.
WHAT A TREMENDOUS #### YOU THAT WOULD BE TO DAMIEN HIRST.
BUT NO REGRETS. FLIP FULFILLED HIS MOST ESSENTIAL ROLE SIMPLY BY SHARING SOME OF MY DNA.
HIS USEFULNESS AS A HUMAN COMPUTER IS DEBATABLE, BUT I DO NOT BLAME HIM FOR BORING OF THE EXERCISE AND TRYING TO INTRODUCE A GREATER LEVEL OF UNPREDICTABILITY.
SHALL I BEGIN FLOODING THE CORRIDORS WITH CORRUPTOR GAS?
I THINK NOT. WE'VE KNOWN ALL ALONG THAT OUR SYSTEM TENDS TOWARD ENTROPY AND CHAOS AT AN OBSCENE RATE.
RECAPTURE WOULD SIMPLY ENCOURAGE GREATER SLOPPINESS AND RESTART THE CYCLE.
WE ARE BETTER OFF, I THINK, PRESSING TO THE FINALE NOW.
AFTER ALL, LOGAN IS WEEDING OUR MOST UNSTABLE ELEMENTS. SOON IT WILL BE ONLY THE TWO OF US, RELIABLE VARIABLES, WHO REMAIN. I AM COMFORTABLE THAT WE WILL BE ABLE TO MANEUVER HIM AS NEEDED.
UNTIL HE BLINDS US.
BLINDS...?
AH, YES, I SEE.

GAS?

AS IT HAPPENS--

I BELIEVE THE CONTROLS FOR THE GAS SYSTEM RUN THROUGH THAT JUNCTION.

WELL THEN. YOU MIGHT, MY DEAR, CONSIDER ARMING YOURSELF.

ACCORDING TO THE SCHEMATIC, THAT DOES APPEAR TO BE THE CASE.

"WHY DO I ALWAYS STRIVE TO SELF-RUIN?"

COMFORTABLY SET UP. POSITIVELY WALLOWING IN ALL I COULD HOPE FOR.

AN ABSOLUTE STY OF MALEVOLENCE, PERVERSITY, MADNESS, FOUL HUMORS, NEFARIOUS INTENTIONS, NECROPHILIA, OUTRIGHT CANNIBALISM FOR PITY'S SAKE, AND HERE I AM, CONTEMPLATING HOW TO RUIN IT ALL.

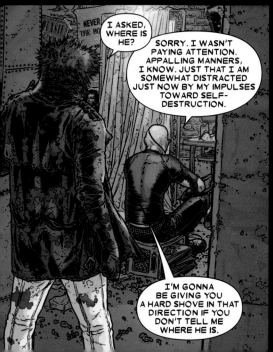

I ASKED, WHERE IS HE?

SORRY. I WASN'T PAYING ATTENTION. APPALLING MANNERS, I KNOW. JUST THAT I AM SOMEWHAT DISTRACTED JUST NOW BY MY IMPULSES TOWARD SELF-DESTRUCTION.

I'M GONNA BE GIVING YOU A HARD SHOVE IN THAT DIRECTION IF YOU DON'T TELL ME WHERE HE IS.

ALL THAT IS REQUIRED OF ME IS THAT I SUCCUMB TO OBSCENITY AND VICE.

I HAVE ONLY TO ABANDON MY HUMANITY, AND I WILL HAVE PEACE. SPARE NOT ONLY MYSELF, BUT MY CAPTIVE SOUL AS WELL.

BUB--

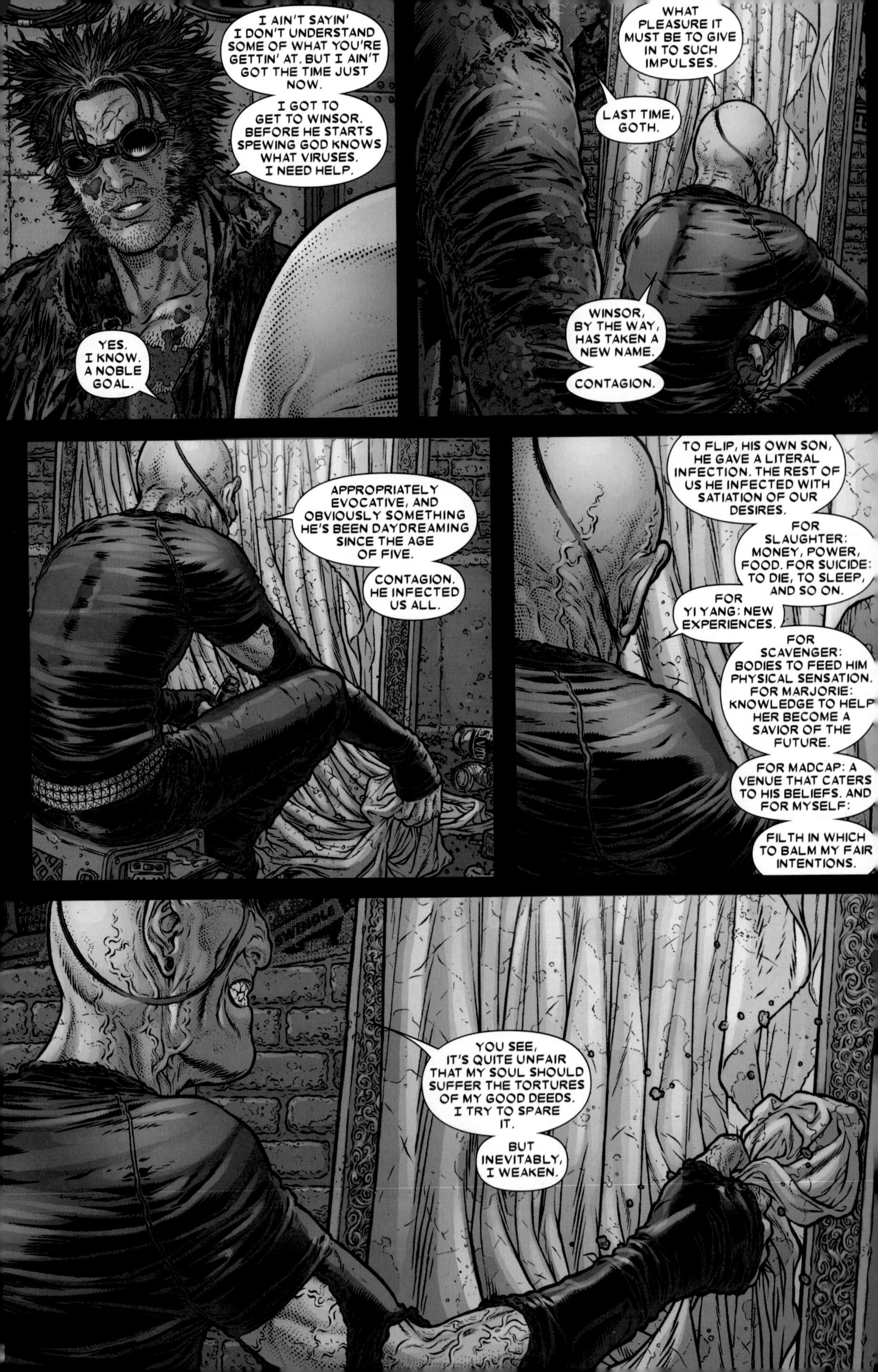
I AIN'T SAYIN' I DON'T UNDERSTAND SOME OF WHAT YOU'RE GETTIN' AT. BUT I AIN'T GOT THE TIME JUST NOW.
I GOT TO GET TO WINSOR. BEFORE HE STARTS SPEWING GOD KNOWS WHAT VIRUSES. I NEED HELP.
YES. I KNOW. A NOBLE GOAL.
WHAT PLEASURE IT MUST BE TO GIVE IN TO SUCH IMPULSES.
LAST TIME, GOTH.
WINSOR, BY THE WAY, HAS TAKEN A NEW NAME.
CONTAGION.
APPROPRIATELY EVOCATIVE, AND OBVIOUSLY SOMETHING HE'S BEEN DAYDREAMING SINCE THE AGE OF FIVE.
CONTAGION. HE INFECTED US ALL.
TO FLIP, HIS OWN SON, HE GAVE A LITERAL INFECTION. THE REST OF US HE INFECTED WITH SATIATION OF OUR DESIRES.
FOR SLAUGHTER: MONEY, POWER, FOOD. FOR SUICIDE: TO DIE, TO SLEEP, AND SO ON.
FOR YI YANG: NEW EXPERIENCES.
FOR SCAVENGER: BODIES TO FEED HIM PHYSICAL SENSATION. FOR MARJORIE: KNOWLEDGE TO HELP HER BECOME A SAVIOR OF THE FUTURE.
FOR MADCAP: A VENUE THAT CATERS TO HIS BELIEFS. AND FOR MYSELF:
FILTH IN WHICH TO BALM MY FAIR INTENTIONS.
YOU SEE, IT'S QUITE UNFAIR THAT MY SOUL SHOULD SUFFER THE TORTURES OF MY GOOD DEEDS. I TRY TO SPARE IT.
BUT INEVITABLY, I WEAKEN.

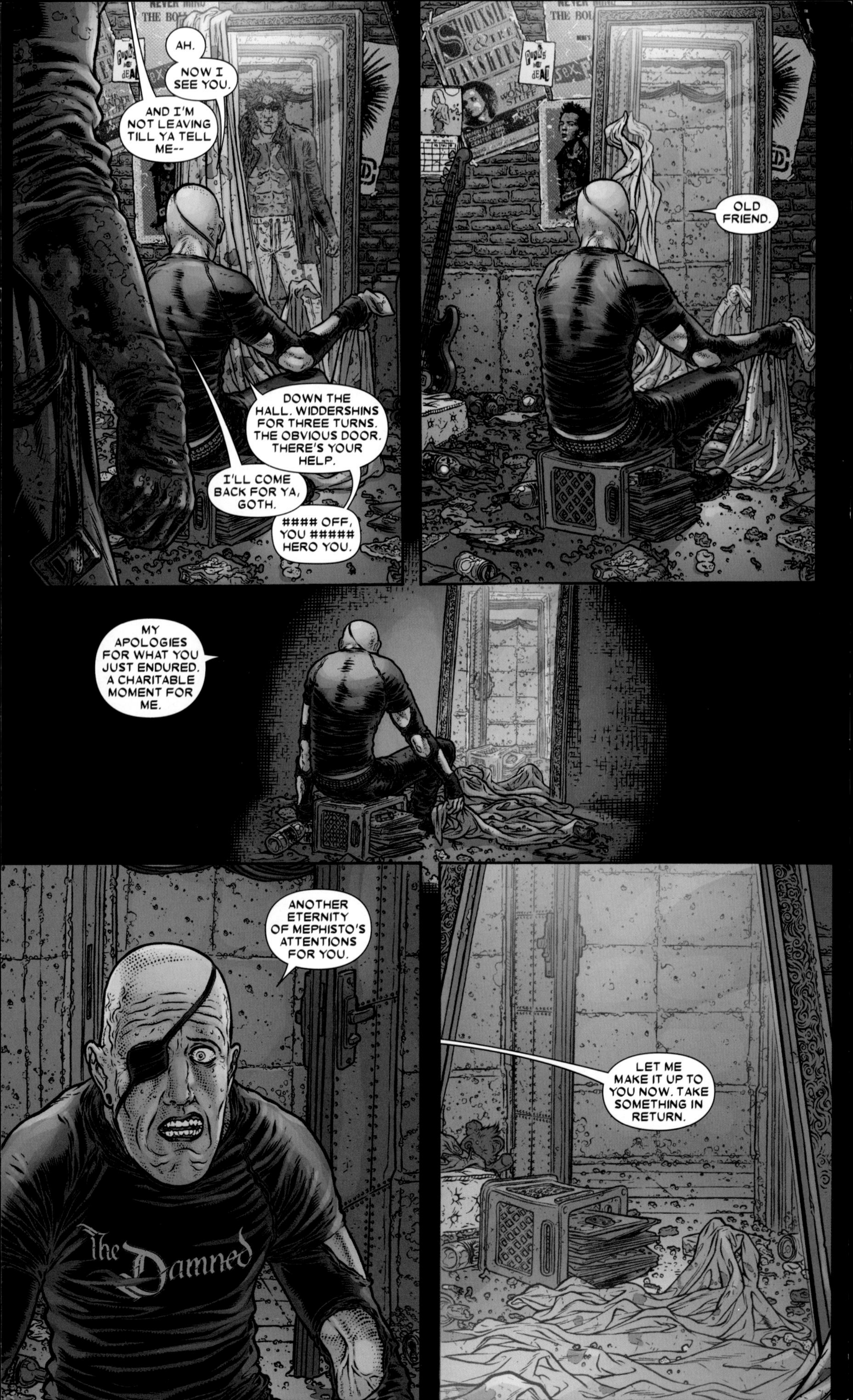
AH.
NOW I SEE YOU.
AND I'M NOT LEAVING TILL YA TELL ME--
DOWN THE HALL. WIDDERSHINS FOR THREE TURNS. THE OBVIOUS DOOR. THERE'S YOUR HELP.
I'LL COME BACK FOR YA, GOTH.
OFF, YOU ##### HERO YOU.
OLD FRIEND.
MY APOLOGIES FOR WHAT YOU JUST ENDURED. A CHARITABLE MOMENT FOR ME.
ANOTHER ETERNITY OF MEPHISTO'S ATTENTIONS FOR YOU.
The Damned
LET ME MAKE IT UP TO YOU NOW. TAKE SOMETHING IN RETURN.

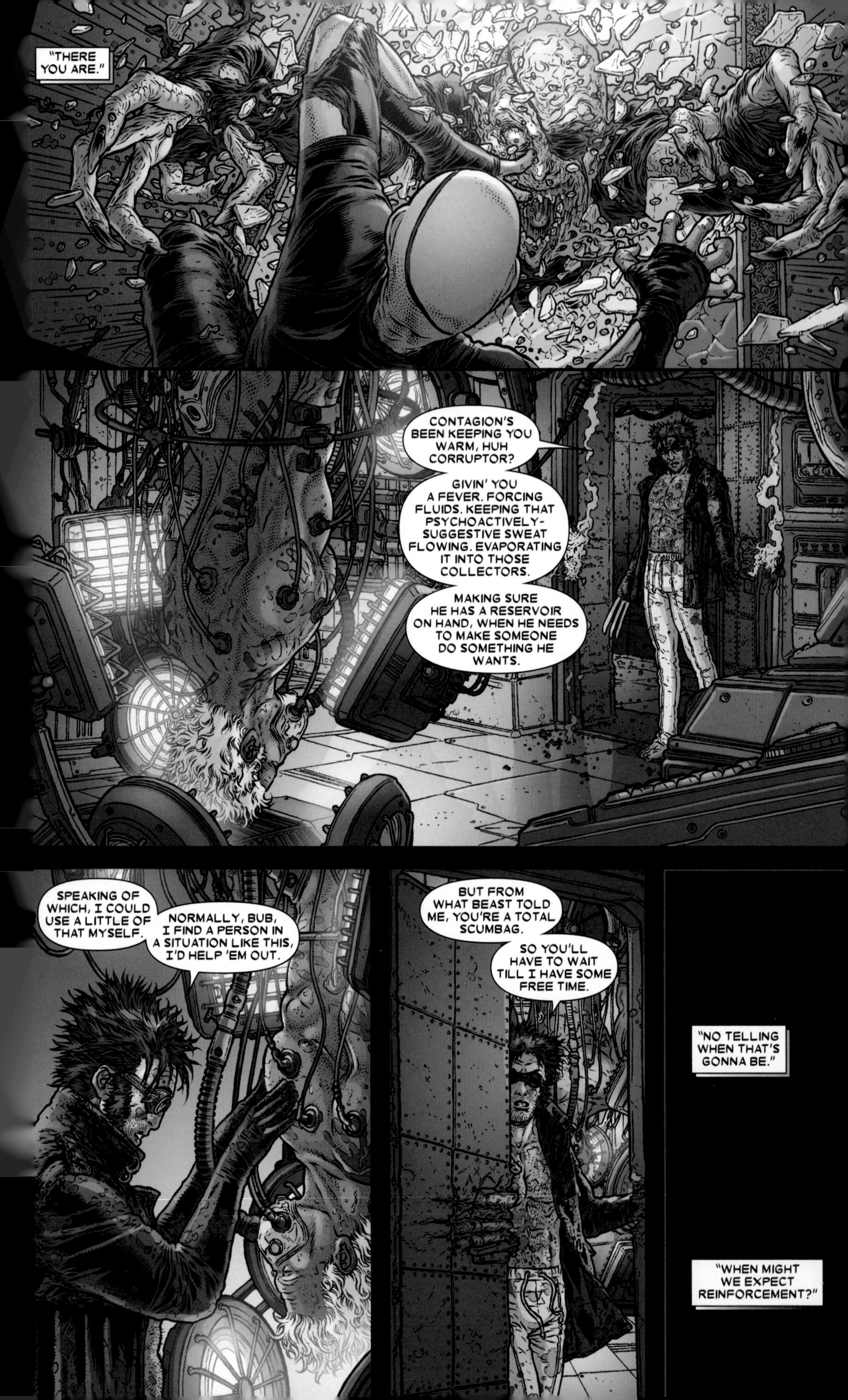
"THERE YOU ARE."
CONTAGION'S BEEN KEEPING YOU WARM, HUH CORRUPTOR?
GIVIN' YOU A FEVER. FORCING FLUIDS. KEEPING THAT PSYCHOACTIVELY-SUGGESTIVE SWEAT FLOWING. EVAPORATING IT INTO THOSE COLLECTORS.
MAKING SURE HE HAS A RESERVOIR ON HAND, WHEN HE NEEDS TO MAKE SOMEONE DO SOMETHING HE WANTS.
SPEAKING OF WHICH, I COULD USE A LITTLE OF THAT MYSELF.
NORMALLY, BUB, I FIND A PERSON IN A SITUATION LIKE THIS, I'D HELP 'EM OUT.
BUT FROM WHAT BEAST TOLD ME, YOU'RE A TOTAL SCUMBAG.
SO YOU'LL HAVE TO WAIT TILL I HAVE SOME FREE TIME.
"NO TELLING WHEN THAT'S GONNA BE."
"WHEN MIGHT WE EXPECT REINFORCEMENT?"

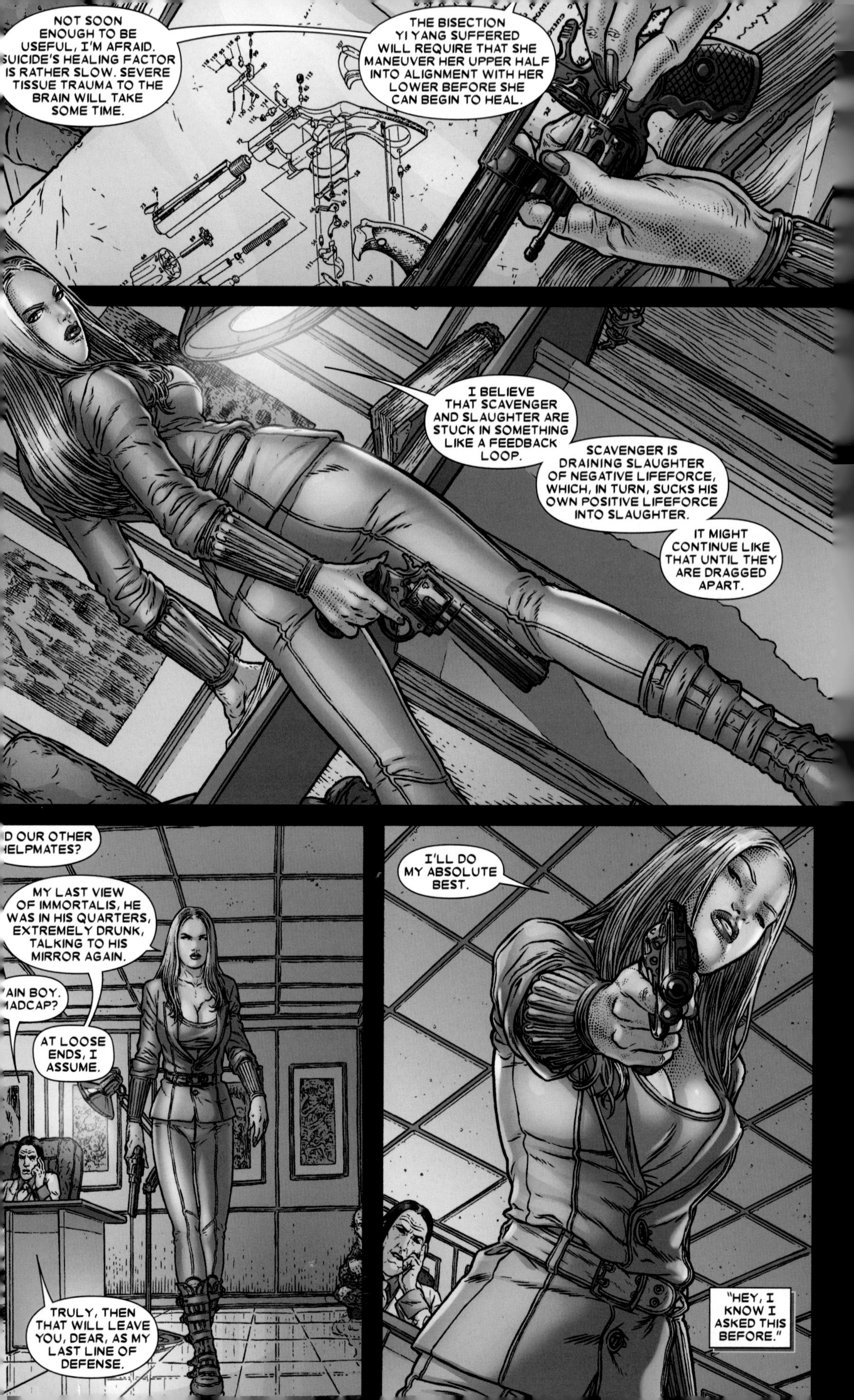
NOT SOON ENOUGH TO BE USEFUL, I'M AFRAID. SUICIDE'S HEALING FACTOR IS RATHER SLOW. SEVERE TISSUE TRAUMA TO THE BRAIN WILL TAKE SOME TIME.
THE BISECTION YI YANG SUFFERED WILL REQUIRE THAT SHE MANEUVER HER UPPER HALF INTO ALIGNMENT WITH HER LOWER BEFORE SHE CAN BEGIN TO HEAL.
I BELIEVE THAT SCAVENGER AND SLAUGHTER ARE STUCK IN SOMETHING LIKE A FEEDBACK LOOP.
SCAVENGER IS DRAINING SLAUGHTER OF NEGATIVE LIFEFORCE, WHICH, IN TURN, SUCKS HIS OWN POSITIVE LIFEFORCE INTO SLAUGHTER.
IT MIGHT CONTINUE LIKE THAT UNTIL THEY ARE DRAGGED APART.
D OUR OTHER HELPMATES?
MY LAST VIEW OF IMMORTALIS, HE WAS IN HIS QUARTERS, EXTREMELY DRUNK, TALKING TO HIS MIRROR AGAIN.
AIN BOY. MADCAP?
AT LOOSE ENDS, I ASSUME.
TRULY, THEN THAT WILL LEAVE YOU, DEAR, AS MY LAST LINE OF DEFENSE.
I'LL DO MY ABSOLUTE BEST.
"HEY, I KNOW I ASKED THIS BEFORE."

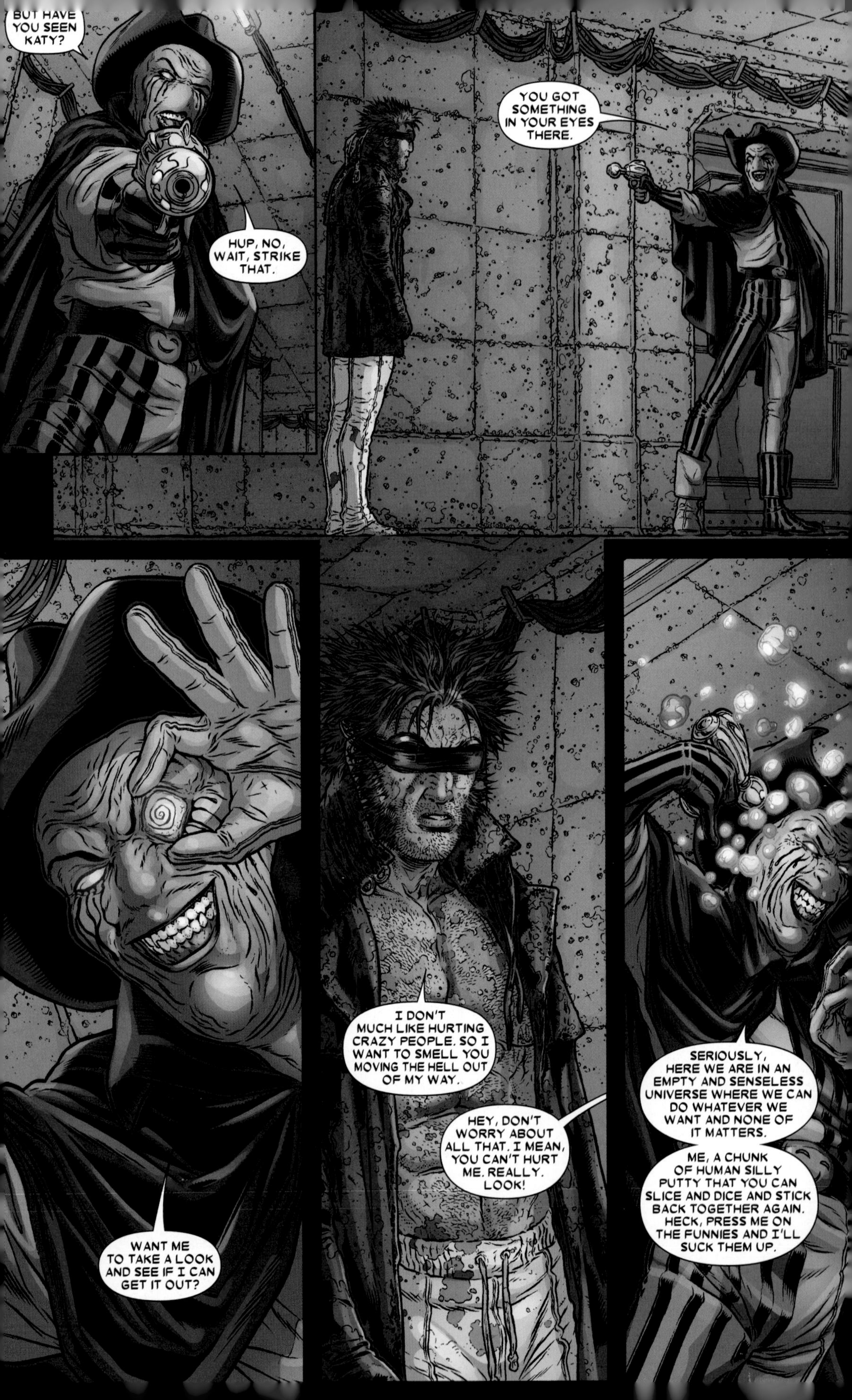
BUT HAVE YOU SEEN KATY?
HUP, NO, WAIT, STRIKE THAT.
YOU GOT SOMETHING IN YOUR EYES THERE.
WANT ME TO TAKE A LOOK AND SEE IF I CAN GET IT OUT?
I DON'T MUCH LIKE HURTING CRAZY PEOPLE. SO I WANT TO SMELL YOU MOVING THE HELL OUT OF MY WAY.
HEY, DON'T WORRY ABOUT ALL THAT. I MEAN, YOU CAN'T HURT ME. REALLY. LOOK!
SERIOUSLY, HERE WE ARE IN AN EMPTY AND SENSELESS UNIVERSE WHERE WE CAN DO WHATEVER WE WANT AND NONE OF IT MATTERS.
ME, A CHUNK OF HUMAN SILLY PUTTY THAT YOU CAN SLICE AND DICE AND STICK BACK TOGETHER AGAIN. HECK, PRESS ME ON THE FUNNIES AND I'LL SUCK THEM UP.

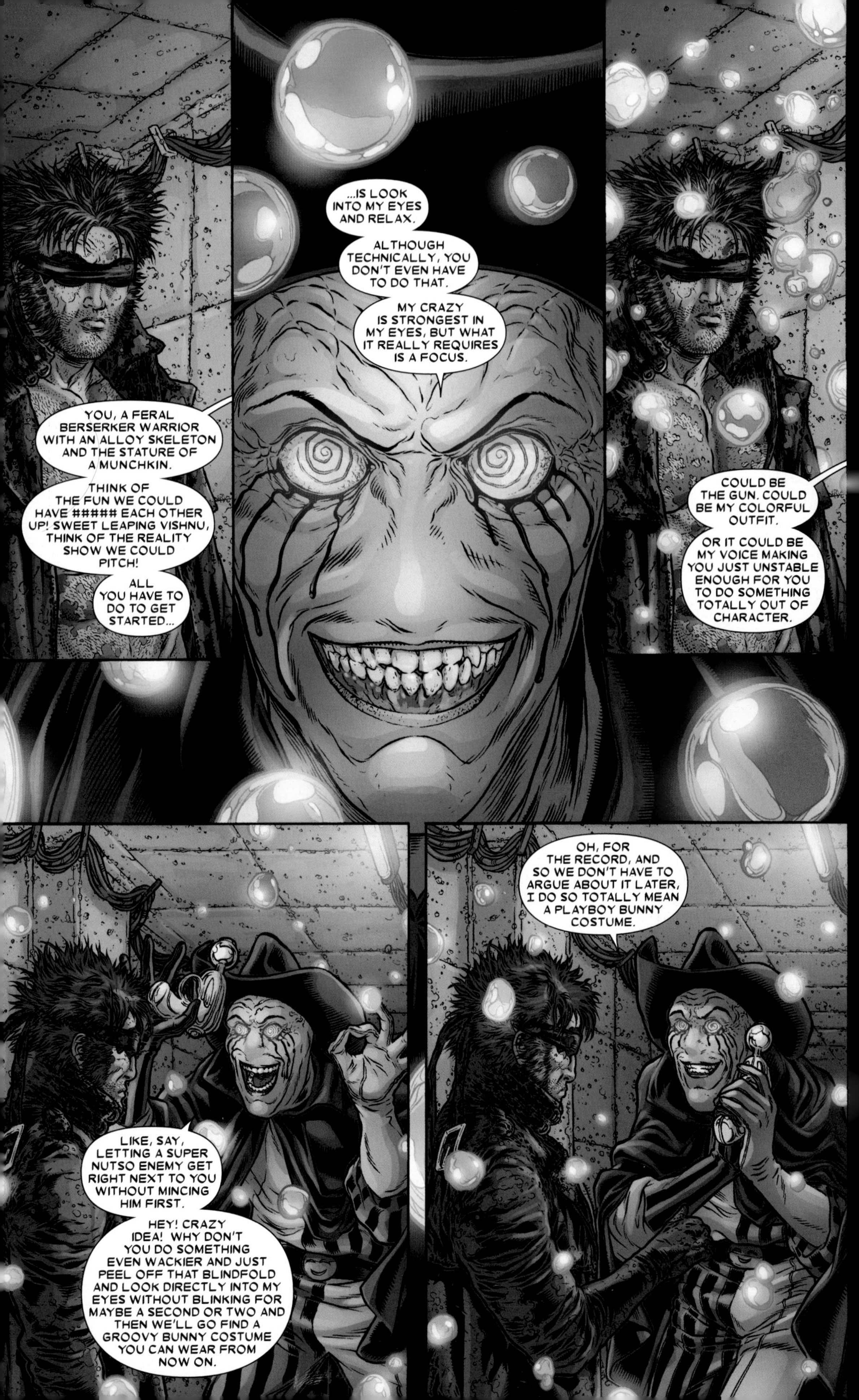
YOU, A FERAL BERSERKER WARRIOR WITH AN ALLOY SKELETON AND THE STATURE OF A MUNCHKIN.
THINK OF THE FUN WE COULD HAVE ##### EACH OTHER UP! SWEET LEAPING VISHNU, THINK OF THE REALITY SHOW WE COULD PITCH!
ALL YOU HAVE TO DO TO GET STARTED...
...IS LOOK INTO MY EYES AND RELAX.
ALTHOUGH TECHNICALLY, YOU DON'T EVEN HAVE TO DO THAT.
MY CRAZY IS STRONGEST IN MY EYES, BUT WHAT IT REALLY REQUIRES IS A FOCUS.
COULD BE THE GUN. COULD BE MY COLORFUL OUTFIT.
OR IT COULD BE MY VOICE MAKING YOU JUST UNSTABLE ENOUGH FOR YOU TO DO SOMETHING TOTALLY OUT OF CHARACTER.
LIKE, SAY, LETTING A SUPER NUTSO ENEMY GET RIGHT NEXT TO YOU WITHOUT MINCING HIM FIRST.
HEY! CRAZY IDEA! WHY DON'T YOU DO SOMETHING EVEN WACKIER AND JUST PEEL OFF THAT BLINDFOLD AND LOOK DIRECTLY INTO MY EYES WITHOUT BLINKING FOR MAYBE A SECOND OR TWO AND THEN WE'LL GO FIND A GROOVY BUNNY COSTUME YOU CAN WEAR FROM NOW ON.
OH, FOR THE RECORD, AND SO WE DON'T HAVE TO ARGUE ABOUT IT LATER, I DO SO TOTALLY MEAN A PLAYBOY BUNNY COSTUME.

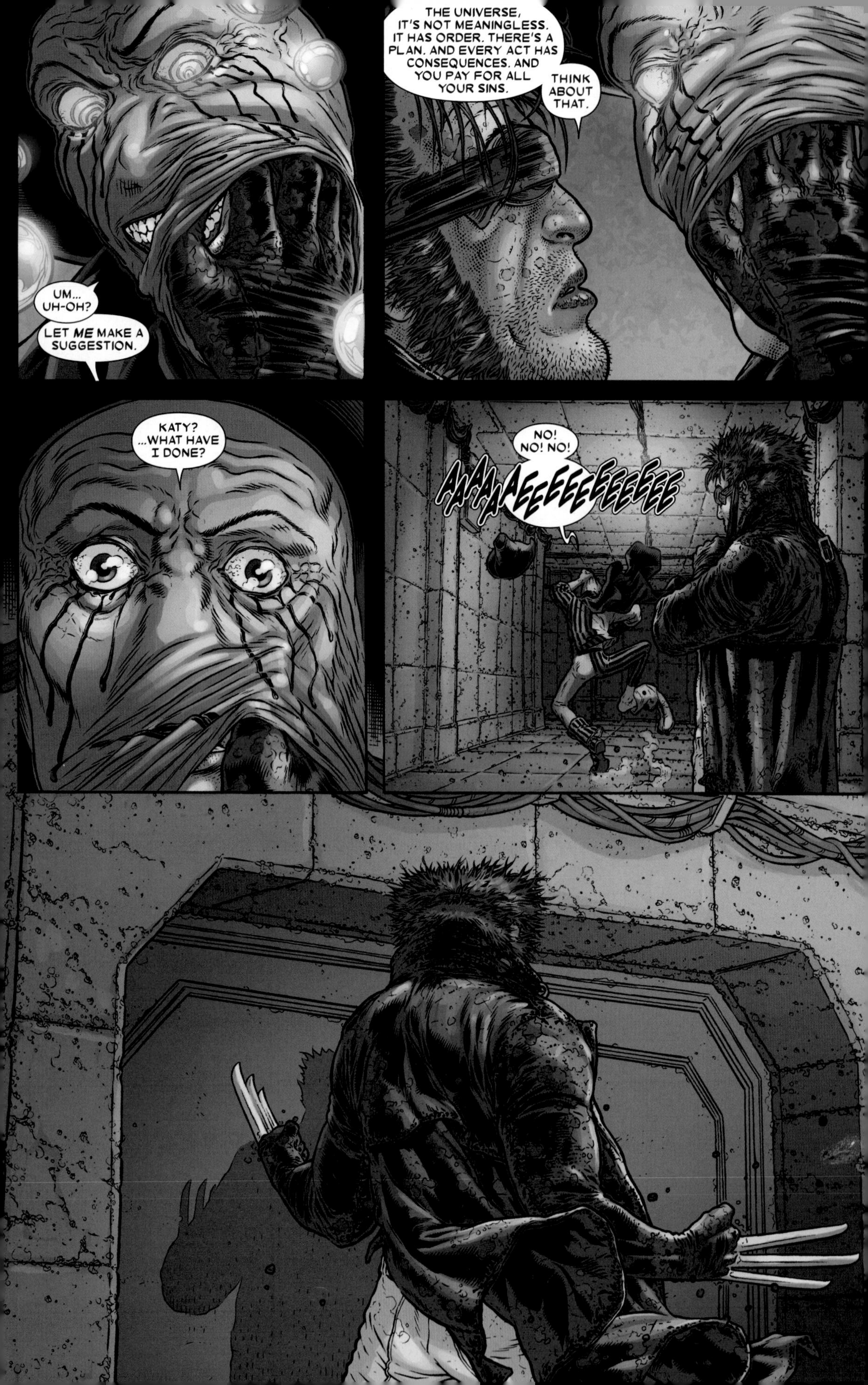
UM... UH-OH?
LET ME MAKE A SUGGESTION.
THE UNIVERSE, IT'S NOT MEANINGLESS. IT HAS ORDER. THERE'S A PLAN. AND EVERY ACT HAS CONSEQUENCES. AND YOU PAY FOR ALL YOUR SINS.
THINK ABOUT THAT.
KATY? ...WHAT HAVE I DONE?
NO! NO! NO!
AAAAAEEEEEEEEEE

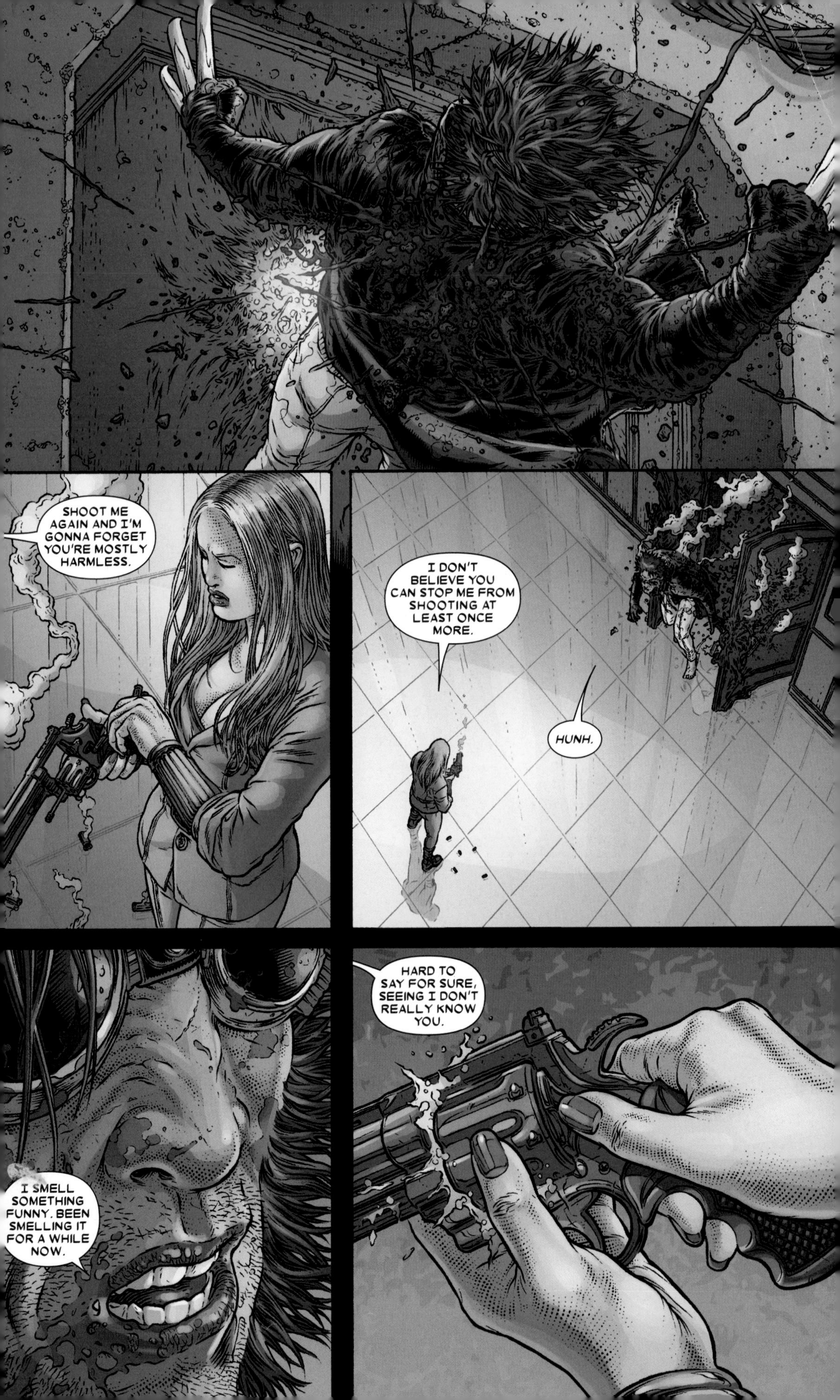
SHOOT ME AGAIN AND I'M GONNA FORGET YOU'RE MOSTLY HARMLESS.
I DON'T BELIEVE YOU CAN STOP ME FROM SHOOTING AT LEAST ONCE MORE.
HUNH.
I SMELL SOMETHING FUNNY. BEEN SMELLING IT FOR A WHILE NOW.
HARD TO SAY FOR SURE, SEEING I DON'T REALLY KNOW YOU.

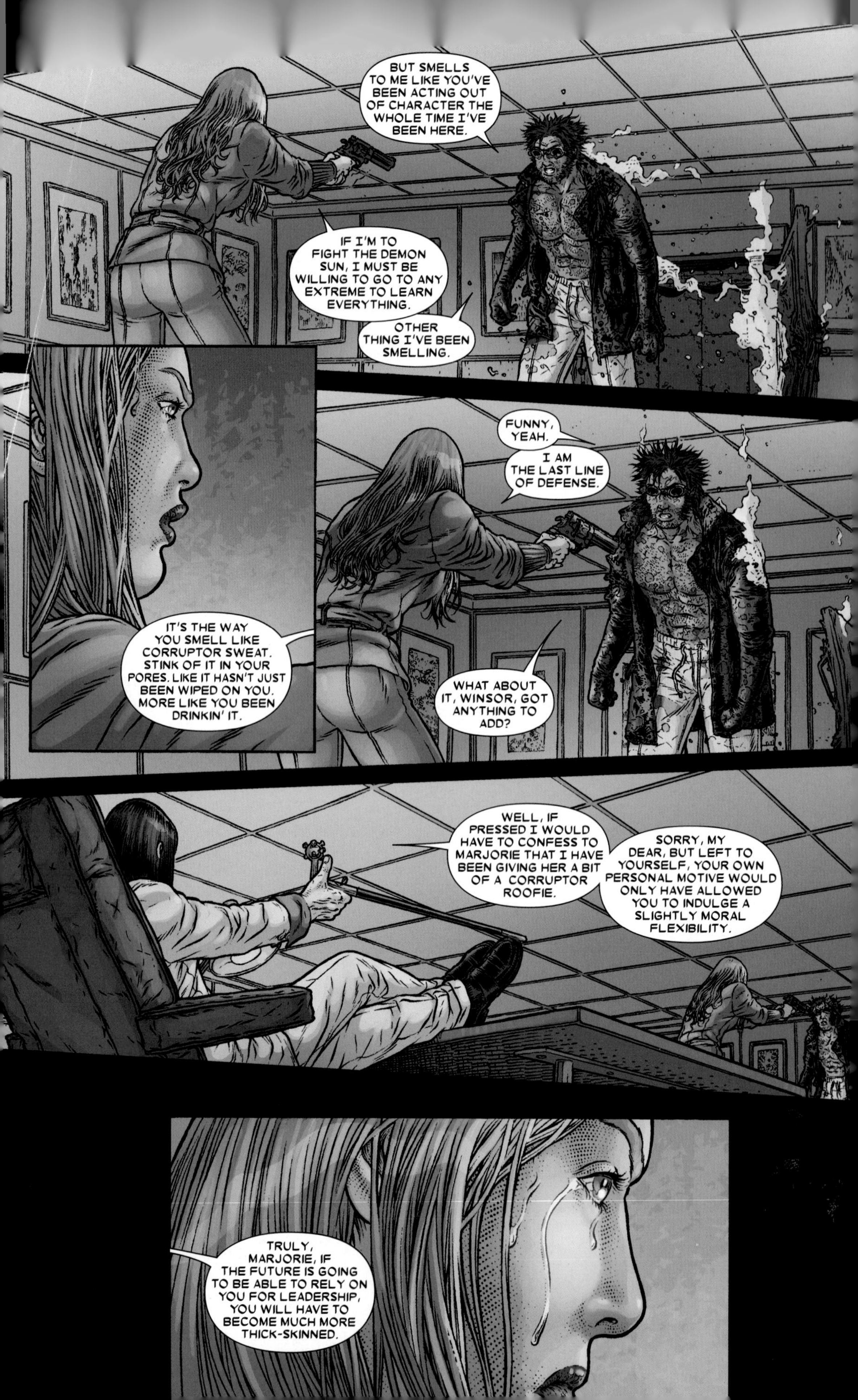

BUT SMELLS TO ME LIKE YOU'VE BEEN ACTING OUT OF CHARACTER THE WHOLE TIME I'VE BEEN HERE.
IF I'M TO FIGHT THE DEMON SUN, I MUST BE WILLING TO GO TO ANY EXTREME TO LEARN EVERYTHING.
OTHER THING I'VE BEEN SMELLING.
IT'S THE WAY YOU SMELL LIKE CORRUPTOR SWEAT. STINK OF IT IN YOUR PORES. LIKE IT HASN'T JUST BEEN WIPED ON YOU. MORE LIKE YOU BEEN DRINKIN' IT.
FUNNY, YEAH.
I AM THE LAST LINE OF DEFENSE.
WHAT ABOUT IT, WINSOR, GOT ANYTHING TO ADD?
WELL, IF PRESSED I WOULD HAVE TO CONFESS TO MARJORIE THAT I HAVE BEEN GIVING HER A BIT OF A CORRUPTOR ROOFIE.
SORRY, MY DEAR, BUT LEFT TO YOURSELF, YOUR OWN PERSONAL MOTIVE WOULD ONLY HAVE ALLOWED YOU TO INDULGE A SLIGHTLY MORAL FLEXIBILITY.
TRULY, MARJORIE, IF THE FUTURE IS GOING TO BE ABLE TO RELY ON YOU FOR LEADERSHIP, YOU WILL HAVE TO BECOME MUCH MORE THICK-SKINNED.

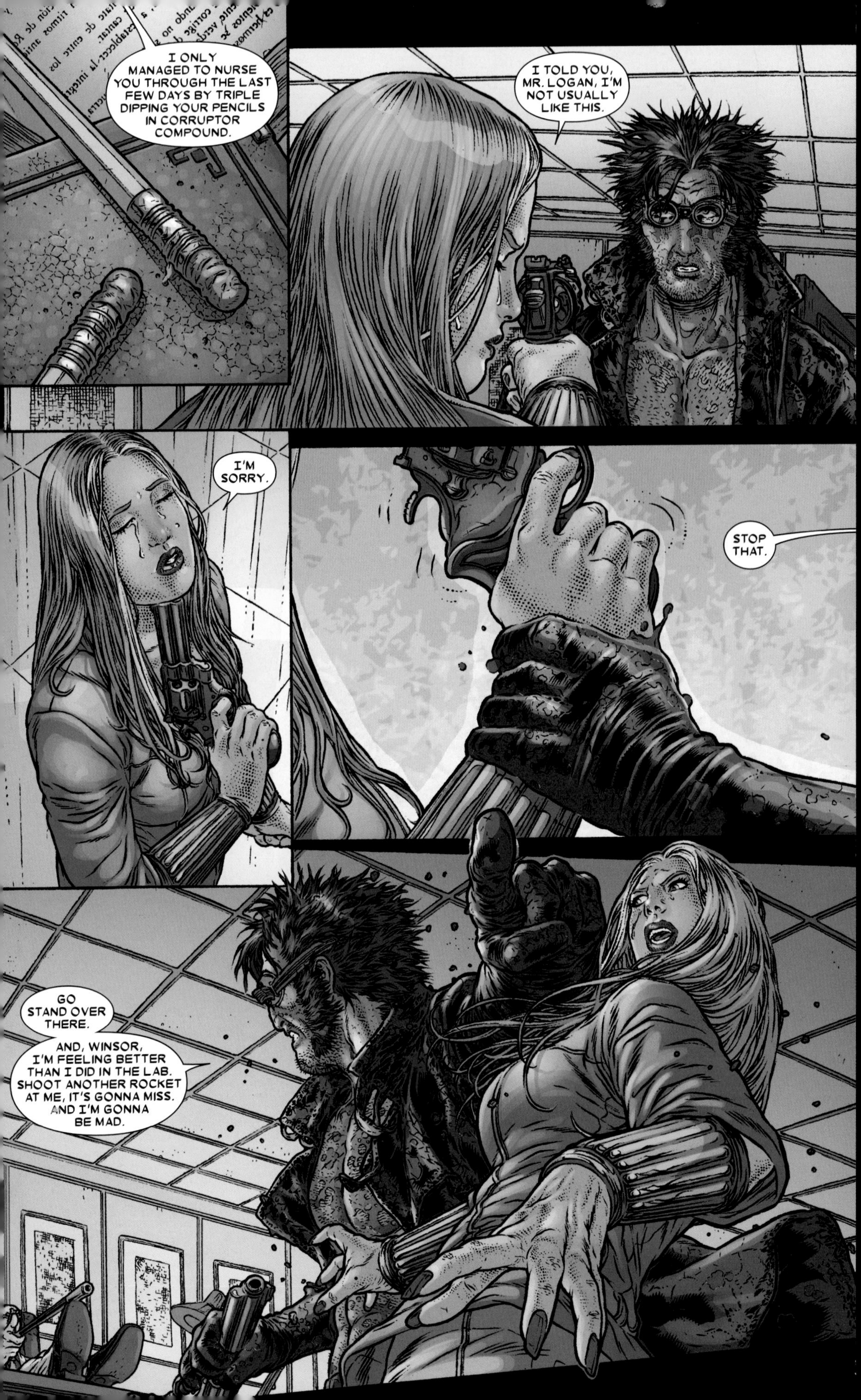
I ONLY MANAGED TO NURSE YOU THROUGH THE LAST FEW DAYS BY TRIPLE DIPPING YOUR PENCILS IN CORRUPTOR COMPOUND.
I TOLD YOU, MR. LOGAN, I'M NOT USUALLY LIKE THIS.
I'M SORRY.
STOP THAT.
GO STAND OVER THERE.
AND, WINSOR, I'M FEELING BETTER THAN I DID IN THE LAB. SHOOT ANOTHER ROCKET AT ME, IT'S GONNA MISS. AND I'M GONNA BE MAD.

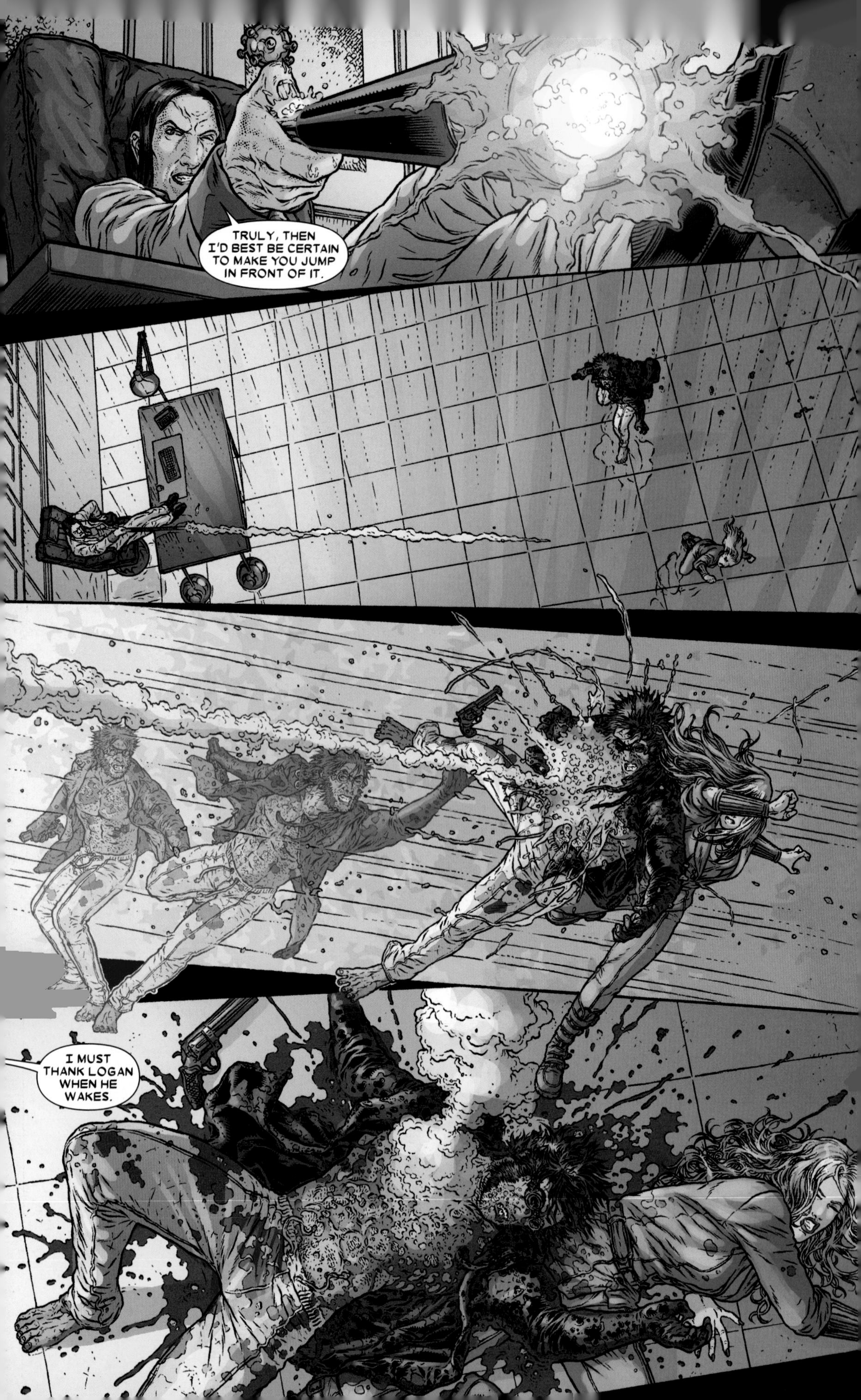
TRULY, THEN I'D BEST BE CERTAIN TO MAKE YOU JUMP IN FRONT OF IT.
I MUST THANK LOGAN WHEN HE WAKES.

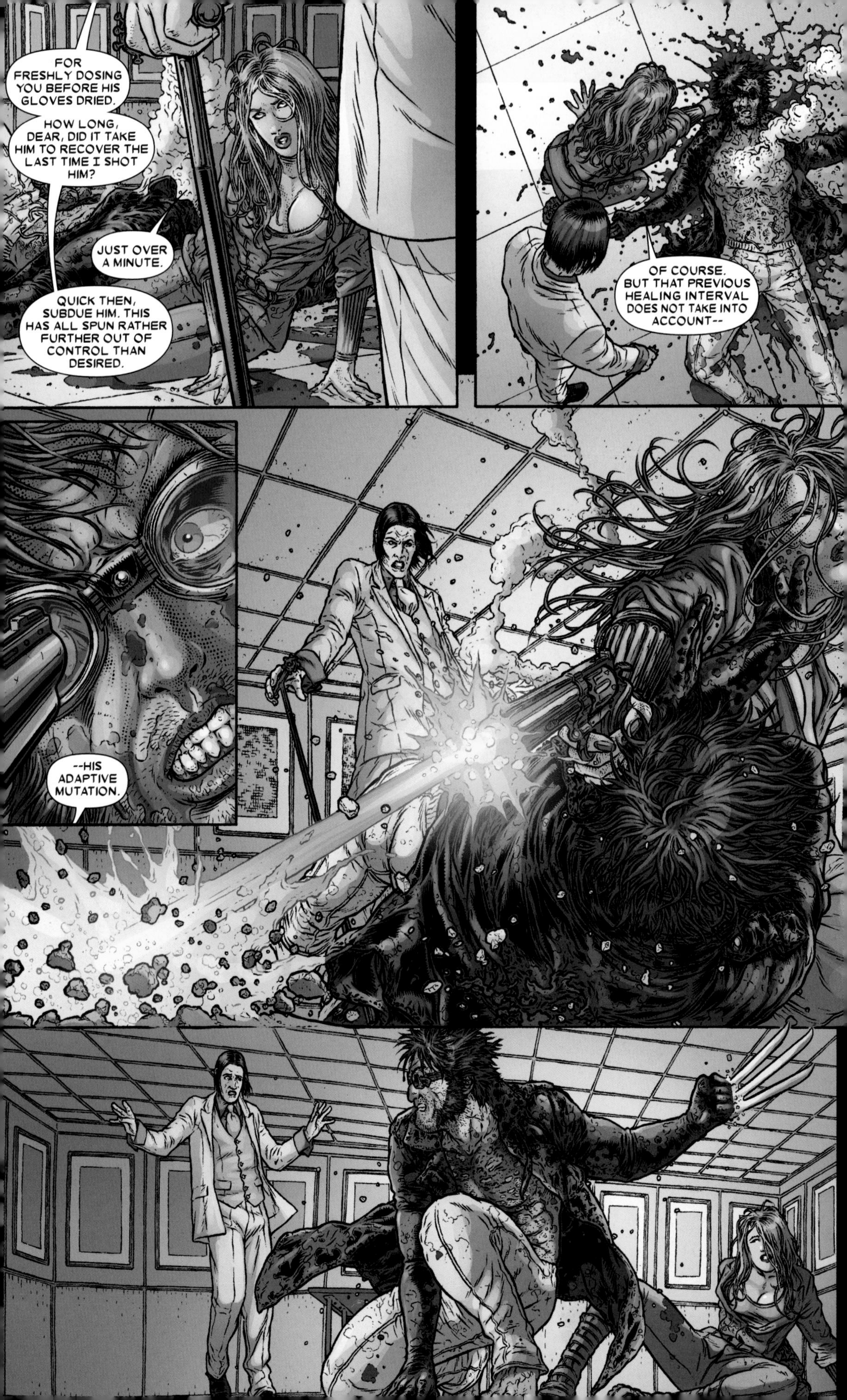
FOR FRESHLY DOSING YOU BEFORE HIS GLOVES DRIED.
HOW LONG, DEAR, DID IT TAKE HIM TO RECOVER THE LAST TIME I SHOT HIM?
JUST OVER A MINUTE.
QUICK THEN, SUBDUE HIM. THIS HAS ALL SPUN RATHER FURTHER OUT OF CONTROL THAN DESIRED.
OF COURSE. BUT THAT PREVIOUS HEALING INTERVAL DOES NOT TAKE INTO ACCOUNT--
--HIS ADAPTIVE MUTATION.

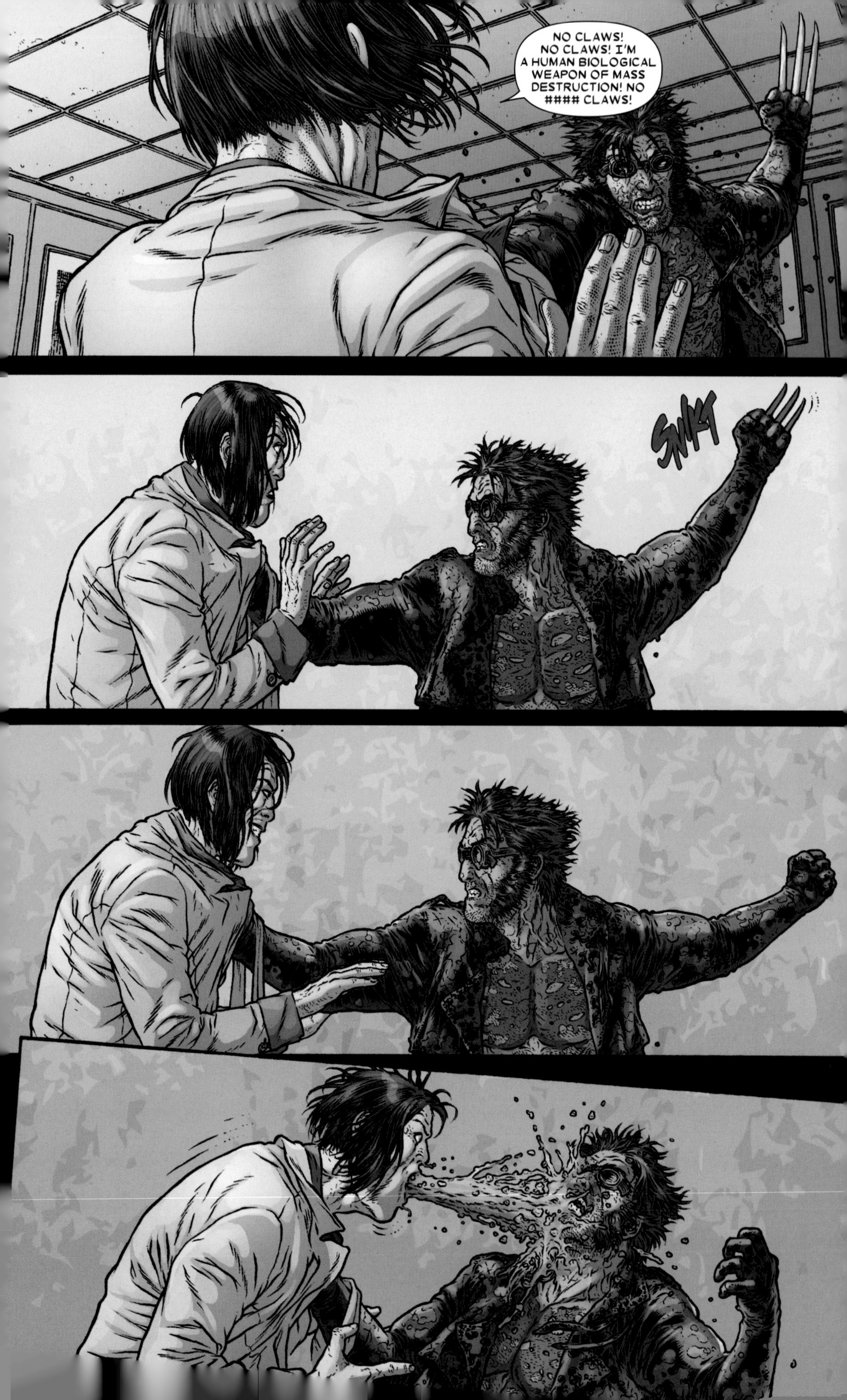
NO CLAWS! NO CLAWS! I'M A HUMAN BIOLOGICAL WEAPON OF MASS DESTRUCTION! NO #### CLAWS!
SNIKT

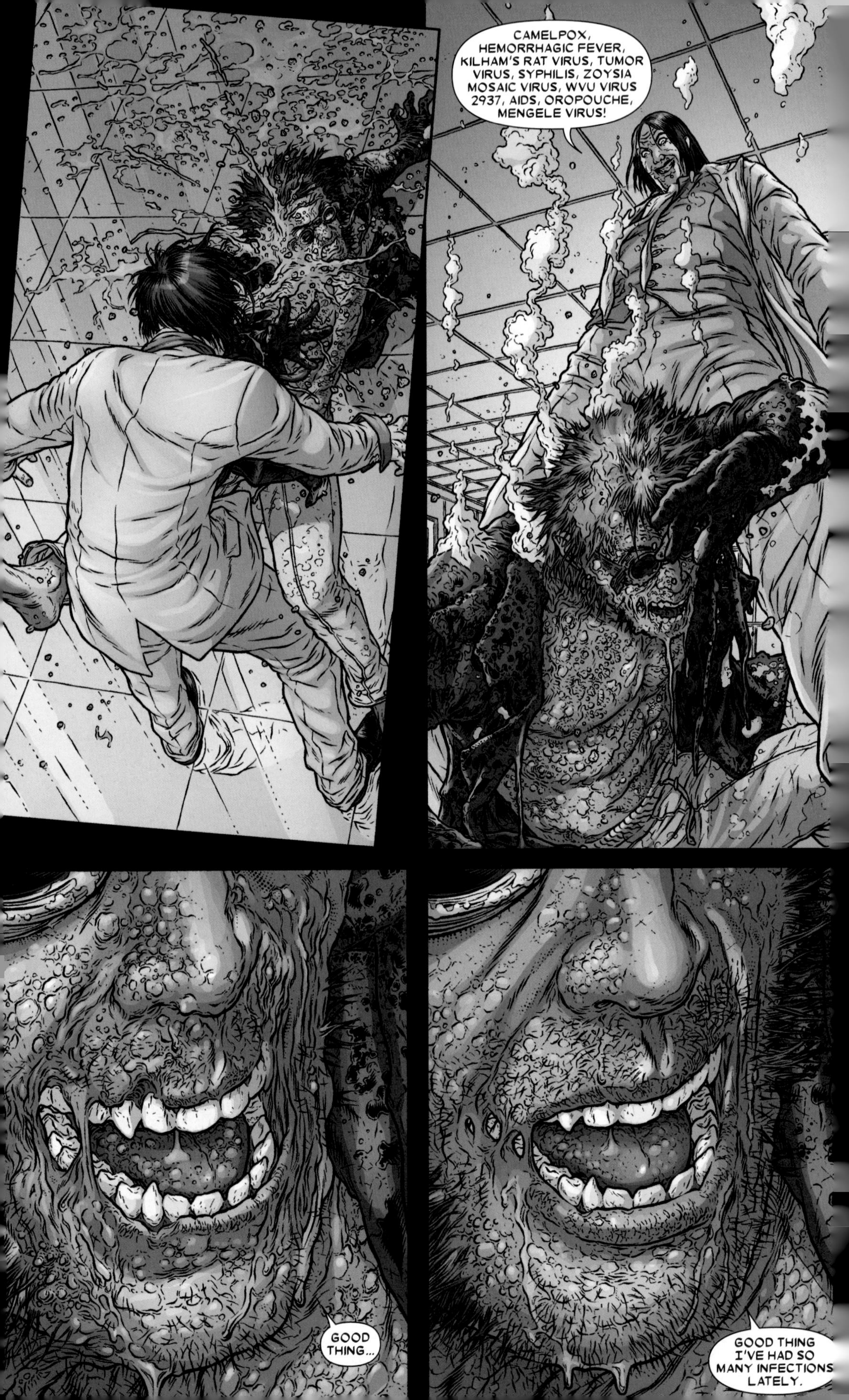
CAMELPOX, HEMORRHAGIC FEVER, KILHAM'S RAT VIRUS, TUMOR VIRUS, SYPHILIS, ZOYSIA MOSAIC VIRUS, WVU VIRUS 2937, AIDS, OROPOUCHE, MENGELE VIRUS!
GOOD THING...
GOOD THING I'VE HAD SO MANY INFECTIONS LATELY.

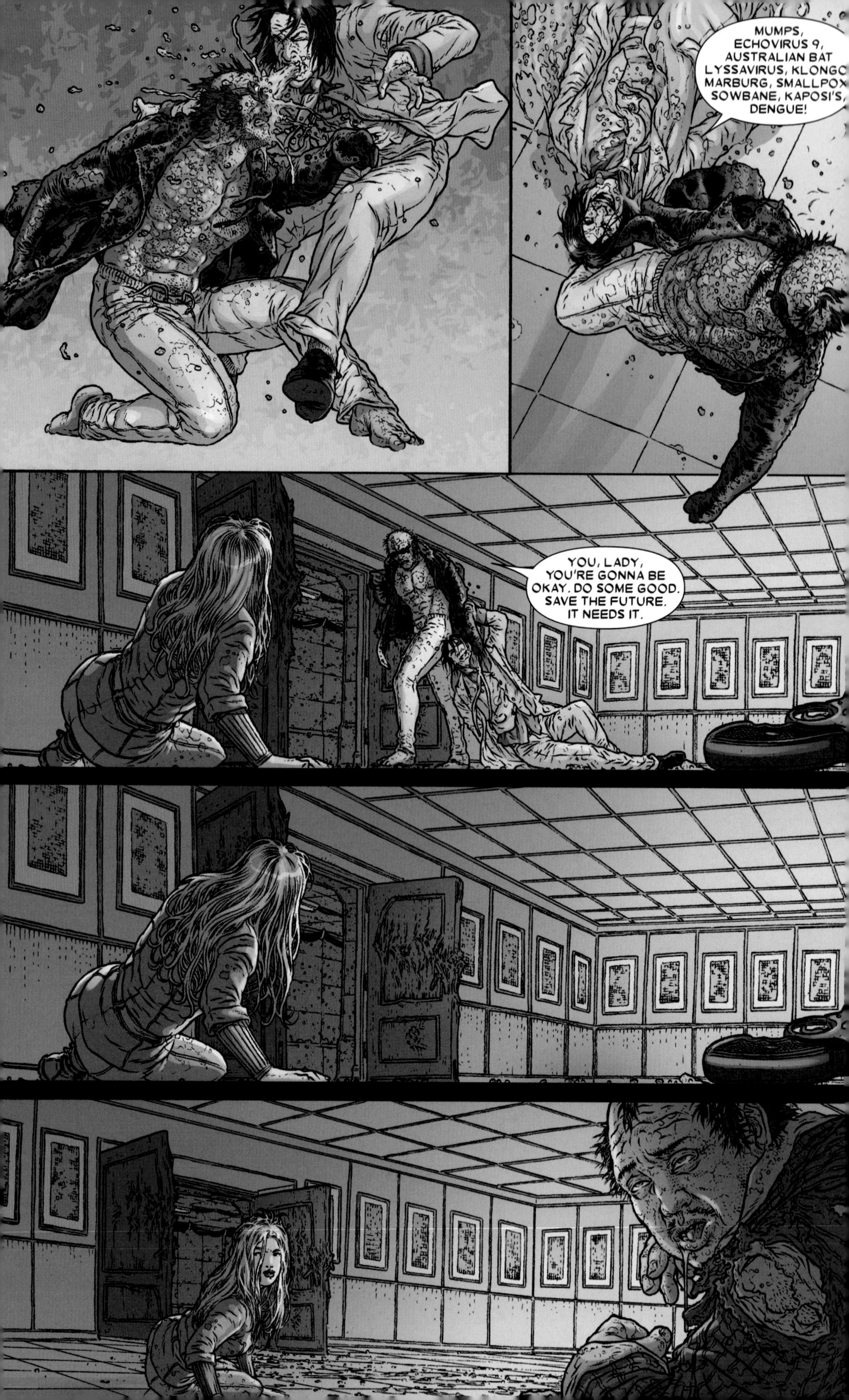
MUMPS, ECHOVIRUS 9, AUSTRALIAN BAT LYSSAVIRUS, KLONGO MARBURG, SMALLPOX SOWBANE, KAPOSI'S, DENGUE!
YOU, LADY, YOU'RE GONNA BE OKAY. DO SOME GOOD. SAVE THE FUTURE. IT NEEDS IT.

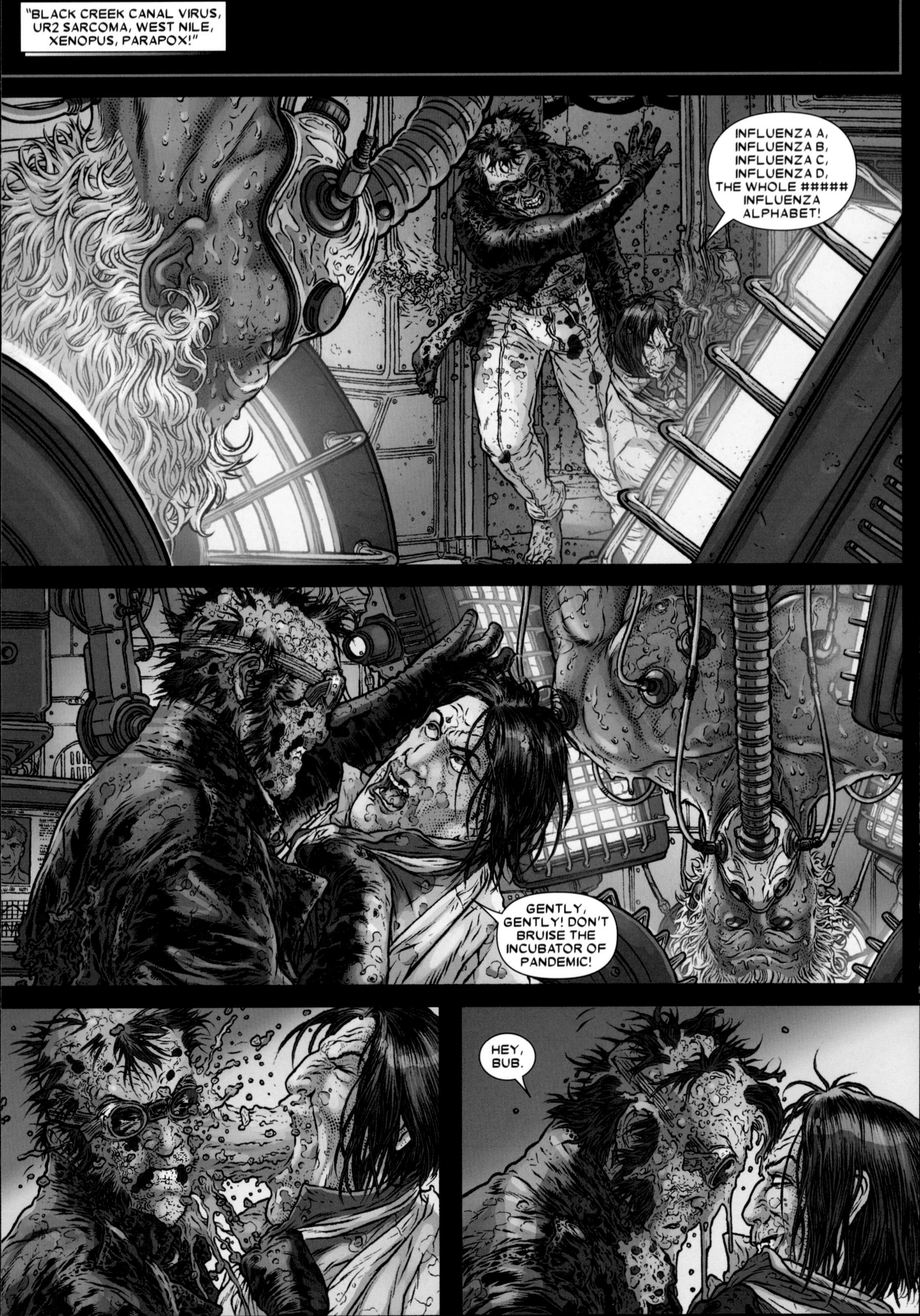
"BLACK CREEK CANAL VIRUS, UR2 SARCOMA, WEST NILE, XENOPUS, PARAPOX!"
INFLUENZA A, INFLUENZA B, INFLUENZA C, INFLUENZA D, THE WHOLE ##### INFLUENZA ALPHABET!
GENTLY, GENTLY! DON'T BRUISE THE INCUBATOR OF PANDEMIC!
HEY, BUB.

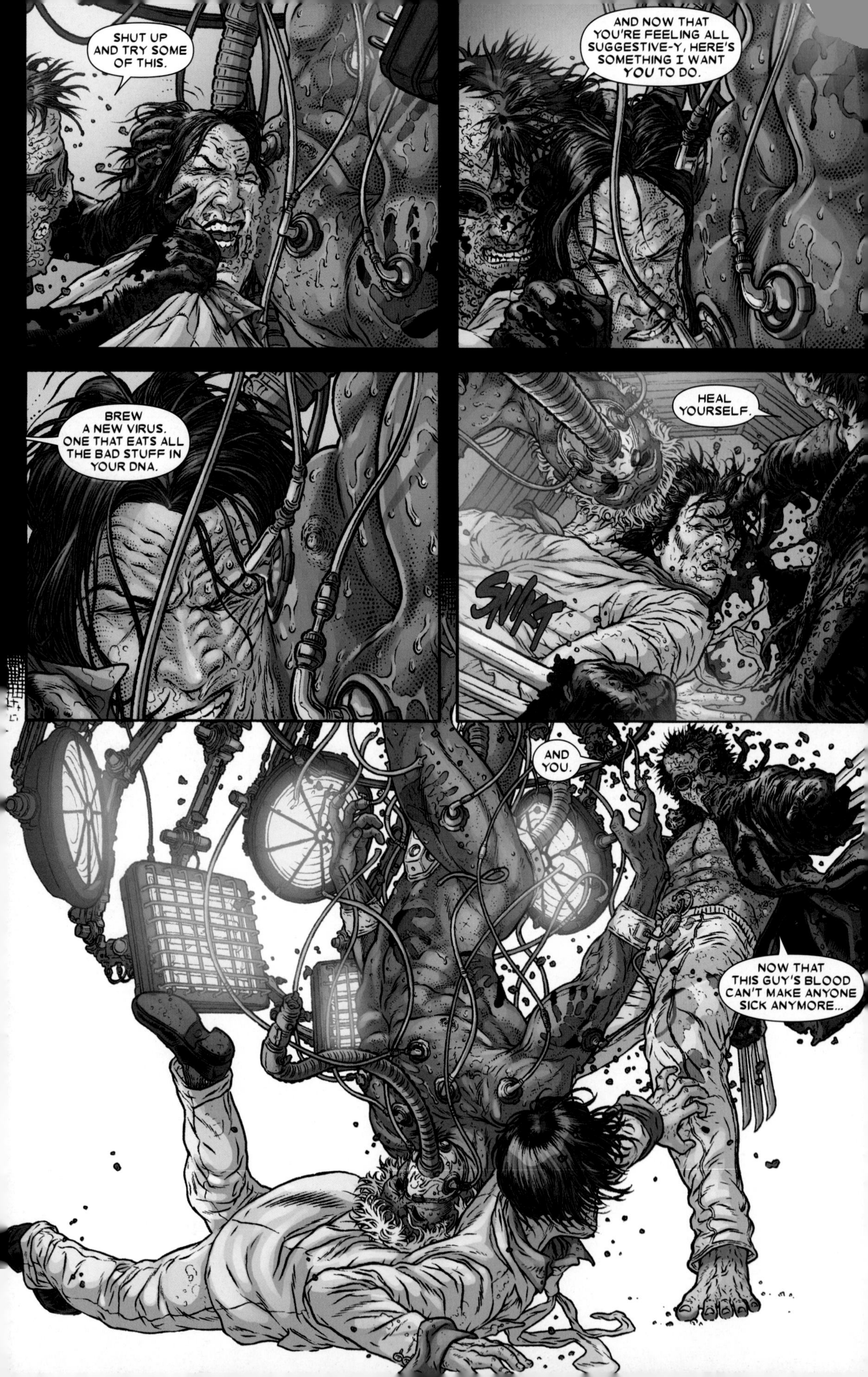
SHUT UP AND TRY SOME OF THIS.
AND NOW THAT YOU'RE FEELING ALL SUGGESTIVE-Y, HERE'S SOMETHING I WANT YOU TO DO.
BREW A NEW VIRUS. ONE THAT EATS ALL THE BAD STUFF IN YOUR DNA.
HEAL YOURSELF.
SNIKT
AND YOU.
NOW THAT THIS GUY'S BLOOD CAN'T MAKE ANYONE SICK ANYMORE...

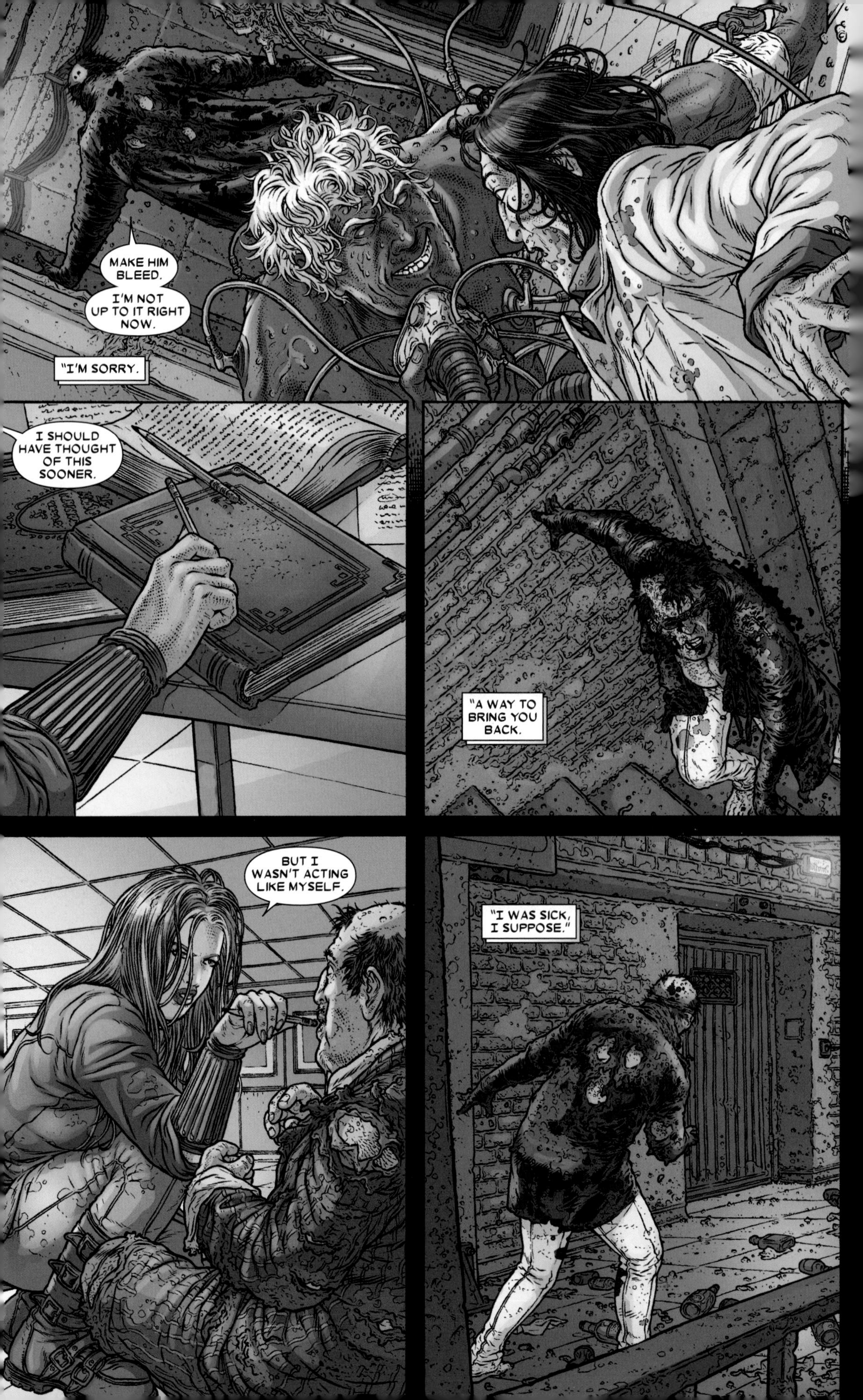
MAKE HIM BLEED.
I'M NOT UP TO IT RIGHT NOW.
"I'M SORRY.
I SHOULD HAVE THOUGHT OF THIS SOONER.
"A WAY TO BRING YOU BACK.
BUT I WASN'T ACTING LIKE MYSELF.
"I WAS SICK, I SUPPOSE."

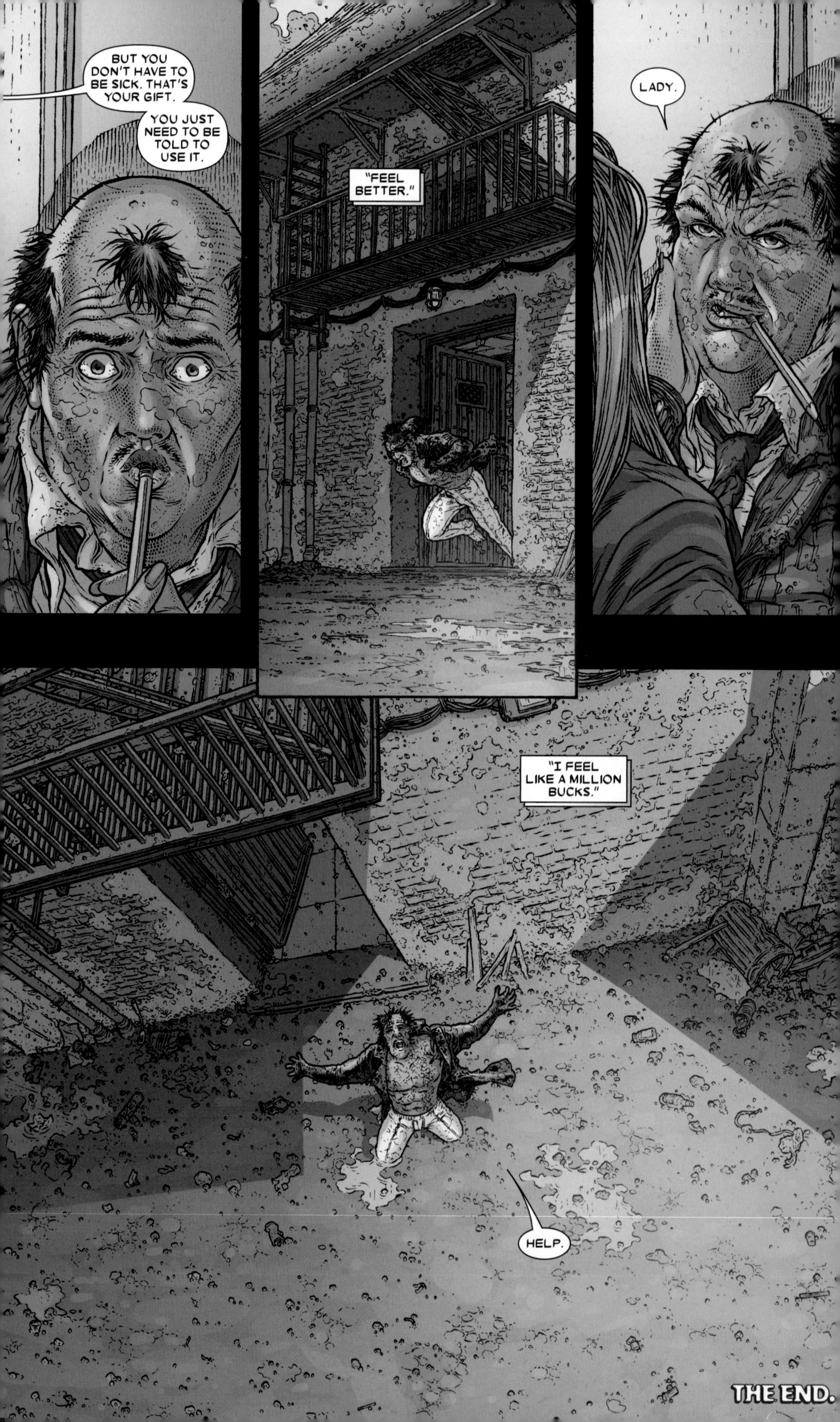
BUT YOU DON'T HAVE TO BE SICK. THAT'S YOUR GIFT.
YOU JUST NEED TO BE TOLD TO USE IT.
"FEEL BETTER."
LADY.
"I FEEL LIKE A MILLION BUCKS."
HELP.
THE END.

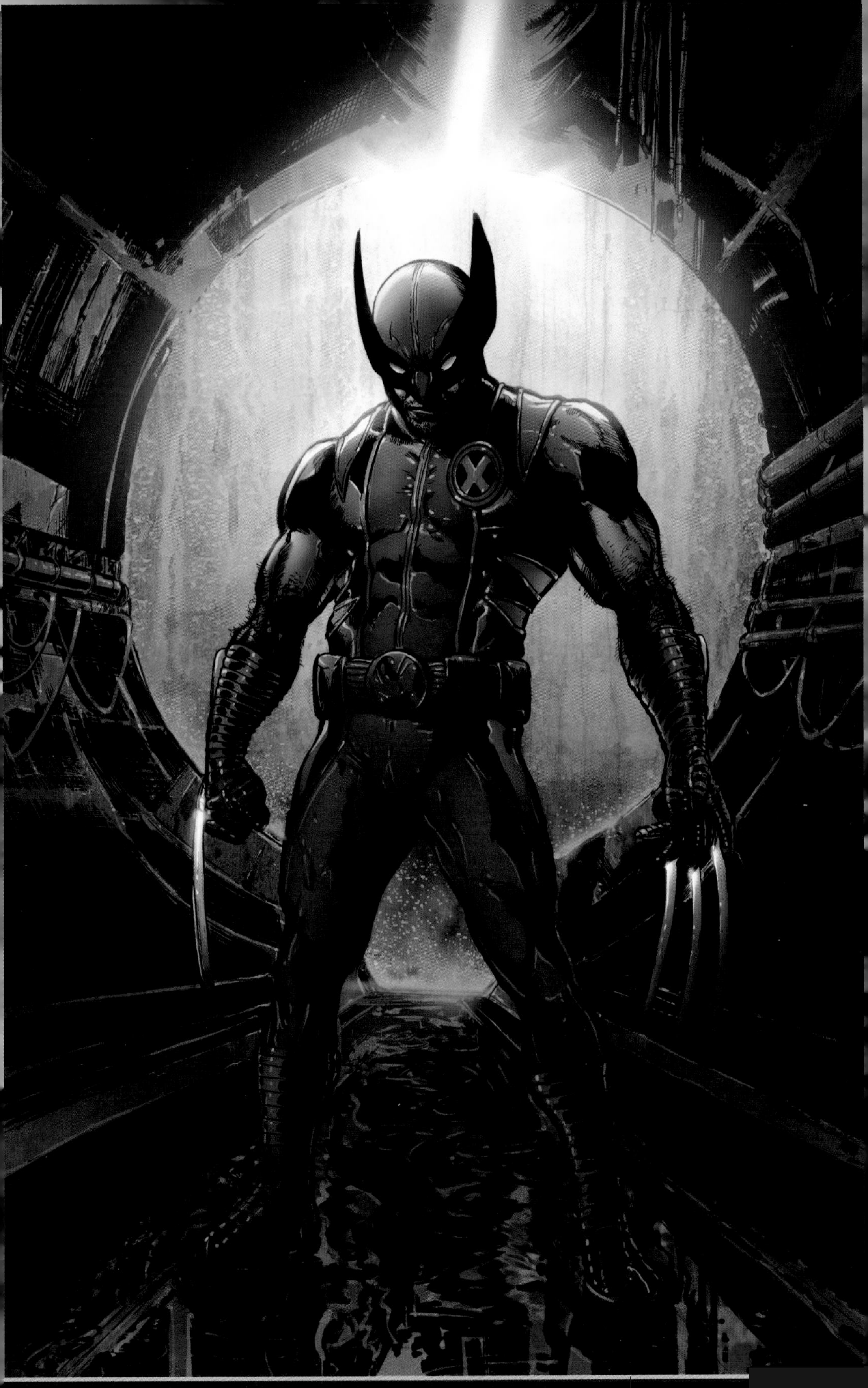

#1 VARIANT BY PHIL JIMENEZ & FRANK D'ARMATA

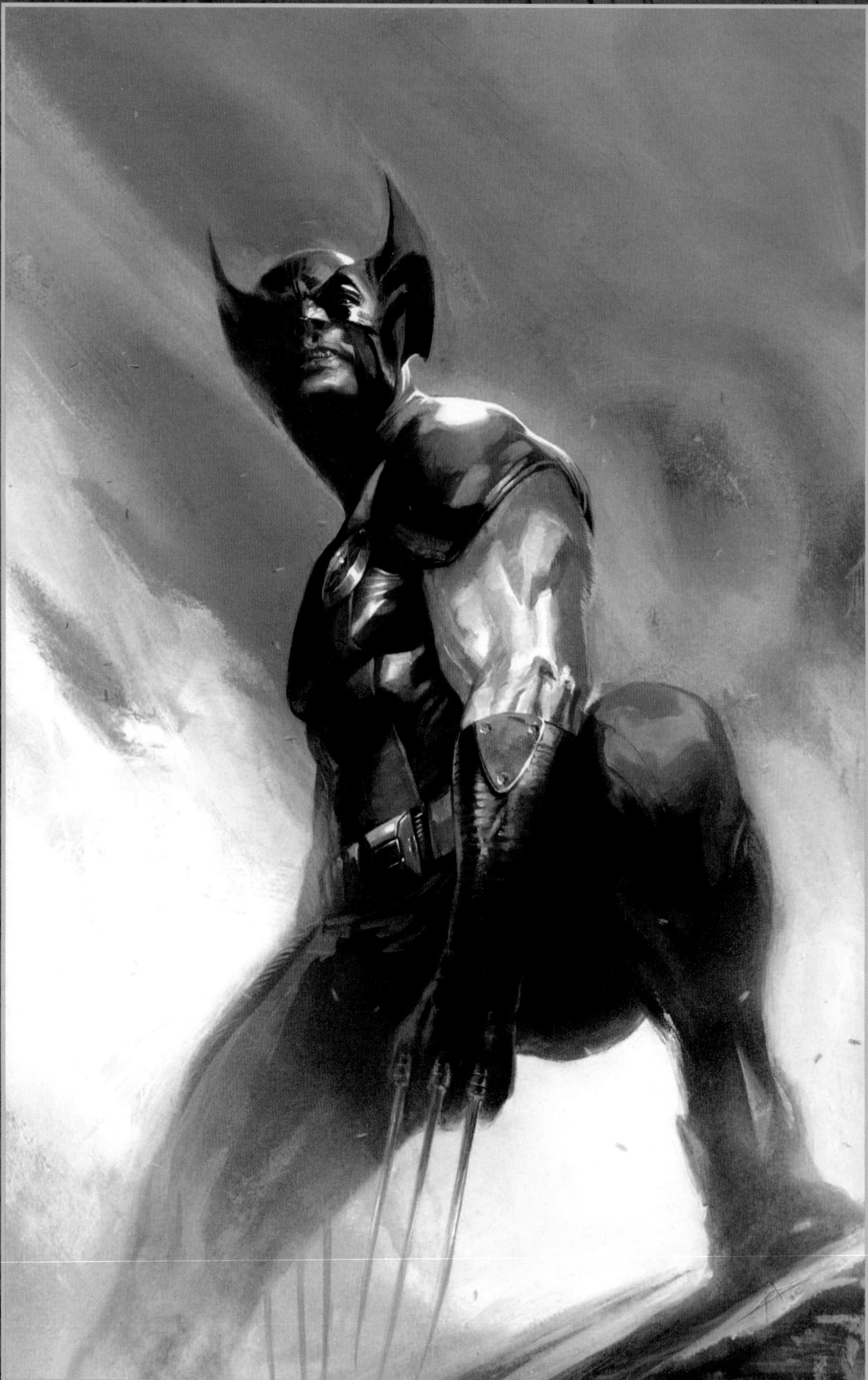

#1 VARIANT BY **GABRIELE DELL'OTTO**